Created and Directed by Hans Höfer

INSIGHT GUIDES
BURGUNDY

Edited by Rosemary Bailey
Photography by Lyle Lawson
Editorial Director: Brian Bell

HOUGHTON MIFFLIN COMPANY

APA PUBLICATIONS

BURGUNDY

First Edition (Reprint)
© 1993 APA PUBLICATIONS (HK) LTD
All Rights Reserved
Printed in Singapore by Höfer Press Pte. Ltd

Distributed in the United States by:
Houghton Mifflin Company
2 Park Street
Boston, Massachusetts 02108
ISSN: 1064-783X
ISBN: 0-395-65986-8

Distributed in Canada by:
Thomas Allen & Son
390 Steelcase Road East
Markham, Ontario L3R 1G2
ISSN: 1064-783X
ISBN: 0-395-65986-8

Distributed in the UK & Ireland by:
GeoCenter International UK Ltd
The Viables Center, Harrow Way
Basingstoke, Hampshire RG22 4BJ

ISBN: 9-62421-162-0

Worldwide distribution enquiries:
Höfer Communications Pte Ltd
38 Joo Koon Road
Singapore 2262

ISBN: 9-62421-162-0

ABOUT THIS BOOK

The region of Burgundy as it is defined today bears only a token resemblance to the original Burgundian empire. But, had history taken a different course, Burgundy could have ended up a separate country. Europe's national boundaries have always had a delightfully arbitrary nature to them, and it was this aspect of Burgundy which particularly intrigued project editor **Rosemary Bailey**. "I felt the fate of Burgundy was a key to appreciating the more flexible frontiers of Europe we are working towards," she says, "and I thought we might learn a great deal from Burgundy's positive regional identity."

Bailey has specialised in regional Insight Guides, having edited *Tuscany, The Loire Valley* and *The Côte d'Azur*, and she especially relishes the challenge of discovering what characterises a particular region and its people. Based in London but a frequent visitor to France, Bailey also contributes articles regularly to various British and foreign publications. In this book, she writes about Dijon and the south of Burgundy, not resisting a brief foray into Beaujolais, nor a few glasses of Moulin-à-Vent.

Visual magnificence

The stunning photography which illustrates this guide is mostly the work of **Lyle Lawson**, an American based (when she isn't travelling the globe) in England. She has brought her keen eye and understanding of what makes a place tick to many Insight Guides, and was editor and photographer of Apa's *Inland Waterways of Europe*. She is passionate about ballooning and barges, and has contributed articles on both activities in Burgundy. Despite the quantity of camera equipment crammed into her MGB sports car, she also managed to load up an astonishing number of bottles of Pouilly-Fuissé.

Bailey quickly assembled an impressive team of expert writers. **Lisa Gerard-Sharp** is a European-based travel journalist and broadcaster, and a regular contributor to the Insight series. While living in Brussels, she found time to explore the old Burgundian empire, which used to include most of Belgium. From her interviews with priests, potters, cattle-breeders, wine growers and a host of others, she has produced a thought-provoking analysis of the Burgundian character and life in the region today, as well as a comprehensive and illuminating guide to the northern *départements* of the region, sampling a variety of fine Chablis on the way.

Peter Graham is also a frequent contributor to Insight Guides, and here he rises to the challenge of explaining the complicated topic of wine in Burgundy, along with a tantalising description of the great cuisine of the region, and a guide to the Côte d'Or itself. Food and wine are his favourite subjects – and, according to his friends, the main reason he moved to France in the first place. He lives in a small village in the Auvergne, writing regularly for London's *Guardian*, *Times* and *Sunday Times*. His most recent book is *Classic Cheese Cookery*, winner of the André Simon Memorial Prize. "One of the things I particularly enjoyed," he says, "was being able to drink a Gevrey-Chambertin with a coq-au-vin made with the same wine."

Bailey was assisted by author **Barry Miles**, for whom Burgundy combined two of his greatest passions, wine and Romanesque architecture. In this book, he introduces the

Bailey

Lawson

Gerard-Sharp

Graham

Miles

region's architectural heritage by explaining how and why the great monasteries and churches were built, and bemoans the fate of the greatest of them all, Cluny, lost to an early breed of property developer. He particularly approves of the fact that the monks devoted as much of their energy to wine cultivation as they did to building churches.

John Ardagh is a familiar name to Francophiles, as the author of many books on the country, including the perennially popular *France Today*. His portraits of writers Colette and Lamartine capture their profound attachment to the Burgundy landscape and the literary inspiration they drew from it.

Rowlinson Carter is another frequent Insight contributor, and his dramatic history of the Valois dukes and their court fleshes out the tortuous history of the period with a wealth of detail and gossip.

Ward Rutherford is a broadcaster and author of numerous history books, including a popular account of Celtic mythology. Here he brings his knowledge of the period to the early history of the first Burgundians.

Journalist **Caroline Bailey** participated in the religious community of Taizé, and has contributed a thoughtful description of its role today.

Exhaustive information

This Insight Guide combines Burgundy's history with a detailed guide to the region, enriched by the personal observations of the people who actually live there. It begins with an exploration of the essential character of the province, Burgundy as a "state of mind".

Today Burgundy is a "lost kingdom", a pale reflection of its former glory, and we first of all track the complex forces that have shaped it. After establishing the historical context, we look at contemporary Burgundy, its local politics and the compelling details of provincial life. The hugely important subject of food and wine is dealt with next, including interviews with food producers and winemakers who describe for themselves the pleasures and pressures of their business.

The Places section journeys round the region, describing in detail the sights to be seen and providing essential background information. Although recommendations are often made about restaurants and especially wine, basic factual information, listing hotels, restaurants, museums, activities, and a wealth of travel advice, is reserved for the Travel Tips section, found at the back of the book for easy reference.

Jill Adam, who compiled Travel Tips sections for the *Brittany, the Loire Valley,* and *Côte d'Azur* Insight Guides, and also edited the *French Farm and Village Holiday Guide* for some years, has compiled the exhaustive listing of information for this book. She welcomes any opportunity to spend more time in her house in southwest France.

Jane Sigal, a Paris-based food writer, has contributed a knowledgeable survey of restaurants in the region, including not only some of the finest cuisine in France but also many good-value humbler establishments.

Jill Anderson guided the text skilfully through a variety of Macintosh computers in Insight Guides' London editorial office, and proof-reading and indexing were completed by **Carole Mansur**.

Ardagh

Carter

Rutherford

Adam

History

Features

Places

Maps

TRAVEL TIPS

Compiled by Jill Adam

For detailed information see page 309

Burgundy has been called *un état d'esprit*, a state of mind. It is the invisible bridge between northern France and the Midi, a transition from the cerebral north to the earthy south, from adulthood to a fantasy French childhood. Every Parisian is a born-again Burgundian at heart.

Henri Vincenot, traditionalist and professional Burgundian, equated northern Burgundy with *la zone parisienne*. In French eyes, Vincenot's books have done for Burgundy what Pagnol and *Jean de Florette* did for Provence. Full-bodied wine, glittering fish-scale roofs and Romanesque churches suggest a semblance of unity in a subtle province. Burgundian hallmarks exist but are elusive, belonging to character rather than to architecture. Burgundy in the blood presumes an irrepressible spirit. It is tinged with religiosity and nostalgia but tempered by mischievous gaiety and wit as sharp as Dijon mustard.

Even in the 15th century the region was reputed for its climate and rich living. Philip the Bold's family came to Burgundy "to enjoy better air and nourishment unavailable in Flanders". The region officially designated Burgundy today encompasses the *départements* of Yonne, Nièvre, Côte d'Or and Saône-et-Loire, but this area bears only a passing resemblance to the Burgundy of yore, which at various stages extended as far as Provence, and included most of Belgium, as well as parts of the Netherlands and Switzerland. In the Middle Ages the original Kingdom of Burgundy established in the 5th century was always looked back on as a legendary home: the "lost kingdom".

The classic image of Burgundy is of golden vineyards and gentle slopes. But real Burgundy is a patchwork of prosperous wine country and fertile pastures interspersed with poorer plains and woodland. Each view has its chauvinistic champions and evokes a dreamy nostalgia for a childhood never-never

land. Madame de Sévigné, that indefatigable letter-writer, was born in the Auxois and loved the lush countryside and air "which you have only to breathe to get fat". Her grandmother, Jeanne de Chantal, owned the Château de Bourbilly, a short ride from fattening Époisses, the village which produces Burgundy's best cheese. "I have just arrived in the château of my forebears," she marvelled. "Here are my beautiful meadows, my little river and my magnificent windmill, just where I left them."

The hilly Mâconnais is a landscape famously sentimentalised by Lamartine. The Romantic aristocratic poet lived in rural bliss near the village of Milly. As a child he loved his creeper-clad manor and "the sweet and melancholy voices of the little frogs that sing on summer evenings". As an adult, Lamartine owned local vineyards but regularly returned to his childhood home to relive his boyhood.

This landscape remains an inspiration: the Rock of Solutré, a prehistoric site, is the object of a Whitsuntide pilgrimage by François Mitterrand and his followers. The descent naturally ends in the Pouilly-Fuissé vineyards at the foot of the cliffs.

Preceding pages: *Habit de Vigneron* by Bonnar (17th century); flying the flag; Burgundy canal barge; Beaune market; grape-picking; wedding at Auxonne. <u>Left</u>, snail-grower, Jean-François Vadot. <u>Right</u>, 18th-century wine merchant's sign.

Less celebrated is the secretive landscape of the Puisaye, with its lakes, neat hedges and slender trees. As Colette's childhood home, its fate is sealed as Colette country. Born in 1873 at St-Sauveur-en-Puisaye, on the edge of Burgundy, this self-appointed *reine de la terre* describes her rural childhood in the *Claudine* books. "If you came to my home on a fine summer's day, you would find a dark garden devoid of flowers, and in the distance, would watch the mountain turn bluish, its slopes covered with pebbles, butterflies and thistles tinged a dusty mauve – you would forget me." But, as Burgundy's best-loved writer, her presence is pervasive.

When Shakespeare spoke of "waterish remote, as do the misty marshes and valleys of La Bresse. To the west, the rolling countryside around Charolles is home to placid white Charolais cattle, a celebrated export second only to wine.

Yet to outsiders, the Burgundian landscape is forever linked to wine. The Côte d'Or, named for the rich colour of the earth, is a narrow ribbon stretching south from Dijon. The buff-stone villages in the vineyards have a pampered look, in keeping with the cosseted proprietors. Comtesse de Loisy, for example, belongs to an old family of *vignerons* in Nuits-St-Georges. The canny countess recently traded 12 bottles of Clos de Vougeot Grand Cru 1947 for an Alfa Romeo.

Burgundy", he visualised Flanders, then part of Burgundy, but the image remains apt in the watershed of France. The Yonne is the traditional waterway to Paris; the Loire marks the western border of Burgundy; and the Saône wends its way through the southern vineyards. With 700 miles (1,100 km) of navigable rivers and canals, the region is a veritable paradise for barging.

A third of the territory is forested, from the watery Puisaye to the northern plains of the Châtillonais. The Morvan is the dark heart of Burgundy, a rugged interior dominated by mountains, forests and fast-flowing streams. Devoid of literary champions, it remains

"The buyers pleaded. I told them the wine was too old to travel, but finally I gave in." Even so, she kept a bottle back, claiming its fragrance of mushrooms and autumn leaves epitomised a Burgundian childhood. As Colette wrote: "My homeland enchants me, intoxicates me, but leaves an after-taste of bittersweet nostalgia".

The Côte d'Or offers rich civic architecture, champagne-coloured villages in serried ranks of vines. Clos de Vougeot and La Rochepot are sumptuous châteaux at ease with their surroundings but the Hôtel-Dieu in Beaune draws the deepest admiration. On leaving Beaune, Henry James remarked: "I carried away the impression of something mildly autumnal – something rusty yet kindly, like the taste of a sweet russet pear."

The sensuous and spiritual landscapes complement one another perfectly. Burgundy may keep its feet on the earth but has its head in the clouds. The Romanesque churches are hymns to the spirituality of the province, as is the proliferation of religious foundations.

If the landscape is deeply civilised it is thanks to the monastic tradition that swept Burgundy in the Middle Ages. Until the construction of St Peter's in Rome, Cluny was the largest church in Christendom, and enjoyed phenomenal power for hundreds of years. Corruption and laxity were, however,

As a leader he was a fanatic, embroiled in every controversy, and launching the doomed second crusade at Vézelay. But to his credit 500 Cistercian abbeys flourished in his lifetime and 3,000 a century later. Simple monastic estates like La-Pierre-Qui-Vire survive in Burgundy today, living the contemplative life and producing the Zodiaque series on Romanesque architecture.

Burgundy has always been characterised by a universal religious impulse, and today shelters a wide spectrum of religious foundations. Roger Schutz founded Taizé here in 1944; it is now a huge flourishing community. Burgundy is also home to the Buddhist monastery at Dettey, the largest in Europe,

inevitable and eventually the reforming figure of St Bernard appeared on the scene.

He was a young nobleman born near Dijon in 1090 who joined Stephen Harding's Cistercian community at Cîteaux. While Harding ran Cîteaux, St Bernard roamed France, preaching, debating and founding abbeys, including Clairvaux and Fontenay. As a monk he adhered to the original Benedictine precepts of obedience, silence, contemplation and penitence, preaching a pared-down Christianity, a reaction against Cluniac excess and luxury.

<u>Left</u>, *en famille*. <u>Above</u>, Clos de Vougeot chefs.

while 1992 saw the opening of France's first Islamic theological institute nearby. Not for nothing is Burgundy known as *le toit du monde occidental*, the religious roof over the Western world.

Churches provide the natural stage for Burgundy's procession of master craftsmen. In Autun, the presence of Roman remains inspired church sculpture, imbuing the figures with harmony and a haunting sense of loss. Gislebertus d'Autun's *Eve*, captured at the moment of temptation, is one of the most vibrant Romanesque sculptures ever made. Luckily, medieval sculptors ignored St Bernard's admonitions against ornament: "In

God's name, if you are not ashamed of these idiocies, why at least are you not sorry to incur such expense?"

Nor was expense spared in the time of the Grand Dukes, when the Flemish influence was paramount. Arts and crafts were the acceptable face of cultural imperialism. Sculptor Claus Sluter left his mark in Dijon with his magnificent *Moses*. Roger van der Weyden, another Flemish master, painted a poignant *Last Judgement* to adorn the Hôtel-Dieu at Beaune. The golden triangle of Beaune, Brussels and Bruges grew opulent under lavish Burgundian patronage. The Italianate châteaux of Ancy-le-Franc and Tanlay boast exquisite Renaissance marque-

equation between *douceur de vivre* and *joie de vivre*. Contrary to this rollicking image, Gaston Roupnel defines his fellow Burgundians as "those who pause on their journey, with the time and inclination to marvel".

"Burgundian" may be a byword for opulence and excess but the regional temperament is quieter, more perceptive, patient and pragmatic. Artists tend to be unsentimental and robust. Colette was never self-consciously a "writer" but turned her hand to anything; Vincenot was also a sculptor and carpenter; even Lamartine, the precious poet, was an amateur *vigneron*.

Humour is typically understated, teasing or ironic, occasionally delighting in the mis-

try, a decorative talent which survived the passing of the Dukes. Even at the end of the Ancien Régime, classical châteaux, including Versailles, continued to benefit from Burgundian good taste.

The Flemish inheritance colours the Burgundian character. The stereotype is of a red-faced, simple-minded, hot-blooded womaniser. This *Joyeux Bourguignon* (Jolly Burgundian) is a stock figure in racy 16th-century literature. Such satirical and scatalogical tales echo Rabelais, the product of a similarly merry wine-growing region, the Loire. But this flamboyant temperament owes much to astute public relations and to a simple

fortunes of others. An air of detachment masks a quiet faith, a closeness to nature and a sense of continuity. Burgundian lore stresses that a new thing succeeds only if it is deeply rooted in tradition.

An epicurean image is confined to the Côte d'Or. Yet even here it is muted: conviviality is reserved for visitors or festivals. Beaune is Burgundy's wine capital but its cellars are synonymous with secrecy.

Writer Jean-François Bazin, a Burgundian born and bred, believes that the wine-growers are discreet by nature. They are tolerant on all matters – except for the superiority of Burgundy: "Bordeaux is often prescribed for the sick but our wines are for the healthy."

Caustic humour is a common link throughout Burgundy, best reflected in stories. Equally typical is a sceptical, irreverent tone of distant mockery. In the words of writer Jules Renard: "We're put on earth to laugh. We won't be able to laugh in purgatory or hell and laughter wouldn't be fitting in heaven." Bussy-Rabutin, the author of a satirical novel about Louis XV's court, was a true Burgundian in his witty mischief-making. As Robert Speaight remarks: "A country which produced both St Bernard and Bussy-Rabutin may claim to have reconciled within its borders the extremes of human nature."

aime mieux y croire que d'y aller voir" (people would rather take it for granted than go and see for themselves).

Chauvinism is justified by the richness of the province yet even famous Burgundians are modest, from Nicéphore Niepce, the inventor of photography, to Gustave Eiffel whose tower dominates the Paris skyline. Eccentrics are rare in such a balanced region. None the less, the transvestite Chevalier d'Eon made his mark in Louis XV's employ and even fooled Casanova about his true sex. This diplomat, spy, swordsman and bonvivant allegedly introduced red Burgundy to Britain. Xavier Forneret, Lamartine's contemporary, lived in a Gothic tower near Beaune

St Bernard aside, Burgundians are no saints, even in the church. St Bernard himself had selective compassion, railing against spendthrift abbots and scantily clad women alike. In modern times, Chanoine Kir best exemplifies the priest who is more spirited than spiritual. As mayor of Dijon after 1945, he was a truculent, caustic character remembered both as a war hero and as the populariser of Kir.

A Burgundian expression holds that *"On*

Left, firemen's fête at Ligny-le-Châtel. **Above**, bandsmen at the Bague festival, Semur-en-Auxois.

and slept in a coffin. When not playing the violin, he wrote poetry which later inspired the French Surrealists.

Burgundy also boasts Pierre-Athanase Larousse, a fitting son for a place so preoccupied with language. Larousse pored over his famous dictionary, "my brain and heart swelling with Burgundian sap". The language is as soft as the landscape. In Burgundy, Auxerre is rolled as "Ausserre" and Auxois melts into "Aussois". The dialects reveal Celtic and Flemish influences. *Tu es un vrai bourguignon* has been a Flemish expression for a bonvivant since the days of the Grand Dukes. Despite the trend towards *cuisine légère* most Burgundians still favour *cuisine traditionelle*, food enriched by wine, wine enhanced by food. Henry James relished the "poetry" of Bresse butter: "*'Nous sommes en Bresse et le beurre n'est pas mauvais,'* the landlady said, with a sort of dry coquetry."

Burgundian appetites are nothing if not robust. Jugged hare, *jambon de Morvan, boeuf bourguignon, poires Dijonnaises* and Burgundy-drenched *coq au vin* are traditional fare. Henry James also gorged himself on eggs in Bourg-en-Bresse: "*La plus belle fille du monde ne peut donner de ce qu'elle a*; and it might seem that an egg which has succeeded in being fresh has done all that can be reasonably expected of it." The region

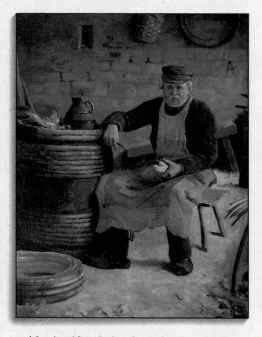

prides itself on being *bien dans son assiette*, at ease with its soul and stomach. The hearty attitude to food reflects an equally earthy approach to life.

Even the mystical writings of Romain Rolland are suffused with sensuousness. He describes an idyllic country childhood in which "the taste and smell of the resin, of the honey, acacia and warm earth have entered my flesh and bones forever". Sensuousness and sensuality often merge. Réstif de la Bretonne, a friend of Madame de Staël's, supposedly kept a calendar of his mistresses, one for every day of the year.

Earthiness is arguably a Gallic legacy.

Certainly, there is a Celtic flavour to Burgundian folklore. Vercingétorix fought the Romans all over Burgundy but was crushed at Alésia, a defeat spelling the end of Gaul. Despite the conquest, the deities of the Roman pantheon did not obliterate Gallic cults. Vercingétorix' misty-eyed appeal is to Celtic sensibilities. There are plans to turn Bibracte, the Celtic camp in the Morvan, into a theme park: Ancient Gaul by way of Asterix.

The archetypal Celt was Henri Vincenot, whose moustache recalls both Vercingétorix and the Jolly Burgundian of yore. The story-teller lived in the fertile farmland of the Auxois until his death in 1985. He used Burgundian settings and his peasant stock as a source for his novels. This modern folk hero defied the Romanisation of France, calling himself "a Celtophile, Celtomane and above all, a Celt". His *Livre de Raison de Glaude Bourguignon* is a work of Burgundian resistance to all colonisation. Vincenot's novels show that the native character has survived the loss of Gauls and Grand Dukes.

In *Pape des Escargots*, his best-known work, Vincenot tells the story of a snail-breeder in the tiny village of Saffres on the Côte d'Or. The biggest snail is fattened up and then ceremoniously eaten on the family feast day. Not for nothing is the snail the regional symbol, occupying church capitals, and decorating Dijonnais town houses, as well as one's plate. It is modest, sensitive, shows its horns from time to time, but mostly goes quietly about its business. The snail is the soul of Burgundy, a province *bien dans sa peau*, happy in its shell.

Vincenot coined the phrase *civilisation lente* to describe the snail's pace of the province. Sensible visitors travel at the speed of the slowest canal boat, indulging in a leisurely wine-tasting, with time to discuss vintages and note the recipe for *gougères*, crusty cheese pastries. Trails around Romanesque churches and Renaissance châteaux create an appreciative Burgundian appetite. Henry James "came away with a strange mixture of impressions – of late Gothic sculpture and thick *tartines*". Colette's advice is as sound as ever: "Burgundy is like a pig: some parts are more memorable than others but every bit is edible."

Left, traditional *sabotier*. **Right**, *sabotier* Romain Doré in St-Père-sous-Vézelay today.

EVROPA MVNDI PARS QVARTA:

Julio cesare imperante · A theodoto dimersa · nominatur pars tercia ·
Sed uere est quarta · nam asia et in? partes duas & affrica tercia · europa &
Habet europa maria XI · insulas XL · prouincias XX · oiaturos XXVI ·
inter opida CXXI · flumina XXI · Gentesq; diuersas numero XXXVI
Regna ii que se colore rubeo circuscripta ad romanos francosq; ptinent img in
EVROPA dicta e ab europpa filia agenoris regis lybie · uxoris iouis :·

The historical boundaries of Burgundy may have wavered but its devotion to wine has not. The Romans first discovered the symbiosis of wine-grape and Burgundian soil, as one vineyard, the Vosne-Romanée, famous for its high-quality reds, still recalls. But it was earlier occupiers, the Celts or Gauls, who could be said to have been its first serious oenophiles. Ferocious warriors, prodigious lovers and voracious eaters with a weakness for roast boar, the Celts were so addicted to wine that it was said they would swap a slave for a jugful, a servant for a single swallow.

The region had, of course, been inhabited long before the arrival of the Celts in the 1st millennium BC. Indeed, the Rock of Solutré near Mâcon has lent its name to the Solutrean Culture which flourished 23 centuries ago. Distinguished for its jewellery and cave-paintings, its craftsmen invented the technique of pressure-flaking of flint, enabling them to produce arrow and lance heads as delicate as the laurel and willow leaves after which they were named.

The Celts continued this love of the beautiful. With their productive farms yielding grain in abundance, they were able to exchange the surplus not only for wine, but for works of art from all Europe, as grave-goods found in a burial chamber on the hill of Vix and now in the Châtillon-sur-Seine museum testify. Besides Baltic amber work, silver cups and bronze wine jars from Tuscany, they included the remains of a funerary chariot. In it was the skeleton of a Gallic princess, adorned with bracelets and pearl necklaces and crowned with a gold diadem.

Most sensational of all was the Vase de Vix, a magnificently decorated bronze krater or urn from Greece large enough to hold at least five fully grown adults. Though its function may have been decorative, it might equally have had a ritual purpose since one Celtic method of human sacrifice was to hold the victim's head down in a container of water until they drowned.

Preceding pages: Roman inscription, Cluny. Left, Burgundia at the centre of medieval map of Europe. Right, statue of Vercingétorix.

Always a loose and quarrelsome confederation of tribes, the Celts were capable of temporary unification to launch some military adventure. In 390 BC, the Senones, whose capital was at Sens, were the prime movers in an invasion of Italy in which Rome was seized and held to ransom for seven months.

The Vix princess belonged to the Sequani tribe and in 60 BC their neighbours, the Aedui, believing themselves under threat from her people and their allies, the Helvetii,

appealed to the Romans for support. That they gave it was due solely to their fear that Gaulish inter-tribal strife might jeopardise their possessions in southern France and Spain. And what ensued was to change the course of European history.

In a lightning campaign in 58 BC Julius Caesar, the Roman commander-in-chief, defeated the Helvetii outside the Aeduan capital, Bibracte (now Mount Beuvray, near Autun) and seized the Sequanan capital, Vesontio (now Besançon).

However, Caesar was profoundly distrustful of his Aeduan allies and particularly of Dumnorix, younger brother of the king who was making a bid for leadership. During the winter of 53–52 BC he decided on the total subjugation of Gaul and, in the early spring, began the redeployment of the limited forces at his disposal.

Before its completion his fears were confirmed. At a secret conclave in the Aeduan capital the most powerful of the Gaulish chieftains had banded themselves into an anti-Roman league led by the young Vercingétorix, king of the Arvernians (what is now the Auvergne).

The first assault came while Caesar's vastly outnumbered legionaries were on the march. The defeat, which seemed inevitable, was turned into victory by superior organisa-

tion and discipline and a badly mauled Vercingétorix was forced to pull back to Alésia (Alise-Sainte-Reine) where his statue now stands. Pursued and besieged by Caesar, he held out for six weeks only, forced to surrender when an Aeduan relief column failed to reach him. He was taken to Rome in chains, paraded by Caesar at his triumph, then secretly strangled.

Despite the devastating blow dealt to the Gauls' morale by the failure of this, the biggest and most promising of all their revolts, the country remained turbulent, and total subjugation was not achieved until the reign of Augustus, who succeeded Caesar in 45 BC. Razing Bibracte, he built a new capital called Augustodunum, in his own honour. Although the name has since been eroded to Autun, its remains, including a 15,000-seat amphitheatre, testify to a past when it was "sister and rival to Rome".

The next four centuries saw Rome's conversion to Christianity while, at the same time, its hold on its dominions grew feebler. It was now that those who were to give their name to Burgundy entered the scene. From original homelands on the southern shores of the Baltic, the Burgundi had been pushed westward by a variety of enemies finally to reach the easternmost borders of the Roman Empire. Here a century and half of contact had so conditioned them that they spoke of themselves as Romans and had adopted Christianity. The Romans, believing the Burgundi might form a buffer against the hostile Huns and Germans, encouraged them to settle along the banks of the Saône, thus laying the foundations of modern Burgundy.

There was to follow a period of several centuries in which Burgundy passed through different hands and, like a patch of oil tossed on an ocean, would sometimes expand, sometimes contract, sometimes split into several parts. The first expansion, in the 5th century, took its borders to the west bank of the Rhine. Then, in the middle of the century, a rash quarrel with Rome led to almost total annihilation and the massacre of the ruling dynasty, a disaster recounted in the medieval German Nibelungenlied, later used by Wagner as the basis of his *Ring* cycle.

Those who survived were deported to an area round Lake Geneva in what is now Savoy. None the less, they were soon expanding once more, this time north and west and into the Rhône and Saône valleys.

It was during this period that there occurred what may have been the precursor to the later alliance between Burgundy and England. To the north the British – led, according to legend, by King Arthur – had just established a defensive line against the invading Angles and Saxons. The Burgundian king, Gundioc, is known to have numbered among his allies one Riothamus from "over the water". Geoffrey Ashe in *The Discovery of Arthur* argues that "Riothamus", roughly "Great King", was none other than Arthur himself. After a defeat at the hands of Goths in about 470, Riothamus (or Arthur) withdrew to Burgundy where he died. Ashe suggests he was buried at Avallon near Vézelay, rather than in England at the traditional "Avalon" usually identified with Glastonbury in Somerset.

What came to be known as the Second Burgundian Empire reached its peak under Gundioc's son, Gundobad – an achievement which, however, involved him in the murder of his brother, Chilperic, and his wife. Forced, for his own safety, to shut their two teenage daughters up in a convent, a chance encounter by one of them, the spirited Clothilde, with Clovis, the legendary 20-year-old king of the neighbouring Franks, led to romance. Eventually Clothilde es-

crucifixion. The fact that a number of experts have asserted that it was probably a refectory bread knife failed to save it from seizure centuries later by Adolf Hitler, convinced that his own destiny was bound up with it.

The links between the Burgundian and Frankish royal families were strengthened when one of Clovis's four sons married Sigismund's daughter. But, as was inevitable in such a union, it was the more powerful partner, in this case the Franks, who were to dominate and much of the future was to be a struggle by Burgundy to free itself from Frankish domination.

When Clothilde's last surviving son Lothar, king of the Franks from 558, died in

caped and married Clovis in AD 493. Clovis was converted to Christianity and helped establish the powerful link between church and state which dominated so much of the Middle Ages.

In 516 Gundobad was succeeded by his son Sigismund, canonised for his endowment of the monastery of St-Maurice d'Agaune which acquired an international reputation as the home of the lance supposedly used to pierce the side of Christ at the

Left, coin with head of Caesar, Mt Beauvray museum. **Above**, Celtic pottery, Châtillon-sur-Seine.

561, his empire was divided among his five sons, with the fourth, Guntram, receiving Burgundy. This would eventually be extended to include territories in Provence, Italy and northern central France.

In 570 Guntram's younger brother, Siegebert, married the daughter of the Visigoth king of Spain, Brunhilde. Renowned as a beauty, her ambition and iron will were to make her enemies who, in her old age, subjected her to a cruel and humiliating death. With only one brief intermission, the Frankish occupation of Burgundy lasted 150 years when the torch of independence was raised once more. Its bearer was St

LA·ROYNE·CLOTILDE
LE·ROY
CLOVIS
S·REMY
AVRELIEN

Leodegar (or Léger), Bishop of Autun, who, in 675, fought an epic battle on his people's behalf against the Frankish chief minister, Ebroin, before being tricked into giving himself up to be blinded and beheaded.

Had he survived six years more he would have seen his homeland free, although, like most of France, faced with a new threat from the Saracens. With their advance temporarily brought to a halt at the gates of Sens in 731, Charles Martel defeated them decisively at Poitiers the following year. However, for the Burgundians, relief was tempered by their re-subjugation to the Frankish kingdom a year later.

But their overlords were not without problems of their own. Although in 771 their domains were consolidated into the Holy Roman Empire by Charles Martel's grandson, Charlemagne, who was responsible for the Carolingian "renaissance" of art and learning, territorial quarrels among heirs followed his death. These were partially resolved when his grandson, a second Lothar, inherited the title of Holy Roman Emperor. Resonant as the title was, in practice he was master of only one of the three strips into which Charlemagne's empire had been divided, the one that included Provence and Burgundy. Even his permanent possession of this was doubtful as, to the west, he was faced by a covetous step-brother, Charles, surnamed the Bald.

Charles's territorial hunger had temporarily to be curbed by the common need to meet the menace of the increasingly bold Norman raiders. The truce ended in 878 after a legendary figure in the independence struggle, Gérard of Roussillon, governor of Burgundy and Lothar's chief minister, defeated them. Charles promptly returned to the attack. Gérard vanquished him at Vézelay, only to be defeated himself at Vienne a year later.

However, the family squabbles which had fragmented the Holy Roman Empire persisted so that when Charles's brother-in-law Boso succeeded Gérard as governor in 879, though proclaimed king of Burgundy, he was actually ruler only over the area from Autun to the Mediterranean which came to be known as "Lower Burgundy".

Its counterpart, "Upper Burgundy", from 888 ruled by Boso's brother-in-law Rudolf

Guelph, included what is now Savoy as well as a considerable portion of Switzerland. From about 931 Upper and Lower Burgundy were merged, but the Burgundian kings still found they had little authority over one group of their nominal vassals, the counts in the area north of the Rhône in what was called Cisjurane Burgundy.

In 888, Boso's brother Richard the Justiciar had been given command of the forces fighting the invading Normans. Returning victorious, he so reorganised the administration of Cisjurane Burgundy as to make himself effective ruler. In 923 his son, Raoul, who had succeeded him two years earlier, became king of France, giving the dukedom to his younger brother, Hugh I.

Most of what had been the united kingdom of Upper and Lower Burgundy passed into other hands through marriages to become the Kingdom of Arles. At about the same time one of the rebellious Upper Burgundy counts, Raynald III, by refusing to do homage to its king, was finally acknowledged as a "free count" (franc comte), thereby giving his territory the name of Franche-Comté.

The region which the world was to know as Burgundy, though it was subject to further additions and subtractions, had come into existence as an independent French dukedom, its throne occupied by Capetian royal family dukes until the 14th century.

Its close relationship with the French crown notwithstanding, Burgundy preserved a surprisingly large measure of independence. The period was one of political stability in which Burgundy could be said to be participating in international events. Hugh I led a crusade against the Saracens in Spain, taking Toledo in 1084, and, in 1146, St Bernard of Clairvaux preached the second crusade at Vézelay.

At the same time, the arts and especially architecture, expressed in the building of the great churches, were flourishing. During the period which became known as Romanesque, roughly 10th–12th centuries, Burgundy's great Romanesque abbeys were created and spread their influence far and wide.

The peace and stability of the Capetian rule provided the opportunity for such developments. The Capetian line came to an end with the death of Philip of Rouvres in 1361, but under the Valois dukes who now acceded the fortunes of Burgundy were renewed.

Left, the *Baptism of Clovis*.

BRUNHILDE

I n 570, two daughters of the Visigoth king of Spain, Brunhilde and Galswintha, left home betrothed to the King of Burgundy. Fortunately for all concerned, there happened to be two kings of Burgundy, but even so the girls were entering what historians subsequently called the "Merovingian nightmare".

The nightmare is the rich backdrop to a wealth of legend, literature and music, everything from parts of *Beowulf* to the Anglo-Saxon poem *The Wanderer*, from William Morris's epic *Sigurd* to Ibsen's *The Vikings at Helgeland*, and perhaps above all to Wagner's monumental opera, *The*

Ring of the Nibelung.
According to Wagner, the people among whom the sisters were to settle were a tribe of dwarfs called the Gibichungs whose king, the Nibelung Alberich, had stolen the Rhine gold during their migration to a new homeland. Wagner was doing the first Burgundians (because that's who they were) an injustice, and it seems he was influenced by a 5th-century description of an altogether different Germanic tribe. "A foul, stunted, misshapen tribe, scarcely human, with a fearful swarthy aspect, shapeless lumps for heads, pin-

Above, Brunhilde, played by Norwegian soprano, Kirsten Flagstad. **Right**, monastic culture.

holes for eyes, and the cruelty of wild animals."
If the true Burgundians were in any way remarkable, it was owing to their habit of smearing themselves with rancid butter, which they found powerfully attractive, and bleaching their long hair with lime. Where Wagner comes closer to historical reality is in his evocation of a vanquished tribe clinging to its former identity in the shape of ancient regalia, specifically a lance, a sword and the signet ring which is the resounding motif of the opera. The tribe split, and it was to the respective kings of the two halves, Siegebert and Chilperic, that the Visigoth sisters were married. Both brides experienced immediate difficulties. Chilperic, whom Galswintha married, had a mistress of long-standing named Fredegund who was not about to be usurped. Galswintha bore the king a son but was strangled soon afterwards. And, according to one of the sagas, Brunhilde's loss of virginity simultaneously robbed her of certain supernatural powers.

No matter: Brunhilde had plenty of determination left, and her attempts to avenge her sister's murder led to 40 years of warfare. On the death of Siegebert, Brunhilde's husband, she was forced very much against her will into marriage with her nephew Merovech, Chilperic and Galswintha's son.

Brunhilde had a son of her own who succeeded to both Merovingian thrones but died soon after. The thrones then passed separately to his infant sons, Theodoric and Thierry, with Brunhilde acting as regent to both. She was forced to surrender Theodoric's regency but remained with Thierry in the Époisses château, about 8 miles (13 km) from Semur and one of the oldest fortified sites in Burgundy. Life with grandson Thierry at Époisses was said to have been so depraved that Columban, an Irish monk called in to bless the collection of royal bastards, refused to eat with the ménage. Pressed to say why, he merely stood at the table in silence, whereupon every vessel on it spontaneously exploded.

Despite grave doubts about her private life, Brunhilde the regent ruled with a firm hand. In 613 she was back at war, leading her army in battle on the shores of Lake Neuchâtel in Switzerland. At age 63, she was taken prisoner by the Franks and tortured for three days, tied by an arm and a foot and her long white hair to the tail of a stallion, which was then whipped into a gallop with the unfortunate Brunhilde in tow. In Wagner's version of events, it would seem she got off relatively lightly. ∎

21000–17000 BC: The Solutrian Era (named after the Rock of Solutré near Mâcon).

58 BC: The Celtic Aeduan tribe seek Roman help against the Sequani and Helvetii.

59 BC: Caesar defeats Helvetii near Bibracte (Mount Beuvray), the Aeduan capital.

52 BC: Vercingétorix's rebellion against Romans ends with his surrender at Alésia (Alise-Sainte-Reine).

AD 1–3: Augustodunum (Autun) replaces Bibracte as Aeduan capital.

AD 3–4: First Christian missionaries.

AD 443: Burgunds from the Baltic settle in Saône valley under Roman protection.

457: The County of Burgundy, with Geneva as capital, established by King Gundioc.

474: Reign of Gundobad. Second Burgundian Empire reaches its peak.

534: Franks occupy Burgundy.

616: Burgundy, under Clothar II, separated from Frankish empire.

657: Forced reunion with Franks by Ebroin.

720: Saracens reach northern Burgundy.

737: Charles Martel defeats Saracens and makes himself master of Burgundy.

843: Lothar I becomes ruler of Burgundy and Provence.

856–858: Raids by Normans.

859: Normans are defeated by Gérard of Roussillon.

868: Gérard defeats Charles the Bald.

871: Gérard defeated; succeeded by Boso.

880: Richard the Justiciar, his brother, given title of duke of Burgundy.

888: Rudolf Guelf becomes King Rudolf I of Transjuran Burgundy.

919: Magyar invasions.

923: Raoul, eldest brother of Richard the Justiciar, becomes King of France. Hugh, his younger brother, becomes Duke of Burgundy.

933: King Rudolf II reunites the Kingdom of Burgundy.

936: Separation of Duchy of Burgundy and Duchy of France, which includes Paris.

937: Magyars ravage the Lyonnais.

940: Foundation of Cluny abbey.

951: German influence increases after marriage of Conrad's sister to Otto I.

955: Otto routs Magyars, ending incursions.

973: Majolus, abbot of Cluny, begins expulsion of Saracens.

987: First Capetian king ascends throne of France.

1006: Holy Roman Emperor Henry II captures Basle from Burgundy.

1015: Robert Capet of France takes Burgundy.

1021: Robert Capet's second son, also Robert, becomes hereditary duke of Burgundy.

1078: Hugh I, Duke of Burgundy, leads crusade to Spain.

1084: Burgundian troops take Toledo from the Saracens.

1098: Order of Cistercians founded at Cîteaux.

1146: St Bernard preaches the second crusade at Vézelay.

1164: Hugh III, Duke of Burgundy, does homage to king of France.

1178: Frederick Barbarossa becomes King of Burgundy.

1186: Struggle between Duke Hugh III of Burgundy and Philip Augustus of France.

1193: Holy Roman Emperor Henry VI awards crown of Burgundy to Richard the Lionheart.

1281: Anglo-Burgundian alliance thwarts attempts to restore peace between France and Burgundy.

1315: French retreat from Burgundy.

1346: French defeat at Crécy.

1348: Burgundy ravaged by Black Death.

1361: The death of Philip of Rouvres ends the Capetian ducal line.

1364–1477: The four Valois dukes bring Burgundy to the height of its power.

1415: Decisive English victory at Agincourt turns Hundred Years' War in their favour.

1429: Joan of Arc passes through Auxerre on way to relieve the siege of Orléans.

1430: Joan of Arc captured by Burgundians at Compiègne.

1431: Joan of Arc is burnt at Rouen.

1477: Charles the Bold marries his daughter Mary to the Holy Roman Emperor. Beginning of Habsburg dynasty. Louis XI of France seizes most of old Burgundian kingdom.

1480: Margaret of Bourbon vows to build the monastery at Brou but work does not begin until 1506.

1513: Troops of the Holy Roman Emperor invade Dijon.

1526: Charles V briefly recovers the duchy.

1567: Auxerre invaded by Protestants.

1600: Henry IV invades Burgundy.

1602: Duchy of Burgundy annexed to France and enlarged by addition of Bresse, Bugey and Valromey.

1642: Briare Canal and Rogny lock-system completed.

1723: Burgundy Académie founded

1750: University of Burgundy founded.

1787: Second Lieutenant of Artillery Napoleon Bonaparte posted to Auxerre.

1789: Outbreak of French Revolution. Rioting in Champagne spreads to Burgundy.

1814–15: The Allied nations invade Burgundy when Napoleon I rejects conditions of

1890: Briare canal-bridge is constructed.

1906: Abbey of Fontenay, turned into paper mill during Revolution, restored.

1914: On 5 September, from his headquarters at Châtillon-sur-Seine, General Joseph Joffre, commander-in-chief of the French armies, issues the order which launches the Battle of Marne and brings the first major German reverse of World War I.

1934: Brotherhood of the Knights of Tastevin founded at Clos de Vougeot to promote wines of Burgundy.

1940: Ecumenical religious community founded by Father Roger Schutz at Taizé.

1940–44: French resistance fighters use the forests of the Châtillonais as a base.

the Congress of Châtillon-sur-Seine.

1815: First wine auctions held at Hospice de Beaune.

1832: Burgundy Canal opened.

1836: The works at Le Creusot by Joseph-Eugène and Adolphe Schneider become an important iron-founding enterprise.

1841: Steam hammer invented at Schneider factory.

1871: Burgundy occupied by Prussians.

1880: Entire French wine crop destroyed by Phylloxera insect.

Retable of the crucifixion, Salles des Gardes, Dijon.

14 Sept 1944: Troops of General Leclerc's division and the army of Lattre de Tassigny make contact.

1949: All Schneider factories amalgamated as the Société des Forges et Ateliers de Creusot.

1970: Société des Forges Creusot amalgamates with the Compagnie des Ateliers et Forges de la Loire to form Creusot-Loire. Morvan Regional Nature Park designated.

1974: Tibetan monastery opened at Château la Plaige, Luzy.

1981: François Mitterrand becomes President, from his base in Château-Chinon. TGV begins service to Dijon.

& Filio & Spiri_ tui san_

cto. R. Chri stus.

Post. Resp. dicitur Prosa Victimæ. ut in die Sancto
Paschæ. ad Vesperas. Pagina

IN ASCENSIONE DOMINI.

IN PRIMIS VESPERIS.

Ant. Cant. & Succ.

V Enit hora. Pf.

Nisi Dominus æ-

dificaverit domum; I. f.

Ant.
Subd.

D e- us. Pf. Beati omnes

qui timent Dominum. 7. a.

It is quite a feat of the imagination to picture how the small medieval French towns (for there were no great cities) looked before the building of the great cathedrals. The roads were muddy tracks, for the most part not even levelled, and the people lived in rude mud and wood shacks.

Towering over the hovels and the small Carolingian churches were the massive, overgrown ruins of long abandoned Roman towns: vast amphitheatres, triumphal arches and colonnaded temples covered with weeds and undergrowth, and gigantic aqueducts bigger than the towns themselves, spanning valleys with ease. The Romans built to last and during the great period of building known as the Romanesque, from about AD 950 to 1150, a huge number of Roman buildings were still standing.

In fact the very building of the great medieval churches resulted in the demolition of these Roman edifices and the reuse of their conveniently dressed stone. This had always been common practice; for example, in Carolingian times, Charlemagne used the columns from Ravenna in the cathedral of Aix-la-Chapelle. Nor was it just columns and dressed blocks they plundered; these early builders were not averse to reusing the occasional Roman capital, particularly in the construction of smaller, country churches.

Only one architectural manual has survived from Roman times, *The Ten Books on Architecture* by Vetruvius, in which he explains the proportions of columns, the floor plans of basilicas (an aisled building with a clerestory level for light) and the techniques of buttresses. After the Dark Ages, this was our only key to Roman construction. It was inevitable that medieval builders were influenced by the architecture around them, and that their own work should become known as Romanesque.

The Middle Ages were fantastic times. Though the threat of barbarian invasion was not over, relative political stability enabled agriculture to flourish and the population to

Preceding pages: medieval manuscript, Auxerre. **Left**, Vézelay, central aisle. **Right**, the founding of Cîteaux.

grow. The way was prepared in the late 5th century when Clovis, king of the Frankish settlers, built an enduring state from the ruins of the Roman Empire, but it was Charlemagne who ushered in the new age.

He created an orderly political system and enlarged the boundaries of Christendom by his military conquests, establishing strong ecclesiastical and political links with Rome wherever he went. He recognised that the Roman church was perhaps the greatest surviving inheritance from antiquity and it

could be said that his coronation as Roman Emperor at Christmastide AD 800 marked a new beginning for Europe. His tremendous energy and flair for innovation encouraged Carolingian art and architecture to flourish, merging the best of the old with new ideas.

His church architects developed many brilliant new ways of building, anticipating many Romanesque characteristics, but scholars hesitate to say that Romanesque architecture began during the Carolingian Renaissance, preferring to date Romanesque proper from the time of Otto the Great of Germany (936–73). This is because Carolingian sculpture, manuscripts and painting differ more sharply from the later Romanesque work and they prefer to group all Carolingian art and architecture together. However, because the Roman component in Carolingian architecture is very strong, the term Carolingian Romanesque is often used to describe their buildings.

Central to the growth and stability of French society was the spread of Christianity and the development of monasticism. The Benedictine order, founded in Italy at Monte Cassino in 529 by St Benedict of Nursia, spread at amazing speed throughout Europe. In the early Middle ages the stable monastic community acted to establish international order at a time when temporal government was to reform the Benedictine order and bring a civilising influence over much of Europe. Cluniac monks spread throughout the continent and within only a few years had established 1,450 houses and dependencies, bringing order and stability to a brutal and feudal world. Solving the problems caused by the construction of this many monasteries brought about a considerable advance in building technique in western Europe.

The monasteries had other civilising effects on their surroundings: they imposed the rule of law and gave the people a unified Christian world view. By implementing the feudal system of government they established new hierarchies of power which ena-

had broken down. An important monastery often consisted of 1,000 or more people, bigger than most towns of the time. The architectural problems involved in planning and building were on the scale of whole towns but even more monumental and integrated. The sophisticated solutions to building on this scale laid the groundwork for the great age of the cathedrals.

After Saracen, Norman and Magyar raids ended the Carolingian Renaissance, the Benedictines became corrupt and lax. However, at the beginning of the 10th century, William the Pious, Duke of Aquitaine, founded in the small village of Cluny, a monastery which bled them to extend their influence and beneficence into every area of society. In Burgundy, to feed the mother house of Cluny required 40 farms, each with its own chapel, and this brought about great advances in animal husbandry and farm management. It was the monks of Cluny who selected and planted the Chardonnay and Pinot Noir grapes in Burgundy, which today make some of the finest wine on earth.

Cluny organised pilgrimages to Santiago de Compostela and encouraged the Christian re-conquest of Moorish-occupied Spain. In pursuit of this cause Cluny built or enlarged vast basilicas all along the pilgrimage route, though they were not the only order to do so. Cluny was also responsible for the first crusade to drive the heathen from the Holy Land: Urbain II, who preached the first crusade in 1096, was from Cluny.

This was the greatest period of religious building France has ever known. In the three centuries between 1050 and 1350, several million tons of stone were quarried in France to build 80 great cathedrals, 500 large churches and tens of thousands of parish churches. More stone was quarried than in ancient Egypt during its entire history. The foundations of some of the cathedrals were as deep as 30 ft (9 metres) below ground, in certain cases forming a mass of stone as large

talism, that passed down the centuries and was responsible for the great scale of medieval church buildings.)

Not surprisingly, the first people to revive the old Roman ways of building were the Italians; in fact, *Lombardus* became the word for a mason in the early period. Until the monasteries and towns grew larger, masons, bell-founders, glass-makers and fresco painters worked as travelling bands. All across Europe bishops were calling out for skilled masons for their new churches, and craftsmen from Lombardy spread out from Milan, bringing their particular local interpretation of Romanesque with them. Burgundy was one of their destinations: William

as that above the surface. The buildings rose to astonishing heights, 30 or even 40 storeys, high even by today's standards for a small town.

Eventually there was a church or chapel for approximately every 200 people in the country, and in many of the towns, the entire population could attend the same service. (Early Roman Christianity provided only one church for each city in which the whole community was expected to meet. It was this traditional idea, and the notion of monumen-

Left, monks carrying relics. **Right**, cultivating the world.

of Volpiano, who began work on the abbey church in Dijon in 1001, brought craftsmen from his native Lombardy.

The Treaty of St-Clair-sur-Epte in 911 finally put an end to "Norman fury" and laid the foundations for the great Norman duchy. In the ensuing peace an architectural and intellectual revival began in the northwest, in Aquitaine and in Burgundy. Because of its rivers, Burgundy was uniquely situated to receive and exploit the new ideas and to select the best of the old: it had easy contact by way of the Loire with the architectural school of Western France; it was connected to the Empire by way of the Saône and knew about the Lombard First Romanesque style by way of the Rhône. There was a cult of relics with its consequent flow of pilgrims bringing new ideas, and monastic developments were growing apace.

Until the middle of the 12th century Burgundy was, comparatively speaking, the safest part of France. To the east were the Huns and to the north the Normans, while the Saracens kept up the pressure from the south. As a consequence, monks brought the relics of their saints from outlying parts of the country to the safety of the interior: Mary Magdalen was brought from St-Maximin to Vézelay, where her cult later brought riches to the abbey and town. Lazarus (who, legend

has it, brought Mary Magdalen in a rudderless boat to Marseille) was taken to Autun where he is buried behind the high altar; the church still possesses the oriental cloth in which his body was wrapped. St Baudèle was brought from Nîmes to Beaune; St Philibert's relics made a long journey from Noirmoutier to Tournus; St Médard, the 5th-century bishop of Noyon, was brought from Soissons to Dijon.

The peace of Norman France did not stop the pyromaniac Hungarians from visiting in 937 and 955, stirring the Burgundians to think seriously about fireproof vault construction. St-Philibert in Tournus was one of the monasteries which suffered most from the Hungarian invasion. The monks rebuilt it, however, and the new crypt was dedicated in 979. The ambulatory of their new church was derived from St-Martin in Tours, which had the first ambulatory, radiating chapels in procession behind the altar. It was the beginning of specifically French development in Romanesque architecture.

The plan and structure of Tournus shows a marked influence from the west of France, except in the St Michael chapel and the original belfries which were Lombard First Romanesque in style – the Burgundians were picking and choosing as they pleased. The result, after 150 years of labour when conditions were still very primitive, was an advanced church of the greatest importance to the history of medieval achitecture.

What Kenneth John Conant (the medieval scholar responsible for excavating Cluny earlier this century) called "the most spectacular of the Burgundy accomplishments in the Early Romanesque style, a very instructive example which summed up the progress of church architecture in the 10th century", was the Cluniac abbey church of St-Bénigne in Dijon. It was an entirely vaulted church, 305 ft (95 metres) long, begun in the first year of the new millennium.

Like Tournus, it was a *summa* of what had thus far been created in church architecture: the east end had a highly elaborate three-storey rotunda, essentially the same scheme as the Holy Sepulchre in Jerusalem, built over Christ's tomb, and probably copied from the Early Christian St-Pierre in Geneva, built around the year 600, which uses the same scheme. St-Bénigne had nine towers and turrets, which is a Carolingian arrangement, and was vaulted, which was Roman. Only the crypt remains of this amazing structure but it is well worth visiting.

The main problem facing the medieval architect was getting enough light into the building without weakening the walls. It was always a hit-and-miss business – we marvel at how long these buildings have remained standing only because we never knew the ones that fell down, often within a few years of being built.

The prototype of all Romanesque churches is the Roman basilica or hall – originally a very simple structure consisting of a central space, or nave, with collaterals or aisles on either side. A light wooden roof topped the building. No light could reach the central nave directly, since only the aisles had light from the outside walls. In Italy, with its strong sunlight, this was not much of a problem and small windows pierced in the outside walls provided all the light needed, reaching the nave through the triforum, the upper level of arches above the columns.

In order to light the nave directly, the next step was to raise the roof of the nave higher than the aisles so that windows could be pierced in it, creating a clerestory (literally "clear storey"). Since the nave only had to support a wooden roof, the loss of strength involved did not compromise the solidity of which collapsed shortly after, or even during, construction. The vertical downward thrust caused by the tremendous weight of the stone roof tended to made the walls bulge or thrust outwards as soon as openings were made in the clerestory.

The problem was the barrel or tunnel vault (*berceau*) which is the main characteristic of early French Romanesque churches, and particularly those of Burgundy. Unfortunately it makes the building top-heavy. This was the chief, if not the only, architectural problem that the builders of these early churches faced. Different parts of the country approached the problem in different ways: the Normans copped out and used

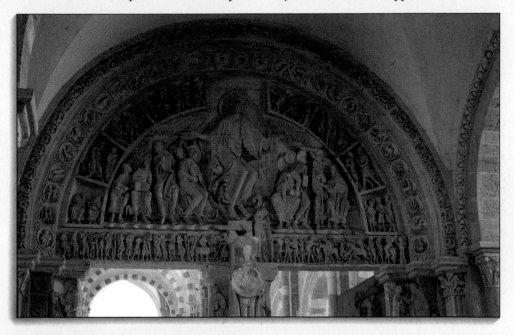

the building to any great extent and the roofs of the aisles now became lean-tos, preventing the walls from bulging.

In the northern, greyer climate of France, however, the problem was much greater. The builders wanted their churches to be fireproof, an important consideration in an age when enemy invasion was a constant threat. This, as well as the climate, dictated that they should vault the basilica in stone, not wood, posing a difficult structural problem as evidenced by the number of naves

Left, capital from Cluny. **Above**, tympanum at Vézelay.

wooden roofs but the Burgundians took such risks that in some of their experiments the stability of their churches was seriously threatened; the nave of the great church at Cluny fell down on more than one occasion.

Finally, after 200 years, it was the innovative Burgundian architects (or builders, for that was what they were) who solved the problem when they discovered rib-vaulting and the flying buttress – inventions which paved the way to Gothic with its unbroken columns soaring toward heaven and huge windows beyond the wildest dreams of Romanesque builders.

The builders of Cluny III were determined

to achieve direct lighting of their nave at all costs so they made their barrel vault as light as they dared, pointing the arch to diminish the outward thrust, a feature which later became one of the hallmarks of the Gothic style. They were never tempted to abandon the barrel vault, however, because the Cluniac psalmody, which was admired and imitated throughout western Europe, sounded its most beautiful when sung in a tunnel-vaulted church.

Another new feature, peculiar to the churches of Burgundy, was the narthex, or entry vestibule, built on to the west end of the nave. This can be open, as in St-Benoît-sur-Loire, or closed as at Vézelay or Tournus. It

was used as an anti-chamber where pilgrims waited their turn for admission. (These were all abbey churches, not generally open to the public.) The narthex alone at Cluny was five bays long, bigger than most parish churches. In some churches they were used as a prætorium where the abbots held their court, so they had a civil as well as an ecclesiastical use. At both Paray-le-Monial and Tournus, the narthex is double-storeyed. In fact, at Tournus the upper storey is a complete church in itself, called the *église supérieure*, originally intended for use as a sanctuary in times of danger.

Burgundian churches are of an unusual spaciousness but often have an unassuming barn-like exterior, relieved only by elaborate portals. Autun is often thought the most beautiful Burgundian church, provided you face away from the ugly 15th-century choir. Paray-le-Monial is cited for the airiness and beautiful proportions of its nave. All of these churches can be seen as forging towards the Gothic order as they strive to unify the interior into an orchestrated space.

Burgundy is also famous for its stone carving: the magnificent tympani at Autun and Vézelay; the capitals at Cluny and Sanlieu are considered national treasures; the wall-paintings at Berzé-la-Ville are possibly the best in France.

Under the puritanical strictures of St Bernard of Clairvaux and the Cistercians, Romanesque architecture took a more ascetic turn, producing the stark unadorned beauty of the abbeys of Fontenay and Pontigny. The Cistercian order banned the use of coloured glass, decorated floors, towers and carved capitals. St Bernard criticised his Cluniac brethren for their cloisters covered with "horrible beauties and beautiful horrors… disgusting apes, ferocious lions and monstrous creatures".

One of the daunting things about visiting these buildings is the business of Romanesque and Gothic. While it is generally true that if it has a round arch it is Romanesque, and if it's pointed it's Gothic, it is more useful to bear in mind the age of the building. There was an enormous difference between a church of the mid-11th century and one of the 13th century.

The differences are in the hundreds, or even thousands, of small technical advances made by the builders and incorporated in the next generation of buildings – a 250-year span of innovation and discovery which was to be followed by a further 250 years during which practically no progress was made at all in building construction.

During the course of their labours the Burgundian masons invented most of the features – the flying buttress, the pointed arch and the rib vault – which gradually combined to create the Gothic style, and paved the way for the great airy cathedrals of the 13th century.

Left, vaulting at St-Philibert, Tournus. **Right**, Paray-le-Monial, east end.

CLUNY

In 1132, the citizens of Cluny watched awe-struck as a procession of 1,212 monks, their voices raised in song, passed down the wide staircase from the abbey gates and entered their great abbey church. The monks entered the nave beneath the huge polychrome tympanum of Christ in glory, its brilliant colours now protected from the elements by the newly constructed narthex (or porch) after 20 years in the open. A double avenue of columns, 56 in all, led the eye to the high altar, and beyond that, painted on the half dome ceiling of the apse, a huge figure of Christ against a background of gold.

The greatest artists in Christendom had been assembled to paint these walls with scenes from the lives of the saints, all in glowing Byzantine colours of deep reds and blues. The capitals were carved by the unknown "Master of Cluny" a medieval genius whose work influenced countless other sculptors; a man capable of taking risks, of carving figures in motion, their clothing billowing in the wind, of making stone live. Like all the other stonework, the capitals were brightly painted, shining in the direct light which poured in from the high clerestory level.

Each day and night, for hundreds of years, the great church echoed with massed male voices as the 138 psalms of the day and night services were sung and the hours were recited by the two to three hundred monks always in attendance. The eight modes of Gregorian chanting, which was held in high esteem at Cluny, are shown on the eighth and ninth capitals of the choir; four to each capital and each represented by a musician. Each musical tone had religious as well as musical symbolism to the medieval mind and the Gregorian capitals are justifiably famous, though they suffered greatly at the time of the demolition. The chanting at Cluny was so important that the barrel vault was always employed in new Cluniac establishments because it provided the best echo for the chant. It was, said the monks, "as though Easter was celebrated every day in the abbey."

The monastery of Cluny was once the greatest power in Europe, deferred to by popes and kings, controlling the lives of tens of thousands of people, able to start crusades, and, though not possessing an army of its own, armed with the ultimate deterrent: excommunication. It had a fabulous income and controlled much of western Europe from a huge monastery built around the largest and most beautiful abbey church in the world, Cluny III, the pinnacle of Romanesque artistry and technical achievement. In fact, if the church had been any more advanced in its techniques, it would have been Gothic – as it was it already had flying buttresses and its barrel vault was slightly broken (both definitions of the Gothic order).

Cluny controlled more than 10,000 monks in over 1,600 monasteries, from Germany to Spain, Scotland to Switzerland, Italy to the Vistula in Poland, as well as more than 800 daughter houses in France including the great churches of Vézelay and Moissac. There was a saying, "Wherever the wind blows, there is rent for Cluny abbey."

Cluny was founded and endowed as a Benedictine monastery on 11 September 940 by Duke Guillaume of Aquitaine in the grounds of one of his houses. It was a good location, at the centre of a road network and yet surrounded by a great forest, parts of which survive to this day. Guillaume made it subject only to the Pope, a vital decision because interference by civil powers was common at the time.

Of the first church, Cluny I, built in 926, nothing remains. The second, Cluny II, was consecrated in 981 while the monastery itself was being rebuilt, but this, too, proved to be much too small to accommodate the growing numbers of monks. We still have its ground plan, part of which is marked out in a remaining chapel of Cluny III.

It was St Hugues of Semur (1049–1109) who conceived and began the stupendous building programme of the abbey church of Cluny III. He was the sixth abbot of Cluny and during his 49-year rule Cluny reached the apogee of its influence. In England William the Conqueror offered to pay in gold for the honour of having Cluny-trained monks as members of his clergy. Hugues refused the offer but a number of monks from Cluny were placed in English abbeys, notably Lewes and Wenlock. The Cluniac plan, utilising a double transept, appealed very much to the English and was used in many of the great British cathedrals even though no further examples were built in France.

In 1083 St Hugues visited the famous monastery of Monte Cassino, home of the Benedictine order of which Cluny was a part. Cluny was already too small for the size of its congregation and the vast size and sumptuous Byzantine paintings and mosaics of Monte Cassino inspired him to rebuild Cluny on a monumental scale.

From 1085 onwards the abbey became a building site; the design of the new building was carefully worked out, and combined the the most advanced ideas of architecture from all over Christian Europe. The work began on 30 September 1088, and in 1095 Pope Urbain dedicated the five altars in the choir and by 1100 both transepts had been completed except for the towers. At the time of Hugues's death in 1109, the entire east end, with its radiating chapels and towers, and half of the nave had been completed. The nave vault was completed by about 1120 but it collapsed soon afterwards and had to be rebuilt. The church was finally consecrated in 1130 by Pope Innocent II, and it was two years later that 1,212 monks processed through the magnificent building.

down more than 13 ft (4 metres), was a monumental labour in itself. Cluny survived the Revolution, and the painting of Christ on the apse was apparently still fresh and brilliant on the day it was blown to pieces by early 19th-century property developers, 700 years after it was painted. Now all that remains are a few fragments; the south tower of the transept, a gateway and a few capitals in the museum. It is possible to piece together how it must have looked by visiting other buildings in the area which were profoundly influenced by Cluny; this is best done by first visiting Paray-le-Monial, which, though smaller, is very similar to Cluny III in everything except the length of its nave. It gives a good sense of the architectural form of the original abbey.

It took just over 40 years to complete; an immense edifice 608 ft (187 metres) long, with four major steeples, two towers and double aisles in decreasing height. It was the longest building in Christendom for 500 years until the construction of St Peter's in Rome, which is only five feet longer. The organisation of building such a structure, the opening of quarries, making of scaffolding, recruiting and housing the workmen was a formidable task. The scale of the work itself was much larger than anything that had gone before it; just digging the foundations, which go

High altar at Cluny's new church is dedicated by Pope Urbain in 1095. Abbot Hugues is on right.

The abbey at Tournus, the sculpture of Vézelay, and the paintings at Berzé-la-Ville, give some indication of the richness of the decoration.

Most of what is now known about Cluny comes from the indefatigable work of the American archaeologist, the late Kenneth Conant, who painstakingly excavated the site and did many drawings reconstructing how it must have looked.

Imagination is necessary fully to appreciate its lost glories. But in Cluny today the massive abbey church, though long destroyed, still exerts a tremendous power. It is like an ancient ruined skyscraper, immensely larger than anything built in Cluny since, still controlling the lives of the townspeople who tore it down. ■

Another great flowering of art and architecture was seen under the Valois dukes, self-styled "grand ducs de l'Occident", who ruled Burgundy for the next century and a half. After petering out at the death of the last Capetian incumbent Philip of Rouvres in 1361, the Duchy of Burgundy was revived as a reward for the youthful petulance of Philip, fourth son of King John the Good of France. The 14-year-old prince had fought stoutly at his father's side during the Battle of Poitiers in 1356 and was not in the least overawed when taken prisoner, along with the king and half the French nobility, after a crushing English victory. He slapped the face of an English knight who in his opinion did not show due deference to the King of France, no matter what the circumstances.

Father and son were bundled off to England. The terms of their captivity observed the courtesies of a chivalric age, and indeed Edward III laid on a banquet to honour their arrival. Philip's stand on dignity was as vigilant as ever, and when a butler presumed to put food in front of the King of England before a King of France, he was given a sharp lesson in priorities with another resounding slap in the face. "Truly, cousin," sighed Edward, "you are indeed Philip the Bold." A famous 13th-century French king had been so called, and the nickname stuck. Philip's father promised that he would reconstitute the Duchy of Burgundy and give it to him.

In so doing, he created the illustrious line of Valois dukes, who were to become synonymous with the peak of Burgundy's glory. There was hardly any substance to the title or the duchy when the promise was made good. The whole of France was in a pitiful state, and not only because of the disastrous run of the Hundred Years' War with England, Poitiers being just one of a series of defeats. To make matters worse, the Black Death was raging, Paris was ungovernable, peasants everywhere were in open revolt, and gangs of disaffected mercenaries had taken the law

Preceding pages: 15th-century tapestry of wine-making. Left, wedding of Philip the Good and Isabella of Portugal. Right, John the Fearless and the Duc de Berry visiting Charles VI.

into their own hands. The Kingdom of France had not yet achieved any degree of ascendancy over the principalities, duchies, baronies and counties which made up the patchwork of feudal Europe. It was only a modest part of modern France and was overshadowed by many if not most of its neighbours, like Normandy. The kingdom was so short of money, in fact, that John was unable to meet the instalments on the ransom agreed with England. True to the spirit of the age, he dutifully returned to England and surren-

dered his person. Replying in kind, Edward laid on another banquet, an occasion marred by a wholly unexpected development. It seems, if some sources are to be believed, that John acknowledged the gesture too fulsomely and at the height of the celebrations dropped dead of drink.

With the French kingdom passing to Philip's elder brother Charles V (1364–80), Philip's only chance of making his inheritance, the Duchy of Burgundy, more than a name was through judicious marriage. Margaret, daughter of the Count of Flanders, and the former fiancée of Philip of Rouvres, was a candidate with mixed qualifications.

Plain to the point of wincing ugliness, she was nevertheless extremely rich, or would be when her father died. Her inheritance encompassed large parts of what are now Holland and Belgium as well as Franche-Comté. The count had justifiable misgivings about Philip's prospects, but these were adequately met by the French king who, if unable to help with money, was at least able to declare the Duchy of Burgundy hereditary. Philip and Margaret were married in Ghent in 1369 to the ultimate satisfaction of all concerned. They could have moved into in any one of a number of suitable ducal residences, but Philip was particularly keen to establish Dijon as a dynastic capital. The

town had existed in Roman times and grown in importance under the Capetian dukes. Philip himself had been living in Dijon for five years prior to the wedding.

The population of Dijon at the time numbered only a few thousand, and the skilled labour required to realise Philip's ambitious plans for the town was brought in from Flanders. He renovated and enlarged the Capetian residence, whose focal point was a massive square tower, some of which survives and is the oldest part of what is now the Palais des Ducs.

Philip's other major undertaking was to build outside the city walls the Chartreuse de Champmol, a monastery which he envisaged as a dynastic mausoleum. Margaret's contribution was to build a ducal bath-house. The cauldron for heating water eventually had a capacity of 5,000 gallons (23,000 litres). It took six men, three days' work and an enormous quantity of wood to bring the water up to the required temperature, a task performed once a month.

Ordinary living conditions, however, were squalid. Drainage was practically nonexistent so, in keeping with the times, all manner of rubbish and waste was simply dumped in the street. Philip called the town council together to discuss pavements and drains, but the finance was not forthcoming. Trenches filled with stones and covered with sand were dug down the centre of the major thoroughfares; paving did not materialise until the end of the 17th century.

Noble houses had roofs of coloured tiles in geometric patterns such as may still be seen on the Hôtel-Dieu in Beaune (founded 1443) and many architectural flourishes, introduced by the craftsmen brought in from Margaret's Low Countries. Lesser houses were wooden and thatched. The greatest contrast of all, however, was between the incredible extravagance of the knightly tournaments which went on for days, and the menace in the alleys of the town when darkness descended. A great number of traders were constantly passing through Dijon, and their presence attracted a floating population of "thieves, gamblers, adventurers, and scoundrels of all kinds", as described in William R. Tyler's lively account, *Dijon and the Valois Dukes of Burgundy*.

Nevertheless, Dijon prospered. The marriage of Philip and Margaret had effected a potent mixture of Burgundian ambition and Flemish wealth. Dijon became established as one of the major cities of medieval Europe and the centre of the most glorious period of Burgundian history. Philip the Bold was revered as a statesman and great patron of the arts. The junior line of the House of Valois was soon in a position to challenge its senior, the future kings of France proper. King Charles V, who had sanctioned Philip's marriage, died prematurely, suceeded by his 11-year-old son Charles VI. The boy was undoubtedly stupid and very likely mad. His uncle the Duke of Anjou showed what he thought of the future under the boy-king by running off with the contents of the treasury and the royal jewels. He had to be bribed with the promise of a fair share to bring the rest back. The compromise seems to have been satisfactory because the duke lent his influential voice to an arrangement which installed Philip of Burgundy and another of the king's uncles as regents.

Any hope of Charles being capable of ruling without regents receded as years went by. He started seeing and hearing things, with unpredictable results. He was once travelling with his entourage when he got it into his head that they were all traitors. Flailing at them with his sword, he was subdued with difficulty and taken home in

tinely pocketing half the revenues destined for the royal treasury. Philip had to wait until 1384 to get his hands on Margaret's colossal inheritance. While her father was still alive, he created a good impression by dealing efficiently with sedition in the Flemish towns, especially in Ghent. On the count's death, his responsibilities widened and he proved to be an excellent administrator with a special interest in the arts, manufacturing and commerce.

The one blindspot throughout Philip's career was the management of money. Neither the money he expropriated from King Charles nor the liquid element of Margaret's inheritance lasted long as change in his

disgrace. "His debaucheries, his violent passions, and the intoxicating influence of royal power," it was noted, "predisposed his weak head to an attack of madness which was brought about by sudden excitement and by sun-stroke." His incapacity was put beyond doubt when he decided he was made of glass. Acting as regent, Philip cannot have been too disappointed. What little money he had, plus a huge loan, had gone towards the cost of his wedding. As Charles's regent he could at least draw a salary, a euphemism for rou-

Left, crown of Philip the Bold. Above, Order of the Golden Fleece, Palais des Ducs.

pocket. He died with lands of inestimable value but absolutely no cash. His gold and silver plate were sold to pay for the funeral.

Philip's son and successor as duke of Burgundy appeared to be a chip off the old block and was dubbed John the Fearless (1404–19). He rushed off to the crusade of 1396 and launched himself at the Turks "with a total disregard of all the rules of tactics". It was nearly his undoing. He escaped the fate of 10,000 French troops who were captured and beheaded only because of the sultan's rather naive assumption that his family could and would pay a handsome ransom. The money was raised somehow, and John returned to France with undiminished ambition. There was a struggle for power between the Burgundians and the Armagnacs, led by the Duke of Orleans, who was Charles VI's brother and ruled France during Charles's periods of insanity. John had the duke assassinated. He was followed into a dark alley by John's hirelings and knocked senseless.

The same gang had previously botched a similar assignment, so they took the precaution of lighting a wisp of straw and holding it to their victim's face to satisfy themselves that he was dead. There must have been some doubt because one of the chronicles is quite specific about what happened next: "The right arm was cut in two places, at the elbow and at the wrist; the left wrist was thrown to a distance, as if from the violence of the blow; the head opened from ear to ear; the skull broken, and the brains scattered all over the pavement."

The murder of the powerful and popular duke caused an uproar which persuaded John that he had better retreat to Flanders, which of course formed the larger part of his inheritance. From there he issued statements which sought to justify the murder. He also despatched a priest, one Jean Petit, to preach sermons in his defence. The duke's death was necessary for ten reasons, the priest told congregations, and he ticked them off. They included heresy, plotting against the throne and having tyrannical tendencies. The wretched Charles was wheeled on to add his seal of approval. The murder, he agreed, was for the common good.

John returned to Paris to play the worthy saviour and to be "most affable to all sorts and conditions of men". At the same time, however, he secretly recruited a private army of thugs among the butchers of Les Halles. Confident that his back was covered, he made speeches promising the poor a reduction in taxes. To the upper classes he gave assurances that their privileges were secure and that he would increase the number of noble fiefs. In modern parlance, John was running for king and as such was throwing down a challenge to the old feudal party whose figurehead had been the murdered Duke of Orleans. The Orleanists consolidated their alliance with the Armagnacs and prepared to do battle under the Count d'Armagnac. Armagnacs and Orleanists versus Burgundians pitted the west and the

south of France against the north and the east. The former wore white scarves, the latter blue caps with the cross of St Andrew and a fleur-de-lys in the centre. The Burgundian slogan was "*Vive le Roy!*" Having fortified himself in Paris, John opened proceedings by ordering his butchers to root out any Armagnac supporters in the city.

Across the English Channel, Henry V watched these developments with pleasure. A divided France was an opportunity to seize the whole of Normandy and to consolidate the provinces he had already conquered. The English crossed the channel and laid siege to Harfleur. Under this provocation, the French factions dropped their differences to mount a challenge. The ensuing battle was fought famously at Agincourt.

Although the combined French armies heavily outnumbered the English, the result was a rout. "Never was there a more complete, or more humiliating, defeat," said a contemporary French account, "the proud French knights had been vanquished, not by English noblemen and gentlemen, but by merely archers on foot, by mercenaries five times less in numbers." The number of French knights killed was put at 8,000.

Curiously, John the Fearless seems to have kept his distance, although he expressed disgust at the outcome and "announced loudly his intention of chastising the English, and of restoring the king to the full enjoyment of his power". Actually, says a contemporary in a terse aside, "his only desire was to reconquer his own authority". Exploiting the disarray among his French rivals, he sent his army into Paris to continue the purge of Orleanists and Armagnacs. The Provost of Paris tried to stop the carnage but was brushed aside. "In the devil's name," the butchers protested, "plead no more for them." One of the chronicles pictures the provost turning his head aside in sad resignation and saying: "Do what you please."

In the meantime, the English advance swept through Normandy. The French lords again appealed for unity, and John was specifically given guarantees of personal safety if he presented himself at Montereau to plan the next phase of resistance. The assurance came from Tanguy Duchâtel, one of the king's advisers, and when John stepped on to the bridge at Montereau on 10 September 1419 it was Duchâtel himself who crept up behind him and buried an axe in his head. "The unfortunate duke," says one account, "fell on his knees and was immediately despatched." After this treachery, the Burgundians allied themselves with the English. Philip the Good (1419–67), son of John the Fearless, became the new Duke of Burgundy, and attended the treaty of Troyes which in 1415 recognised Henry V of England as King of France as well. The feeble-minded King Charles, still soldiering on, was demoted to dauphin and ordered out of the palace and into the Hôtel St Pol to make way for Henry. Charles was one of those held responsible for the murder of John the Fearless, and at his trial he was found guilty and

Burgundy and the controversial Isabelle of Bavaria, Charles's widow, were among those who swore allegiance to the babe. In 1429 Joan of Arc emerged to defend the dauphin, Charles VII, and determined to drive the English from France. She was captured at Compiègne by the Burgundian army, then in alliance with the English.

Philip the Good handed her over to the English in 1430 for a vast ransom, and she was subsequently burnt at the stake. However, the English had by then been reduced to a toe-hold in Calais and possession of the Channel Islands. France emerged from the period of English occupation with Charles VII (1422–61) as king. Philip, Duke of Bur-

sentenced to be paraded through the streets of Paris in a cart. Perhaps he did not understand what was required of him, but in any case he failed to appear for the parade on the appointed day and was stripped of his residual rights to the French crown.

Henry V and Charles VI died within six weeks of one another in 1422. The heir to both English and French crowns was Henry's grandson Henry VI, who was all of nine months old. Few people thought the dual kingdom would last, although the Duke of

gundy, abandoned the English cause and did well out of tortuous negotiations which saw Charles installed on the throne. In effect, he demanded and received 400,000 crowns to recognise the arrangement. His deal with the French king meant that the Duchy of Burgundy now became an independent principality encompassing part of Holland, nearly all of Belgium, Luxembourg, Flanders, Artois, Hainault, Picardy and the land between the Jura and the Loire.

The relationship between king and duke was uneasy, representing as it did a new twist in the struggle for supremacy between monarchy and the old feudal order. Instead of

Above, Detail of retable of Saints and Martyrs, Palais des Ducs.

JOUSTING

In 1442, a general challenge was issued to the knights of Europe to assemble at the village of Marsannay-la-Côte on the road between Dijon and Nuits-St-George for a tournament of arms at dawn on 11 July the following year. Such tournaments were the opportunity for knights to show off their martial skills, and this promised to be the grandest ever staged.

Knights had the choice of mock battle, on foot with pairs of carefully matched battle-axes or swords or mounted, when the knights charged at one another from either side of a fence in suits of armour weighing about 200 lb (100 kg).

The Marsannay tournament was a battle for an ancient tree known as *"l'arbre de Charlemagne"*. The home team, 12 knights hand-picked by Pierre de Bauffremont, Lord Charny, were in possession of the tree, and the outsiders had to wrest it from them. Rather than a general mêlée, the rules specified a succession of single combat in the tradition of champions.

The identity of the challengers was the subject of intense speculation, especially when one of the newcomers was revealed as Pedro Vasco de Saavedra, a Spaniard whose prowess was legendary. If any of the local knights were to stand a chance against him, it would have to be Charny himself.

The Duke of Burgundy, then Philip the Good,

invited the Duke of Savoy and the two of them and their entourages spent the night of 10 July at Nuits-St-George. They were up early enough to be at the tree at sunrise for the preliminaries, when the challenger's champion chose his method of fighting, signifying by a touch on one of two shields whether to fight on horses or on foot.

The champion Saavedra rode up. He approached the shields, leant forward and touched first one and then the other – sensational! To choose to fight on both horseback and on foot was almost unprecedented. At 8am Saavedra reappeared for a formal introduction to the duke. He wore a short tunic and hat and was dressed entirely in black. Charny then presented himself. Compared with the understated Spaniard, he cut an astonishing figure. His horse was decorated with his coat-of-arms; six following were caparisoned with gold-threaded crimson satin. The first contest, at 9am, would be with battle-axes.

The armour developed specifically for tournaments had, in the interests of safety, deviated considerably from its military origins. At the cost of mobility, it was made heavier to resist the thrust of a lance and the pounding of sword, mace and battle-axe. The tips of lances were blunted, and in some cases the horses' chests were protected with a kind of mattress filled with straw. The contestants crossed themselves and laid into one another with their battle-axes. The flurry of blows quickly added up to the quota under the rules, whereupon the duke threw down his white stick to end the contest.

The tournament continued for six weeks and over the course of several encounters the two knights developed such respect for each other that Charny offered the Spaniard the position of chamberlain in his household. The umpire's verdict at the end of contests involving all the knights was that the home-side had successfully defended the Tree of Charlemagne.

Ten years later – in 1435 – Burgundy and the Christian world in general were devastated by the news that Constantinople had fallen to the Turks. Philip the Good was at the forefront of the clamour for a crusade, and a series of tournaments like that at Marsannay were quickly arranged to drum up enthusiasm for the cause. Knights were only too eager to test their tournament skills in earnest and it became a matter of inescapable honour so to do. Almost to a man they signed up and set off. What they were left to discover was the reality of warfare against a ferocious, mobile enemy. Few came back. ∎

having to "borrow" armies from the feudal lords in time of need, Charles VII found the money to raise an army whose loyalty was exclusive to him. By appealing directly to the bourgeoisie and peasants, he diverted the chain of feudal allegiance. It was altogether new for people to look for leadership beyond the confines of the estates to which they owed their livelihood. The Count de St Pol was one of the nobles who sensed that they were being usurped and he expressed his objections. The king had him sewn into a bag and dumped in a river. At this even the Duke of Burgundy, it was said, "felt the necessity of keeping quiet".

Philip's only recourse was to keep the provinces and Dijon in particular flourished under Philip the Good; the population doubled in size and the court was famous for its luxury and culture. But Burgundy had become far too rich for the king's liking, and the hostility between Burgundy and France boiled over when Philip died and was succeeded by his tempestuous son Charles le Téméraire (1467–77). His name is translated sometimes as Charles the Bold and sometimes as Charles the Rash, and there is a case to be argued for both.

As the contest between Louis and Charles lifted the Duchy of Burgundy to the apogee of its power and as swiftly to its destruction, it may be worth quoting Sir Walter Scott's

king's enemies simmering, and in this he was supported by the king's son Louis. The son's intrigues so tormented Charles that eventually, convinced that Louis was out to poison him, he could not bring himself to eat anything at all and literally starved to death.

Philip and Louis found a *modus vivendi* to begin with, although rigorous protocol was required to keep their relationship on an equitable footing. The civility between them was shattered on the former's accession as Louis XI. The Duchy of Burgundy had grown stupendously rich on its Flemish

Above, Knights tilting in full armour.

assessment of the two protagonists. Louis, he wrote, "was by nature vindictive and cruel, even to the extent of finding pleasure in the frequent executions which he commanded. But, as no touch of mercy ever induced him to spare, when he could with safety condemn, so no sentiment of vengeance ever stimulated him to a premature violence. He seldom sprung on his prey till it was fairly within his grasp, and till all hope of rescue was in vain; and his movements were so studiously disguised, that his success was generally what first announced to the world the object he had been manoeuvring to attain."

Sir Walter clearly had his preference, and he described Charles as one who "rushed on danger, because he loved it, and on difficulties because he despised them. As Louis never sacrificed his interest to his passion, so Charles, on the other hand, never sacrificed his passion, nor even his humour, to any other consideration." Louis and Charles began to circle one another like gladiators.

With wholly uncharacteristic naïvety, Louis was the first to fall into a trap. He accepted an invitation to a conference with Charles in Péronne, which was in Burgundian territory. Of all their various difficulties, the most pressing was Liège, where the king had blatantly been urging the popu-

lation to cut themselves off from Burgundy and come over to him.

In Péronne, Philip greeted Louis "most cordially, embraced him, and led him to the castle, where lodgings had been prepared for his reception". He gave no intimation that the lodgings in question were in fact the tower, a doom-ridden place notorious as the place of execution of an earlier king known as Charles the Simple. Louis was securely locked up before he knew what was happening. Ignoring the advice of aides who wanted Louis put to death there and then, Charles had devised a strategem which would cause Louis more discomfort than a quick death.

He was made to wear a cap emblazoned with the Burgundian cross of St Andrew, dumped in a cart, and driven through the streets of Liège. To add a note of piquancy, and no doubt to the puzzled amusement of the citizens of Liège, the king was required to keep up a cry of "*Vive Bourgogne!*" throughout. Feeling very pleased with himself, Charles then released the king. He was free, a chronicle records, "to depart wherever he wished to go, having spent the three most anxious weeks of his life".

No sooner was he back in the relative safety of France than Louis replied in kind. Cardinal Balue and the Bishop of Verdun, both staunch Burgundy supporters, were locked up in iron cages, where they remained for 10 years. They were still in their cages, and Louis and Charles were still at loggerheads, when Charles received a letter. It was from Frederick III, the Habsburg Holy Roman Emperor, and it contained the fascinating proposal of marriage between his son, Maximilian, and Charles's only child, his daughter Mary. The proposal was not without flaws, but Charles saw it as the chance to settle scores with Louis at a stroke.

Frederick III was the most glorious figure in Christendom. A Habsburg duke by birth and therefore ruler over vast domains, he was also the elected King of Germany and Holy Roman Emperor, ordained by the Pope in Rome and regarded as semi-divine. Beneath the trappings, however, Frederick had to contend with appalling personal, dynastic and financial problems. The Turks were threatening his borders, he was plagued by a belligerent brother, he had lost Hungary and had twice been besieged in his palace by his own furious subjects. During the second siege, he had been reduced to eating the palace pets and then the vultures which settled on the roof with a view to eating him. Above all, he was broke.

Charles, on the other hand, had taken to flaunting the Duchy of Burgundy's wealth, most of it derived from the Flemish provinces. The cloaks he wore were generally made of gold thread and his favourite sword was embedded with diamonds which spelt out the Pater Noster in full. Charles understood perfectly well that in proposing marriage between Maximilian and Mary the emperor had designs on his money, but he would happily part with money in exchange for something which the emperor could give him. Charles believed that as emperor Frederick was empowered to make him a king, and in a broad sense that was true. Frederick could create a kingdom out of thin air if he wished, but Charles needed one that would put him on at least a level pegging with the hated Louis XI of France. Frederick might even agree to make him King of the Romans, the formal status of the heir-designate to the imperial throne and one next to which the Kingdom of France could not hold a candle. If Frederick baulked at conferring a suitable kingdom, Charles was confident that a brisk review of his financial situation would change his mind.

A meeting between Frederick and Charles was arranged in Trier for 30 September 1473, and in their different ways both were playing for psychological advantage. Charles arrived on a black horse draped in gold cloth. He wore gleaming armour and a short cloak dripping with diamonds and rubies. He was accompanied by 14 heralds-at-arms, 100 heavily-muscled bodyguards and a band of trumpeters. Fastidious to the last degree, his fingernails were as long as talons and manicured to perfection.

Frederick had to borrow money simply to make the journey. His robe was dotted with pearls but had clearly seen better days. Frederick was not too concerned about such details. He believed that his whole persona exuded dignity and that he was a direct descendant not merely of Augustus Caesar but of King Priam of Troy. He had done the genealogical research himself and no one dared to contradict him. All his possessions were engraved with the letters A E I O U, and while these might have appeared to be just the vowels of the alphabet they were actually an acronym (a secret not uncovered until his death) for *Austriae Est Imperare Orbi Universo* – "Austria (by which was meant the House of Habsburg) is Destined to Rule the Whole World". He arrived in Trier with the 14-year-old Maximilian in tow.

When they came face to face, Charles begrudgingly made token submission by bending a knee, but in case Frederick got the wrong idea he then pointedly snubbed the emperor's invitation to ride alongside him.

Frederick was welcome to think he was descended from King Priam; Charles preferred to model himself on Alexander the Great, son of Philip of Macedon. He attached some significance to the fact that his father was also a Philip.

Although Charles was technically the guest in Trier, he took care of all the arrangements. Frederick, who could well recall eating vulture, was given a place at a table festooned with 800 pieces of silver and gold plate which Charles had brought along. Dukes of Burgundy, he explained, were not comfortable eating off anything less. Charles was so confident of the outcome of the marriage negotiations that he had already

seen his jewellers and had his head measured for a suitable crown.

The negotiations lasted two months. They were prolonged by issues with wider implications than marriage. Pope Pius II, who tended to regard the emperor as his military right-hand man, was keen to see a Habsburg-Burgundy alliance, without which Frederick could not afford to mount a campaign against the Turks who had captured Constantinople in 1453 and were threatening not to rest until they stabled their horses in the Pope's palace in Rome. The Pope hoped to secure a commitment from Charles which would enable Frederick to lead another crusade. With

Boundary between Holy
Roman Empire and France

Territory at the accession
0f Charles the Bold 1467

French Royal Domain
placed under Burgundian
Control in 1435

Territory added by Charles

Ecclesiastical Lands

FRIESLAND

Utrecht

ZUTPHEN

HOLLAND

ZEALAND

BRABANT

GUELDERS

HOLY
ROMAN
EMPIRE

FLANDERS

Calais

Liège

LIMBURG

ARTOIS

HAINAULT

NAMUR

Abbeville

Péronne

Amiens

LUXEMBURG

RETHEL

Paris

Rhine

Nancy

Orléans

Seine

KINGDOM

OF

FRANCE

LORRAINE

BRISGAU

UPPER
ALSACE

DUCHY OF
BURGUNDY

Dijon

NIVERNAIS

COUNTY OF
BURGUNDY

Nevers

SWITZERLAND

Burgundy in 1477

80 km / 50 miles

Charles making it plain that there were plenty of better-heeled suitors for Mary's hand, Frederick played his cards carefully. He was determined to hold the Kingdom of the Romans in reserve for young Maximilian, so he suggested instead that Charles consider becoming King of Burgundy, a defunct kingdom which shared only its name with Charles's existing duchy. Frederick proposed a reconstituted kingdom along the lines of the "Middle Kingdom" as envisaged at Verdun in 843 when, following the collapse of Charlemagne's empire, it would have served as a buffer between Germans and Franks.

Added to the considerable territory which the Valois dukes of Burgundy had acquired by various means, the kingdom under discussion would have given Charles dominion over a solid mass of territory from the northern tip of the Netherlands to the Italian Riviera and a sizeable portion of modern Switzerland as well. Ironically, it would not include the nuclear Duchy of Burgundy itself. As Charles did not need reminding, that was technically subject to Louis of France and therefore not within Frederick's remit.

Charles liked the idea. A lot of proverbial water had passed under the bridge since the Middle Kingdom had originally been outlined, and while the inhabitants might at first ask questions about being arbitrarily bundled together as his subjects, he was confident that he had the arguments, and if necessary the force, to make them acquiesce. It might not be the Kingdom of Rome, but it was undoubtedly a kingdom which would put the loathsome Louis to shame.

Agreement was reached in principle and Charles, mindful of the Pope's interest, promised to put 10,000 troops at Frederick's disposal to fight either the Turks or, even better, Louis XI. With that he ordered his craftsmen to prepare the abbey church of St-Maximin for his coronation. He wanted two thrones, one for himself and one for the emperor, who would of course place the crown on his head. Benches for distinguished guests would be arranged in tiers on scaffolding around the church.

For his part, Frederick was quietly congratulated by a Habsburg cousin for having pulled off "the greatest piece of luck that had

Philip the Good by **Roger van der Weyden.**

for long befallen the house of Austria". The date for the coronation would be set as soon as Frederick had consulted his astrological charts. He settled on 25 November and Trier went into a frenzy of activity for the great occasion. As the preparations neared completion, something began playing on Frederick's mind. He never revealed what it was. Some of the chroniclers thought that he detected in his charts a warning that Charles was riding for a fall. Others suggested that he took a personal dislike to Charles. Whatever the real reason, in the hours of darkness of the very morning on which the coronation was due to be held, Frederick slipped out of Trier and took Maximilian with him.

Charles was thunderstruck by the discovery that Frederick had walked out. He was stuck with a town full of important guests, a redundant crown, and a betrothed daughter facing an indeterminable future. The only message Frederick left for him was that he might be willing to reconsider the matter sometime in the future. The Archbishop of Trier was none too pleased either: Frederick had left word for his numerous creditors that all bills should be sent to him.

Reconstituting the ancient Middle Kingdom as the Kingdom of Burgundy had taken root in Charles's mind, and it was not long before the disappointed dignitaries who had filed out of Trier were reconvened, on this occasion in Dijon. He treated them to a magnificent banquet on the same gold and silver plate which had seen service in Trier and then announced his intentions: he would unilaterally create the Kingdom of Burgundy and, if necessary, crown himself.

High on Charles's list of priorities was to declare war on Louis, and to this end he proposed to engage the support of England. Edward IV of England was his brother-in-law (Charles had allied himself with Edward by marrying his sister, Margaret of York) and the proposition which Charles put before him had at least the virtue of simplicity. If Edward would help him defeat Louis, he

could become King of France while Charles proceeded with his plans to become King of Burgundy. The only condition was that Edward would cede to him unfettered sovereignty over the Duchy of Burgundy which, as we have seen, was still, painfully, part of the French kingdom as then was. The duchy could then take its place at the heart of the new Kingdom of Burgundy.

The scheme did not work. In fact, everything that Charles attempted fell to pieces, leading to speculation that he had lost his senses. As he stumbled from one futile military campaign to another, it was said that his troops completely lost sight of where they were and whom they were supposed to be fighting. One of his troops was reputed to have approached an officer for enlightenment. "This war, I think," the officer is said to have replied, "is over some sheepskins."

The chroniclers confessed to being at a loss. "If only he could have tempered his greatness of spirit with moderation and prudence," wrote Thomas Basin. "But, as it happens often with princes, he prided himself on his own judgement and listened only to his own wisdom, rejecting good advice most of the time or listening to it little, and making up his mind according to his view of what he wanted done."

In 1476 the string of débâcles caught up with Charles and left him a broken man. Edward of England, initially not unwilling to go along with Charles's plans, had been bribed to abandon him. Louis employed Swiss mercenaries to inflict punishing defeats. Charles achieved what many would have considered practically impossible: he exhausted the Duchy of Burgundy's wealth. The Emperor Frederick, who had unwittingly set the train of disaster in motion, chose the nadir of Charles's despair to pop up again. Was Mary still free and willing to marry Maximilian, he asked. He could have her, Charles replied, on any terms he liked, in fact unconditionally.

A few days later, Charles was with his troops at Nancy trying to forestall an attempt by Lorraine to secede from his domain. His forces were overwhelmed and in the mêlée Charles went missing. The following morning, his naked body, stripped of its armour, was dragged out of a frozen lake. It had already been half-eaten by wolves and could be identified among the pile of dead only by the remarkable fingernails.

The postscript is that Maximilian and Mary duly married, and with that the Duchy of Burgundy ceased to have a history to call its own. Part of the Duchy passed to the Habsburgs and Louis XI occupied the remainder, which consisted of Burgundy, Mâconnais, Auxerrois and Charolais. In the space of just two years, the wealthiest state in Europe crumbled, its identity lost to the Habsburgs and to France.

Left, chapterhouse window, Palais des Ducs. **Right**, the book of hours of Mary of Burgundy, 15th century.

After the glories of the Grand Dukes, Burgundy was cut down to size by the upstart French kings. For the Burgundians, there was no question of redrawing the map of the world but rather of remoulding the province into a comfortable shape, and of ensuring independence within the new frontiers.

More a retrenchment than a dilution of Burgundian identity, the period still produced leaders of national stature. The Condé dynasty helped shape the Wars of Religion and the *Frondes*, the struggles against absolutism. The radical province also claims St-Just, the ideologue of the French Revolution, not to mention Napoleon's greatest generals, and, more recently, wartime Resistance heroes such as François Mitterrand.

The duchy ended with the death of Charles the Bold near Nancy in 1477. Even if this defeat spelt the end of the Burgundian empire, the Valois dukes could bask in royal connections. Burgundian glory embraced Edward III of England and anticipated François I, the Renaissance King of France. Emperor Charles V, his equal on the world stage, also claimed Burgundian blood and planned to recapture the lost province before being buried in the Chartreuse de Champmol, the traditional tomb of the Grand Dukes. It was not to be.

Repeatedly humiliated by the Burgundian dukes, Louis XI eagerly desired the fall of the duchy. Louis wasted no time in informing his new Burgundian subjects that they were "*de la couronne et du royaume*". The dynastic marriage of Charles's daughter, Marie de Bourgogne, to Emperor Maximilian of Austria in 1478 temporarily foiled plans for French hegemony: Flanders and many Burgundian enclaves went to the Empire. However, in 1479 Louis invaded Burgundy and, after occupying Dijon and Beaune, built fortresses to secure his kingdom. Dijon's Palais des Ducs became the Logis du Roi.

In 1493 the Treaty of Senlis formalised the dismemberment of the Burgundian empire:

Preceding pages: interior, Château of Bussy-Rabutin. **Left**, Marguerite de Brou. **Right**, Drapers' Guild window, Semur-en-Auxois.

Artois, Flanders and the Franche-Comté would stay in the emperor's hands while Burgundy fell to Louis XI. Both leaders wished to settle the succession with a marriage between the emperor's daughter, Marguerite d'Autriche, and the dauphin, the future Charles VIII. Instead, Charles married Anne de Bretagne while Marguerite, a pawn in the political power game, married Philibert le Beau of Savoy. Sadly, Marguerite's stay in Bourg-en-Bresse, her ancestral estate, was as short-lived as her marriage.

On the death of her brother in 1504, she moved to Mechelin as Regent of the Low Countries and the Franche-Comté. There she brought up the future Emperor Charles V, Maximilian's grandson. As the last heiress of the Burgundian dukedom, Marguerite made her memorial the luminous monastery at Brou. The craftsmanship is a tribute to her Burgundian heritage, a monument created by French and German masons, guided by Flemish and Burgundian sculptors. Her enigmatic motto adorns the church: "*fortune infortune fort une*" ("through good and bad fortune, one woman remains strong").

Yet the territorial sharing of the spoils had

serious consequences: Burgundy became a buffer between the French crown and the Empire and remained so for two centuries. As a royal precaution, Avallon, Beaune and Chalon were heavily fortified by successive kings. In 1513 Dijon was besieged by the emperor's Swiss forces, and again in 1636. Much to the crown's displeasure, Burgundy exploited its mastery of the borders. Spanish and French coinage were both in circulation so currency deals were rife, as was fiscal fraud, smuggling and the training of mercenaries. Profiteering was rampant in Bresse, Charolais and Château-Chinon, enclaves controlled by the emperor. Only Louis XIV's annexation of the Franche-Comté in

the Saône fostered trade from Rheims to Lyon while the Loire linked Nevers with Orléans and Tours. In Nevers, the Duc de Gonzaga established luxury industries, a glassworks and factories for faïence, fine pottery still made today.

Despite assimilation by France, Burgundian towns defended their privileges. The region still clung to fragments of foreign policy, purchasing Bresse and Bugey in 1601. Even so, Burgundy was reduced to the status of a province ruled by a governor, a crown appointee. The governor, intendant and bailiffs, drawn from the ranks of the nobility, created an administrative caste that survived until the Revolution. The ruling

1678 ended Burgundy's buffer role and ushered in an era of peace and prosperity.

Not that Burgundian merchants were strangers to prosperity. At the turn of the 16th century, the wool merchants of Semur-en-Auxois vied with the drapers of Dijon and the wine merchants of Beaune. Iron foundries flourished in the Châtillonais and the fairs at Chalon and Dijon attracted traders from as far afield as Flanders and Italy.

By the middle of the century, the wooded heart of Burgundy began to be exploited: paper mills were created while the rivers were used to float firewood to Paris, a trade that continued until 1914. Navigation along

class accepted the king's authority on condition that he allowed considerable autonomy. Self-government and lenient taxation were the price for peace in the province. Yet, against its will, Burgundy became embroiled in the Wars of Religion, providing national leaders on both sides.

The first Huguenot centres were Dijon and Nevers but the new faith soon spread to Chalon and Mâcon. In 1547, the inspirational preacher Théodore de Bèze resigned his priory at Vézelay and joined Calvin in Geneva. After succeeding Calvin, Bèze was a calming influence over his compatriots.

Protestants dominated the professional

and artisanal classes while the nobility, bourgeoisie and the rural population clung to the Catholic cause. Significantly, the regional administration, the *Parlement* and the *États*, were staunchly Catholic. However, moderate Catholics spared Burgundy a bloody St Bartholemew's Day Massacre.

Prince Louis de Bourbon, the Protestant leader of the Burgundian Condé family, was killed at Jarnac in 1569, the climax of a series of Catholic victories. But the tide turned the following year when the Huguenot Henri of Navarre won at Arnay-le-Duc. Led by the Duc de Mayenne, Governor of Burgundy, the Catholic League met in Dijon Parliament while the Protestants plotted in the Château

routed the Catholics at Fontaine-Française. This decisive victory over Mayenne and his Spanish troops was the turning point of the war. The King converted to Catholicism but not before his supporters had desecrated Auxerre Cathedral and destroyed the "vipers' nests", châteaux belonging to prominent opponents.

Luckily, most Burgundian châteaux survived the onslaught. Politics aside, Tanlay is a tribute to a less troubled age. Like the refined châteaux of Ancy-le-Franc and Sully, it is a product of the Renaissance, shaped by Italian painters and Burgundian master craftsmen. These moated châteaux boast mullioned windows, sculpted fire-

de Tanlay, the home of their leader, Gaspard de Coligny. Tanlay remains a political commentary on the troubled times: the Tour de la Ligue, a turreted tower, contains witty mythological representations of the contemporary protagonists.

In 1589, despite royalist sympathies, Burgundians sided with the Catholic Duc de Mayenne. Henri IV responded by besieging Autun and other Catholic strongholds. After gaining control of Dijon in 1595, Henri

Left, château of Ancy-le-Franc, a 17th-century engraving. **Above**, a 17th-century etching, Cormatin Château.

places, frescoes and busts of Roman emperors. In Nevers, the Gonzaga's Italian court provided a channel for Renaissance ideas. Not for nothing does the city boast "the first Loire château".

On a smaller scale, the region abounds in Renaissance *hôtels particuliers* typified by the Hôtel de Crôle in Auxerre, with its sculpted facade adorned with pilasters and ornamental gargoyles. Above all, Burgundians excel in the decorative arts, particularly sculpture. In Montréal, the church stalls reflect a Burgundian earthiness, matched by a daring pulpit: bare-breasted Bacchanalia at play in the vineyards. In Dijon, the talent of

BUSSY-RABUTIN

The handsome old Château of Bussy-Rabutin, 40 miles northwest of Dijon, enshrines one of the oddest sagas of the 17th century — as you can see from the bizarre satiric frescoes in its main rooms. Here the outrageous and flamboyant Roger de Rabutin, Count of Bussy, was exiled to his country seat by Louis XIV for lampooning court life, and then took a lonely revenge by decorating his walls with bitchy cartoons and comments on his ex-mistresses and other celebrities of the day. Few stately homes remain so expressive of the personality of their former owner — in this case, a witty, womanising renegade.

Secluded in a narrow valley, amid majestic trees, the château itself is quite striking. Part 17th-century, part much older, it has pepperpot towers, a moat, a fine Renaissance courtyard, and a terraced garden with pools. The Bussy-Rabutins, a leading Burgundy family, bought it in 1612 and then rebuilt it.

Roger, a cousin of Madame de Sévigné, led a life of lurid melodrama. As a soldier, he kept changing sides in civil conflicts ("The best officer in my army – for songs," said Marshal de Turène, who hated him). In 1659 he took part in the notorious "debauch of Roissy", near Paris, where gays and libertines sang obscene songs to hymn-tunes and a priest baptised a frog. Bussy's role was to improvise lyrics poking fun at Louis XIV's love-life. The young king was not amused and sent Bussy on a first exile to Burgundy. Here he wrote his *Histoire Amoureuse des Gaules* (a pun, for *gaule* can also mean stick, or phallus, in slang): this stylish novella was a wickedly accurate portrayal of certain ladies at court, thinly disguised, and their adulteries. A copy found its way to Paris, where Louis was prevailed upon to send Bussy to the Bastille, although he had just been elected to the Académie Française.

Released after a year, Bussy then returned to exile, and set about turning his château into a sardonic memorial to the follies of his age. Few of the murals he commissioned are of much artistic quality, but they shed fascinating light on his quirky character, and on the decadent times of the Sun King.

The château today is State-owned. The guided tour will take you first to the Salle des Dévises, which has a remarkable mural of Versailles then half-built, as well as allegorical paintings with Latin inscriptions. One is devoted to Madame de Sévigné who had formerly rejected his bid to become her lover: she is depicted as a jug pouring cold water on hot coals, with the tag, "She is cold and enflames me."

The Salon des Grands Hommes has 65 paintings of military leaders, many caustically captioned. Cromwell is there, "condemned by his great crimes to eternal notoriety". But Bussy's scorn falls most fiercely on his faithless mistress Marquise de Montglat whose desertion hurt him deeply; she is shown as the moon, "with more than one face". His bedroom is decorated with portraits of mistresses of French kings, clearly an obsession with him, including such famous beauties as Agnes Sorel and Diane de Poitiers.

The Tour Dorée in the west tower has the château's most ornate decor, including a ceiling that Bussy called "*le ciel somptueux d'un lit d'amour*". Round the walls are portraits of ladies of the court, tartly captioned – the Marquise de las Baume ("she would have been the prettiest and most lovable, had she not been the most unfaithful"), the Duchesse de Choiseul ("very well informed, notably about other people's faults"), and others.

Here Bussy-Rabutin died in 1693, aged 75. He had a nasty character, arrogant, hot-headed and malicious, but he also had style and candour. Perhaps the clue to this rebel and *provocateur* lies in the family motto, "*Et si omnes, ego non*" – "If others are for it, I'm against." ∎

Hugues Sambin enlivens the door of the Palais de Justice, the former regional Parliament. Inspired by Roman statuary, the master craftsman sculpted a riot of garlands and lions but couldn't resist adding a final flourish with the humble Burgundian cabbage. Sambin was a quintessential Renaissance man: a military engineer, art historian, court entertainer and imaginative sculptor as well as a committed Protestant.

After the Wars of Religion, Burgundy's convalescence was slow, hindered by creeping centralisation. The *Parlement*, although unelected, acted as a barrier between the people and the king, protecting Burgundians from excessive royal demands. The province

With royal authority, they kept the peace, dispensed positions and favours. As leader of Louis XIV's army, Le Grand Condé crushed the first *Fronde* uprising in 1648 but after a clash with Mazarin, switched sides and led the second *Fronde* revolt in 1650. He was aided by La Grande Mademoiselle, the king's cousin, who also detested Mazarin. After inciting Orléans and Paris to rebellion, she stood on the towers of the Bastille and fired the cannon on royalist troops.

Perhaps fortunate only to be exiled to St-Fargeau, her desolate Burgundian château, she is recalled in a *son et lumière* that recreates these momentous events. Despite popular support for Condé, his Spanish forces

was largely self-governing yet suffered from increasingly heavy taxation. In 1630 Dijon's *vignerons* rebelled against a centrally imposed wine tax. The *États de Bourgogne* acted as the royal tool for tax collection yet could also be stubbornly independent. In 1659, after Dijon had failed to ratify the royal taxes, Louis XIV exiled the *États* to loyalist Noyers-sur-Serein and then severely curtailed the power of Parliament.

The Princes de Condé, already local lords, became governors of the province in 1631 and remained in power until the Revolution.

Revolutionaries: Paris Tribunal 1792.

overstepped the mark; the uprising was quelled and the Prince subsequently exiled.

Condé was, however, spared the expense of life at court. Madame de Sévigné complained that the *noblesse d'épée* were burdened by debts. Courtiers like Marigny, one of her witty correspondents, were ruined at Versailles and slunk back to Burgundy in disgrace. Nor was Madame de Sévigné's cousin Bussy-Rabutin forgiven for his satire on court manners. Exile to Burgundy at least enabled Bussy to decorate his château with veiled allegorical insults to Louis XIV, his former master. But the courtly ambience, defined by Bussy as *"une société de prudes, cocottes, sottes et hommes galants*," was at odds with the spiritual tenor of the times.

The 17th century saw a religious revival and renewed church building. Bussy himself had studied with the Jesuits in Autun but the Order was also well-established in Dijon. Jeanne de Chantal, Madame de Sévigné's grandmother, founded the Order of the Visitation while Anne de Xainctonge, a Dijonnaise, established an Ursuline convent in Dôle. In Paray-le-Monial, St Marguerite-Marie Alacoque had heavenly visions, a prelude to the cult of the Sacred Heart that suffuses the city today.

Yet, apart from a Carmelite convent in Dijon and a church in Nevers, Burgundy responsible for Versailles. In Louis XV's day, Burgundian cabinet-makers were valued at court; rococo ornamentation and lacquered *chinoiserie* were *de rigueur*.

On the eve of the Enlightenment, Dijon came into its own as an intellectual centre. An *Académie* and law faculty were founded in 1723, followed by the Université de Bourgogne. In the 1750s the Academy was at the forefront of French thought, introducing Rousseau's revolutionary ideas to a wide public. The President of the Parliament had the largest library in Burgundy, a collection ranging from illuminated manuscripts and chivalric tales to the latest scientific works. This formed the basis of the first public

CLUNY – Affiche du XVIIIe siècle

avoided the baroque. Instead, the province threw itself into classical architecture, from the abbey at Chalon to the reconstruction of monastic buildings at Cluny.

Burgundy might have lost its political independence but it flourished artistically. Louis XIV's reign saw the triumph of French classicism. Dijon created the Place Royale, fit for a king, belatedly adding a statue of Louis XIV in 1721 to curry royal favour. As for châteaux, few rival the formal grandeur of St-Fargeau, partially rebuilt by Le Vau, the architect of Versailles. Bussy-Rabutin's château boasts classical elements and a garden landscaped by Le Nôtre, the designer library, opened in 1701. Perhaps as a reaction against such edification, the bourgeois were nostalgic for a pastoral fantasy: travel books and paintings indulged the fashion for sweet shepherdesses and cowhands in *scènes galantes*.

The provincial aristocracy mingled with the enlightened *haute bourgeoisie*. Comte de Buffon, the naturalist and royal gardener, had a residence there and designed Dijon's botanical gardens. The city offered free classes in anatomy, chemistry and astronomy, with particular encouragement to *sages-femmes*, the blue-stockings once mocked in Molière's plays.

Encyclopédistes like Diderot mixed with Jean-Philippe Rameau, Bach's contemporary, and the major French classical composer. The new drawing academy later educated François Rude, the Romantic sculptor. For the moment, however, classicism was in the ascendant. Symmetrical mansions took the place of half-timbered medieval houses. Soufflot, from the Auxerrois, left the region with a classical legacy, including his grandiose hôtel in Irancy, his home town.

One of the most colourful figures of the period was the Chevalier d'Eon, Louis XVI's roving ambassador and enigmatic secret agent. His spying activities in England and Russia led him to dress as a woman, trolled by the *noblesse* while the *États* represented the nobility, clergy and the urban bourgeoisie. The Third Estate rallied to the revolutionary flag, supported by the *petit-bourgeoisie*, peasants, rural clergy and intellectuals. St-Just, born near Nevers, was the great philosopher of the Revolution. The Nivernais remains the most radical region in Burgundy. The storming of the Bastille was followed by uprisings in Dijon and Beaune. Dijon's newly-finished États de Bourgogne was abandoned until it was rechristened as the Hôtel de Ville. Yet thanks to widespread support for the Revolution, the region was spared the bloodshed that occurred in the Vendée. Still, in radical Mâcon a bonnet

aided by his feminine Christian names and build. He so liked his disguise that "his sex was sometimes open to speculation in Paris or London but never in Tonnerre". The Quentin Crisp of his age retired to Tonnerre during the Revolution and later died in London, after having made Burgundian wines as celebrated as his sex.

The Revolution was generally welcomed in Burgundy. It was as much a reaction against Burgundian authoritarianism as French absolutism. The *Parlement* was con-

Left, sale notice for the stone of Cluny. Above, Cluny before it was torn down.

decorated with *fleur de lys* was enough to invoke fears for "the safety of the Republic". While reactionary Catholic farmers in Charolles protested, the merchants and small landowners on the Côte d'Or took advantage of the forced sales to consolidate their gains. As émigrés' estates came under the hammer, land speculation was rife. However, close ties between the nobles and the local people meant that châteaux changed hands but were spared. In Époisses, for instance, the owners had long allowed local merchants to store their grain and wine in the castle cellars. As a result, the *châtelains* kept their heads and several wings of their home. However, in keeping with events, the château was later sold as a *Bien National* to the highest bidder. If most châteaux escaped lightly, churches were not so fortunate. While Fontenay Abbey was converted into a paper mill, most monasteries were destroyed. Cîteaux Abbey was vandalised while Cluny was gutted and sold off for building material.

The monks at Lugny expressed the resignation of many: "Since our misfortunes aid the prosperity of France, let our losses enrich the common good." But the Revolution also built. Writing from Saulieu in 1790, Abbé Courtépée praised the enlightened authorities for "street lighting, paved roads and the covering of medieval moats". The Burgun-

so did Carnot and Junot, Napoleon's patriotic Burgundian generals. In Fixin, near Dijon, is François Rude's romantic statue of *Napoleon Awakening to Immortality*, a tribute to a local hero.

In 1870 the province swarmed with German troops: there were 8,000 in Semur-en-Auxois alone. Enlistment faced the town's weavers, tanners, millers, wine merchants, horse-breeders and hemp-gatherers. Despite such a motley crew, Burgundy inflicted some of France's only defeats on the enemy in Dijon and Nuits-St-Georges. Fittingly, Maurice de MacMahon, from Semur-en-Auxois, became president of the Third Republic after the demoralisation of the

dians did not allow revolution to affect business. *Faïences patriotiques*, Revolutionary pottery, did a roaring trade. On the designs, an anchor symbolised hope, an oak meant moral strength, a mirror truth and a snake prudence.

Départements were artificially imposed in 1791 and the last shreds of Burgundian autonomy faded. However, the *Ancien Régime* was not mourned and few citizens supported the Restoration. Burgundians were largely in favour of Napoleon, seeing him not as an enlightened despot but as the spirit of the Revolution. Just as the great Vauban had distinguished himself in Louis XIV's wars,

Franco-Prussian War. After 1830, depopulation was Burgundy's biggest problem, only partially stemmed by industrialisation. In keeping with its industrial heritage, the region was a pioneer. The Grande Forge, set up by the Comte de Buffon in the 18th century, was one of the biggest French foundries of its day. A period sketch shows dignitaries in fine frock coats holding lanterns over grimy foundry-workers. While visiting monarchs enjoyed the spectacle as pure theatre, the workers compared it to hell.

Buffon's foundry was near Montbard but later industry centred on the south, between Nevers and Chalon-sur-Saône. The names are atmospheric enough: Le Creusot, Montceau-les-Mines and La Machine. Adopting British techniques, Le Creusot steelworks introduced coke-fired production and prospered by building machines, cannon and other armaments. Eugène Schneider took over the factories in 1836 and quickly produced the first French steam engine. After his first sale to Britain, the triumphant Schneider was congratulated in Parliament. Selling trains to the British in 1865 was as rare as selling planes to the Americans in the 1990s. A town square displays the famous Schneider power-hammer, claimed to be sensitive enough to crack a walnut without damaging the kernel.

Burgundy's prime Charolais cattle. The vineyards, once the preserve of the monks and nobles, became the property of the bourgeoisie and, after the Revolution, were sold to the highest bidders. Even so, many of the most famous wine estates remained intact. Clos de Vougeot belonged to a single proprietor until the end of the 19th century. But from 1870 Phylloxera devastated the region, leaving only the *grands crus* to build from.

Despite such troubles, the period was far from fallow. The landscape near Lamartine's village of Milly was celebrated by the Romantic poet. Our pleasure in the rolling countryside also owes much to the invention of photography by a fellow Burgundian,

At its height, Schneider rivalled Krupps, employing over 10,000 workers. But such industrialisation would have failed without excellent communications. The opening of the Canal du Centre, linking the Saône to the Loire, coincided with the expansion of Le Creusot in 1794. The advent of the railway meant that Dijon's population grew from 20,000 in 1800 to 70,000 by the end of the 19th century. Yet Burgundy remained agricultural at heart. The flight from the land was slowed down by the successful breeding of

Left, industrialisation at Le Creusot, 1847. **Above**, 1858 foundry-workers.

Nicéphore Niepce. The spiritual landscape was shaped by Lacordaire, the leader of the liberal Catholic movement. His Dominican foundation still survives in Flavigny-sur-Ozerain while his birthplace in the Châtillonais, ancient Templar country, is now a convent.

From the *Frondes* rebellions to the Revolution, regional ties counted for more than national loyalty. The writer Edme Bardet puts it thus: "Burgundy, like all places off the beaten track, resembles a family. Although separated by rank and fortune, the family members are united by deeper bonds." In short, still backwaters run deep.

"*Une Tradition de Tradition*" is the region's slogan, a faith rooted in radical politics and pragmatic economics. Burgundy's republicanism has survived into this century. In 1914 the region was awash with patriotism while 1941 saw the emergence of France's most active Resistance cells. More recently, the "Mitterrand decade" has seen the election of smooth socialist stars, much in their master's mould. Yet this passion for politics is tempered by an old mercantile spirit. Even at the height of World War II, the region kept the Reich supplied with fine wines. The land knows how to exploit its natural charms; today's tourist trade is merely an extension of traditional Burgundian hospitality.

On the eve of World War I, Burgundy's radicalism and early industrialisation aligned it firmly with the left. An influx of refugees to the industrial south led to the expansion of Le Creusot and Monceau-les-Mines, aided by a burgeoning arms industry. While the war was fought elsewhere, Burgundy contributed arms and men. The aftermath brought inflation and strikes in the mines, steelworks and railways.

The inter-war years saw a political polarisation: Dijon, the Châtillonais and Charolais harboured Conservative pockets but the Saône-et-Loire was, after Marseille, the most left-wing region in France. The Catholic response to communism was politicised priests, such as Canon Bélorgey in Dijon. His spiritual successor was Chanoine Kir, an impassioned priest turned journalist who remained a formidable political force for 30 years. Kir's partiality for wine and *cassis* is celebrated in the Burgundian liqueur that bears his name.

The region had a special significance for the Nazis, not merely as a strategic border zone with munitions factories. Himmler formulated the idea of a Burgundian state with its own army, currency and laws – the hub of a mythical empire formed by the Franche-Comté, Benelux and Switzerland. He tried to

revive a spirit of Burgundian nationalism, saying, "What have the French ever done for Burgundy except pickle it in wine?" This "return" to the Teutonic fold failed to inspire Burgundians.

It took the Wehrmacht only five days to occupy Burgundy in June 1940. Most towns were declared *villes ouvertes* to deflect the wrath of the invading troops. Over half the population fled south, joining a stream of Belgians, Dutch and French in search of security. A mythical sense of safety beyond

the Loire led hordes of refugees to block the bridges at La Charité and Nevers. One fleeing dignitary, the Grand Duchess Charlotte of Luxembourg, lost her retinue near Château-Chinon and was swept onwards alone.

The remaining citizens quickly learnt to protect their property with a *Haus bewohnt* (house occupied) sign. There was no organised resistance but stranded French forces and rash individuals did battle in Saulieu and Sens. Cavalry officers from the military school at Autun daringly charged an armed convoy. In Tonnerre a lone *ancien combattant* donned his fireman's uniform and guarded the city gates until he was shot

Preceding pages: early mechanical threshing. **Left,** World War I memorial, cathedral window, Semur-en-Auxois. **Right,** World War II Resistance monument, Quarré-les-Tombes.

down. Paul Meunier, a farmer near Vézelay, helped the mayor burn a list of *garde civile* members before rushing to mass to warn his neighbours of the approaching tanks.

According to the terms of the Armistice, Chalon bounded the demarcation line between Occupied and Vichy France. Chalon and most of Burgundy therefore remained under tight control, with the industrial might of Le Creusot and Monceau-les-Mines harnessed to the German war machine. Dijon stayed as the administrative centre, with military bases at Auxerre, Autun and Nevers. By contrast, Cluny, Charolles, Mâcon, Tournus and Bresse lay in Vichy France. They enjoyed a more liberal regime

until full occupation of Burgundy in 1942 rendered any distinction meaningless.

As elsewhere, Maréchal Pétain commanded massive support at first. On 17 June 1940 Madame Lemaire shot a German officer in Cosne-sur-Loire, traditionally taken to be the first act of resistance against the occupying army. However, other individual gestures soon followed, from feeding deserters and hiding arms to forging documents and helping Jews cross the demarcation line. When Pétain's "peace with honour" degenerated into shortages, round-ups and deportations, Burgundian resolve stiffened. By the end of 1940, the first *Résistant* cells

emerged in the Nièvre. These included communist steel workers in Nevers, socialist teachers in Charité-sur-Loire and clandestine Gaulliste supporters in the Morvan. Maréchal Leclerc was helped to flee Avallon disguised as a priest. At the same time Michel Debré, de Gaulle's future prime minister, escaped from a German camp at Autun. Hairdresser Georges Moreau from Clamecy insisted that a Nazi officer wait his turn so his salon was closed. In response, he set up Le Loup *maquis*, a network which came to control much of Burgundy.

Robert Morlevat, mayor of Semur-en-Auxois since 1937, was one of the few officials to play an early role in the Resistance. In 1941 the Vichy government appointed its own mayors but Morlevat had his council reinstated. He later limited deportations and turned a blind eye to arms caches. After refusing to swear an oath of allegiance to Pétain in 1943, he and the council were removed. They left the chamber carrying a bust of Marianne and swearing to return. They had to wait only until September 1944, when Semur was liberated by the Resistance and Morlevat returned as mayor.

Naturally, first-hand stories of collaboration are scarce. Insofar as generalisations are possible, Dijon and the Yonne harboured more *collaborateurs* than the rest of the province. After Liberation, it was here that revenge killings were widespread. Profiteering was the more acceptable face of collaboration. The day Dijon surrendered, one astute wine merchant stood in the deserted city centre, waiting to sell crates of Burgundy to the victorious troops.

Other Dijonnais started a factory to produce German side-cars. Elsewhere, profiteers supplied champagne to officers' favourite bars or to private beaches on the Saône. Yet life for most citizens was both fraught and tedious, with painful daily compromises and grim acquiescence. There were petty regulations on everything from the etiquette of pedestrians to obligatory attendance at military bands and the correct temperature for serving apéritifs.

The war was not without its ironies: Nazis unsuspectingly gave lifts to grandmothers struggling home to feed clandestine rebels on their farms. The station master at Luzy spent the day repairing trains and tracks that he had sabotaged the night before.

The *maquis* at Luzy was operated by a Scottish teacher and an English parachutist. The British SAS established close links with such networks and parachute drops brought vital arms as well as fishing rods, pipe tobacco and other odd items. In return, the locals claim that Michel Hollard saved London by warning the Allies of a secret base with 15,000 flying bombs intended for London. Burgundy provided ideal camouflage for the Resistance, from the forested plains of the Châtillonais to the mountainous Morvan. The *Résistants* often ignored the demarcation line. Roland Champenier, a celebrated leader, travelled between the Nièvre and Paris, hiding in abandoned farms

Resistance centre it is fitting that France's Resistance museum should be in St-Brisson, a hamlet destroyed with Dun-les-Places.

In Cluny, Danielle Gouze, later Mitterrand's wife, was so horrified by the Jewish deportations that she joined the Resistance as a nurse. Allied success elsewhere aided the freedom movement but in Burgundy, unlike most of France, it was the *Résistants* themselves who secured their liberation.

August 1944 saw the Battle of Cluny and the liberation of the first Burgundian town. This was followed by the Battle of Autun and the merging of the French army and Resistance forces. The French and Allied forces travelled up the Saône corridor, catching the

or on sandbanks in the Loire. The effectiveness of the Morvan Resistance brought fierce reprisals, from hostage-taking to deportation. In 1944, the villages of Montsauche and Planchez were torched.

In June, the SAS-aided *maquis* murdered troops and sabotaged plants so the Germans responded with the massacre of civilians in Dun-les-Places. Mitterrand attends the memorial service every year, and made it his first engagement after his election as president in 1981. Since the Morvan was the

retreating German army in Burgundy.

The liberation of Dijon occurred in September, followed by the integration of French regular and Resistance forces at Châtillon and the historic meeting of the Allied armies from Normandy and Provence. Where the French forces failed in June 1940, the *Résistants* succeeded in summer 1944, bringing a revival of national pride. There were mixed feelings towards the Allies.

In Nevers and Le Creusot, hundreds of civilians were killed in Allied bombing raids, while the historic heart of Nevers was gutted. Historian Jean-François Bazin com-

Left, the Nazis in Dijon. **Above**, 11 September 1944, Liberation; the first tanks roll into Dijon.

ments wryly: "The building of British and American planes often outpaced the training of Allied pilots."

Nièvre was formally attached to Burgundy in 1945, echoing its "annexation" under German rule during the war. In Dijon, Chanoine Kir's victory speech compared the Liberation to the Burgundian defeat of the Swiss on the same day in 1513. Since the Mayor of Dijon had fled in 1940, Kir was elected and ran the city for 23 years. Politically, Dijon, like its leader, remains ambiguous. As victim of Parisian magnetic power, it is one of the most isolated French cities, with a sparsely populated hinterland and confusing political links.

Henry Miller, Dijon remains the only Burgundian town with any cosmopolitan pretensions or cultural status. Elsewhere, the Mitterrand connection has brought better cultural and educational facilities. New colleges and *maisons de culture* are designed to curb the young brain drain to Paris. As a supreme tactician, Mitterrand remained "Sunday mayor" in the Morvan until the presidency. His political obituary has often been written but his protégés are in place and seem secure in this socialist fiefdom. His successors at Château-Chinon are also *amis du Nivernais*, designer socialists with the popular touch. Whether out of loyalty or cunning, Mitterrand still remains on the

In elections, Dijon favours the right while the left wins in its immigrant suburbs. Yet in Presidential elections, the city voted decisively for Mitterrand, arguably a vote for the local boy. The Yonne and the Côte d'Or are broadly centrist but become more conservative in the wine belt. By contrast, the Nièvre and the Saône-et-Loire, the other two *départements*, vote left. The industrial belt around Montceau-les-Mines remains resolutely communist whereas Nièvre votes socialist. In the last legislative elections, the Nièvre was the sole French region in which every *canton* (constituency) voted socialist.

While its suburban soul is ridiculed by

Château-Chinon electoral register. The Mitterrand Mafia, the so-called *fraternité nivernaise*, has influence stretching beyond Burgundy. Friends in the Elysée are essential if a politician is to attract heavy state subsidies to his region. The major figure is Pierre Bérégovoy, mayor of Nevers. But as finance minister and the prime minister, he has brought an economic rigour to the region. Henri Nallet, Mayor of Tonnerre, is derided as the Justice Minister implicated in the Socialist Party's slush fund scandal, but as mayor, is praised for attracting new industry to his depressed corner of the Yonne.

As the crossroads of France, Burgundy

offers a confusing choice of directions. Sens, Auxerre and Nevers fall under the Paris spell while Chalon and Mâcon identify with Lyon. Only Autun and Beaune clearly look towards Dijon. As a result, Burgundy's four *départements* have differing outlooks. The Côte d'Or and Saône-et-Loire are the most popular, with good communications, a balanced economy and a share of the wine wealth. By contrast, the Yonne suffers from depopulation and the Paris effect. But this rural exodus is most marked in the Nièvre: the Morvan averages only 10 inhabitants per kilometre. New industry is concentrated in the Saône-et-Loire, leaving the Nièvre to cope with the reconversion of outmoded

nuclear and electronics fields. The steel industry along the Loire is in decline but metallurgy is still Burgundy's most important sector, based in the triangle of Montceau-les-Mines, Chalon and Le Creusot. The Schneider firm grew rich on arms manufacture but now specialises in precision engineering, making the bogies for TGV trains.

While Monceau is home to Michelin, Avallon has its own tyre company employing a workforce of 1,000. Pneu Laurent was founded in 1945 by the present mayor of Avallon. Burgundy has maintained its reputation for craftsmanship and design: Semur produces accordions and harmonicas while Nevers and the Puisaye are renowned for

plants. Naturally, the Saône-et-Loire's per capita income is 25 percent higher.

Burgundy's trading vocation has been bolstered by the advent of high-speed TGV trains. The region is rarely associated with industry yet is at the forefront of nuclear research. More humbly, Burgundy boasts the invention of the egg-timer. The old industrial heartland has gone high-tech: Montbard manufactures cores for nuclear reactors while in Salives, near Dijon, nuclear arms are designed. Chalon also works in the

Left, technology: the TGV comes to Burgundy.
Above, prosperity: château and Jaguar.

pottery. Kodak has a research centre in Chalon near where Nicéphore Niepce invented photography. Oddly, Beaune boasts the world's biggest factory for casino chips. As for tourism, Romanesque architecture and wine are the twin attractions. Only French visitors outnumber the British and Germans. While the British have pioneered barging along the canals, the Germans favour green tourism in the Morvan.

Dijon is primarily a commercial and administrative centre, aided by its proximity to Paris. However, the city is justly proud of its food industry: mustard, gingerbread, *cassis* and chocolate vie with dairy products, ham and snails. Burgundy still lives off the fat of the land, even if farmers account for only 11 percent of the workforce. Cereal covers the Châtillonais, the northern plains, while fruit, especially cherries and pears, grows near Auxerre. Forestry is still the Morvan's major industry: while Christmas trees supply Paris, the solid oaks end up in Autun's furniture factories. Further south, the Nivernais and Charolais are cattle country while the Bresse boasts France's only *appellation contrôlée* chicken. But to the wine-lover, the Côte d'Or epitomises Burgundy.

Burgundian wines have every reason to get drunk on their success. Vineyards represent only 1 percent of land yet generate 25

Burgundy's cheaper wines suffer competition from the Midi while the fashion for white wine risks eclipsing the reds. However, the finest vineyards remain priceless and rarely change hands. Even so, institutional investors are tempted by the profits: wine is safer than houses, more interesting than shares and most suitable for corporate hospitality. As a result, prices have soared, tripling between 1989 and 1991. To local approval, AXA, Auxerre football team, acquired prize Romanée vineyards in 1990. But Beaune's prestigious Maison Jadot was bought by Americans, including part of the sacred Clos de Vougeot estate. Japanese investments are also bitterly resented in Bur-

percent of agricultural revenue, with over 50 percent of wines exported. The creation of the Confrérie des Chevaliers du Tastevin in 1934 helpfully coincided with the start of the *appellation contrôlée* system. Since then, wine professionalism and profits have gone hand in hand. Dijon University was the first in France to offer courses in oenology, including a highly-valued degree in wine.

Local celebrities can also affect the wine trade. In Tonnerre, Justice Minister Henri Nallet recently established a major replantation programme while actor Gérard Depardieu's buying into Burgundian vineyards caused other stars to follow suit.

gundy. Takashimaya department store now controls a third of the top producers in Auxey-Duresses. Not that resentment is ever a bar to business. Centrifugal forces suck the region towards Paris but Burgundian identity survives. Visiting civil servants are constantly surprised by the commitment to the old province by politicians and citizens alike. Mayors happily define themselves as *un ami du Nivernais* or *un vrai Bourguignon*. If regionalism is a French religion, it finds its purest form in Burgundy. This is provincialism raised to an art form.

Above, promotion: buglers at Clos de Vougeot.

MITTERRAND'S MORVAN

Thanks to its Celtic roots and bitter climate, the Morvan often goes against the mainstream. The natives are wary of outsiders, and are as tough and inflexible as their granite mountains. But one outsider, François Mitterrand, has been part of this austere landscape for almost 50 years. In his book, *L'Abeille et L'Architecte* (The Builder and the Bee), Mitterrand declares: "I love the forest: my path in life often brings me back to the forests of the Morvan."

Mitterrand was born in Jarnac, cognac country near Bordeaux, but his career belongs to Burgundy. As a *Résistant* untainted by Vichy, he was "parachuted" into the Nièvre to fight a parliamentary seat. In 1946, at the age of 30, he was elected a *député* of the Morvan and this remained his political power base until the presidency. His wife, Danielle, had a family home in Cluny and a background in the Resistance so this tied the Burgundian knot. The president's pilgrimage to Solutré, the great rock near Mâcon, is now an annual reward for his disciples.

After being made mayor of Château-Chinon in 1959, Mitterrand became Président du Conseil Régionale and cultivated a brand of consensus politics. In local posts, as in the presidency, he was a wily pragmatist, with a team characterised by personal loyalty rather than shared ideology.

Beaten by de Gaulle, Mitterrand cultivated the political backwoods and fought again in 1981. It was in the Hôtel du Vieux Morvan in Château-Chinon that Mitterrand learnt he had become the first Socialist President of the Fifth Republic. Ginette Chevrier, the manageress, cried with delight. Mitterrand had stayed in Room 15 for 22 years, and in May 1991, Chevrier was one of the first Morvan friends invited to the Elysée to celebrate his golden decade.

Despite his mythological ascension from *Tonton* to *Dieu*, Mitterrand remains loyal. "*Bonne chance pour demain*," reads the president's postcard to a Morvan mayor in the 1989 local elections. Marchand, the mayor of Gouloux, had been elected unopposed since 1954 so luck was a mere formality in a tiny village with little more than a waterfall and a clog-maker to its name. The mayor first met Mitterrand in 1949, following an illegal wolf cull. A councillor had been killed in the chase and the *commune* fined 7 million francs. Mitterrand fought the case and the fine was reduced. Marchand returned to clog-making

while Mitterrand went on to the presidency. But in 1984 Marchand was in hospital in Chalon and forbidden phone calls, despite insisting that one was from the Elysée. "The nurse took me for a lunatic until I showed her a presidential letter."

Mitterrand is renowned for sending postal greetings to Morvan folk from all over the world. He never bothers with addresses but sends his *"fidèles pensées"* care of "Nièvre, France".

Little love is lost between the president and Nevers. Mitterrand has always found the Morvan *"une terre de fidélité"* compared with the "shifting sands of Nevers". Mitterrand's greatest fans are at Château-Chinon. His former deputy, Simone Bondieux, says admiringly: "We always called him President – we knew he would succeed."

Wine merchant André Emery confirms local legend: "He never has any money on him and doesn't wear a watch; his house is insignificant – he'll never be rich." But a *gendarme* gives Mitterrand the highest accolade: "Not once did he ever try to get out of a speeding fine."

Mitterrand's views on his adopted home are at one with his penchant for nature imagery and purplish prose. "My roots remain here – my writing contains the breath of the region as an accent would the speech." Mitterrand has chosen this patch of *France profonde* in which to cultivate his secret garden. In this shrine to *Mitterrandie*, the mood is *fin de règne* but, as Ginette Chevrier says, "*C'est sa place.*" ∎

Clochemerle, the archetypal provincial village, belongs to Burgundy. Writer Gabriel Chevalier said he based it on Gueugnon, his childhood haunt in the Charolais, although other villages also claim the honour. "Part agricultural village, part industrial town, Gueugnon was where I learnt about provincial life." There he found his inspiration for a social satire centred on the installation of a public lavatory. The cast included a ruined *marquise*, a vicious hunchback, a lecherous widower, bosomy haberdashers and an old maid madly in love with the local priest. This Burgundian soap opera may be drawn with a broad brush but the provincial theme strikes a chord with visitors. Real life is less scandalous but equally robust.

The small-town atmosphere is captured in photographers' studios all over Burgundy. The portraits in the window provide a projection of the town's self-image. Avallon may offer chaste maidens attending first communion yet, in Chalon, carnival revellers are caught in full flood.

But spontaneity is rarely part of the picture. Nevers focuses on the unexpected formality of a family picnic. Paray-le-Monial shows scenes of Sunday best while Charolais farmers pose awkwardly at a rural wedding. In Toucy, potters display their wares for a publicity shot. In Châtillon, weekend fishermen hold aloft a stuffed salmon. Dijonnais new graduates boast the bourgeois sophistication of bankers. Clamecy's enthusiastic canoeists are a contrast to the shots of chic wine merchants in Beaune. In Chablis, a dignitary looks smug in his wine confraternity costume. In Auxerre, a stolid couple celebrates a life of mutual boredom.

Burgundy prides itself on its provincialism, its claim to the mythical status of *France profonde*, deepest France. The social composition supports Burgundy's singularity. Compared with the rest of France, there is a higher proportion of farmers, wine growers, craftsmen, traders and family-run enterprises. Salaries are below the national average and *cadres* (executives) are few and far between.

Preceding pages: grape-picking, Santenay. **Left,** off to the fields. **Right,** a winning smile.

This social mix fosters traditionalism and political moderation, a pattern broken only by the impoverished but radical Nièvre.

Demography also plays a part: Burgundy is underpopulated, particularly in the rural Yonne and Nièvre. Here too, Burgundians are growing old gracefully. The population is considerably older than elsewhere: 18 percent are over 65 compared with a national average of 13 percent. But this already high figure doubles in rural areas, especially in parts of the Puisaye, Bresse and Morvan.

Mitterrand is typical of the region. Temperamentally, he shares a faith in the sanctity of provincial life. His 1981 presidential campaign presented an avuncular sage with *France profonde* in his soul. According to Alain Schrifès, an acerbic French journalist, "Giscard might read the *Financial Times* but only Mitterrand could tell you when it was going to rain. A hat on his head, a rose in his hand, roots underfoot, the president would let time find its own solutions." Cottage-garden socialism was the essence of *la force tranquille*, the slogan which shaped the region to his own rustic image.

"*Une ville quelconque*," remarked Zola of

"Anywhere-ville". Burgundy has its share of tedious towns, from Gueugnon and Clamecy to Montceau and Tonnerre. But behind the brickwork beats a provincial heart. Tonnerre is a slice of local life, from petty politicking to the "Paris effect", the economic blight caused by the escape of the young to Paris. This crumbling town in the Yonne is not grand enough to attract buyers of second homes and is too shabby to tempt tourists. Instead, it is left to the locals to manufacture sofa beds and video recorders, telling occupations for a sedentary population.

Burgundy is a pawn in the game of political patronage. A notable tendency is to *parachuter* (inject) the president's man into

Parisian scandal) which mattered only if it cost Nallet his ministerial post.

More important was the mayor's impact on the economy, from welcome state subsidies to the setting up of new firms and clubs. He has encouraged the replanting of vines, both Pinot Noir and Chardonnay. The prestigious neighbouring vineyards of Chablis benefit from having a friend at court and appreciated a visit from Nallet in their hour of need during the frosts of 1991. Complaints about an absentee mayor are outweighed by the prestige of having a personal grandee in Paris. As a local accountant says: "Up there, they play politics. Down here, we just balance the books."

local politics. Usually a powerful national figure, the "parachutee" is rewarded with a secure political base while his mentor bolsters a regional fiefdom. Tonnerre, an insignificant town of 6,000 people, was amazed to receive a minister as its mayor in 1989. A presidential commitment to consensus still allows scope for imposed appointees.

Henri Nallet, Minister of Justice and mayor of Tonnerre, has recovered from a bumpy landing. Despite allegations of the minister's involvement in a slush fund scandal, the local consensus is that Nallet has revived sleepy Tonnerre. But to most locals the affair was a mere *sale affaire parisienne* (dirty

A typical town council meeting in April 1991 approved a pay rise for the firemen and the replacement of obsolete fire extinguishers in the town gym. After agreement on how to spend a citizen's bequest to the town, the mayor and councillors retired for a drink. The bar discussion ranged from the effects of unemployment to the lack of street lighting in Rue Fosse-Dionne. After brooding on the impact of disastrous spring frosts on the wine trade, Nallet was soundly beaten at table football. The mayor's limousine then swept him off to the Parisian bright lights and his more lucrative weekday job as France's Minister of Justice.

The mayor, priest, lawyer, school-teacher and merchant were once notables, stock figures in provincial society. The old order may have faded but the mayor and the priest still have symbolic importance in the countryside. In 1987 Senator Signé replaced François Mitterrand as mayor of Château-Chinon. He is a seasoned politician as Machiavellian and as enigmatic as his mentor.

Priests command little political power and summon only wavering respect in the provincial heartland. Religion is a thorny issue in Burgundy so spirituality is accompanied by scepticism or anti-clericalism. Mitterrand's 1981 campaign poster set his face against the backdrop of a cosy village, which

tions. The Charolais farming families have always been devout while Paray-le-Monial, a pilgrimage centre second only to Lourdes, is linked to the cult of the Sacré Coeur and has a long tradition of mysticism. It is no coincidence that this pocket is sandwiched between Autun and Lyon, the two most powerful medieval bishoprics.

Elsewhere, the Yonne is the least Catholic part of Burgundy, not that the full-blooded enthusiasm for religious festivals reflects a *déchristianisé* image. In Vézelay, the July Fête de la Madeleine draws vast crowds. While St Bernard's hairshirt principles are not shared by his fellow Burgundians, the Bernard de Clairvaux spectacle is moving.

would have been cosier still if Mitterrand, fearful of clerical overtones, had not insisted that the church tower be airbrushed out.

Perhaps, not surprisingly, the places with the greatest number of practising Catholics are those once dominated by the abbeys of Cîteaux, Cluny, Fontenay and Pontigny. Cîteaux remains a working Cistercian community where Trappist monks have time for contemplation and the production of the celebrated Cîteaux cheese. But Paray-le-Monial and the Charolais boast the largest congrega-

Left, Bresse chickens; off to market in Bresse. **Above**, village café.

Held at the reconstructed monastery of Clairvaux, "the passion that shook Europe" is re-enacted by a local cast every summer. Nevers draws pilgrims to the tomb of St Bernadette of Lourdes. But the greatest congregations materialised for Pope John Paul's pastoral mission in 1986. His tour, to Taizé, Paray-le-Monial and Vézelay, touched upon the sacred spots of Burgundian heritage.

In trading terms Burgundy seems a bastion of traditionalism. The region, once renowned for its hardy peasants: Burgundian cowboys, known as *galvachers*, roamed France while *flotteurs* supplied the capital with firewood, floating convoys of logs downstream.

Nourrices morvandelles nursed orphans in Paris and the provinces. These trades may have died out by 1914 but cheese-makers, clog-makers and thatchers stlll survive.

In the Morvan, many traditional trades appear in different guises. The woodcutters remain but forestry is a sensitive issue, dividing technocrats, ecologists and local people. The ancient forests of birch, beech and oak are struggling to survive against the intrusive planting of conifers. Christmas trees and pine furniture are big business in the Morvan.

But provincial Burgundy moves with the times, its artisans adapting traditional skills to tourism and popular taste.

Survivors of the rural recession include

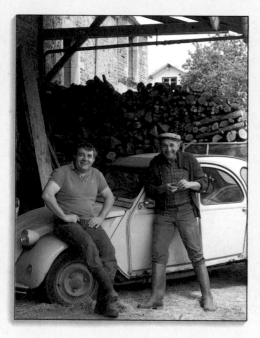

the Pierlot family of potters in the Puisaye, a region known for its stoneware. In the sandstone Château de Ratilly, the family exhibit rustic pots and run a summer school to supplement their income.

Further south, in the tiny village of St Pèresous-Vézelay, Romain Doré works as a *sabotier*, a clog-maker. He is proud of belonging to the eighth generation, an authentic tradition matched by his medieval workshop. He uses ancient tools and carves only wood grown on the slopes of Vézelay: walnut, oak, elm and ash.

Sylvie Julien, a traditional glass-maker, also works in the shadow of Vézelay. Unlike the instinctive Romain Doré, she waxes lyrical about "the relationship between light and matter", and rails against the modern world: "who will be left to adorn the cathedrals of the future?"

Benoît Andriot in Monthélon, near Autun, combines cattle-breeding, his first love, with work as a *chambres d'hôtes* host. The cost of producing beef has doubled in the past 15 years without a commensurate rise in farm prices. Despite slender profit margins, he abhors the trend towards mechanisation and the excessive use of hormones in meat production. By contrast, his cattle "live a balanced, natural life", free to graze wherever they wish.

Looking like a caricature of the ruddy-faced farmer, he relishes sheepdog trials and recently led a delegation of Charolais farmers on an export drive to Canada. Yet his joviality masks a passion for regional history and folklore. Andriot regrets that his children will not follow in his footsteps but realises the drawbacks of the rural life. Although a member of a dying breed, this modest and cultivated farmer is the quintessential Burgundian.

Lifestyles are changing in traditional wine-growing regions, from the patrician Côte d'Or to the poorer Beaujolais. Claude Carlier, the director of Clos de Vougeot, is the epitome of a sophisticated *gestionnaire*, as smooth as his prized product. In the Beaujolais, ruddy-faced peasants in berets have given way to white-coated oenologists with a wine degree, the *licence de la vigne* from Dijon University. Technologist Olivier Venot typically tastes 77 different wines to determine the blend of Gobet's Beaujolais Nouveau.

William Fèvre led a Chablisien delegation to confront their Californian competitors on enemy soil in the Napa Valley. "Chablis of California must stop taking our name in vain," fumed the French growers. At stake is both Burgundian prestige and the lucrative Japanese market. Still, Chablis has cornered the Vatican market – Domaine Defaix supplies Pope John Paul and Vatican officials with Chablis vintages.

Provincial life is a hotbed of petty rivalries and *problèmes de voisinage*, quarrels among neighbours. Ever meddlesome Burgundians are in their element. Disputes over inheritance are the bane of provincial life, with offspring squabbling over the division of spoils, often one tiny smallholding. A bourgeois couple complain about the grasping *mentalité paysanne* that covets a neighbour's success. After selling honey as a sideline, they were shocked when neighbouring farmers followed suit. But this "peasant mentality" is common sense in its purest form.

Marc Meneau, chef at the famous L'Espérance, in Vézelay, arouses mixed feelings. He is admired as the local boy made good, the star who attracts celebrities in helicopters; others begrudge his success. Meneau's fans point to his investment in projects like the restoration of St-Père church. The chef himself is more interested in promoting Burgundian cuisine: "It's just as much part

the wine associations. A sense of solidarity pervades the Côte d'Or vineyards.

To outsiders, the sumptuous tiled roofs of the Côte d'Or overshadow the simple slates of the Morvan. But Burgundy also means the lichen-covered cottages of the Puisaye, low brick houses of the Bresse and warm stone farms of the Charolais. To pessimists, gentrification spells the end of genuine rural life. Still, it saves villages from a slide into low-brow lethargy, with cafés replaced by video shops. Clamecy, once the centre of the logging trade, is a village in decline. A cheerful welcome cannot disguise the cultural void, steep unemployment and grimy facades.

No such fate has befallen the wine-grow-

of our culture as is our artistic heritage."

Culinary matters are also uppermost in Chaumard, a lakeside village in the Morvan. Each of the three restaurateurs advises against eating elsewhere: "They use nothing but frozen food down the road." Yet Burgundy is neighbourly in the warmest sense of the word, from its political leaders downwards. Mitterrand's postcards expressing *sincères amitiés* are treasured by citizens. Wine-growers will help rivals with a troublesome harvest, either as an individual gesture or through

ing communities. Gevrey-Chambertin is sleepy and smug – typical wine country. Ten acres, the average patch, produces a good living. The sleek cars outside *vignerons'* homes in Nuits-St-Georges and Fixin are proof of what the Fisc, the tax office, terms *signes extérieurs de richesse*. Traditional market towns thrive, such as earthy yet appealing Charolles. At the Wednesday market, tough farmers bid for the prized white cattle as well as pigs, sheep and chickens. Farmers gossip below the orange-tiled roofs while, between the canals and the scruffy allotments, bustling traders sell every form of pâté and sausage. Pragmatism and conti-

Left, farmers near Saulieu. **Above**, postman discusses the news of the day, Sacquenay.

nuity are a recipe for success in the land of plenty. Charolles's setting, within the spiritual triangle of Taizé, Cluny and Paray-le-Monial, means that the church is central. There are summer concerts in Romanesque chapels, and folklore festivals, often followed by a rich *entrecôte charolaise*.

Leisure is equally robust. Fans of AXA Auxerre, the best regional football team, flock to matches. Canal and river banks are generally lined with motionless fishermen hoping to tempt perch, carp and even catfish. Oddly, Burgundians prefer cycling along canal towpaths to barging itself. Quiet pursuits include mushroom-picking or hiking near Solutré.

is in the tradition of Flemish burlesque, with wise fools offering a witty commentary on modern manners. Satire aside, it is also a Mardi Gras release, an excess of licence before Lenten abstinence.

The Fête de la Vivre, held in Couches every 20 years, parades a mythical beast, part dragon and part snake. The creature, a sorcerer's familiar, was blamed for destroying the crops in medieval times and so is ceremonially burnt. Burgundians are susceptible to magical, pagan tales.

Celtic beliefs and Christianity coexist. On Shrove Tuesday, the village near the abbey of Pierre-Qui-Vire re-enacts a Gallic ceremony: broth is sprinkled on houses to ward

Burgundy has a reputation for conviviality and spontaneity, best appreciated at festivals. The water jousting ceremony at Clamecy recalls the region's former dependence on the river trade. In industrial La Machine, citizens celebrate the Fête de Sainte Barbe, the patron saint of miners. The goose fair at Toucy and the snail festival at Blaisy-Bas confirm the Burgundian fixation with food. In Semur, the Fête de la Bague is the oldest horse race in France, run since 1639. It takes its name from the prize, a gold ring engraved with the city arms. Even more significant is Chalon-sur-Saône carnival, second only to that of Nice. As a medieval Fête des Fous, it

away spirit-snakes, the evil woodland masters. Montréal sees the survival of ancient spring rite. Bundles of twigs, known as *mais*, are propped against doorways. Left by amorous boys, these sexist signs suggest that the young girl inside is ripe for matrimony.

Ancient superstitions linger, especially in the marshy Bresse and the austere Morvan. In the 19th century, the Morvan was known as "a land of savages, witches and wolves", myths perpetuated by storytelling shepherds and woodcutters. In the 1950s witchcraft was still practised in rural Morvan, linked to animal sacrifice and the cult of wolves and black hens. Nowadays, feasts for the dead, a legacy of Gallic rites, are still offered in some parts. A belief in herbal remedies is widespread in the mountains, although roast lizard is no longer considered an effective cure for epilepsy.

The Bressans are born storytellers, conjuring up images of white ladies swirling in the dense mists over the marshes. An owl's cry heard during the day predicts a pregnancy in the neighbourhood. After the christening, the godfather and godmother must pray that the baby "be neither a simpleton, brat, dribbler nor stammerer". In the past, mothers put a collar of wolf's teeth around the baby's neck as spiritual protection. The loss of the child's first tooth was a rite of passage: the child tossed the tooth into the fire, promising to reclaim it on Last Judgement Day. After a death, the clock, windows and television screen are covered; even vases are emptied "in case the departing soul drowns". Folklore still lurks below the surface.

Burgundian regionalism is renowned, touching émigrés and residents alike. *Régionalisme* is one of the biggest sections in local bookshops; schoolchildren even study an anthology of Burgundian literature. A wariness of outside influences underpins provincial society: in this respect, the Japanese have recently replaced the Americans in local demonology. Regional identity reinforces provincialism, as does the cultivation of rural dialects, customs and festivals. The Burgundian paradox lies in its spiritual passion for earthly pleasures and its pragmatic approach to spiritual matters.

Scratch the surface and literary peasant roots are unearthed. Vincenot's *La Billebaude* is a portrait gallery of modern peasants and a homage to a gamekeeper grandfather who taught him *l'art de chasse et l'art de vivre*. During his childhoood, peasant costumes and beliefs were common in the Auxois. Paul Meunier, a self-styled peasant storyteller, records the folk history of Asquins, near Vézelay. As the great-grandson of the village miller, he recounts the cherry harvests, labours of the month and the slaughter of the family pig. Proverbs are revealing: "Labour is a gypsy child who doesn't obey any law." At its most pretentious, Burgundy indulges in a *mitage du paysage*, an idealisa-

tion of pastoral living and provincial life. At its truest, it is a rootedness in the region that comes before all else. Burgundian roots are essential to provincial status, no matter how humble. Certain *vigneron* families trace their ancestry to the days of the Grand Dukes.

Vineyards are a fertile source of superstition. Spring vigils chill the workers to the bone, bringing the most dangerous moments for frost just before dawn. Given the sacredness of wine, incantations against hail are not unknown. In Chablis, April moons symbolise destructive power so *vignerons* may still resort to Faustian pacts with nature.

Superstition and religion are natural allies in Burgundy. La Chablisienne, the wine co-

operative founded by the Curé of Poinchy, controls a third of the local trade. In 1990 the Archbishop of Sens blessed the harvest and officiated at the St-Vincent wine festival. On a smaller scale, Noyers also pays its religious dues: a Madonna on a medieval gateway is hung with grapes in grateful thanks for a successful harvest.

In 1952 the Burgundian wine confraternities played hosts to their rivals from Bordeaux. Clos de Vougeot witnessed an unprecedented display of pageantry, with a grand mass and processions of trumpeters, heralds, archers and singers. But the role of the orders is not limited to camaraderie and

Left, folk dancing in Dijon. **Right**, adding a fresh lick of paint.

public relations. Their solemn duty is to spread Burgundian culture and maintain the traditional wine festivals.

Les Trois Glorieuses describes a trio of harvest festivals. The first is the Chapitre de la Confrérie des Chevaliers du Tastevin, a banquet held at the Château de Clos de Vougeot. The following day is the Vente des Hospices de Beaune, the wine auction treated as a benchmark for Burgundy wines. Then comes *La Paulée* at Meursault, a literary banquet at which *vignerons* present their finest bottles. *La Fête des Vins* follows a week later. By contrast, *St Vincent Tournante* is a January procession, based in a different wine village each year. *Tastevinage* is also a

spring event, held in the Cistercian cellars of the Clos de Vougeot. The wines are put before a jury of 200 wine writers, growers and brokers. The jury then assesses each bottle's *honnêteté, caractère et qualité*.

Historically, Beaujolais was Burgundy's poor country cousin but the popularity of Beaujolais Nouveau is changing that. The *Clochemerle* series was filmed in Vaux-en-Beaujolais but *vigneron* Gérard Texier remarks: "The cast came to drink our wine but we've never seen the series." Still, visitors feel the convivial *Clochemerle* effect. Michel Déflache attributes any jollity to Beaujolais: "The people are extrovert and so is the wine."

Even a shy Japanese importer was found clog-dancing in front of Vaux's lavatorial tourist attraction, naturally inscribed as "*La Pissotière de Clochemerle*".

Dijon is Burgundy's window on the world, a city that has grown without sacrificing its soul. Outsiders would say that its soul was always resolutely provincial. As a dormitory town of Paris, Dijon attracts a shifting population and also appeals to Swiss and German property speculators. Still, only Dijon has any cosmopolitan pretensions, with its clutch of Parisian intellectuals and sizeable foreign community. At best, its status as regional capital makes it a magnet for the arts. A lively student population ensures an experimental attitude to culture. Recently, a fashionable crowd gathered in a deconsecrated church to watch a play by Lacarrière, who lives in nearby Sacy. His reveries on passion and mortality held the audience spellbound.

But at heart Dijon is bourgeois and conservative, a city of civil servants, academics and office workers drawn to the Burgundian good life. Dijon's gastronomic fair is a byword for Burgundian sumptuousness as well as cuisine. Its bustling ethnic markets seem untypical of Burgundy: Italian and Algerian traders jostle for space; a gypsy has trained a mongoose to sit on a pony and beg. Yet behind the exoticism are Burgundian signs and symbols. La Petite Flamande sells snails beside stalls stacked with jars of mustard; nearby, bourgeois students join Dijonnais matrons in browsing for junk. They are bound by a mercantile yet convivial approach that embodies the spirit of this countrified capital, and of Burgundy itself.

Immersion in provincial life is one of the chief pleasures of Burgundy. A balloon flight over rolling countryside reveals gilded roofs, pointed weathervanes, fields of sunflowers and Charolais cattle. A smooth descent may alight upon a boldly painted barge, a bicycle race or a Burgundian wedding. Such cameos may be glimpsed from the ground as easily as from a hot-air balloon. "Good wine is an inward emotion," said Henry James; so is provincialism. Behind the lace curtains are cultured farmers and cunning *vignerons*. Burgundy has its finger on the pulse of provincial France.

Left, wine-maker , Côte d'Or. Right, taking shelter in Tanlay.

"No wine is as earthy as red Burgundy... And no wine accompanies dusk as intimately, and is such a friend of the night, as the wine of Nuits-St-Georges, which is nocturnal in its very name, dark and twinkling like a summer evening in Burgundy. It shines blood-red on the threshold of the night like the fires of the setting sun on the crystalline rim of the horizon. It kindles red and deep-blue glints in the purple earth, in the grass, and in the leaves of the trees, still warm with the tastes and aromas of the dying day. With the arrival of night, wild animals go into their dens deep in the ground; the boar crashes noisily through the dense undergrowth; the pheasant, with its short and silent flight, swims in the twilight already floating above the woods and fields; the nimble hare slides on to the first moonbeam as though on to a silver tightrope. It is the hour of Burgundy wine."

— Curzio Malaparte, *Kaputt*.

This paean to Nuits-St-George is entirely typical of the lengths writers will go to in order to express their passion for Burgundy wine. And it inspires not only passion but deep confusion in anyone attempting to understand the fiendishly complicated business of growing and selling Burgundy.

Who, for example, said that "Burgundy, and in particular Côte d'Or, is... excruciatingly difficult to comprehend," and "to a large extent... an unfathomable mystery"? A novice wine buff? Or maybe a chauvinistic Bordeaux château-owner? Neither: it was none other than Robert Parker, one of the world's greatest experts on Burgundy (and Bordeaux, for that matter). You have been warned.

Before looking at why some Burgundy wines pose such a problem, let's first define what we are talking about. The *appellation contrôlée* wines of Burgundy (Grande Bourgogne), come from five areas: Chablis and the Auxerrois, Côte d'Or (Côte de Nuits and Côte de Beaune), the Chalonnais, the Mâconnais and Beaujolais. Beaujolais, then, is technically a Burgundy, though rarely referred to as such. Despite its adjective,

Preceding pages: Pinot Noir grapes. Right, tasting the vintage, Côte d'Or.

Grande Bourgogne produces only about half as much wine as Bordeaux (excluding Beaujolais, only a quarter).

Beaujolais is the easiest to understand of all the Burgundy *appellations*. It has only three categories: Beaujolais, Beaujolais-Villages and 10 named growths – the Institut National des Appellations d'Origine (INAO) allowed Régnié to join the club in 1988; it comes in a single colour (red) and is made from a single grape variety (Gamay).

The relatively recent marketing success story of Beaujolais, and more particularly Beaujolais Nouveau, is well known. It is alleged that Parisian journalists marooned in Vichy-run Lyon during the Occupation re-

quality and price. This is the result of a syndrome which has also taken its toll, though to a lesser degree, in Chablis and Côte d'Or.

It works like this: your vines produce, let us say, 50 hectolitres per hectare of excellent wine, which you lightly chaptalise to make it smoother (chaptalisation consists of adding sugar to the fermenting must to boost its alcoholic content); it sells like a bomb; demand outstrips supply, so you put up your price; but you are also tempted to cajole your vines (by pruning techniques, selection of clones and so on) into producing ever greater yields; the quality of the wine automatically goes down, as does its alcoholic content;

To Paris 175 km

LES FOURNEAUX   Fleys

La chapelle-Vaupelteigne

FOURCHAUME   Fyé

245

Serein

269

BOUGROS
LES PREUSES
VAUDESIR
GRENOUILLES
VALMUR
LES CLOS
BLANCHOTS

MONTÉE DE TONNERRE

MONT DE MILIEU

VAUCOUPIN

BEAUROY

Poinchy

Chablis

Serein

To Dijon 145 km

To Auxerre 14 km

CÔTE DE LÉCHET

Milly

Chichée

244

LES EPINOTTES

VOSGROS

Chablis

1300 m/ 0.8 miles

VAILLON

GRAND CRU

PREMIER CRU

272

MONTMAINS

turned to the capital after the war with stories of a deliciously light and fruity red wine they had discovered called Beaujolais. But even without the hacks' efforts to publicise the wine, it is doubtful whether any advertising copywriter could have come up with a more alluring brand-name than Beaujolais (with its suggestions of *beau* and *joli*). Many of the growth names, too, are melodious (Brouilly, Chiroubles) or full of sensual (Saint-Amour, Juliénas) and visual (Moulin-à-Vent, Fleurie) associations.

In recent years, though, Beaujolais sold to consumers outside the Beaujolais area has tended to be distinctly less attractive, in both

your consumers are accustomed to a certain strength, so you overdo the chaptalisation a bit. The resulting wine is an undrinkable brew that produces instant migraine.

In 1988, the French consumer magazine *Que Choisir?* caused a bit of a scandal when it was able to prove, through nuclear magnetic resonance tests, that chaptalisation had boosted the alcohol in some Beaujolais wines by as much as 4°, way above the permitted level of 2°. There has since been a swing back to non-chaptalised or less chaptalised wines on the part of some more intelligent growers. If buying Beaujolais on the spot, try to track them down, or invest in a reliable up-to-date wine-buying guide (such as the Gault-Millau or the Hachette). And steer clear of all but the most reliable *négociants* (Pierre Ferraud, Louis Tête, Georges Duboeuf).

The Mâconnais area, like Beaujolais, which it adjoins to the north, is also relatively straightforward to understand. Its most prestigious wine – many would say it was overrated and overpriced – is the white Pouilly-Fuissé, a Chardonnay that sells well on the US market. Otherwise the Mâconnais produces an ocean of unpretentious, largely white wines under the Mâcon *appellation régionale* which vary widely in type, depending on grape variety and soil, as well as

Middle Ages on, by Chablis and the Auxerrois. That this was once one of France's principal wine-growing areas can be seen from the adjective *vineux* in some place-names. In the 19th century the railway, which opened up the capital to cheaper wines from the Midi, and the arrival of Phylloxera, together caused wine-growing in the region – which for climatic and geological reasons was never an easy option – to go into serious decline. Many vineyards were grubbed up and put to other uses.

It is only in the past few decades that the trend has been spectacularly reversed, mainly as a result of vineyard extension. Production of Chablis, for example, rose 16

Mechanical grape-picker, Chalonnais.

in quality. Mâconnais wines, like Beaujolais, benefited from shrewd advertising, though at a much earlier date. In 1666, a giant of a man called Claude Brosse decided to take two barrels of his red Mâcon to Paris on spec, shipping it by oxcart. He somehow managed to sing the praises of his wine to Louis XIV in person, and immediately received an order from the royal cellars.

Because of easy waterway communications via the River Yonne and the River Serein, a substantial share of the Paris wine market was cornered, from the end of the

times between 1945 and 1990, and could increase further if more vineyards are planted (as they are legally entitled to be).

Those interested in lesser-known, recently replanted *appellations* should sample some of the red and white wines of distinct character and reasonable price that are dotted all over the Yonne *département*, They include Irancy, Epineuil, Saint-Bris-le-Vineux, Chitry and Coulanges-la-Vineuse.

These wines, however, are dwarfed in quality and price by the area's most celebrated name, Chablis. At its best, this Chardonnay can be a superbly intense wine. But recently it has been in such demand,

WINE CONFRATERNITIES

The vinous motto "*Jamais en Vain, Toujours en Vin*" belongs to the *Confrérie des Chevaliers du Tastevin*, the most celebrated wine confraternity in France. The tradition of bacchic brotherhoods goes back to the Middle Ages when *confréries vineuses* abounded in Anjou, the Bordelais and Burgundy. They provided practical support and camaraderie, under the banner of St Vincent, patron saint of *vignerons*.

After the Revolution, Burgundy's loss of political power whittled away regional pride; the wine confraternities were relegated to folklore. As a result, most wine-tasting orders date from the

20th century. The success of Burgundy's *Chevaliers du Tastevin* has spawned countless imitators. In the 1930s, Burgundian wines were not selling. Desperate wine-growers at Nuits-St-Georges revived the festival of St Vincent, citing an old saying, *Si nos caves sont pleines, nos coeurs débordent* (If our cellars are full, our hearts are overflowing). In reality, their hearts were far from overflowing. The growers hit upon an inspired idea: invite their friends to drink Burgundy wine. "They will then discover that, as in St Bernard's day, these are the finest wines in Christendom".

The idea was perfect public relations, soon robed in chivalric splendour and housed in a dreamy château. In 1934 the *Chevaliers du Tastevin* acquired Clos de Vougeot, a walled wine estate built by St Bernard's Cistercian monks. Its 50 hectares are shared by a total of 70 owners, making it a symbolic spot for such a joint venture.

The *Chevaliers du Tastevin* organise 17 chapters a year and during the grand *disnées* (banquets), folkloric rituals initiate newcomers in Burgundian ways. The colourful ceremony, inspired by Molière, uses dog Latin and archaic French. The dinner is a homage to Burgundy, from *oeufs en meurette*, eggs poached in red wine, to vintage Meursault and Montrachet. Merry drinking songs include the refrain, "*Toujours buveurs, jamais ivrogne*" (ever drinkers, never drunk).

The *intronisation* (initiation ceremony) requires the postulant to swear an oath of fidelity to Burgundian wines and to make a speech. As initiates, Princess Grace of Monaco, General de Gaulle, François Mitterrand, Ronald Reagan and George Bush have all drunk from the *tâtevin*, the traditional wine-tasting cup.

As far as such anachronistic rituals are concerned, "*le nouveau c'est l'ancien*" remains the rallying cry. In Racine's day, *confréries* had no compunction about adopting the ceremonial of an ancient religious or chivalric order; it was a respectful nod to history, with no trace of mockery. The *Chevaliers* likewise plundered the past: their costumes resemble the academic gown of Rabelais; titles such as *Chef du Protocole* and *Grand Chambellan* are redolent of another age.

The *confréries vineuses* also play an essential part in protecting the quality and reputation of Burgundy wines. In 1950 the pioneering *Chevaliers du Tastevin* formalised this in *Tastevinage*, an annual *dégustation*. More quality control than competition, it judges whether the Burgundy is typical of its *appellation* and, more subjectively, whether it is a wine fit to offer friends. The dual aim is to reward the grower for high quality wine and to signal the symbiotic relationship between producer and consumer. The successful bottles are pronounced *tastevinées*, strictly numbered, and labelled with the prestigious *Tastevinage* seal.

The hushed atmosphere could not be more different from the boisterous initiation ceremonies. One celebrates Burgundian verve while the other honours the mystical nature of wine, with praise such as "*il est grand, le mystère de la foi*".

Purists might wince at the fake folklore and public relations but beyond the bold pastiche, a genuine Burgundian spirit prevails. Clos de Vougeot is the shrine of wine, symbolising its central importance to the region. ∎

especially outside France, that it has suffered from the Beaujolais syndrome. To avoid nasty surprises, you can to some extent trust the INAO classification of Chablis.

But there is more than meets the eye to the INAO categories and their respective qualities. It is here that we start moving into the forest of complications that bedevil comprehension of top Burgundy wines. To understand the problem, one needs to know a little about their history. While it is known that there were vines in Burgundy when the Romans left Gaul (they may even have been introduced there by Julius Caesar – an old grape variety used in Irancy is called César), the development of wine-growing in Chablis

detect its characteristics by tasting the soil. The Cistercians divided up what is now Clos de Vougeot, in Côte d'Or, into three separate entities, which they called, in ascending order of quality, Cuvée des Moines, Cuvée des Rois and Cuvée des Papes. So it has been known for centuries that distinct wines can be produced by different parcels of a single vineyard, depending on their orientation, altitude, exposure, slope and soil (recent research has shown that in the Côte de Nuits alone there are 59 different types of soil).

Matters were further complicated by the French Revolution. The church's vast estates in Chablis and Côte d'Or were confiscated and sold off in small lots. Two centu-

and Côte d'Or was largely the work of medieval monks, particularly the Cistercians. Despite their concern with matters spiritual, they displayed great temporal sophistication when it came to wine-making. They also realised the value of great wine as a bargaining counter or diplomatic tool.

The monks naturally needed to know the "market" value of wine from this or that vineyard. So they initiated the lengthy process of classifying parcels of land that is still being continued by the INAO today. It seems they were so skilled that they could even

Grape-picking, Moulin-à-Vent, Beaujolais.

ries later, intermarriage between wine-growing families and the Napoleonic law which requires property to be divided up equally between all progeny have together resulted in a pattern of vineyard ownership in Chablis and Côte d'Or that forms a gigantic mosaic of tiny, often widely separated, parcels of land. Some are owned by individual growers, who may market their own wine, or sell all or some of it to *négociants*; others are in the hands of *négociants*, who may blend the product of one vineyard with wine from another of the same *appellation*. When the mosaic of ownership is superimposed on the intricate pattern of appellations and growths, the result looks like a scrambled TV picture. If you add to the equation the fact that not all wine-growers or *négociants* are equally interested in getting the best out of their vines because in many cases they are certain of selling all their wine at a good price, irrespective of its quality, then buying Burgundy starts looking like a lottery. Even the INAO classifications are not always a model of clarity. About half the 40-odd *premiers crus* in Chablis can replace their actual name with that of a more famous neighbour. Thus the 50-acre (20-hectare) Chablis Premier Cru Chapelot is entitled to masquerade under the name of its more highly ranked 12-acre neighbour Montée de Tonnerre.

tract maximum benefit from the presence of a *grand cru* on their territory by simply annexing its name to their own. Thus, the villages of Aloxe-Corton, Chambolle-Musigny, Vosne-Romanée, Gevrey-Chambertin, Chassagne-Montrachet and Puligny-Montrachet, for example, were once simply called Aloxe (pronounced *Alosse*), Chambolle and so on.

With the possible exception of Clos de Vougeot, whose multiplicity of ownership (70 growers share 50 hectares!) makes for a certain irregularity of quality, you are unlikely to be disappointed by any of the *grands crus* – always supposing you are able to lay your hands on, and afford, a bottle or

The situation in Côte d'Or is even more confusing, even if there is no blatant name substitution as in Chablis. It divides into Côte de Nuits, which produces mainly reds, and Côte de Beaune, where both whites and reds are found. The area boasts no fewer than 32 *grands crus*, scarce and very expensive wines that are recognised as being among the very finest in the world. Their very names conjure up sensations of a vinous nirvana – the French singer and bon viveur Pierre Perret wrote a song consisting almost entirely of names like Richebourg and Corton-Charlemagne.

Historically, communes have tried to ex-

two. Two of the finest wines of them all are generally thought to be the white Montrachet (pronounced *Mon-rachet*) and the red Romanée-Conti.

Where buying becomes more complex is in the next two categories down, the *premiers crus* and the *appellations communales*. Mention of a *premier cru* on the label generally provides a certain guarantee of quality. However, a wine which simply calls itself Chassagne-Montrachet, for example, is an *appellation communale*; it will have come from any vineyard in that large commune and may not necessarily be worth the hefty price being asked for it.

Communes less prestigious than Chassagne-Montrachet, in that they have no *grand cru* on their territory, are often a better bet. Some very good Burgundies can be picked up, in both the *premier cru* and *appellation communale* categories, in Fixin, Pernand-Vergelesses, Savigny-lès-Beaune, Beaune, Volnay, Monthelie (also spelt Monthélie; pronounced *Mon-tli* by locals), Auxey-Duresses, Saint-Aubin and Santenay. Greater caution is needed when it comes to Pommard, Meursault and Nuits-St-Georges, because of their high reputation, particularly on export markets, and correspondingly steep prices. Greed and the law of supply and demand are responsible for

lès-Beaune and St-Romain. Wines from the hills of Côte d'Or, which go under the *appellations régionales* of Bourgogne Haute-Côtes de Nuits and Bourgogne Haute-Côtes de Beaune, are also good.

Although the wines of the Chalonnais cannot compete with the finest of the Côte d'Or names, they have been steadily improving, and now provide some of the best value to be found in Burgundy. They include some *crémants* (lightly sparkling wines) which can rival lesser champagnes and are 50 percent cheaper. Since 1990, wines from the Chalonnais that do not come from its four *appellations communales* (Rully, Mercurey, Givry and Montagny) have been entitled to

Burgundy's spectacular price hikes in some years (such as 1989). These are usually followed by much talk of crisis and an easing of prices. But, even allowing for inflation, the figures for Burgundy exports between 1975 and 1990, for example, look good: they rose by 68 percent in volume and by 622 percent in value.

Probably the best value for money in Côte d'Or is provided by lesser-known communes which cannot even boast a *premier cru*. They include Marsannay (which got its *appellation communale* in 1987), Chorey-

1983 Aloxe-Corton *premier cru*.

the *appellation régionale* Côte Chalonnaise. For the time being at least, it would seem that the ethos of the enthusiastic Chalonnais growers is "we try harder". One feels that a Chalonnais wine might have been the kind of thing James Thurber had in mind when he wrote his celebrated cartoon caption: "It's a naive domestic Burgundy, without any breeding, but I think you'll be amused by its presumption."

In Burgundy, as in Beaujolais, a wine-buying guide is a vital asset. Not all growers are equally meticulous about the sanitary conditions of their equipment or equally prepared to invest in expensive new oak

THE VIGNERON

St-Romain is one of the least-known of Burgundy wines and perhaps for that reason it is very good value. It got its *appellation communale* only in 1947 and boasts no *premier cru*. Its geographical location also sets it apart: it is higher up and farther west than any of its fellow Côte de Beaune *appellations*.

The road leading up to the village of St-Romain from Auxey-Duresses runs along a deeply gouged valley dominated by grandiose cliffs – a foretaste of the landscape of the Côte d'Or hinterland. The upper part of the village, St-Romain-le-Haut, is a secluded cul-de-sac of warm-

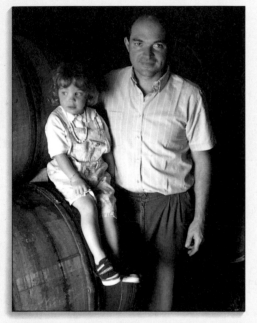

coloured old stone houses and a 15th-century church, with the vineyards beyond. On the left stands the handsome 17th-century home of one of St-Romain's top growers, Alain Gras.

Gras, a small muscular man with a weatherbeaten face and melodious voice, is not one to waste time on pleasantries: he immediately suggested a visit to his *salle de dégustation*. Out came the bottles and glasses – Burgundian growers, unlike *vignerons* in some other areas, are notable for their willingness to pull a cork on a finished wine rather than siphon out a sample from the barrel.

After attending the Lycée Viticole in Beaune,

Above, Alain Gras and his daughter Clémentine.

Gras worked as a home help before doing his military service. Then his father gave him a tumbledown house he had acquired through the ancient and rather macabre system of *viager* (whereby the buyer acquires a property by paying the seller an annuity for as long as the latter lives).

"In those days – the late 1970s – St-Romain wines were even less known than they are today," Gras said. "And the two hectares of land that came with the house, although entitled to the *appellation*, were being grazed by cows. I put vines there instead, bought up parcels of other vineyards here and there, did up the house, and then in 1982 made my first wine."

He pointed to a photograph of his *vigneron* great-grandfather. "He lived to be 100, and my grandfather is still going strong at 93. Perhaps it has something to do with the fact that we never drink *vin ordinaire*, just our own wine!"

Gras's 10 acres (4 hectares) of St-Romain vines, which are located at an average altitude of 1,250 ft (380 metres), produce about 16,000 bottles of wine a year, half of it white (Chardonnay) and half red (Pinot Noir). He also owns 5 acres lower down in the Auxey-Duresses *appellation*, which yield about 6,000 bottles of red. Every Burgundy grower has his or her own wine-making techniques, partly out of personal inclination and partly because of differences in soil, altitude and so on. Gras prefers fairly traditional methods. They are – for the technically minded – 25 percent new oak barrels; 100 percent de-stemming; 12–14 days' maceration; fermentation at about 73°F/23°C (white) and 86°F/30°C (red); chaptalisation if the year has not been particularly sunny; malolactic fermentation in vats (white) and in barrel (red); and fining with infusorial earth. Gras bottles his wine almost a year after the harvest, in August (white) and September (red).

Gras has never had any problem selling his wine – in fact, rather the reverse – because St-Romain in general, and his St-Romain in particular, is considered such good value. In the days when the dollar was strong, a group of 18 American importers once came to sample his wine. They had been doing the rounds of a large number of prestigious Burgundy growers. "A fellow from Florida said my St-Romain would make a nice picnic wine," Gras recalled drily. True, both his white and red St-Romains are lightweights compared with a good Meursault or a Volnay. But they have such breeding that the best place for them to be brought out of a picnic hamper would be the lawns of Glyndebourne. ∎

barrels – and some have even been known to use oak shavings to flavour their wines.

Nor will even reputable growers necessarily agree on what is the best method of vinification. Some de-stem all their grapes before pressing, others a certain proportion, yet others none. They have different opinions on such questions as yields per hectare, maceration before fermentation, fermentation temperature, filtration and fining. Those more interested in quick profits go for big yields, bottle early, and both fine and filter in order to save time. A badly made Burgundy can be disgusting, particularly when a certain quinone forms in the wine which, with age, gives it a nose that has been variously described as "almost decaying" or reminiscent of "dead mouse" and even "faeces".

In the 1980s, the consulting oenologist Guy Accad set the cat among the pigeons by recommending up to 10 days of cold maceration before fermentation, to give the wine a darker robe; he also urged the use of old-fashioned organic fertilisers. Over a dozen growers use his services and put him in the same league as such legendary Burgundy wine-makers as Henri Jayer and André Porcheret; others call him "a sorcerer", which is not a compliment in Burgundy country. But there is a growing awareness among the more intelligent growers and négociants (such as Leroy and Leflaive) that too many insecticides, fungicides and modern fertilisers damage not only the balance of the soil but the actual taste of the wine.

The reliability of Burgundy *négociants*, most of whom both own vineyards and buy in wine, is a vexed question. Historically, partly as a result of the Flemish connection, they have always been skilled exporters. Exports went up by 50 percent in the 1980s, and today nearly half of all Burgundy finds its way abroad.

This has not always worked in favour of quality: some *négociants* tend to produce heavier wines that go down better on export markets. Where the handful of good *négociants* (Leroy, Leflaive, Jadot, Faiveley and Roux, for example) score over the growers is that because they are not so vulnerable to climatic accidents, they can guarantee supply of a given wine. The variation in wine-making methods from one Burgundy grower or *négociant* to another is far greater than in, say, Bordeaux. The only respect in

which the great Côte d'Or *appellations* are more straightforward than their Bordeaux counterparts is in the vine varieties used: Pinot Noir (a notoriously difficult grape to grow and vinify) for red wine and Chardonnay for white. The differences with Bordeaux do not end there. Visiting a top Bordeaux château is often a much more formal affair and it is not always possible to taste the wine you may wish to buy.

Burgundian *vignerons*, whatever their wealth – and it may be considerable – prefer casual dress or even overalls; they are fully prepared to let you sample their wares (in a few cases asking for a nominal payment), sometimes opening a bottle of vintage wine

for you which they do not bother to decant. When the tasting is over, they may then inform you that they have no wine to sell.

Stendhal's description, in 1837, of the Burgundians as being "small, wiry and ruddy-faced" still holds today. They often live to a ripe old age (this may have something to do with the excellence of their everyday drinking wine). They are loud, bluff and fiercely individualistic people, who in their transactions still use pre-Revolutionary land measures, the *ouvrée* (512 sq. yards/428 sq. metres) and *journal* (8 *ouvrées*). They are not very good at pulling together, and it was not until the mid-1980s that they got round to forming the Bureau Interprofessionnel des Vins de Bourgogne, a trade association covering the whole of Burgundy with the exclusion of Beaujolais.

The Burgundians are also very chauvinistic about their wine. For them, and many would agree, there can be no better wine than a *grand cru* Burgundy. They will have to keep on their toes, though: at the 1991 Olympiades du Vin, a blind tasting organised by the wine fair Vinexpo, it was no surprise when the Chardonnay category was won by a 1986 Montrachet from Domaine Ramonet; but sharing second place with another well-known Burgundy came a 1988 Coldstream Hills from Rising and Shantell Vineyards, Yarra Valley, Australia.

For the time being, though, the Burgundians see claret as their greatest rival. Their motto might almost be *"Bordeaux, connais pas!"* Or they may say, dismissively, "I think Bordeaux is often prescribed for the sick… Our wines are for the healthy."

Their dismissive attitude is heartily reciprocated. The Bordeaux-born novelist Philippe Sollers wrote in 1986: "Burgundy is not wine, but a beverage to make sauces with. When you drink Burgundy you have the awful feeling you're drinking something that has bled; what's more, you can taste the appalling heaviness of the soil. In my view, then, anyone who likes Burgundy (or Beaujolais for that matter) is – not to put too fine a point on it – a nerd."

Describing the glorious sensations produced by a really big Burgundy is notoriously difficult. Wine writers resort to a huge variety of associations; these range from grilled and marinated meat, Arab mare, toast, tobacco, cinnamon, clove, lavender honey, dead nettle, mignonette and hawthorn blossom to the more familiar winespeak terrain of vanilla, mango, almonds, cherry (wild, raw or cooked), plum, raspberry, blackcurrant and so on.

Hyperbole is a distinct temptation; Chambertin, for example, has been memorably described as "the good lord himself sliding down your gullet in a pair of velvet trousers". And Roald Dahl once remarked that drinking Romanée-Conti was like having an orgasm in one's mouth and nose at the same time.

Right, The wine harvest.

"We went as often as we could afford it to all the restaurants in town, and along the Côte d'Or and even up to Morvan, to the Lac de Settons, the Avallon… and down past Bresse. We ate terrines of pâté ten years old under their tight crusts of mildewed fat. We tied napkins under our chins and splashed in great odorous bowls of *écrivisses à la nage*. We addled our palates with snipes hung so long they fell from their hooks, to be roasted then on cushions of toast softened with the pâté of their rotted innards and fine brandy. In village kitchens we ate hot leek soup with white wine and snippets of salt pork in it."

– M.F.K. Fisher, *Long Ago in France.
The Years in Dijon.*

Burgundy's near-religious devotion to food has not diminished since the legendary food writer M.F.K. Fisher's pilgrimages in the region in the 1930s. Open the Michelin guide at the restaurant map of France, and you will find that Burgundy has a concentration of one-, two- and three-star establishments unparalleled elsewhere in France, except for the Paris area. They cluster like metal filings, as if magically attracted there by some invisible gastronomic magnet. The restaurant map in the Gault-Millau food guide shows a similar pattern.

The excellence of Burgundian restaurants is nothing new. Towns and cities like Sens, Auxerre, Avallon, Saulieu and Dijon have always been staging posts on the main route south from Paris to Lyon and Geneva. Competition for travellers' custom on such a well-frequented route was inherently likely to spawn inns of repute. When travel by motor car became popular during the inter-war years, people like Jean Parizot of the Buffet de la Gare in Dijon and Alexandre Dumaine of La Côte d'Or in Saulieu became nationally famous and triggered off a self-perpetuating tradition of gastronomic excellence: once a restaurant gains a high reputation under one chef, there is often extra motivation for the next to do equally well.

The Burgundians themselves, of course, will tell you that the high quality of their region's cuisine is the natural result of their innate gourmandise. They will point to ancient culinary inscriptions in the Dijon archaeological museum and talk of a mysterious conjunction of the invading Burgundian tribes and the Gallo-Romans in the 5th century which produced a unique gift for gastronomy.

That is as may be – other regions of France would probably dispute the right of Burgundian cuisine to a special place at the

top of the tree. The fact remains that the dukes of Burgundy gave considerable priority to matters culinary. This is evident from the size of their kitchens, as Curnonsky reminded us: "Whereas other sovereigns built a hearth in a kitchen, the dukes of Burgundy designed a kitchen in a hearth; in other words, the four walls of the chamber were simply an enormous machine for cooking, spit-roasting, boiling, grilling, casseroling and frying. Bustling squads of scullions worked away in the middle of the vast room, hemmed in by revolving spits, seething cauldrons, sizzling pans, puffing casseroles and bubbling soups."

Preceding pages: Marc Meneau's restaurant, Vézelay. **Left**, the ingredients for *matelote d'anguilles*. **Above**, tomato and mustard tart.

It was Philippe le Bon who is thought to have been responsible for the first written "menu", when, for a banquet he held in 1457, he displayed an "*escriteau*" (placard) listing the dishes to be served. The Bishop Princes of Sens certainly enjoyed their food and liked to eat in comfort: they made indentations in their dining tables to accommodate their bellies. The tradition of good food has been kept alive by the numerous gastronomic clubs that flourish today in the region, and by Dijon's important international food fair. Dijon's two main culinary specialities, *pain d'épices* and mustard, have long historical roots. *Pain d'épices* (a cake similar to gingerbread) was introduced to the area from

French Cheeses (the definitive work on the subject) Patrick Rance tells us that the creamy Chaource and the marvellously rich-smelling Époisses, which is regularly washed with *marc* or white wine, were probably first made in the Abbaye de Pontigny and Abbaye de Fontenay.

The making of proper unpasteurised Époisses almost died out recently, but has started up again. Cîteaux, a delicate Reblochon-like cheese made in the Abbaye de Cîteaux, is in such short supply that it is available only from the monastery itself and in local restaurants. Abbaye de la Pierre-Qui-Vire produces a similar, more recently devised cheese, La Pierre-Qui-Vire.

Flanders during the reign of the dukes of Burgundy. Mustard, brought to Gaul by the Romans, was particularly appreciated by Philippe le Bel, who would give away barrels of the condiment to guests, so they could make it known elsewhere. This no doubt helped to create Dijon's reputation as a mustard producer. Dijon mustard is made from mustard powder and verjuice (the juice of unripe grapes) or white wine.

Several of the cheeses of Burgundy also have a long history: they have been made in monasteries since medieval times by monks whose diet was restricted to fruit, vegetables and dairy products. In his highly readable

When Rance asked one of the monks there if they washed their cheeses in *marc*, he replied: "No, we prefer to drink that separately." Burgundy also produces several goat cheeses of various shapes and sizes, one of which, Bouton de Culotte ("trouser button"), is little more than a mouthful. Cheese (Gruyère) goes into a Burgundian choux-pastry speciality called *gougère*, whose delicate, unassertive flavour makes it a wonderful accompaniment to wine.

Burgundian cuisine, like all cuisines to a greater or lesser extent, was shaped by the availability of certain ingredients. It is the wide variety and the excellence of those ingredients, combined with a frequent use of red wine, that made Burgundian cuisine what it is today.

Although vegetable dishes are often imaginative (cardoons with bone marrow, for example, or kidney beans in red wine), the predominant ingredients are meat and fish. Wild produce is especially prized, and there are numerous recipes calling for freshwater fish, crayfish, frogs, snails, pigeon, quail, thrushes, boar and venison, as well as wild mushrooms (morels, cèpes, chanterelles and fairy-ring mushrooms).

Domestic animals have long been carefully bred for their culinary qualities. The off-white Charolais cattle that are a familiar

that out of gratitude to the Marquis de Treffort the council voted that he should be made a gift of two dozen fatted poultry." When Henri IV conquered Bresse in 1600, he remarked on the delicacy of the chicken he had tasted.

Two centuries later Brillat-Savarin, never at a loss for a pat apophthegm, gave his verdict: "Queen of poultry, poultry of kings." By the 1920s its fame had spread throughout France and it began to command higher prices. Fraudulent Bresse chickens appeared on the market, so in 1936 a special *appellation contrôlée* was created (the only one for a meat product in France).

Bresse chickens are free-range white

sight in the fields of Burgundy produce renowned beef. Elsewhere in France they are often crossed with other breeds to enhance the latter's culinary qualities.

Poultry from Bourg-en-Bresse has long been highly esteemed. Four centuries ago it was already a prestigious enough product to be thought worthy of being offered as an official gift. According to the Bourg-en-Bresse archives for 12 November 1591, the people of the town were "so joyous at the departure of the Romans [the Savoyards]

Left, variety of onions and shallots. **Above**, Dijon specialities: mustard and cassis.

Beny poultry reared in a strictly defined area and fed on a diet of maize and whey only. They have an aluminium ring on one foot, and a stamp on the base of the neck. Their flesh is indeed remarkably flavoured (this is especially true of Bresse capons, France's most expensive poultry product). But care has to be taken, before cooking a Bresse chicken, to remove the wads of yellow fat from its stomach cavity and to prick the fatty areas of skin. The nickname of the people of Bourg-en-Bresse, *ventres jaunes* (yellow bellies), may derive from the yellowish tinge of their poultry.

The charcuterie of the Morvan, and in

SNAIL-HUNTING

The French name for the edible snail (*Helix pomatia*) is *escargot de Bourgogne*. It is so named because it was once particularly common in the vineyards of Burgundy. Nowadays the use of weedkillers has largely driven snails out of the vineyards, and three-quarters of all edible snails consumed in France are imported from Eastern Europe. In the 19th century, however, there were still battalions of snails in Burgundy, if local writer Henri Vincenot is to be believed. He claims that engineers building the Paris-Lyon railway line toyed with the idea of sending trains up and over the ridge west of Dijon separating the

Rhône and Seine river basins. When they worked out how steep the incline would be, requiring trains to climb 650 ft (200 metres) in only 1¼ miles (2 km), they feared that the thousands of snails which were bound to be squashed would make the rails so slippery that locomotives would slither to a halt. So they decided to drive a tunnel through the ridge instead.

The *escargot de Bourgogne* is a pretty good traction engine itself. Scientific tests have shown that a single individual can carry a weight of up to 9 oz (250 gm) on top of its shell. When it comes to dragging rather than carrying, the creature is capable of shifting a weight of 9 lb (4 kg). The snails' other great forte is munching and they are

as happy munching hemlock as cabbage leaves, which means they may be poisonous unless they are starved ("purged") for a week or two before being eaten.

Once in the kitchen, the poor creatures are covered with salt, to make them give up their slime, and then washed. They are now ready for cooking, usually for an hour or two in a *court-bouillon* before being finished off in any number of ways. Usually they are put back into their shells with lashings of garlic butter and heated in the oven. This preparation, which is called *escargots à la bourguignonne*, is extremely popular. The first recorded *escargots à la bourguignonne* recipe dates from 1825 and calls for *fines herbes*, which might at that time have included a little garlic, among other things. The delicate flavour of snails is brought out in several interesting recipes from other French regions. Ingredients can include: parsley and aniseed; sausage meat, onion, tomato and slivered almonds; raw ham, anchovy, spinach and walnuts; onion, tomato, orange peel, savory, fennel and saffron.

Burgundy has given *Helix pomatia* its official French name. But the snail goes by an impressive number of local names elsewhere in France: *carnar* (Lorraine), *egorgo* or *carcalou* (Auvergne), *bavou* or *luma* (Poitou), *ekerbo* (Normandy), *escarabotte* (Limousin), *cagaraulau* (Languedoc), *cagouille* (Charente), *cantereu* (Comté de Nice), *tapada* or *carago* (Provence) and *carsaulada* (Roussillon). Even Burgundy itself has a local name: *canigo*.

Although the French are very much identified with the eating of snails, this has not always been the case. The first known French recipe for snails is given in an anthology known as *Le Ménagier de Paris* (*c.* 1390), which says that "*escargolz*" are "for rich people". But Philip Hyman, who has researched snail recipes exhaustively, suggests that, at Parisian tables at least, the mollusc suffered a virtual eclipse for two centuries.

Several other peoples have eaten snails at various times – the Romans (who were the first to farm them), the Italians and even the British (18th-century Newcastle glass-makers and now day-trippers to Calais). The Swiss, however, are not noted for their fondness for the mollusc, perhaps out of embarrassment that their national characteristic is perceived by the mercurial French to be slowness. Hence the joke about the Frenchman who goes snail-hunting with a Swiss friend, who catches only one snail. "Didn't you find any others?" asks the Frenchman. "Yes. One. But it got away." ∎

particular its lightly smoked raw ham, is highly prized. Farther south, in the Chagny area, a succulent and very thick sausage called *judru* is made. Pork marinated in *marc* and cut up into chunks, rather than minced, goes into the sausage, which is matured for six months. Traditionally, the meat for *judru* comes from pigs that are sent out into the woods round Chagny to feed on acorns and the occasional viper, which, it is alleged, lends their flesh a special flavour.

Three Burgundian pork-based specialities only rarely encountered on restaurant menus are *rigodon*, *ferchusse* and *gruotte*. *Rigodon*, from southern Burgundy, a curious dish of salt pork or ham baked in a mixture of milk,

aspic mixed with liberal quantities of garlic and parsley. When cut, it presents an attractively appetising mosaic of red-pink ham and dark-green parsley. Some modern chefs inexplicably prefer to mash the ingredients together, thus robbing the dish of its visual effect. *Jambon persillé* is often oversalted by charcutiers and restaurant chefs. It is easily made at home, however, where that particular pitfall can be avoided.

Because of Dijon's reputation as the mustard capital of France, any dish using the epithet *dijonnais* implies use of the condiment. One of the most successful marriages of the cooked mustard taste (which is appreciably more aromatic and less pungent than

eggs and a little flour, is reminiscent of the medieval *lait lardé*; in times when bread was baked at home it would be put in the oven after the loaves had been taken out.

Ferchusse is also linked to a specific event in the calendar of the domestic economy, the killing of the pig. It is a stew consisting of the pig's heart, liver and lights. *Gruotte* is similar, but made from wild boar.

The best-known pork-based dish from Burgundy is *jambon persillé*. It consists of roughly-cut pieces of cooked ham pressed down into a bowl and held together with

Above, Burgundy bistrot meal.

its raw flavour) is with kidneys, in *rognons à la dijonnaise*.

Perhaps the most distinctive characteristic of Burgundian cuisine is its frequent use of red wine. The classic explanation, proposed by Burgundians and non-Burgundians alike, is that this is only natural, given that the region is famous for its wines. Yet the cuisine of other major wine-producing areas, such as the Bordelais, is not similarly vinous in character. It is possibly true that red Burgundy is more suited to the stewpot than the more astringent Bordeaux; but, equally, trying to come up with a neat explanation is probably an impossible task.

However that may be, the list of red-wine-based recipes is impressive. They range from simple dishes such as *trempus* (pieces of toast dipped in sweetened red wine) and the already mentioned kidney beans to the famous and often traduced *coq au vin*. All the recipe books tell you to use the same wine in that dish as you intend to drink at table. The price of really good Burgundy being what it is nowadays, this poses something of a problem, and there is no harm in using an excellent *bourgogne ordinaire* in the dish and putting something much bigger and pricier in your wine glass.

The essential ingredient of *coq au vin* is not so much the wine as the bird, which

treated in much the same way as the cock in *coq au vin*. In *saupiquet*, an ancient dish from the Morvan (a recipe for it appears in a 16th-century cookbook by Jean Reynier), Morvan raw ham is lightly cooked and served in a sauce of vinegar, shallots and juniper berries. The Burgundians have a fondness for fish-meat combinations, which produces such interesting dishes as *poularde aux écrevisses* and *poulet en matelote,* in which the chicken is cooked with eel in a red-wine sauce.

The words *en meurette* indicate a red-wine sauce. The most common such dish is *oeufs en meurette,* in which the sauce, slightly thickened with *beurre manié*, accompanies

should be – and this is where many restaurants fall down – neither too young nor too old. When properly made, the dish (which also contains pickling onions, lightly smoked bacon, mushrooms, garlic, *marc* and *bouquet garni*) should have a pronounced but not over-gamey taste. Many chefs insist that it should be eaten only after being reheated the day after it is made. Alexandre Dumaine always marinated the bird for at least 12 hours before cooking it; his personal touch was to add a tablespoonful of uncooked wine to the sauce at the very end.

Another celebrated dish is *boeuf bourguignon*, in which stewing beef is

poached eggs, pieces of bacon and mushrooms. It is usually served with deep-fried croûtons, whose crispness contrasts well with the rich and velvety sauce. Brains and freshwater fish, particularly eel or carp, also thrive *en meurette*.

Pauchouse (or *pochouse*), Burgundy's most famous freshwater-fish dish, uses white, not red, wine. Just as the paternity of the cassoulet is fought over by Toulouse, Castelnaudary and Carcassonne, so *pauchouse* exists in two slightly differing forms, one from Verdun-sur-le-Doubs, and the other from nearby Seurre. Although the two recipes differ little, both villages are adamant that theirs is the "genuine" version.

As often happens in France, their location in different departments (Saône-et-Loire and Côte d'Or respectively) has exacerbated their rivalry down the years. In Verdun-sur-le-Doubs, where there is an active Confrérie de la Pauchouse, the dish is made with eel, burbot, pike, perch, onion, shallot, garlic, *beurre manié* and Bourgogne Aligoté. The amount of garlic used varies from one clove to a whole head. The Seurre version calls for cream to be added to the sauce at the last moment.

Modern chefs generally prefer to thicken their sauces in a lighter way than with *beurre manié*. Michel Lorain of La Côte Saint-

ingredients that customers at pricey restaurants expect (foie gras, lobster, truffles and caviare), they have on the whole remained remarkably faithful to the spirit of Burgundian cuisine. In particular, they have explored new possibilities of red-wine sauces and fish-meat combinations: *feuilleté de moelle et girolles au vin rouge* (Jean-Pierre Billoux at Digoin), *dorade au vin rouge à la fondue d'échalote* (Loiseau), *carpe au vin rouge aux lanières de queue de boeuf* (Jean-Pierre Gillot at Moulin de Martorey in Chalon-sur-Saône), *gratin de pommes de terre au vin rouge* (Lorain).

But what distinguishes those chefs, like their colleagues Marc Meneau at Vézelay,

Jacques, for example, emulsifies the sauce of his *pauchouse* with cream and egg yolks. Whereas Parizot of the Buffet de la Gare in Dijon used to spend two hours over his *oeufs en meurette* imperceptibly thickening its flour-based sauce, Bernard Loiseau of La Côte d'Or lends it consistency by beating in a fine purée of cooked carrots and butter.

But although there has recently been a detectable trend among the new generation of top Burgundy chefs towards a systematic, and ultimately anonymous, use of the kind of

Jean-Pierre Silva at Le Vieux Moulin in Bouilland, Jacques Lameloise in Chagny and Georges Blanc in Vonnas, is their constant quest for perfection at both the invention and the execution stages.

In that, they are worthy successors to that greatest perfectionist of them all, Alexandre Dumaine. Towards the end of his life he was very ill and suffered fits of delirium. In his moments of lucidity he would talk obsessively of nothing but cooking. According to his wife, he said: "I think I now know how to make a good *coq au vin*." "But you've been making it for 30 years," his wife said. "I was just practising!" Dumaine replied.

Left, Colette Girand making chèvre cheese near Saulieu. Above, the finished product.

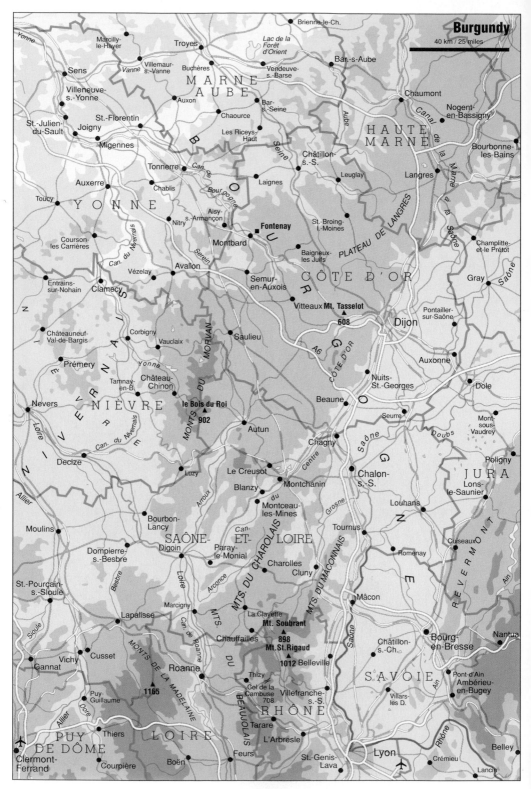

Burgundy offers a rich and diverse landscape to the traveller. The following pages journey from the Yonne, with its great rivers and wide cereal plains, and Chablis, offering the first taste of Burgundy wine, then head south into the heartland, the religious mystique of Vézelay and the great abbey of Fontenay. Then we go west to the Nièvre and the black granite heart of the Celtic Morvan,with, further south, the ancient Roman remains at Autun, echoed by its magnificent Romanesque cathedral.

Burgundy's capital, Dijon, follows with its great museums, its glittering tiled roofs and fine restaurants, a prelude to the celebrated red earth of the Côte d'Or and some of the finest wines on earth. The trail continues through the wine country of Chalonnais to southern Burgundy and its abundance of Romanesque churches, the earth-hugging wooden houses of the Bresse and the rich pastureland of the Charolais. Finally we encounter the south, heralded by the hilly contours and terracotta roofs of Mâcon and Beaujolais. Traditional Burgundy, which at one time extended over vast swathes of Europe, spills over today's boundaries and we have been equally profligate in our explorations.

Within these generous limits there are treasures to be found. Wine, of course: magic names like Gevrey-Chambertin, Romanée-Conti, Clos de Vougeot. And food, undoubtedly: *escargots*, mustard, fine Charolais beef, *appellation contrôlée* Bresse chickens and pungent Époisse cheese.

Cultural riches abound. One of Burgundy's great gifts to the world is its Romanesque architecture and within its boundaries are some of the finest examples in Europe – from the still thriving shrines of Vézelay and Paray-le-Monial and the great monastic foundations of Fontenay and Pontigny, to the sad emptiness of Cluny and literally hundreds of stunningly simple small chapels. The architectural tradition continues with the extraordinarily preserved Hôtel-Dieu in Beaune, the great Gothic cathedral of Sens, the flamboyant Gothic splendour of Brou, and many sumptuous Renaissance châteaux.

Whether your interests are cerebral, sensual or *sportif*, architectural investigation, wine tours, or rock-climbing, Burgundy supplies a feast for every visitor and rewards many return journeys. For the French, Burgundy is their mythic childhood home, their lost kingdom, and even for a first-time visitor Burgundy can strike a peculiarly nostalgic chord.

Preceding pages: Hospices de Beaune; Romanesque church at Semur-en-Brionnais; choirstalls at Brou; Joubert statue, Pont Vaux.

THE YONNE

In a region of rivers, the **Yonne** reigns supreme. The French dispute whether the Yonne or the Seine flows into Paris. Convention favours the Seine but Burgundians are adamant: at the confluence in Montereau, the Yonne is the greater. This is also a pointed reminder that, but for a quirk of medieval history, France would be Burgundian.

As the closest region to Paris, the Yonne suffers rural depopulation yet remains deeply conscious of its Burgundian identity. After all, Colette settled in Paris yet was passionate about her homeland: "I belong to the country I've left behind." Chablis is an equally celebrated ambassador. Just for good measure, Auxerre regularly beats Paris at football.

Rising in the Morvan, the Yonne is known as the *enfant terrible* because of its chaotic flow. By the time it reaches Basse-Bourgogne and its historic heart at Auxerre, it has acquired stature. Burgundian borders are as fluid as the river. Sens is the official gateway to the region but Auxerre is a warmer, more informal Burgundian welcome. Historically, the towns north of Auxerre were not part of the Burgundian kingdom. If geography is any guide, the Yonne's cereal plains should belong to Champagne. If architectural frontiers apply, then Burgundy begins not in Gothic Sens but in Romanesque Pontigny. If wine is a definition of Burgundy's borders, then these should be redrawn at Chablis, Burgundy's first great white wine.

The *département* resembles a Burgundian snail, with Auxerre curled inside a variegated shell. Sens and Joigny join the river Armançon to form an outer circle, embracing Burgundy's châteaux country. On the western rim, watery Puisaye has little in common with these Renaissance glories. Closer to the Burgundian heartland, the placid

Preceding pages: fields of mustard near Chablis. **Left,** Auxerre from the river.

river Serein forms an inner circle to the east: Pontigny and Chablis are quintessential Burgundy. The lifeblood of the region is the Auxerrois wine route stretching south along the River Yonne. After Auxerre, the rivers Yonne and Cure belong to the Morvan mountains.

Gateway to Burgundy: Orchards and rich cereal plains signal the Sénonais, traditionally known as Burgundy's granary. **Sens**, situated on the right bank of the Yonne, is an ancient city at the crossroads of Burgundy, Champagne and the Île-de-France. The city's heyday was in the 12th century so the rectangular Roman grid has long since given way to an oval-shaped medieval nucleus. As a major ecclesiastical centre, Sens welcomed St Bernard, Pope Alexander III and Thomas à Becket. The Archbishop of Sens held sway over northern France, spearheading the Gothic revolution and inspiring great Gothic cathedrals from Amiens to Chartres, Canterbury to Jerusalem. Sens's pre-eminence only ceased in 1622: Paris became an archbishopric

and Sens subsequently lost the primacy.

Leafy boulevards now trace the line of the old city walls, but the **cathedral** still sits at the medieval heart. Given the tradition of Romanesque architecture in Burgundy, Sens Cathedral owes more to the simplicity of St Bernard than to the soaring verticality of High Gothic.

The result is a fusion known as Burgundian Gothic: the austerity of a Cistercian abbey allied to the grace of Gothic ribbed vaulting. If it is reminiscent of Canterbury Cathedral, that is only natural: it was William of Sens who rebuilt the airy choir. Although begun by Archevêque Sanglier, St Bernard's follower, Sens spans five centuries. Yet the cathedral's spirit survives a Renaissance belfry and flamboyant Gothic flourishes. The vivid windows are arguably the finest in Burgundy and include a glittering tribute to Thomas à Becket, a reminder of the Archbishop's happy exile in Sens.

Le Palais Synodal, adjoining the cathedral, forms part of the Archbishop's Palace, now an ambitious museum complex. The building itself is an architectural trail through Sens, with Gothic, Renaissance and classical wings built on Gallo-Roman foundations. The religious and historical collections cover prehistoric times to the present. The siting of exhibits in former dungeons, kitchens and chapels makes an atmospheric whole. The highlights are the Roman mosaics and Le Trésor. Set in a converted chapel, the treasury is the richest collection in France. Byzantine reliquaries vie with Flemish tapestries, altar cloths and ancient silks used to wrap relics.

The cathedral quarter enjoys a market bustle on Mondays and Fridays. Before leaving, wander along the narrow Grande Rue and admire the half-timbered houses between here and Place Victor-Hugo. For a gastronomic feast, try Hôtel du Paris or Le Clos des Jacobins, set in a former monastery. As a Burgundian initiation rite, what could be more apt than garlicky *escargots*, wine-drenched *oeufs en meurette* or *boeuf bourguignon*?

Joigny is a compact medieval town further along the meandering Yonne. Behind the uninspiring riverside rises a golden town covered in jagged brown tiles. Joigny suffered a great fire in 1530 and was rebuilt in stone. The town is full of quiet charms, mostly lurking in tiny squares at the end of steep passageways. A leisurely climb reveals views of the 18th-century stone bridge, an ivy-covered tower, two squat medieval city gates and tumbledown ramparts. Several half-timbered houses escaped the blaze and retain their naive carvings of foliage, grapes and garlands. Joigny offers three Renaissance churches, all rebuilt after the great fire. St-Jean, once the château chapel, has a fine barrel-vaulted nave while St-Thibault presents an equestrian statue of the saint setting off on a hunting trip.

St-André, tucked into the heart of the *vignerons'* quarter, sports a doorway sculpted with vines. The vineyards of Lower Burgundy were ravaged by Phylloxera in the late 19th century and, unlike in the Côte d'Or, the growers here lacked the resources to replant.

However, a revival of the *Vignoble Auxerrois* is underway, beginning with Vin Gris in Joigny. As a gastronomic centre, Joigny boasts À La Côte St-Jacques, one of the finest restaurants in France, where chef Michel Lorrain prides himself on Burgundian dishes.

Joigny is a traditional Burgundian crossroads: from here, roads lead south to Auxerre, east to châteaux country along the river Armançon, or west to the mysterious Puisaye.

La Puisaye: Despite the fame of Colette, her region remains off the beaten track and singularly unknown. The success of the pottery industry and the cultural events at St-Fargeau have drawn French visitors but few foreigners. Nor are the natives convinced that La Puisaye has a future. On average, the Yonne has fewer than 8 inhabitants per square mile, half that in La Puisaye.

Colette herself did not excel in regional public relations. While *she* loved La Puisaye, "you'll look for it in vain, only seeing a rather sad landscape that casts a shadow over the forests, a quiet

Sens Cathedral sculpture.

COLETTE COUNTRY

Sidonie-Gabrielle Colette (1873–1954), perhaps the 20th century's best-loved French woman writer, spent a magical childhood in a grey stone house in the Rue de l'Hospice in St-Sauveur-en-Puisaye – a house with three small gardens, full of cats, dogs and children. Colette lived here until she was adult, with her adored mother "Sido" and her father, a former Army captain, and she was educated at the local school. Later she moved to Paris, and became known for her very adult and mildly shocking studies of love, jealousy and music-hall life, such as *Chéri* and *Gigi*.

But some of her best work evokes the more innocent world of her Burgundy childhood and that house, which lives on in the pages of two of her most captivating books, *La Maison de Claudine* and *Sido*: "A large solemn house, rather forbidding... that smiled only on its garden side... I shall never be able to conjure up the splendour that adorns, in my memory, the ruddy festoons of an autumn vine borne down by its own

weight and clinging despairingly to some branch of the fir-trees... Both house and garden are living still, I know; but what of that, if the magic has deserted them? If the secret is lost that opened me to a whole world – light, scents, birds, and trees in perfect harmony, the murmur of human voices now silent for ever – a world of which I have ceased to be worthy? It would happen sometimes long ago, when this house and garden harboured a family, that a book lying open on the flagstone of the terrace or on the grass, a skipping-rope twisted like a snake across the path, or perhaps a miniature garden, pebble-edged and planted with decapitated flowers, revealed both the presence of children and their varying ages... it was then, from beneath the ancient iron trellis sagging to the left under the wisteria, that my mother would make her appearance, small and plump in those days when age had not yet wasted her."

These books are above all a portrait of her mother – "the personage who, little by little, has dominated all the rest of my work". From this wise, warm-hearted and unusual woman Colette derived not only her love of animals but her feeling for nature, and her books are full of sensitive descriptions of the rural sounds and smells of her childhood: "No summer, save those of my childhood, enshrines the memory of scarlet geraniums and the glowing spikes of foxgloves. No winter is now ever pure white beneath a sky charged with slate-coloured clouds foretelling a storm of thicker snowflakes yet to come, and thereafter a thaw glittering with a thousand water-drops and bright with spear-shaped buds."

Colette's mother was steeped in country lore, and had remarkable insights into how animals could foretell changes in the climate – a cat digging in its paws tight, or a squirrel hoarding quantities of walnuts and cob-nuts, meant there was going to be a hard winter. Colette's own feeling for animals (especially cats), and her minute observation of their lives, are qualities rare in French literature: Jean Giono and Maurice Genevoix are two of the few French writers who can compare with her in this respect.

And it was a gift that came from her childhood home: "To those who live in the country and use their eyes everything becomes alike miraculous and simple." ■

The young Colette with cat.

but poor village, a watery valley." Colette's description of her birthplace, **St-Sauveur-en-Puisaye**, is accurate yet tinged with the same quiet charm that pervades the region. At the age of 12 she called herself *la reine de la terre* and later infused her childhood with a sensual nostalgia. Her home remains in Rue Colette, as described in *La Maison de Claudine*. A Colette museum is being created in the village château so expect pottery cats galore.

Just outside St-Sauveur, on the road to St-Fargeau, is the **Poterie de la Bâtisse**, a pottery manufacturer that has been in business since the 18th century. La Puisaye is justly famous for its simple brown stoneware, called *grès*, and for its elegant, highly-crafted blue faïence. Just south of St-Sauveur is the **Château de Ratilly**, a chance to glance at a weathered Burgundian château while selecting home-made ceramics. However, the pottery capital is **St-Amand-en-Puisaye**, a quaint village that lives off its ochre-rich clay. Many of the potters here are 10th-generation.

St-Fargeau, the most magnificent château in the region, is a reminder that La Puisaye has always had more than its fair share of feudal landowners. Anne-Marie-Louise de Montpensier, Louis XIV's cousin, was exiled here in 1652. She spent her time profitably, recasting a feudal hunting lodge as a classical château. The highlight of the visit is the endless eaves. The summer *son et lumière* performances are as well-attended as those in the Loire Valley châteaux.

La Puisaye is a landscape unlike any other in Burgundy: houses made of brick and timber; orchards and meadows bounded by neat hedges; tunnels of greenery; copses of oak and beech; pools and marshes. It makes for a secretive race of people. As well as being home to potters and woodcutters, La Puisaye has sheltered exiles and outsiders, from Jansenist priests to *maquisards*. It is a place of legends: tales of ghostly *dames blanches* and werewolves have not been diluted by an influx of newcomers.

Ratilly Château.

Villiers-St-Benoît has a appealing rural museum representing an 18th-century bourgeois home. In the same village is a Gothic church with a dramatic 15th-century mural, the *Dit des Trois Morts et Trois Vifs*, showing three nobles who encounter three ghoulish spectres while out hunting. **La Ferté-Loupière**, east of Charny, boasts a similar church mural, this time accompanied by a rare *danse macabre*, a cortège of kings and babies, nobles and cardinals, all escorted to eternity by grim skeletons.

The Vanity of Human Wishes need not dissuade one from trying La Puisaye specialities, such as honey and buttercup-yellow goat's cheeses. If leaving the region near Briare in the northwest, consider dining in Auberge des Sept Écluses, in **Rogny-les-Sept-Écluses**. There are scenic views of the Canal de Briare's series of seven locks, designed to cope with the falls in water levels on a canal linking the Seine and Loire. This amazing ladder of locks pre-dates Isambard Brunel by 200 years.

Auxerre, unlike much of the Yonne, looks towards Dijon not Paris for its identity. In that sense, it is truly Burgundian, the cultural capital of Basse Bourgogne. The city is pronounced "*Ausserre*" in soft Burgundian tones, a softness in keeping with the view from the Pont Paul-Bert: spires and red-tiled roofs mirrored in the limpid river. As a Gallo-Roman town, Auxerre retains some of its ancient walls. Under St Germain, a 4th-century bishop, Auxerre's spiritual influence radiated throughout Christendom.

Materially, the city owed its wealth to an active port and its prominence on the wine route. After the struggle between Burgundians and Armagnacs, Auxerre joined the French crown in 1477. Peace brought prosperity and renewed church-building. Economic decline was gradual but, in the 19th century, the river lost out to the railways and Auxerre found itself off the main Paris-Lyon trade axis. Auxerre is still an economic backwater, with little industry but a pleasant lifestyle.

La Ferté-Loupière.

Recently, however, the well-restored town centre has been pedestrianised, pleasure cruisers have revived the river and the AXA team has brought football fame to the region.

On Rue Joubert is a shabby Renaissance gateway that once signalled an abbey but now introduces the **Église St-Pierre**. The representation of Ceres and other harvest symbols is a reminder that this was the wine-growers' parish. The *vignerons* shared the former church with the monks but, denied the use of the belltower, decided to build a grander church on the same spot. The Gothic tower and Renaissance facades are grimly imposing but the spartan interior is somewhat disappointing. Just around the corner is Église St-Pélerin, containing Auxerre's first church: the chevet and a deep well remain from the 4th-century basilica.

The streets between here and the town centre disclose the city's Roman past. Rue des Boucheries has some remains of Gallo-Roman walls, while Rue Lacurne-Ste-Pallaye is interrupted

by an ancient tower. Nearby is the lively heart of Auxerre, **Place Charles-Surugue**, built over the Roman forum. The square has a fountain, half-timbered houses and a jaunty statue of Cadet Roussel, an 18th-century eccentric. He was mocked for "having a home for swallows, a house without rafters or roof". A tiny loggia connected his house to the medieval clocktower around the corner. The **Tour de l'Horloge** remains, with its quaint 15th-century sundial showing the phases of the sun and moon and a Latin motto: "When I die, you die, but in dying, I am reborn."

Place de l'Hôtel de Ville, the other side of the tower, has an imposing classical town hall built on the site of the medieval château. The square is lined with half-timbered houses, all blending brick and beams in a fishbone design. Notice the wizened statue of Marie Noël, a local modern poet whose lyrical *Chansons* were often set to music.

Rue Philibert-Roux boasts several period mansions including, at number 3, a Renaissance facade topped by gar-

Timber-framed houses, Auxerre.

goyles. From here, take Rue Fourier to the Gothic **St-Etienne Cathedral**. Despite the decapitation of statues by the Huguenots, the facade is a delicate Gothic masterpiece. The expressive tympanum above the main doorway depicts a triumphal scene, surmounted by interlaced rose windows. The cathedral's dimensions are not as impressive as at Sens but there are compensations. The lightness of the interior is created by an architectural illusion which hides the true function of the support columns. Described as diaphanous, this design creates an impression of grace and weightlessness.

The vivid stained-glass windows, dating from the 13th century, rival those in Chartres and Bourges in their conception and symphony of colours. The high windows in the choir show Christ in majesty, echoing the theme of the frescoes in the barrel-vaulted Romanesque crypt. Denis Grivot, an authority on Burgundian churches, calls these frescoes "an ensemble of unparalleled grandeur". The Christ in majesty is surpassed by an unique fresco of a leader on horseback, attended by angels. Painted in shades of ochre in 1100, the scene has diverse interpretations, a mystery heightened by the penumbra. Once thought to represent the Apocalypse, the fresco is now taken to be the coronation of a Christ-king, a scene inspired by Roman coins.

From the gloom of the crypt, ascend the tower to enjoy a very Flemish view of steep gabled rooftops, doves wheeling above the griffons and the river. From here, Rue Cochois leads through the riverside quarter to the **Abbaye St-Germain**, a Benedictine abbey with the finest Carolingian crypts outside Poitiers. The abbey was founded in the 6th century to preserve the tomb of St Germain, the bishop who combated heresy in Britain as well as in Gaul. The initial impression is confusing: a sole Romanesque tower standing aloof from a neo-Gothic facade and an archaeological zone. Above ground, the troubled abbey church has a cool Gothic choir, 18th-century cloisters and the

Auxerre's pedestrianised *place*.

146

newly-discovered tympanum above the north transept. However, the greatest treasure is the series of vaulted underground chapels, containing the most ancient church frescoes ever found in France. Painted in oranges and ochres in 858, they depict the martyrdom of St Stephen. Although naive, the frescoes are painted with vivacity, especially the expressions of hatred and ecstasy. The deepest crypt is a tomb chamber used to conceal St Germain's tomb under mosaics. In this hallowed spot, low barrel-vaulting is supported by Gallo-Roman columns. While the Romanesque church above was pillaged, the double-storey crypts remained intact and, in times of war, sheltered local citizens.

Once back in the daylight, take Rue Cochois to the heart of the shipping quarter: Place St-Nicolas is a picturesque square with a medieval fountain. From the river footbridge is a view over the cathedral, with a glimpse of an arcaded Romanesque gallery on the former bishop's palace. Until this century, wines, grain and wood were shipped downriver. South of Auxerre, the Yonne is *l'enfant terrible du Morvan* but is navigable from Auxerre to Paris. In summer, pleasure boats run dinner cruises. Gastronomically, Auxerre is solid rather than spectacular. Le Jardin Gourmand favours such local specialities as *quenelles de truites au Chablis* and *cerises d'Auxerre*, cherry pastries soaked in kirsch. Appropriately enough for the Burgundian heartland, *escargots au chocolat* are common.

River Armançon East: The river rises in the Côte d'Or and winds its way through Burgundy's châteaux country, often entwined with the Canal de Bourgogne. The Armançon's reputation as *mauvaise rivière et bon poisson* is confirmed by the fishermen sitting on the shady banks. St-Florentin and Tonnerre form the Yonne's outer circle; both have a foothold in Champagne and a foothold in traditional Burgundy. Both towns are curious rather than picturesque, and, despite economic blight, are noted gastronomic halts.

St-Florentin, equidistant from Joigny and Auxerre, was a Roman fort, chosen for its hilly site. It has a remarkable church and fine views over the Armançon valley. The church, perched on the hill, is a fusion of late Gothic and early Renaissance. Apart from the rich statuary, the highlights are the windows from the golden age of Troyan glass-making at the turn of the 16th century.

From here, the scenic Promenade du Prieuré leads up to a grassy square and the remains of a Romanesque abbey and medieval watchtower. Below lie secret passages linking the fortified abbey to the church. From the square are tranquil views over the river, rooftops and flying buttresses encircled by doves. Before leaving, sample St-Florentin and Soumaintrain, the town's reputed cheeses, at La Grande Chaumière.

Tonnerre, a dark stone town, is not immediately appealing but has two unique sights. In the centre of town is the **Ancien Hôpital**, a charitable foundation created by Marguerite de Bourgogne, sister-in-law of St Louis. As Charles d'Anjou's wife, she led a life of luxury in the Loire Valley châteaux yet

Auxerre
240 m / 0,15 miles

was also privy to scenes of Sicilian massacres. A widow at the age of 36, Marguerite, Comtesse de Tonnerre, dedicated her life to improving the lot of her subjects. In return, she was buried in the hospital chapel, and a daily mass was said for her soul until the Revolution. Built in 1293, the hospital is 150 years older than the Hospices de Beaune but lost its glittering tiled roof in the Revolution. The gigantic roof dwarfs the medieval stone building below. Made of local oak and Spanish chestnut, the barrel-vaulted ceiling is exactly as it was in Marguerite's day. Her private apartments were reached by a galleried passageway. According to her biographer, she was not above "touching wounds and washing ulcers". However, she had more faith in her cool, spacious barn than in medieval quackery.

For 350 years this hospital healed patients in these alcoves, often stacked six to a pallet. From 1650 the building was used as a church, hence the tombs inside. On one patch of flagging is a

gnomum, an 18th-century sundial designed by an astronomically-minded monk: a hole pierced in the roof lets light through at midday. Before leaving, look at the Mise au Tombeau, a poignant 15th-century *entombement* and masterpiece of Burgundian sculpture. It was commissioned by a rich local merchant and the figure of Nicodemus is not unlike a fat Burgundian *marchand*. The life-sized sculpture was copied from a Mystery play, explaining the realism of the figures and the dramatic intensity of the scene.

Tulip gardens lead to the Église St-Pierre, a Gothic and Renaissance church currently under restoration. On the other side of the hill is Tonnerre's most mysterious sight, the **Fosse Dionne**. An 18th-century *bassin* contains a bubbling blue-green spring, once used as a wash-house. One can see a sharp shelf which disappears into hidden caverns below. Since the 19th century, divers have explored these rocky galleries but deep water, narrow tunnels, strong currents and poor visibility mean that the depths remain unplumbed. Legend has it that a terrifying *serpent basilic* lives at the bottom. With its moss-covered roof and air of abandonment, this secret spring typifies the quaint charm of Tonnerre.

Many shops have been boarded-up since the 1950s, casting gloom on the town. Given Tonnerre's economic depression and elderly population, the locals could do with another Marguerite. Henri Nallet may be that saviour. Since 1975, Tonnerre has ceased to be a wine-free zone and both white and red grapes have been replanted; the revival of the vineyards has been led by Henri Nallet, the popular local mayor and unpopular Minister of Finance.

Châteaux country: The Canal de Bourgogne and the River Armançon flow past two of the most sumptuous Renaissance châteaux in Burgundy. The moated **Château de Tanlay** lies slightly east of Tonnerre. It was built in 1553 by Louise de Monmorency, mother of Gaspard de Coligny, the Protestant leader murdered in 1572. As a bastion of Protestantism, Tanlay still **St-Florentin.**

receives the Dutch royal family, descendants of the de Coligny line. In 1704 Tanlay belonged to the financier Jean Thévenin, and has been in the same family ever since, currently lived in by another *banquier*, the Comte de la Chauvinière.

A grand gatehouse and bridge guarded by obelisks look across to an Italianate *cour d'honneur*. This was added by Michel Particelli, Cardinal Mazarin's chancellor, as were the classical grounds. Tanlay is a mixture of Renaissance splendour and classical bombast. *Le vestibule des Césars* parades busts of Roman emperors while the upstairs gallery has a playful *trompe-l'oeil* ceiling inspired by Poussin. Paintings of pastoral scenes are a feature of Tanlay, as are the sculpted Renaissance fireplaces in the bedrooms. *La chambre d'honneur* has a yellow damask canopied bed, still used on visits by the Dutch royal family to their ancestral home. According to the imaginative guide, the shortness of the beds is explained by 18th-century hypo-chondria: fear of suffocation prompted people to sleep sitting upright.

The quaint corner tower was where the Protestant leaders plotted during the Wars of Religion. A witty frescoed ceiling contrasts the debauched court of Catherine de Médicis with the noble Protestants. In this Olympian allegory, Catherine is an unflattering Juno, elsewhere portrayed as a double-faced sphinx. Diane de Poitiers is a statuesque Venus while naturally the Admiral de Coligny is Neptune. Tanlay's intimate atmosphere springs from such pictorial in-jokes, family portraits and wedding photos. Just outside the château gates is a lively bar, usually full of Pernod-drinking locals discussing the fortunes of the local football team, Auxerre. Alternatively, try Le Cheval Blanc, a rustic riverside restaurant.

Just north of Tanlay are thick woods concealing several minor châteaux in forest clearings. In an isolated spot is the boarded-up **Château de Maulnes**. This solid pentagonal hunting lodge looks more like a medieval castle. It was built

Tonnere, Fosse Dionne.

in the 16th century by the counts of Tonnerre but was soon abandoned in favour of Ancy-le-Franc. After becoming a glassworks in the 18th century, it was left to decline until a half-hearted restoration in 1965.

It was this sorry château that inspired the legend of Mélusine, the wicked fairy featured in Jean d'Arras's prose romance and A. S. Byatt's novel *Possession*. Here, the fairy temptress waylaid travellers until she fell unhappily in love and drowned herself in the castle well. Until the 19th century, children threw stones into the well, begging her not to harm them. On moonless nights she is heard to lament her fate: "*Maulnes Maulnes, tant que Maulnes sera, malheureuse serai.*" Since Maulnes may last a little longer, locals hope her spirit may soon rest in peace.

From here, a rural route winds through woodland, hunting estates and sheep farms to **Ancy-le-Franc**, a Renaissance château modelled on an Italian *palazzo*. The Duc de Clermont-Tonnerre wanted it fit for a king: Diane de Poitiers, his sister-in-law, was Henri II's mistress. In 1684 the bankrupt Tonnerre family lost the château to the Comte de Louvois, one of Louis XIV's ministers, but later regained it and kept it until the extinction of the line in 1981. Ironically, the Tonnerre's motto was *Si omnes ego non* (others may abandon you but not I). Ancy is currently owned by an enterprising civil servant who would do well to avoid the Louvois' motto: *Mieux vaut être rompu que plié* (better broken than bent).

This Renaissance château heralds classicism with its restrained, symmetrical forms, its four wings anchored by corner towers. The designs are attributed to Sebastianno Serlio, an Italian architect at the French court. Yet while the cool facade is a triumph of Corinthian columns, the interior is surprisingly exuberant. Ancy has the most opulent decor in Burgundy, rivalled only by the Château de Bussy-Rabutin. It was probably decorated by Primaticio, a Bolognese artist working at Fontainebleau. It is virtually a royal palace:

Tanlay Château facade.

150

French kings from Henri II to Louis XIV slept in the gilded *chambre du roi*. The Italian influence prevails in the imperial murals and panelled ceilings inspired by Pompeian frescoes at the Vatican. From the windows are views of an ornamental pool guarded by two sphinxes. The panelled *chambre des fleurs* is a riot of pansies, roses, tulips and other symbolic flowers. Outside are glimpses of a lakeside folly. Quieter tastes may prefer the green-panelled library with 10,000 ancient volumes.

But for a Burgundian treasure, there is only the chapel, arguably the most authentic Renaissance chapel in France. The life of the apostles, prophets and sibyls appear in 24 *trompe-l'oeil* panels. Above is a soft-hued biblical landscape, reminiscent of Burgundian art in Bruges. Just south of Ancy-le-Franc is **Nuits-sous-Ravières**, yet another Renaissance château. After a surfeit of châteaux, continue south to the vineyards of the Côte d'Or or return to base at Auxerre.

River Serein South: Just north of Auxerre begins the most Burgundian of journeys. The demure River Serein flows past the finest Cistercian abbey in France to the vineyards of Chablis, and leaves the region at Noyers, the Yonne's most authentic medieval town. It is a journey of superlatives: Fontenay may be Burgundy's most complete Cistercian abbey but **Pontigny** is the greatest Cistercian church. In 1114, Stephen Harding, the third abbot of Cîteaux, arrived with St Bernard and 11 monks to found the *deuxième fille de Cîteaux*.

Its location favoured independence, situated on the borders of three counties and three bishoprics. A local adage says that on the bridge at Pontigny, three bishops (of Auxerre, Langres and Sens) and three counts (of Auxerre, Champagne and Tonnerre) could all dine together on home soil. Pontigny used its independence to establish new abbeys and vineyards. As in Sens, the Canterbury connection looms large. Pontigny forged close links with three English archbishops: Thomas à Becket,

Tanlay great hall.

PIERRE LAROUSSE

With sales of just over 1 million copies a year, the Petit Larousse (83,500 entries) is one of the best-selling encyclopaedias in the world, and is to be found in almost every French home. Since it first came out in 1905 it has sold about 25 million copies. Larousse, like Mrs Beeton, is a household name. But the 20th-century version of *Petit Larousse* and its bigger brother, the five-volume *Grand Larousse*, are very different from the extraordinarily idiosyncratic 17-volume, 22,500-page *Grand Dictionnaire Universel du XIXème Siècle* (1866–76) that was largely written by that indefatigable Burgundian, Pierre-Athanase Larousse − "My brain and heart swelling with Burgundian sap," as he put it.

He was the son of a village blacksmith in Toucy in the Yonne. Born in 1817, he showed early promise at school, won a scholarship to the École Normale in Paris and became a teacher. A contemporary remembered him thus: "A short, stocky man with a tawny beard and sparkling eyes,

withdrawn and saturnine, a hard worker who was strongly suspected of harbouring subversive ideas."

By the age of 27 he already had greater ambitions: to become a 19th-century encyclopaedist like Diderot in the 18th. As an admirer of the socialist Proudhon, he wanted "to teach everyone about everything".

Larousse spent several years writing and publishing school textbooks, but still found time to assimilate prodigious amounts of data in public libraries, go to the theatre, write plays, read the literary works of his contemporaries, take notes on the behaviour of his fellow Parisians and even taste unfamiliar dishes, if not test the recipes himself (a task probably carried out by the woman he lived with for 30 years before they married). In 1864, he embarked on his *Grand Dictionnaire*, calling on thousands of contributors (including Jules Vallès, Auguste Vermorel, one of the leaders of the 1871 Paris Commune, and the young Anatole France), but wrote most of it himself. Later editions of the encyclopaedia differ from Larousse's in one major respect: the modern notion of objectivity. One of the joys of dipping into the original work is its Johnsonian idiosyncrasy.

Just as Samuel Johnson defines the word "excise" as "a hateful tax levied upon commodities", so Larousse, after discussing the etymology of a cheese tart called *talmouse* and giving a recipe for it, dismisses it as "an indigestible pastry that could appeal only to unrefined stomachs". He also launches into a lengthy discussion as to whether Cambronne actually uttered his celebrated oath at Waterloo ("*Merde!*"). In the same spirit as the universal exhibitions of the mid-19th century, Larousse firmly and sometimes naively believed in the inexorability of human progress: "Progress is eternal: it pauses, sometimes at a moment of glory, sometimes in the mire, but it never stops."

On his death in 1875, his widow and his nephew, Jules Hollier, completed the publication. Hollier went on to expand the Larousse publishing house and to build the foundations of the present-day corporation. Larousse's ideal of broadcasting the seeds of knowledge to people of all classes was maintained with the motto "*Je sème à tout vent*" (still represented by a dandelion clock on the Larousse logo). ∎

Stephen Langton and finally St Edmund. Two were exiled here and the third, St Edmund, died nearby. His tomb here still attracts a pilgrimage on 16 November.

Built between 1150 and 1212, Pontigny is Romanesque in design, Cistercian in spirit and Gothic by accident. A line of lindens leads to the sober west porch. Nothing prepares one for the blinding whiteness of the stone inside. The light bleaches out detail and directs the spirit inwards, just as the Cistercians intended. Technically, it is a transitional church. The side aisles and severe transept use Romanesque groined vaulting, as at Vézelay. The elegant choir timidly ushers in the Gothic age. The perspective of the nave is interrupted by church stalls and a baroque choir screen.

Above all, Pontigny is Cistercian. The minimal decoration, mathematical proportions, harmony of mass and line, all induce serenity, not heightened emotions. The retired Curé at Pontigny has firm views on his abbey: "Cistercian abbeys were not made for the public –

they were preaching to the converted." Statues, images, colours were all redundant. Religious passion was distilled into prayer. Stark it is, the silent quest for God reduced to the play of light pouring in through tall windows.

A walk in the churchyard allows magnificent views of Pontigny's flying buttresses. Seen from afar, the abbey looks like a great upturned boat adrift in the prairies. Others have compared it to a celestial hovercraft. Sadly, the monastic buildings are now a college so the cloisters, dormitory and abbey farms are out of bounds. It was here that philosopher and pacificist Paul Desjardins founded Décades de Pontigny, a lay monastery for leading intellectuals. For 40 years these encounters drew such diverse spirits as André Gide and Thomas Mann. T.S. Eliot used one visit to seek inspiration for *Murder in the Cathedral.*

When not at prayer, the monks fished the rivers for carp and pike, a practice not wasted on the locals today. The sandy banks of the Serein are ideal for

Pontigny, church porch.

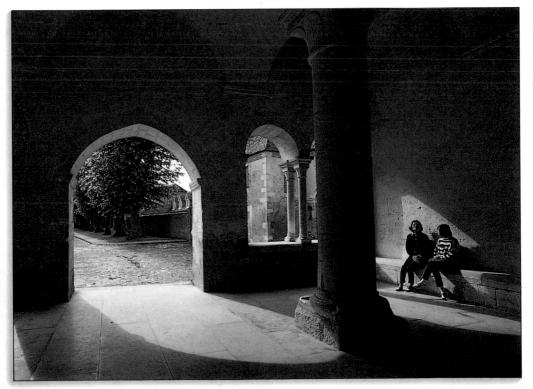

picnics. To sample the freshwater fish, try Le Moulin de Pontigny or a rustic restaurant in neighbouring **Ligny-le-Châtel**. Once there, do not fail to look at the squat Burgundian church with its Renaissance choir.

From Ligny, follow the Serein to **Chablis**, a medieval town snugly nestling in its famous vineyards. A local *vigneron* once punningly pronounced *"À Vézelay, on croit, à Chablis, on a cru"* (Vézelay has faith but Chablis has fine vintages).

Since Roman times, the town has been adept at acquiring special privileges for its vineyards. Chablis has always been rich and even the most modest house exhibits signs of wealth, whether a shadowy Romanesque pillar or a BMW poking out of a solid barn. As a result, the town is only saved from smugness by its tiny scale.

Église St-Martin was founded by monks from Tours in the 11th century. The present Gothic building dates from 1212 and echoes Sens Cathedral but the south doorway is Romanesque, adorned with dove and serpent motifs. The horse-shoes attached to the south porch were brought by pilgrims en route to Compostela: they implored St Martin to protect their mounts. In medieval times, St Martin, not St Christopher, was the patron saint of travellers. By the chevet is the turreted Obédiencerie, an impressive building once owned by the leading monks from Tours.

Clustered behind its medieval town gates, Chablis is a sweet stone town riddled with attractive alleys. Rue des Juifs contains several curious houses, adorned with Romanesque vaults or madonnas in niches. One sculpted Renaissance house is believed to be a former synagogue. Naturally, the creeper-clad wine *domaines* occupy the finest buildings.

Petit Pontigny, in Rue de Chiché, was where the Pontigny monks based their wine estate. These 12th-century stone buildings are now used for the riotous gatherings of the Piliers Chablisiens, the celebrated wine confraternity.

Chablis is the quintessential *vin de*

Grape-picking in Chablis.

luxe and, as such, restaurateurs feel emboldened to over-charge. Even in local bistrots, the mark-up is six times the *vigneron*'s retail price. If dinner is still distant, consider Petit Chablis with *gougères*, crusty cheese pastries. At the other end of the scale, a *grand cru* is a perfect *apéritif* in Hostellerie des Clos. This Romanesque Hôtel-Dieu may have lost *dieu* but has kept the hotel and stocked the cellar with 20,000 bottles of Burgundian wines.

For a simpler yet more atmospheric meal, try Vieux Moulin. Chablis is ideal with seafood, snails, white meat and *charcuterie*. L'Étoile, where Jean Cocteau stayed, produces memorable *andouillettes* and fish dishes. This tiny valley is Burgundy's most controversial wine region. Chablis is not only a microclimate but a microcosm of Burgundy's wine trade. Controversy encompasses frost-control methods, the value of oak ageing, the power of the *négociant* houses and fear of foreign competition. The paranoia of Chablis is not unfounded: its fame has long been abused around the world and its name taken in vain.

Chablis is an oddity among Burgundian wines, stranded 60 miles (100 km) northwest of the wine-growing heartland. Cistercian monks at Pontigny first planted Chardonnay on these steep slopes beside the Serein river in the 12th century. The popularity of Chablis soon spread to the royal courts on the Loire and travelled to Bruges with the Burgundian dukes. Its elegance and breeding still make it one of northern Europe's most sought-after *vins de luxe*.

Production and prices depend on the vagaries of the weather – and these are the most difficult wine-growing conditions in France. A cold spring is necessary to produce the wine's acidity but the late frosts of 1957, 1961 and 1991 had a drastic effect on the harvest. This isolated valley attracts pockets of frost as late as May. Still, methods of frost control have improved dramatically since the 1960s. Petrol-soaked torches and oil-burners fight off frost while water-sprinklers spray the vines to give

Sampling Chablis.

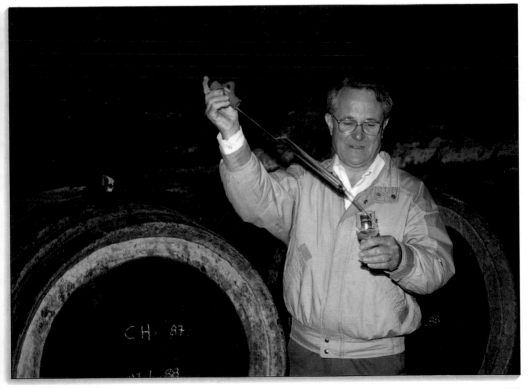

the vines a protective coating of ice.

Chablis is equally exposed to greedy growers responding to the world thirst for Chardonnay. Chablis *vignerons* fear damage to their *image de marque* as neighbouring wine associations seek to extend the Chablis *appellation*. Local growers complained bitterly that Chablis has become a generic term and are outraged that the Americans dare to usurp the Chablis name for their Napa Valley crops.

Local growers have washed their hands of the New World market and now sell mainly to northern Europe. According to *vigneronne* Nicole Adine, Britain leads the Benelux in world demand for Chablis but Italy and Greece are gaining ground. Chablis is an export wine *par excellence*: the French consume only a quarter of the crop. A case of *l'embarras du choix*, perhaps?

The fortune of Chablis is founded on the Chardonnay grape, known locally as Beaunois. The perfect Chablis is described as golden-flecked green, dry, honey-scented, aromatic, with a steely core. It falls into four distinct *appellations*: *petit* Chablis, Chablis, *premier cru* and *grand cru*, grown in a constellation of hamlets around the town. Chablis *premier cru* is produced on the slopes facing east or southeast along the River Serein. Grown in 30 *climats*, these are the most controversial wines which, depending on taste, can surpass a *grand cru* in sophistication or sink to the blandness of an inferior Chablis.

As for the Chablis *grands crus*, these are grown on the sunny slopes overlooking town. The *domaines*, known as "the magnificent seven", are: Blanchot, Bougros, Les Clos, Grenouilles, Les Preuses, Valmur and Vaudésir.

Woodlands and rape fields lead south to **Noyers**, cradled in a bend of the Serein. Noyers is the dreamiest town in northern Burgundy, caught in a medieval time-warp. Its only snag is that this is no secret: classed among *les plus beaux villages de la France*, it is a self-conscious star. The town name comes from walnuts, still common in these parts. In the 15th century the dukes of

Wood carvings, Noyers; town gate, Noyers.

156

Burgundy controlled Noyers castle, its hospices and vineyards. Noyers was a border town, dividing the Tonnerrois from the Auxerrois. The approach is charming: an ancient *lavoir* by the river, two pyramids standing sentinel, ramparts and a medieval gateway.

The streets are as atmospheric as they sound. Place du Marché-au-Blé and Place du Grenier-à-Sel have sloping half-timbered houses and delicate arcades. Petite-Étape-aux-Vins is a tiny square with sculpted facades. Église de Notre-Dame is built in Gothic flamboyant style, with a Renaissance facade. The polished interior looks cosy and well-cared for.

Around every corner are cobbled streets and houses with sculpted Renaissance motifs. Porte Ste-Vérote, a gateway at the end of town, leads out to the fields and quaint wine-growers' cottages. A ruined castle softens up visitors for the inevitable arts and crafts shops.

Proud gardener, Noyers.

"From the top of the hill we saw the stone-covered roofs of **Sacy**, a hamlet planted at the meeting of four vales…

the landscape inspired such lightheadedness that we felt we were the lords of nature." So wrote Réstif de la Bretonne of his home village in 1770. This prolific writer, Jansenist and libertine also set his erotic novels in the Burgundian countryside, and *Le Paysan Perverti*, a cynical portrayal of provincial life, has won him comparisons with Balzac. His birthplace faces the Romanesque church and its octagonal tower. The ivory-hued stone, quarried locally, is the pride of the village. Stretching along a single street are houses enlivened by homely inscriptions carved by *paysans*.

Sacy also boasts a manor house and the Ferme de la Bretonne, an elegant farmhouse on the edge of the village. It once belonged to Réstif but is now owned by another celebrity, travelwriter Jacques Lacarrière. He claims that, apart from television aerials on the barns, Sacy, like its wine, hasn't changed since Réstif's day. In fact, as the grandson of a Burgundian barrelmaker, Réstif de la Bretonne may be best remembered for introducing wine-growing to Sacy. Red and rosé wines are produced, as well as Le Sacy, a dry Sauvignon. However, since the outbreak of Phylloxera in 1905, Frisian cattle have reclaimed many of the vineyards. From Sacy, it is a short or long drive back to Auxerre, depending on the appeal of the *route des vignobles*.

The Auxerrois wine route: Until the 19th century, Auxerre was famed for its red wines but le Clos de la Chaînette is the only reminder of the celebrated Côte d'Auxerre. This *domaine*, founded by the monks from St-Germain abbey, made Alexandre Dumas's favourite wines, including one called Migraines. Curiously, the vineyard and *appellation* now belong to the Yonne psychiatric hospital. But the wines below Auxerre could not be in better health. From Vaux to Vermenton, the banks of the river Yonne abound with *dégustation* opportunities. Most of the villages are sweetly set amongst cherry orchards. Several are clustered around Romanesque churches or peer out of medieval fortifications. **Vaux**, a riverside village just south of Auxerre, used to be a wine-growing area but is now awash with fruit. The slopes are covered with apple and cherry orchards. In spring the pastel landscape is an Impressionist's palette, with lilac by the river, cherry blossom overhead, and rape fields edged with bluebells. In passing, notice an elegant manor house and the Romanesque Église St-Loup, topped by a medieval tower. Le Canal du Nivernais flows just beyond the village.

Escolives-Ste-Camille is a wine village beside the Yonne, just south of Vaux. The Romanesque church has a delicate octagonal tower and arcaded porch. Below is a two-storey crypt designed to house the relics of St Camille. The well-restored upper crypt is adorned with early Christian symbolism. The key to the church is with the Borgnats whose wine estate lies down the road. Virtually opposite the church is a typical walled Burgundian farm but the greatest site harks back to earlier civilisations. At the foot of the hill is a **Irancy**.

rich archaeological zone, with the remains of Gallo-Roman temples, Roman baths and a Merovingian cemetery. Recently, archaeologists have unearthed mosaics and a double-headed Janus, to add to the growing collection of sculptures, coins and jewellery. The Gallo-Roman portico is the finest discovery to date, sculpted with mythological scenes. Notice the bas-reliefs depicting grape harvests, a tribute to Escolives' ancient wine roots.

If grape-picking scenes prompt thoughts of wine, combine archaeology and alcohol with a visit to the local *vignerons*. Régine and Gérard Borgnat run their *domaine* from this converted medieval château. They produce reliable rosé and tangy Bourgogne Aligoté in wine cellars which are reputedly the longest in Burgundy. They are also keen amateur archaeologists and the proud possessors of a Gallo-Roman arch. Theirs is a wine marriage made in heaven: his family owned the ancient cellars and hers owned the vineyards.

In **Coulanges-la-Vineuse**, the drunken village next door, wine literally flows like water. When a fire raged here in 1676, the villagers were so short of water that they tackled the blaze with barrels of wine. The ravaged medieval church was replaced by a classical church in the 18th century. In the presbytery is a Flemish *Annunciation*, by Roger van der Weyden. The main street has several fine facades, a sculpted fountain and an old wine-press.

On the other side of the Yonne are equally famous wine villages. The most vinous is the picturesque **St-Bris-le-Vineux**. The Gothic **Église St-Prix** bursts with flying buttresses and Renaissance flourishes. The ornate church contains 16th-century stained-glass windows and a vivid fresco of the Tree of Jesse, painted in 1500. The Renaissance pulpit depicts natural scenes, from wild boar and snails to corn and wine. St-Bris is an intriguing blend of styles. Two medieval town gates are all that remain of the ramparts. In the compact centre are Renaissance *hôtels* with mullioned windows, as well as stone-

Wheat fields at harvest.

gables, dovecotes and a 17th-century staging post. The post office, once a 12th-century haunt of the Knights Templar, is adorned with a baphomet, a secret masonic symbol of a head and crescent. Even the classical château has been converted into a school and *mairie*.

Running the whole length of the village is a warren of medieval cellars. Given the array of wines and the richness of the vaulting, it is worth returning to the depths.

To disperse the alcohol, one welcome snack is *croquets*, local almond biscuits. Both here and at Irancy, time between wine-tastings can be spent browsing for junk in the *brocante* shops. Just north of St-Bris is **Chitry-le-Fort**, a hamlet with a hulking fortified church, designed for a siege, not spiritual peace. The hamlet is more riddled with holes than a Gruyère cheese.

Irancy, south of St-Bris, is set in a hollow amongst banks of cherry trees and vineyards. It is the sweetest, most traditional wine-growing village, per-

fectly captured in the watercolours of Georges Hosotte, a local artist. Overlooking a cherry orchard is the Église St-Germain, a Gothic church with delicate Renaissance buttresses and a square belfry surmounted by *griffons*. Encircling the church are typical *vignerons'* houses with their characteristic outside staircases.

In medieval times, Irancy was guarded by four gateways but this harshness has given way to Renaissance ease. The main street has a shuttered 16th-century mansion that was the birthplace of Soufflot, the neoclassical architect who has left such a heavy imprint on Paris. On neighbouring facades are opulent Renaissance details, from turrets and mullioned windows to sundials and stone inscriptions. Down below are fossil-encrusted cellars, a reminder that Irancy is home to 25 wine-growing families.

Between Irancy and **Cravant** stretch views of vineyards and valleys framed by cowslips and wild orchids, a fitting end to the wine trail.

River Yonne to the Morvan: Cravant is a crossroads, situated at the meeting of rivers Yonne and Cure. From here one can fork east, following the River Cure to Vézelay or fork west, tracing the Yonne to its wild mountain source in the Morvan. From Cravant to Clamecy, the Yonne is a fast-flowing stream cutting south through woods and valleys. The landscape is as dramatic as any in Burgundy, throwing up sheer cliffs in the face of narrow valleys. Until this century, the Yonne, like the Cure, was used to transport firewood and wine to Paris. Nowadays, the region provides a healthy break from wine-tasting. Instead, it is a backdrop for boat trips, wooded walks and rock-climbing.

In **Cravant**, the tumbledown towers and medieval gates recall a decisive battle fought in 1423. The Burgundian and English armies finally overcame the French and Scottish forces, leaving the region outside French control for years to come. Today, the fortifications are landscaped gardens but the ramparts remain by Promenade St-Jean. A watchtower guards a sturdy Gothic

Rock-climbing, Saussois.

church: three 15th century naves and stained-glass windows accommodate an airy Renaissance choir and square belfry. A walk through the narrow alleys reveals medieval houses, a stone manor and a well-preserved *lavoir*.

Mailly-le-Château, many bends south, commands a dramatic loop in the river. The château, built on a rocky escarpment, belonged to the three Mailly sisters who were all Louis XV's mistresses. Set amongst chestnut trees, the picturesque village has a cluster of medieval houses, a Gothic church and attractive views of the river and Canal du Nivernais. From here, cross the 15th-century bridge over the river and, shortly after a canal bridge, **les Rochers du Saussois** loom ahead. These sheer cliffs are often used for rock-climbing.

A little further upriver is **Châtel-Censoir**, a walled medieval village perched on a hill. On the summit is a fortified church beside a ruined château. The church is unusual in combining Romanesque and Renaissance styles without any intervening Gothic.

After a fire in 1460, the nave and doorways were rebuilt in elaborate Renaissance style by Italian craftsmen. The choir is Romanesque, with sculpted capitals representing fire-breathing mythological beasts. Under the church is an austere Merovingian crypt.

On the other bank, just before Clamecy, are yet more cliffs and a charming 16th-century church at **Surgy**. Clamecy itself is a depressing but untypical gateway to the rugged Morvan.

From Surgy, it is worth making a short detour west to **Druyes-les-Belles-Fontaines**, the region's most dramatic ruins. Perched on a bluff, this 12th-century castle once belonged to the counts of Auxerre and Nevers. Comte Philiphe de Courtenay, Emperor of Constantinople, somehow ran his empire from here in the 13th century. A formidable barbican leads to the lower courtyard, now lined by stone cottages. Once through to the roofless keep, there is little to see but the site itself is atmospheric. At the foot of the hill is **St-Romain**, a harmonious Romanesque

Barging at Mailly-le-Censoir.

church, lying close to Druyes' famed springs and grottoes. From outside, the church chevet resembles a nest of honeycomb domes. Inside, the highlights are the broken barrel-vaulted nave and the carved capitals depicting fighting dragons and devils.

River Cure to Vézelay: This route is not what it seems; the natural landscape conceals a bizarre underworld. Just south of Cravant, vines give way to wooded slopes, heralding the Morvan. The Cure is a brisk mountain stream with weirs that once helped control the Paris firewood supply. **Vermenton**, like Clamecy, is an erstwhile port reduced to green tourism. At the heart of the village is a medieval watchtower and a cluster of 16th-century houses. In the centre is the moss-covered church, with a slender Romanesque tower and a doorway framed by columns of statues. The church is in transitional Romanesque Gothic style with ribbed vaulting, a feature common to churches in the Île-de-France, as is the colonnaded tabernacle below the northwest spire.

From Vermenton to Vézelay, the Cure is a fast-flowing trout stream, often disappearing underground. Across the Yonne from Vermenton is **Reigny**, a ruined Cistercian abbey built beside the River Cure. Now converted into a private home, the scriptorium and luminous Gothic refectory remain, with elegant vaulting supported by slender columns. The dovecote and abbot's house overlook a peaceful scene of grazing Charolais cattle. Just upstream, the mystery begins.

Arcy-sur-Cure's fantastic caves are embedded in limestone cliffs. These caves were discovered in 1666 but have been inhabited periodically since prehistoric times. Buffon, the 18th-century naturalist, regularly came to sketch the animal designs. Over half a mile of galleries can be visited, spanning natural formations and rock carvings. The colours are dramatic, ranging from an emerald green lake to curtains of gold and silver rock. Other chambers contain carvings of mammoths, bison and pilgrimage symbols.

A riverside walk passes caves not yet open to the public, including ones decorated with sculptures of hyenas, bears and wolves. Adjoining galleries contain a medieval burial chamber full of sarcophagi. Just off the shady paths are opportunities for picking strawberries, mushrooms and nuts.

The neighbouring **Manoir de Chastenay** is almost as bizarre as the caves. The Renaissance manor once belonged to the Knights Templar and was a pilgrims' halt on the way to Compostela. As a result, it is adorned with symbols of competing philosophies, from Christian faith to Renaissance mythology and masonic ritual. On the sculpted facade are Santiago cockleshells, a philosopher's stone and a vanitas. The owner delights in explaining this esoteric cocktail of alchemy, numerology and the scriptures. He shows how the medieval mind used divine numbers to unlock the universe. In short, this cryptic visit is reminiscent of a film by Michel Devile or Peter Greenaway. If feeling out of your depth, remember that mystic Vézelay is only a heartbeat away.

Left, St-Germain, Auxerre. **Right**, swan at Tanlay.

THE HEARTLAND

The heartland encapsulates the essence of Burgundy. The region overlaps the Côte d'Or and the Yonne, bordering the great vineyards of the south and the watery landscape of the north. Its châteaux and wines may look like pale imitations but in other respects it rivals or surpasses its neighbours.

The region traces the history of Burgundy, from the Gallo-Roman site at Alésia to the walled medieval town of Avallon. The Forges de Buffon introduce the region's seminal role in the Industrial Revolution while cosy Semur-en-Auxois shows how Burgundy copes with post-industrial society: sleepily.

Sophistication on a small scale is the flavour of the region. Its muted charms have made it the natural home of painters, writers and priests. Flavigny-sur-Ozerain is a tiny village bursting with art galleries, seminaries and celebrity authors in hiding. Not that the region shies away from dramatic set-pieces. The heartland is home to two of the greatest Romanesque treasures in France: the Cistercian abbey of Fontenay and the basilique in Vézelay. Cluny may be a mere shell but Vézelay is the mystic heart of Burgundy.

Perched on a wooded hilltop, **Vézelay** has the allure and self-sufficiency of a Tuscan town. It also has a tradition of painters and mystics that would be equally at home in Siena.

The link is not so spurious as it seems: St Bernard, the Burgundian saint, was equally adored in Siena and his homeland. It was on Vézelay's hillside that he preached the second crusade in 1146. Richard the Lionheart and Philippe Auguste, King of France, followed in his footsteps, inaugurating the third crusade from this spot.

The presence of Mary Magdalene's supposed relics in the basilica made Vézelay a place of pilgrimage. Here, too, Thomas à Becket excommunicated the absent Henry II, King of England. A winding road climbs to the **Basilique**

Ste-Madeleine, a spiritual journey. Medieval pilgrims would have felt a symbolic lifting of the veils, from the uphill toil to the passage from darkness into light. Clustered in the shadowy penumbra of the narthex, medieval pilgrims could ponder the mysteries of the tympanum before flooding into the uplifting nave and rejoicing in the luminous choir. Then as now, the path is crowded, the pilgrims hushed and scepticism suspended. According to the friars who run La Madeleine, the church is designed to be at its most majestic at summer solstice: on 24 June, a funnel of light appears to emanate from the ancient crypt containing Mary Magdalene's relics, acknowleged as genuine by the Pope in 1058.

Vézelay has had many incarnations, first as a 9th-century nunnery founded by Girart de Roussillon at the foot of the hill. It became a monastery in 873 but a Norman attack forced the Benedictines to flee to the safety of the hilltop in 887. Their new foundation was twice destroyed by fire but the present Cluniac

Preceding pages: wheat fields; Semur-en-Auxois. Left, *en famille en bicyclette*, Vézelay. Right, Vézelay, Ste-Madeleine interior.

basilica dates from 1106. The ochre-tinged basilica is an imposing sight, its groined vaulting and high windows embodying the daring of Burgundian Romanesque builders.

In 1295 the Pope declared that Mary Magdalene's relics had never left Provence. Vézelay's credibility was destroyed and decadence set in. The church was allowed to decline and in 1834 Prosper Mérimée reported a sodden nave overgrown with shrubbery. After his advice, La Madeleine was saved from ruin by Viollet-le-Duc. For good measure, Mary Magdalene's relics were placed in Vézelay's Carolingian crypt in 1876. Curiously, Vézelay has no depictions of the saint.

To the medieval mind, the narthex was Galilee and the choir Jerusalem, a passage from witness to transcendence. The doorway from the narthex into the nave is adorned with the most accomplished **tympanum** in France. An ethereal Christ floats in swirling drapery; around him are the converted and unconverted, a fabulous universe em-bracing the bewildered apostles, peasants, hunters, giants, pygmies and pig-snouted heathens. Such animation can blind one to the individuality of the Burgundian statuary all around.

The obscurity of the narthex gives way to the joyous nave, an ochre and cream concoction seemingly liberated from earthly constraints. It, in turn, is outshone by an early Gothic choir, radiating a shell-like translucence. Tournus may feel virginal, Fontenay pure, Autun subtle and Paray-le-Monial graceful. Yet of all Burgundy's Romanesque churches, none is as unselfconscious as Vézelay, as fluent in its mastery of spirit and form.

As at Autun Cathedral, the sculpted capitals reach supreme heights but the dense symbolism can be confusing to modern minds. There are more than 100 of them, on a wide variety of subjects. The *Moulin Mystique* capital shows Moses pouring grain (Old Testament law) through a mill (Christ) while the ground flour (New Testament) is gathered by St Paul. This Bible in stone also

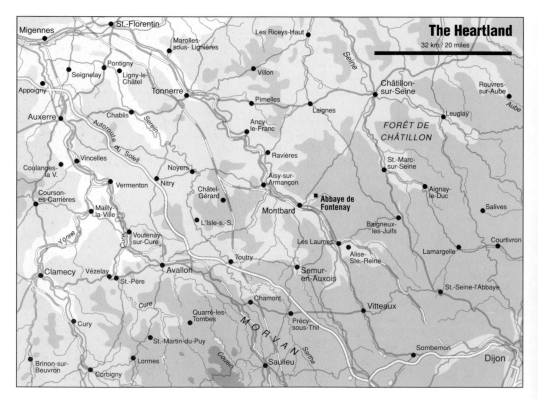

presented humanity with moral tales and vivid depictions of greed, despair and lust. *Le Péché Originel* shows an uninhibited Eve passing an apple to a coy Adam. *La Musique Profane*, like several capitals in Cluny, warns against the corrupting influence of dancing.

The town: Vézelay, like the church capitals, is not afraid of earthiness. Rue du Tripot is named after the brothels that once accommodated tired pilgrims. La Grande Rue also shows that the citizens were human: virtually all these medieval houses have vaulted Romanesque wine cellars. The loveliest lie under the Hôtel de Ville, along with two medieval wine presses. The city vines were wiped out by Phylloxera but have recently been replanted. Despite the reputation of *la colline éternelle*, the wines are abysmal.

Opposite the town hall is the turreted Tour Gaillon, a Renaissance *hôtel* in both senses of the word. In the same street are a cluster of historic buildings, including a deconsecrated church and former convents. Rue St-Étienne boasts two 16th-century houses, one of them lived in by Calvin's moderate successor, Théodore de Bèze, who apparently had his Calvinism softened by his Catholic upbringing here.

The ramparts walk is conducive to contemplation. From the wisteria-hung walls are views of woods and vineyards. In keeping with the painterly landscape, Vézelay has a profusion of antique shops, galleries and silk-screen designers. In summer, Vézelay can be unrelenting. The town teems with Danish pastors, Swiss priests *manqués* and *soixante-huitards* in search of New Age philosophies. For religious sceptics, the earthy bars on Champ de Foire, symbolically outside the city walls, provide relief from an overdose of mysticism. For visitors who insist on closeness to La Madeleine, there is Le Pontot, a sumptuous mansion hotel built over well-stocked Romanesque cellars.

Yet, at heart, Vézelay's air of mysticism is not misplaced. Esoteric bookshops specialise in astrology while restaurants dabble in food cults. Even the

Nuns in Vézelay.

dissolute Serge Gainsbourg was affected by the atmosphere. When visiting Vézelay just before his death in 1991, he resisted entreaties to enter the basilique. Pressed for a reason, the legendary singer-songwriter merely said, "I am unworthy." Vézelay is suffused with a spirituality that subdues unbelievers. It has long seen itself as a bastion against hostile elements, whether heathens or the wilderness below.

While living on the edge of the rugged Morvan, the sophisticated city-dwellers claim it has *"rien à voir avec nous"*. In some ways they are right: the Morvan's farming culture is alien to artistic Vézelay; the Morvan has no vineyards yet Vézelay clings to the remnants of its wine-growing industry; the Morvan's low-roofed cottages cannot compete with Vézelay's elegant mansions; even the city's climate is 5°C warmer than outside.

At the foot of the hill is **St-Père**, a village in Vézelay's shadow. It was not always so: a Gallo-Roman site once commanded this stretch of the River Cure. The archaeological ornaments on display in the local museum include a Celtic bronze panther and a marble Venus. However, the most curious exhibit is an Iron Age catchment well, made from a hollow oak trunk. Beside the museum is an exuberant Gothic church, studded with cherubs and capped with pinnacles. Although built in 1290, the belltower feels flamboyant, with its riotous decoration of griffon gargoyles and triumphant angels.

As the exterior is restored, the creamy white stone dazzles. The facade depicts the Last Judgement, a reminder that this was built as a funerary chapel for rich benefactors. The church is still noted for its charitable works and carries an inscription saying: "spiritual riches need no material domain." By contrast with the overpowering facade, the sober interior embodies Burgundian Gothic style, with a luminous nave and austere tombs. The restraint is breached only by lively sculpted capitals, one depicting a negroid head.

From here, follow the *"sabotier"*

The pilgrims' route, Vézelay; Vézelay's mystic golden glow.

signs to the workshop belonging to Romain Doré, one of the last clog-makers and wood sculptors in the region. Watching him carve a boar's head or wooden goblet may generate an appetite for lunch in L'Espérance, one of the finest restaurants in France. François Mitterrand and Jacques Delors are regular guests at this riverside mill. But villagers are blasé about "folk who arrive in helicopters for lunch". Marc Meneau's restaurant is noted for its *foie gras* and roast turbot with *feuilleté de fromages*. An effusive host and a cellar of Bourgogne and brandies confirm its appeal to French celebrities.

It was here that Serge Gainsbourg chose to live the last winter of his life, well away from Parisian debaucheries. According to Marc Meneau, he spent his days composing and his nights propped up against the bar. Unsuspecting diners were delighted by Gainsbourg's spontaneous performances at the piano, accompanied by his tiny dancing daughter, Bambou.

St-Père borders **Fontaines-Salées**, a sacred Celtic settlement which sprang up around magical springs. This wheel-shaped sanctuary was dedicated to the sun god, Taranis. Within the hallowed site, circular baths and temples were used for druid worship. The Romans had a more pedestrian approach, adding conventional baths. The salty, radioactive water was thought to have curative powers, and to be particularly beneficial for arthritis and poor libido.

In medieval times the springs were celebrated in the epic *chansons de geste*. These minstrels' songs encouraged pilgrimages, thus paving the path to sacred Vézelay. The salty springs were only abandoned in the 15th-century. The Gallo-Roman site can still be visited but its obvious finds lurk in St-Père's dingy museum. Delicate amulets, brooches and hairpins were unearthed in the women's baths. Sadly, the museum spirit is more redolent of arthritic Rome than mysterious Gaul.

Just south of St-Père is **Pierre-Perthuis**, a scenic hamlet with a ruined castle built on a rocky escarpment. Stone bridges span the gorge and the

River Cure; in the distance are misty views of Vézelay. Bringing one back to earth are signs for honey and locally quarried minerals. Between here and Avallon is a lush valley carved by the River Cousin. This is rich farmland with grazing for sheep and Charolais cattle. Bordering the river are old washhouses and dreamy watermills, often turned into inviting inns. Since the valley is only two hours from Paris, these manors and mills are fast becoming *résidences secondaires*.

Like the Haut-Châtillonais, this region, was once the haunt of the Knights Templar. Their austere *commanderies* guarded the Burgundian borders and pilgrim routes. Humble Templar churches half-heartedly addressed the Gothic revolution that was enveloping northern Burgundy. Compared with the Haut-Châtillonais, however, fewer Templar lodges remain. Even so, Saulce has a sturdy 13th-century chapel, the remains of a Templar guard post. In the neighbouring hamlets of Island and Menades, Gothic verticality

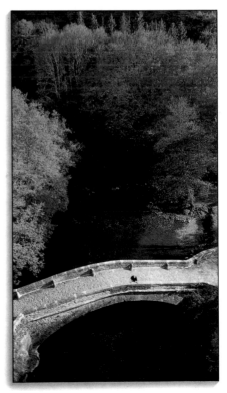

Bridge at Pierre-Perthuis.

and bourgeois manors are triumphant.

Pontaubert is a welcome return to Burgundian Romanesque. This squat church, once linked to a *commanderie* and hospital, also reflects the Templars' preference for Romanesque. The tiered tower may be Gothic but the tympanum, sculpted capitals and the groined vaulting in the nave reflect an earlier sensibility. Before leaving, notice the medieval polychrome statues of the Virgin and St John.

Like many of the bridges over the Cousin, the village bridge was first built by the Templars. Between here and **Vault-de-Lugny**, the Cousin is a fast-flowing mountain river, popular with trout fishermen. Vault-de-Lugny has a moated medieval château and a 15th-century church with striking frescoes. This 16th-century series represents the Passion: chaotic but artful scenes cover the wide nave and choir. From here, follow the river to Avallon, calling at the romantic Moulin des Ruats for a trout-inspired dinner.

Avallon is twinned with Tenterden in Kent, a similar gentrified market town. However, the lofty location and the impressive ramparts are Burgundian enough. Avallon is perched between two ravines and its prominent site has been fortified since Charlemagne's time. The town has had a turbulent history, fought over by the early French kings and the dukes of Burgundy. It was occupied by the English in the Hundred Years' War and pillaged in the Wars of Religion.

A walk along the ramparts gives a sense of Avallon's strategic importance. Although several towers have been razed, most of the bastion remains. In between turrets are plunging views over the rooftops and church to the Cousin Valley. (Walking itineraries are available from the tourist office.)

Église St-Lazare was rebuilt in Burgundian Romanesque style, shortly after Vézelay. Intended to house the relics of Lazarus, the church retains its original Carolingian crypt. But the interest centres on the facade. A tower collapsed in 1633, destroying one door-

Avallon rooftops.

174

way but the remaining two are as exuberantly sculpted as any in Burgundy. Despite a battered tympanum, the large doorway reveals the signs of the Zodiac, the labours of the month and musicians of the Apocalypse. The smaller one is lovely, interweaving flowers and foliage in stylised patterns. The sober interior echoes the vegetal theme in its foliated capitals. A Cluniac nave, groined vaulting and a semi-domed apse are enlivened by polychrome statues.

Despite its fraught history, Avallon is almost too calm. A charming clocktower straddles the narrow Grande Rue. Beside it is the 17th-century Couvent des Ursulines. Rue Masquée, off the Grande Rue, is lined with medieval houses and leads to the fine 17th-century Maison du Prévôt.

Beyond these quaint, cobbled alleys, this is a pragmatic city. The 17th-century Couvent aux Capucins is now a cinema. The local *tribunal* has moved into the ducal castle; the great hall is now the courtroom while the vaulted cellars below are used for receptions.

The most atmospheric spot in town is the Hôtel des Sires de Domecy. The delicate turret over the stairwell and entrance is peculiar to Burgundy.

Parc des Chaumes, just outside town, affords views of Avallon's terraced gardens, ramparts and rooftops. From here, a circuitous route leads east to Semur-en-Auxois.

Close to Avallon is St-Jean-des-Bonhommes, a ruined 12th-century priory with a delicate chapel and refectory. The priory depended on the neighbouring village of **Montréal**. As the name implies, this village has a royal past, dating back to Queen Brunéhaut, regent of Burgundy. The walls of her 7th-century *Mons Regalis* have been incorporated into medieval houses. The village prospered under the Burgundian dukes and acquired the artistic reputation it retains today.

The delightful **church** was finished in 1170 and feels early Gothic with its rose windows and ribbed vaulting. However, pointed Romanesque lancets and delicate capitals reveal that this is a

Avallon, gateway and belltower; fine carving, Église St-Lazare.

transitional work. The naive alabaster altar-piece is thought to have been carved by a Nottingham soldier left behind after the Hundred Years' War. But the highlights are the 16th-century choir stalls, made by the local Frères Rigolley. The misericords are a masterpiece of Burgundian wood-carving. Rough scenes from peasant life are mixed with biblical stories.

From the churchyard are panoramic views over the Serein Valley and the distant mountains of the Morvan. Severe gateways mark the upper and lower entrances to Montréal but the lofty stone village spills out of its medieval towers. High-walled houses sprout turrets and mullioned windows. The stone is softened by creeper-covered walls and neat flower beds. In this well-tended village even the Romanesque priory has been turned into a cosy old people's home.

For similar sights, visit **Île-sur-Serein**, a picturesque riverside village just north of Montréal. Well-restored Renaissance houses, a ruined castle, a medieval church and a former priory provide an attractive setting. Following the River Serein north is the most Burgundian of journeys, but for a direct route to Semur-en-Auxois, follow the D954 through rich farmland. Spare a glance for Savigny-en-Terre-Plaine, an exquisite Romanesque church perched on a windy hill.

Époisses, to the east, is the most welcoming of the châteaux in the Auxois region. The harmonious village nestles amid sloping Burgundian roofs and mellow stonework, its 17th-century houses decorated with elaborate chimney pots and sculpted doorways. The château lies beyond the *basse-cour*, virtually a medieval village in itself. As well as farm buildings and a 13th-century church, there is a dovecote with room for 3,000 doves, a sign of the importance of the feudal estate. Originally a ducal residence, this moated 15th-century château has belonged to the Guitaut family since 1672. The early fortifications remain but several wings were destroyed in the Revolution.

Herding cattle.

A drawbridge leads to the *cour d'honneur* and a well which is decorated with delicate ironwork produced in an early foundry nearby. The château blends medieval towers with Renaissance mullioned windows; rose-coloured roofs are matched by warm stone walls. Inside, a gallery displays portraits of the last four dukes of Burgundy. However, the prevailing spirit is of Madame de Sévigné, a regular 17th-century visitor. Her portrait overlooks a four-poster bed while the library contains her letters. Small wonder that the sparkling marquise preferred this appealing château to dilapidated Bourbilly, her ancestral home nearby.

To the French, however, Époisses means cheese: the local *fromagerie* is the fitting place to sample Burgundy's most famous cheese. Invented by 15th-century Cistercian monks, it is now made by the Berthaut family. Époisses regularly wins the gold medal for traditional cheese at the Concours Agricole de Paris. This creamy cheese requires half a gallon (2 litres) of milk and is dipped in *marc de Bourgogne* every day for two months. The result is a smoky cheese with the texture of old Burgundian pottery. Époisses, best with a glass of Savigny-lès-Beaune, can also be sampled at the local café.

Château de Bourbilly, just south of the village, was once a fief of Époisses. Set in a clearing, the small white château is surrounded by inquisitive Charolais cattle. In Madame de Sévigné's day, Bourbilly was an austere feudal castle, reflecting the personality of Jeanne de Chantal, her saintly grandmother. Jeanne founded the Order of the Visitation and created 80 convents all over Europe. The château today is a charming pastiche, restored in romantic style in Napoleon III's time. The facade is topped by pepperpot towers and mock-medieval crenellations. Madame Darcy, the *châtelaine*, blames the British: an earlier Darcy fell under the spell of Victoriana and, along with the pepperpot towers, added a "Gothick" library. The chapel is charming, however, decorated with frescoes by a monk

Époisses Château.

from La-Pierre-Qui-Vire monastery.

From here, it is a short drive north to **Semur-en-Auxois** and the farmland Madame de Sévigné called "a delicious valley". In its cute way, Semur remains delicious and is an ideal base, an historic centre enclosed by snug walls. During the Wars of Religion, this military stronghold became the home of the Burgundian Parliament. In 1941 Semur was a symbol of Resistance, led by Maire Morlevat, who is still in office. The initial sighting of the town, glimpsed from Pont Joly, is of a turreted bastion perched on a rocky spur above the River Armançon. Semur is stacked around the four towers of its castle keep and merges into the rose-coloured rock.

Porte Guillier, a medieval gateway, leads through the pedestrianised centre to a square lined by half-timbered houses and **Église Notre-Dame**. This priory church depended on the abbey at Flavigny. Dating from 1218, the eclectic church offends purists but delights others. The north portal bears a tympanum with the legend of St Thomas and, beside it, two snails symbolise the region. The interior borrows freely from Burgundian Gothic churches. A narrow nave and spindly capitals emphasise the height of the vaulting. Yet the mood is intimate, from the piped music to the slender nave bathed in light. It is a church one could almost live in.

Much of the statuary is being restored but a faded polychrome Entombment has the expressiveness of Claus Sluter's work. The medieval panelled windows represent local guilds: in one, a butcher is poised to slaughter a cow; in another, drapers are busy weaving Semur's fortune in cloth. Outside are imposing flying buttresses and devilish gargoyles. The church cloisters have been absorbed by the Hôtel de Ville.

The **ramparts walk** is, unlike Avallon's, a rural experience, encompassing former convents, mills and tanneries. Rue du Rempart winds past towers, including Tour de l'Orle d'Or. Named after its glinting roof, this was the entrance to the town, prior to the building of Pont Joly. From the walled

Fête de la Bague, Semur-en-Auxois.

Place de Montbeillard, Rue Basse follows the river's loops to the weir at Quai d'Armançon. The pink-tinged ramparts are overgrown with heather, broom and climbing plants. The scene is completed by a tiny island, mills and terraced gardens, gradually rolling into open countryside. Soon after the Pont Pinard, Escalier du Fourneau climbs steeply back to the high town and a cluster of friendly bars.

Semur does not rest on its laurels. The main museum, housed in a former convent, boasts illuminated manuscripts and Burgundian paintings. The *Fête de la Bague* is the French equivalent to the Italian *Palio*. Held on 31 May, the oldest horse race in France has been run since 1639. The victor receives a gold ring engraved with the arms of the town. In summer, Semur presents ballets, concerts and opera, an appropriate range for a town with a *conservatoire* and an accordion industry. With its period lanterns and alleys hung with flower baskets, Semur narrowly escapes tweeness. But the warmth of local hospitality

Fête de la Bague is the oldest horse race in France.

dispels any doubts. In the words of Sebastien Munster, a 16th-century visitor, the citizens are *"paisibles, doux, débonnaires et charitables"*.

From Semur, a country drive leads to Montbard via the **Château de Lantilly**. It is called *le château aux cent fenêtres* because of its profusion of windows. Although originally medieval, the château is largely classical. Lantilly enjoys sweeping views across the Brenne Valley to Mont Auxois. The location is perfect for the summer concerts and exhibitions hosted by the cultured owners.

Montbard, north of Semur, is marked by economic rise and fall. The presence of forests, rivers and a canal made Montbard a natural candidate for industrialisation. However, its success was entirely due to the local Comte de Buffon. The multifaceted count was a royal gardener, botanist, scientist and industrialist. In essence, he was a product of the Enlightenment, with an encyclopaedic knowledge of the sciences and a belief in progress. In Montbard he

BALLOONING

On 21 November 1783 two men were frantically stuffing straw and twigs into a brazier. Their work was vital: the fire *had* to be kept hot; if there were any let-up, disaster might result. One man took a moment from his labours to gaze below; this made his co-worker slightly nervous, and he remonstrated with his friend: "If you look at the river in that fashion you will be likely to bathe in it soon."

Pilatre de Rozier and the Marquis d'Arlandes were making the first manned hot-air balloon flight. Paris, the River Seine and the King and Queen of France, Louis XVI and Marie Antoinette, were below, and this historic flight lasted less than half an hour. Afterwards, the Queen is supposed to have gushed: "It is the sport of the gods!"

The means of ascent that afternoon was a 78-ft (24-metre) high, blue and gold coloured linen-and-rag "balloon" (or "envelope") called a Montgolfière after its inventors, the Montgolfier brothers.

Raised by heated air ("fire balloon" was

the original name), the earliest models were always in danger of catching fire even before the flight started. Inflation was by hanging the envelope between two poles and building a fire underneath, then achieving the exact mixture of hot-air exhaust and flame height.

The first balloons were almost round with a hole in the bottom. Netting surrounded the balloon both for stability and to hold the attachment lines which kept balloon and basket tethered to one another. Despite technical advances, all flights still begin in much the same manner; the balloon is spread flat on the ground, with the open end nearest the basket, which has several tanks of fuel and a propane burner in it. The basket is tipped on its side with the burner pointing toward the open end of the balloon, and the steel cables at the base of the balloon are attached to the basket supports.

Two people are stationed at the mouth of the balloon to hold it open, with one or two others at the top end. A large fan is set up to blow the heated air into the balloon. The pilot pulls the burner release, and a "whooooooooosh" emits from the small black flame-thrower. Nothing seems to be happening, even when the process is repeated several times. But then, magically, the silk-like fabric takes on a life of its own. In undulating waves, it rises and falls, all the while expanding. As the balloon inflates, those anchoring the top-end leads begin to loosen their grip and allow it to rise. This brings the basket upright, and after a few more flame spurts, all is ready.

As the balloon slowly rises, panic subsides, and in exchange comes a feeling of elation and freedom. Except for the occasional bursts of burner flame, and the quiet comments of the pilot, it is a silent world. There is no feeling of an air current because the balloon is going with it. Flight speed and direction are at the wind's pleasure, although by combining burner blasts with manipulations of the balloon's turning vents, the pilot can make the balloon revolve at will. Altitudes will vary from a few feet to several thousand, depending upon passenger requests and wind conditions. A traditional champagne toast follows the flight, since in the early days pilots carried bottles of champagne to placate angry farmers whose crops might be ruined by visitors arriving unexpectedly from the sky. ■

fostered a metal industry that still survives today.

Landscaped over a ruined château, **Parc Buffon** was laid out by Buffon and remains a tribute to Montbard's greatest son. Bordering the park is Buffon's study, set in a romantic medieval tower. Buffon lived by the belief that "*Il ne faut que du temps pour tout savoir*". Since then, however, ailing components factories have cast a shadow over his legacy. Nowadays, despite the presence of the TGV, Montbard has scant faith in progress. Despite the park, canal views and a cluster of old houses in the town centre, there is little to detain the visitor apart from the local cuisine.

Just downriver is the finest monument to Buffon, **La Grande Forge**. Like all early Burgundian foundries, it required a watery site and massive amounts of wood. Built in 1768, this was one of the biggest French foundries of its day. Until 1866 it produced tools and weapons, including cannon used to attack the British in the Napoleonic wars. Buffon's ironworks were rendered obsolete by the triumph of *forges à l'anglaise*, coke-fired furnaces. The ironworks became a cement factory until 1945 but Buffon's creation has been lovingly restored by Taylor Whitehead and his French wife.

To the modern eye, this industrial complex is delightfully rural. Buffon's main residence was in Paris but his *pied à terre* in Burgundy includes all that a country gentleman would expect: a classical manor, chapel, dovecote and orangerie. As a naturalist, Buffon also installed an aviary and zoo to aid his research on the classification of species. Buffon, like most foundry masters, lived beside his workforce but the master's and minions' accommodation naturally differed.

Four hundred privileged workers lived on site while the foundry's woodcutters and labourers had to fend for themselves. These spartan 18th-century dwellings represented the model housing of the day. Several workers' cottages remain and, despite being occupied by farmers until recently, are fur-

Buffon forge.

nished much as they were in Buffon's time. The foundry itself is the star exhibit, the showcase of the early Burgundian iron industry. Although later eclipsed by Le Creusot steelworks, the 18th century belonged to northern Burgundy. The visit is enlivened by working models and a witty commentary. The blackened brick chimneys of the blast furnace are real enough, as are the water-driven bellows and the rushing mill-race. In the metal finishing workshop the sounds and processes are recreated; only the heat is missing. Given the plans to turn the foundry into a *forge artisanal*, heat and cast-iron souvenirs are not far away.

The foundry must have presented a dramatic picture of early industrialisation. Buffon would invite honoured guests to stand on a monumental staircase overlooking the raging furnace below. From this grand balcony Louis XVI first witnessed the reality of the Industrial Revolution. As half-clad figures loomed out of the pitch darkness, the contrast between court finery and grimy workers must have affected the king. At the very least, the spectacle made a change from a comedy of manners by Molière. Not for nothing does the guide call the scene *un théâtre industriel*.

Yet Burgundy's industrial heritage owes more to St Bernard than to Buffon. In these forests the Benedictine monks were medieval forge masters, first at Fontenay Abbey and later at neighbouring priories. **Prieuré de Vausse**, just west of Buffon's forges, was founded by the monks from Montréal. Although now a working farm, the priory is still visible. The church itself has become a charming library; Romanesque cloisters enclose a rose garden, occasionally overrun by recalcitrant ducks.

Abbaye de Fontenay, west of Montbard, is a Benedictine treasure on a greater scale, the oldest Cistercian ensemble surviving in France. Founded in 1118 by St Bernard, Fontenay was named after the healing springs in this marshy valley. In 1139 the Bishop of Norwich endowed the abbey and, as a **Fontenay Abbey.**

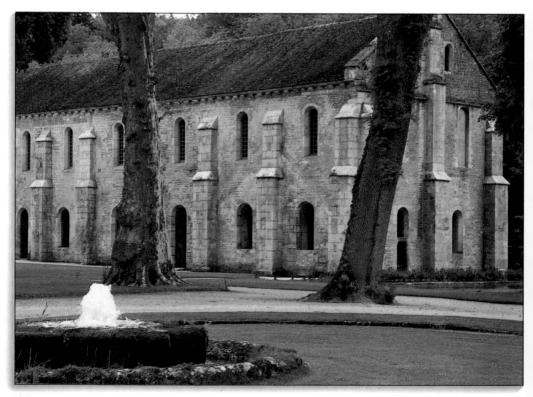

posthumous reward, is buried beneath the choir. But 14th-century prosperity gave way to absentee abbots and 16th-century decadence. After the Revolution, Fontenay became a paper mill until saved by the Montgolfier ballooning family. In 1906 their descendants restored the abbey to its Cistercian simplicity. The Aynard family still lives in the grounds, in an austere house built on the site of the refectory. Rather like the Cistercians, they make their living from fish-farming.

The abbey complex presents a virtually complete view of early Cistercian life. The refectory may be missing but the rest remains, including the kitchens, small prison and an over-restored infirmary. The smoke-blackened *forge* is the best conserved of early Benedictine foundries. For the Cistercians, manual work was a form of prayer, a vocation the Cluniacs had rejected. The self-sufficient monks built a water channel, ran a mill, forge, dovecote and lived off their vegetable gardens and trout-filled ponds; trout even appear on the abbey's arms. Curiously, most manual work seemed to fall to the *frères convertis*, the lay brethren.

Fontenay is faithful to the precepts of St Bernard, at once supremely mystical and functional. But unadulterated by ornamentation, it boasts no belltower, tympanum, coloured glass or decorated capitals. In fact, unlike magnificent Cluniac churches, it does not boast.

St Bernard accepted the Platonist credo that truth lay in proportion so the architecture reflects mathematical design and Christian numerology. The **church** embodies St Bernard's beliefs. The bare facade is pierced by seven narrow windows, a sacred number, symbolising perfection. Three windows are placed above the rest since four represented the earth and three the heavens. This fusion of heaven and earth is echoed throughout the interior.

A dramatic single-storey nave is sustained by pointed arches. The capitals are only decorated with natural foliage, acanthus leaves and aquatic symbols inspired by the marshy setting. The sin-

Fontenay cloisters.

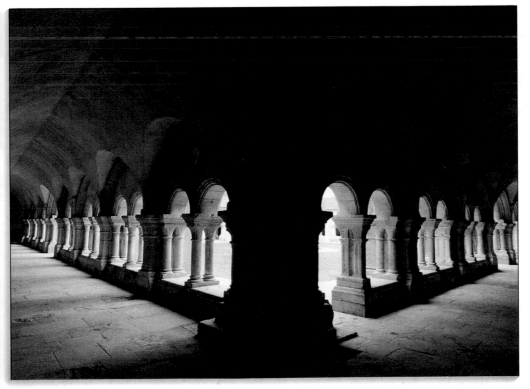

gle statuary is a 13th-century Virgin, the protectress of the abbey. There was a practical purpose behind the absence of ornamentation: St Bernard did not permit anything that could distract the monks from prayer. Yet St Bernard's vision was broader than mere abnegation. His austerity was softened by a burning faith that manifested itself in light rather than imagery. In Fontenay, the mystical symbolism of light is ever-present. The monks were buried in the north of the church so that they would not see the light until the Resurrection.

Upstairs is the dormitory, covered by a ship-shaped oak roof. The 300 monks slept fully-clothed and ready for prayer; only the abbot had enough privacy to test his vows of chastity. The design of the dormitory and latrines is copied by Fountains Abbey in Yorkshire. Nearby, the chapter house was a place for meetings, penance and the business of monastic life. Only *moines de coeur* were allowed here, no *frères convertis*. Naturally, the vaulted scriptorium was designed to be the lightest room. Although the windows are modern, they reproduce the original abstract designs. Next-door is the *chauffoir*, the only warm room in the abbey. Not that the monks' comfort was uppermost in St Bernard's mind: the room sometimes served to warm the copyists' hands but its primary purpose was to stop precious inks from freezing.

The presence of the white-robed monks lingers in the cloisters, an intimate spot. The midday light was intended to illuminate the rigorous patterns on the columns. A walk around the grounds shows the Cistercians' genius for selecting sacred sites, a gift equalled only by the Romans. The mellow stone complements this watery forest clearing. The last scenes of the 1991 movie *Cyrano de Bergerac* were filmed by the fountain. In the romantic twilight, Roxanne cries, "*C'est vous…*" to Cyrano. In real life, however, the actor Gérard Depardieu says that leaves were added to give summer an autumnal air. St Bernard would not have countenanced such fabrication.

Châtillon-sur-Seine.

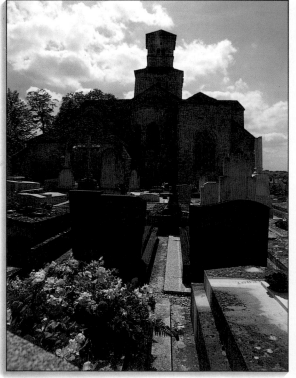

From Fontenay, one can go east to Dijon, south to the Côte d'Or or north to **Châtillon-sur-Seine**, an isolated town with a unique Gallic collection. The journey across the plains was the path taken by the Allies during the Liberation of Burgundy, culminating in the fusion of the French forces. But Châtillon's fame comes from the unearthing of the remarkable **Treasure of Vix** in 1953, found in a Gallic necropolis dating from 6 BC. Celtic tribes then controlled a trade route leading from the Seine to the Mediterranean and lived by barter, trade and patronage. Mont Lassois had already delivered lesser Gallo-Roman finds but the Vix burial chamber was on a royal scale.

The tomb revealed an elaborate funeral litter and the skeleton of a 30-year-old princess, wearing jewels and a gold diadem. Nearby were Attic vases, an Etruscan wine pitcher and the bronze Vase de Vix, the largest yet known from antiquity. Made in Magna Grecia, this *krater* could contain over 1,000 litres of liquid. The vase depicts Gorgons'

heads, and the snake-like legs which reoccur as a theme in Burgundian medieval sculpture. The treasure is on display in the Maison Philandrier, a Renaissance mansion undamaged in the war. Such Celtic wealth remains a mystery in this forlorn frontier zone.

Alise-Ste-Reine is the site of Gallic Alésia, known to French children through the Asterix books. Adults also associate it with the final defeat of the Gauls in 52 BC, and thus with the founding of modern France. After Vercingétorix was declared leader of the Gauls at Bibracte, he led a surprise attack against Julius Caesar. However, the Roman army, strengthened by German mercenaries, beseiged the fleeing Gauls at their citadel of Alésia. Caesar's double *enceinte* kept out Gallic reinforcements and Vercingétorix surrendered to save his people. This first and last leader of a united Gaul was later put to death in Rome.

High above the village is a statue which has become a shrine to Celtic mythomania. The bronze of heroic

Vercingétorix was erected by Napoleon III, who popularised the rediscovery of France's pre-Roman roots.

Alise-Ste-Reine is a curious experience, from the disparate village to the mounds of Gallic earthworks. The exposed, windswept village places symbolism before sights. Even the bistrot is called Au Grill Gaulois. The archaeological zone includes the remains of the forum, Celtic temple and forges. The star finds may be in Paris but the local museum is revamping its collection of spears, coins and silver cups. Nearby is the Renaissance Chapelle Ste-Reine, named after a Christian orphan who was beheaded rather than marry a Roman.

Just outside flows the Source Ste-Reine, said to have sprung up when the saint's head hit the earth. The cult attracted an influx of sick pilgrims so a hospice was built nearby. The 17th-century building still stands, complete with the original pharmacy and library.

Beside the archaeological zone is **St-Léger**, arguably the finest Carolingian church in Burgundy. The domed basilica dates from the 7th century and retains a Merovingian wall and an altar carved with a Byzantine cross. On a ridge overlooking the church is a modern pastiche of a Gallo-Roman theatre, used for summer concerts. For those still oblivious to Gallic glory, there is a prominent statue of Joan of Arc.

Over the brow of Mont Auxois is a witty link to a latter-day Gaul. **Château de Bussy-Rabutin**, named after its 17th-century owner, is the most absorbing stately home in Burgundy. Virtually every painting and bittersweet motto symbolises the life of Roger de Bussy-Rabutin. The sardonic count had much in common with his forebears. With intentional mockery, Bussy even entitled his scandalous account of court affairs *Histoire Amoureuse des Gaules*. This contentious book offended Louis XIV and led to Bussy's banishment to Burgundy. For 16 years of exile, his life revolved around his château, a time enlivened by love affairs and letters.

The moated château, set in gardens designed by Le Nôtre, has a gracious

Bussy-Rabutin painted ceiling.

Renaissance facade and elegant Italianate wings. Inside is a picture of the Burgundy snail which, to Bussy, was a poignant reminder that his home had shrunk to this small shell. "*Je rentre dans mon coquille*," Bussy has noted beside it. But the snail also represents self-sufficiency: the erstwhile courtier and soldier did not waste his time.

Bussy's morganatic wife was banished from the château and paintings of his mistresses soon covered the walls. Most portraits of the Marquise de Montglat, the woman he loved, refer to her inconstancy: "*plus légère que le vent*". But a floral painting contains the plaintive "*Son absence me tue*".

Many paintings are allegorical, both to elevate Bussy's suffering and to disguise key courtiers. A picture of the sun obscured by clouds is clearly a metaphor for the stormy regime of *le Roi Soleil*. A phoenix rising from the ashes refers to Bussy's own fate, although his reprieve happened very late in life. One gallery contains 65 portraits of European soldiers, including Cromwell. In an arrogant flourish, Bussy portrays himself as a Roman emperor.

One room is devoted to portraits of his real and imagined mistresses, including several shared with the Sun King. According to the guide, "If we showed all Louis XIV's mistresses, the room would explode."

Several paintings show the château and gardens as they looked in Bussy's day. The grounds are being restored to their original glory in time for the tricentenary of Bussy's death in 1993. Echoing Versailles, perspectives should be signalled by classical statues, topiary and fountains.

After leaving the château, visit the lovely Romanesque church in Bussy-le-Grand before continuing to **Flavigny-sur-Ozerain**. A dramatic location and history seem a heavy burden for this mild town. As the seat of an 8th-century bishopric, it was the religious centre for the Auxois, with a powerful Benedictine abbey. Flavigny was loyal to the crown and during the Wars of Religion shared the Burgundian parliament with

Wall panel paintings, Bussy-Rabutin.

Semur. Its religious authority remains: in 1848 a Dominican monastery was established, now run by an English priest. Recently, a controversial *seminaire intégriste* has swollen the religious ranks. This right-wing order is fighting for a return to cassocked priests, Latin mass and traditionalism. These rival organisations are Flavigny's bread and butter, but have divided the town.

Flavigny is perched on a rocky spur overlooking two deep ravines. Beyond the severity of the ramparts and medieval gates is an intriguing nucleus. Richly-decorated houses are a legacy of Flavigny's 16th-century prosperity. This mellow stone town reveals Renaissance turrets, mullioned windows, romantic balconies and madonnas in niches. Flavigny's charm lies in its wealth of discreet details rather than in one outstanding site. Even so, the eclectic **Église St-Genest** contains a galleried nave, Romanesque chapel and Burgundian sculptures. But most of the famous 15th-century Flemish choir stalls and misericords have been stolen.

Abbaye de St-Pierre boasted a renowned scriptorium whose manuscripts are now in the Vatican collection. The ruined abbey contains fine 8th-century crypts supported by Roman columns and Byzantine pillars. The abbey crypts, church and remaining buildings have been subsumed by an *anises* factory, *bons-bons* originally made by the Benedictines. A professed interest in aniseed drops unlocks a visit to the crypts. Flavigny retains its religious complexity and traditional craftsmanship. As a chic address for Parisian weekenders and media folk, the village has sprouted an art school and craft shops. Sunday painters and amateur builders help one another renovate their Renaissance arcades.

Flavigny is well-disposed to tourism, seeing it as a chance to reduce the influence of the clergy. On Sundays, the terraces and ramparts witness processions of rival priests of different nationalities and orders. In Le Trop Chaud bar, however, there tend to be sly jokes about defrocked priests.

For a Burgundian departure, one can sip from the **Sources de la Seine** at Chanceaux. As proud *Bourguignons* like to remind Parisians, the capital's river rises here. Napoleon III, a victim of *la gloire de la France*, commandeered the site for the city of Paris. Since the languid nymph Sequana embodies the spirit of the Seine, Haussmann was ordered to create a nymph-encrusted grotto over the springs. An early bronze of the nymph was found nearby but is now in Dijon museum. Even so, the wooded site is more atmospheric than the statuary.

If Burgundy represents religion, Romanesque architecture and wine, then the heartland lives up to its name. Druids, St Bernard, the Templars and traditionalist modern priests have all left their legacy in stone. But quibblers will send wine-lovers south to the Côte d'Or: only a vintage Meursault has the edge over the splendours of Vézelay. St Bernard might disapprove of such indulgence but Serge Gainsbourg would give his blessing before disappearing in a puff of Gitanes.

Left, artist at work. **Right**, Flavigny-sur Ozerain, church interior.

The region is as elusive as its celebrated son, François Mitterrand. **La Nièvre** is the official name for a *département* with a slippery soul. This is not the traditional Burgundy of wine and song. The jolly Burgundians of yore are confined to the vineyards of the Côte d'Or. Without wine and rich pastures, there is little good fortune to toast.

Like a black granite heart, **the Morvan** occupies the centre of the region. This is the land of the Gauls, with a separate language and culture. The Morvan is also a central mystery, its myths striking a chord with current French Celtomania. For visiting earthlings, its appeal lies in rustic cuisine, rugged landscape and a chance to flee vintage charts and Romanesque masterpieces. Yet around Mitterrand's black heartland is a cluster of warmer influences. Auxois, to the east, is a generous Burgundian landscape looking towards Dijon. Autun, in the south, is the Roman heart of Burgundy with its Romanesque cathedral an echo of the imperial past. Nivernais, to the west, was for long an independent duchy with the Burgundians only one of many masters.

Significantly, all these regions feel marginalised by the wealthy Burgundian wine belt and vote left, though there are signs that the region may move towards the mainstream. Perhaps then Nièvre's wandering soul will feel *bien dans sa peau*, at ease with itself.

Contrasting influences make this Burgundy's most diverse region. Autun and Saulieu boast a rich religious heritage and gastronomic heights. The Auxois and Nivernais prairies are home to Charolais cattle and the occasional château. In summer, the Morvan becomes the green belt of Burgundy while rural canals make Nièvre the ideal barging base. Travelling west leads to the charming medieval towns on the river

Preceding pages: Burgundy Canal at Châteauneuf; Nevers Cathedral. Left, Commarin Château.

Loire. The centre of Nièvre may be a wine-free zone but the Loire's Pouilly-Fumé vineyards amply compensate.

Stretching westwards from Dijon is **L'Auxois**, a soft, watery landscape celebrated by Henri Vincenot, the modern regional novelist. In his tales, truculent farmers are at odds with each other but at one with the gentle scenery. This rich region was once the granary of Burgundy but is now better-known for its cattle and cheese. Made in brown-tiled farms, Époisses cheese joins prime beef on the local menus. Before starring in *boeuf bourguignon*, Charolais cattle laze around lush meadows. This is the watershed of Burgundy: tumbledown mills border the Armançon and Serein rivers; the Canal de Bourgogne runs idly by, silenced by the railways.

Commarin was Vincenot's childhood home and attracts literary pilgrims in search of snails and *douceur de vivre*. *Escargots* are particularly tasty in the area but Vincenot also described the snail as the secret heart of Burgundy. Commarin has a remarkable château which has belonged to the same family for over 600 years. Guarded by stone lions, the château presents a feudal face with classical features. The towers, moats and wooded grounds are a prelude to an opulent interior. Renaissance tapestries and imperial busts are a backdrop to furniture that has been *in situ* since 1750.

A short drive south leads to medieval **Châteauneuf**, with its commanding views over the plains. This crumbling citadel is encircled by Burgundian merchants' houses. From here, follow the Canal de Bourgogne to **Pouilly-en-Auxois**, the point where the canal disappears underground for 1¾ miles (3 km). Built in 1822, this fine piece of engineering pre-dates Brunel. Now a backwater, Pouilly was then a thriving port supplying Paris with firewood. By the 16th century, Normandy's forests were depleted and Burgundy became the capital's chief supplier until the age of coal. The wood was felled in the Morvan and floated down the Yonne, Cure and, later, along the canals.

Barging on the Burgundy Canal, Châteauneuf.

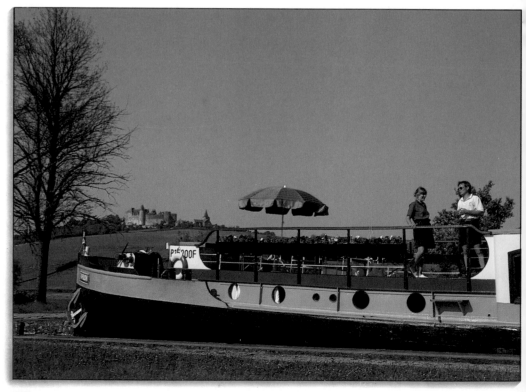

Just west is **Chailly-sur-Armançon**, best known not for its watery landscape but for its Renaissance château, now Burgundy's most exclusive hotel. Mike Sata, a Japanese industrialist, fell in love with Chailly and after spending £10 million on renovations, persuaded the French Prime Minister to open it in 1990. Since then, the Japanese have supplanted the Americans in Burgundian folklore. Villagers talk in awe of these exotic imperialists, arriving for lunch by helicopter, then sweeping off to examine their vineyards in the Côte d'Or. The keynote is not envy but puzzlement at such a frenetic pace of life. Burgundians rarely sacrifice pleasure to speed: "Don't hurry a good wine" is a motto with wider implications.

After resisting a pampered stay in Chailly, there are further temptations in **Saulieu**, a gastronomic halt since the 17th century. Saulieu owes its prosperity to its position on the old Lyon–Paris trade route. Wine, fish, grain and wood were exchanged at Saulieu's fairs. Merchants then restored themselves with hearty portions of ham and *andouillettes*. The town was at its industrial peak in the 1860s, with clog and tile factories in town and tanneries on the river. In the 20th century, Saulieu was blighted by rural depopulation and war. As the Resistance centre of the Morvan *maquis*, Saulieu experienced fierce fighting, deportations and executions. Recently, the town has waved the flag of green tourism, presenting itself as the gateway to the Morvan.

Cynics say that Saulieu's gastronomic revival stems from the building of the N6 motorway: after an early start, Parisians could make Saulieu for lunch and Lyon for dinner. But the A6 autoroute bypassed Saulieu in favour of the vineyards of Beaune, bons-vivants still flock to Saulieu. Bernard Loiseau's Restaurant de la Poste rules the roost.

Loiseau is a skilled exponent of *cuisine légère*, a light touch which does not apply to diners' wallets. Typical dishes include snail and nettle soup; rabbit livers; endives in a truffle sauce; pikeperch in red wine; and red mullet with

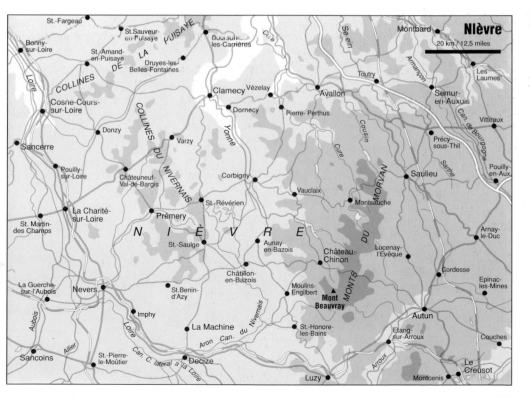

sea-urchins and beans. François Mitterrand invites favoured colleagues here, whilst EC President Jacques Delors chose this Burgundian inn for his talks with Soviet leaders on the future of the USSR. When the negotiating team withdrew to the Japanese Château de Chailly, the press joked that this was a chance for the Russians and Japanese to settle their age-old territorial dispute.

Saulieu is pleasingly Burgundian in its hearty hospitality, rustic cuisine and Romanesque architecture. **Basilique de St-Andoche**, the town's notable Romanesque church, is best seen on a summer's afternoon. The sombre granite interior is then relieved by light beamed on to the sculpted capitals. The church honours the Greek missionary who brought Christianity to Saulieu before Saulieu brought martyrdom to him. Inside is his 8th-century marble tomb, carved with pagan and Christian symbols. Despite a collapsed Carolingian crypt, 15th-century chapels and an 18th-century choir, the church still feels early Romanesque. The choir and transept were torched by English marauders during the Hundred Years' War but later alterations do not detract from the barrel-vaulted Cluniac nave.

The nave's pictorial capitals contain all the symbolism of Romanesque architecture. An eagle with outstretched wings represents spiritual striving; a phoenix symbolises eternal life; bees build a nest in arum leaves, a sign of solidarity and companionship.

Elsewhere, grotesque heads peer out of acanthus leaves and griffons devour a wolf. Dancing goats and fighting bulls are linked to the signs of the Zodiac. On the remaining space, ferns, acorns, arum and acanthus leaves are entwined. The capitals were carved by a disciple of Gislebertus of Autun, one of the greatest sculptors of the Middle Ages. These distorted, naive shapes are infused with feeling but do not attain the stylistic perfection of the capitals in Autun Cathedral. Before leaving, look at the medieval stalls, carved with inscrutable animal motifs. One features a hunting centaur while another depicts a **Bernard Loiseau's Restaurant de la Poste, Saulieu.**

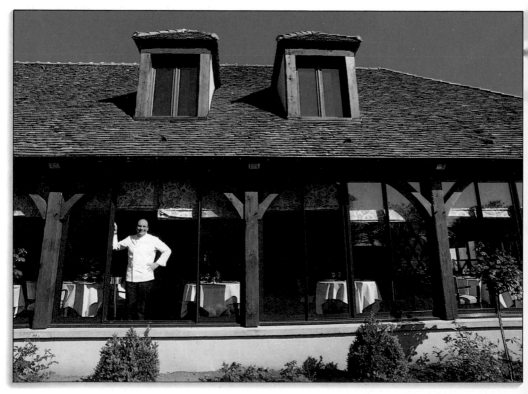

dog clutching a Camembert in its mouth. The hunting influences are natural in a region famed as a game paradise.

Next door is the **Musée Régional**, a chance to view the animal studies made by François Pompom, a local sculptor doomed to oblivion by a silly name. Pompom's sculptures of animals in motion are only too realistic portrayals of chickens and ducks. His 19th-century imagination lacked the poetry of his Romanesque counterparts. But the best works can be seen outside: a bull adorns the square dedicated to the sculptor while a fierce condor guards his grave.

Saulieu dominates a windswept ridge overlooking the Morvan so healthy pursuits are *de rigueur*. The thickly-wooded terrain is dotted with bridle paths and picnic sites as well as a trout-filled lake. A well-marked 2-mile (4-km) walk leads to Lake Chamboux while other trails weave through plantations of Christmas trees to unexpected glades. After such exertions, follow in the footsteps of Madame de Sévigné and indulge in a Burgundian feast – or at least a drink in a workmanlike art nouveau bar.

The Morvan has long been the butt of Burgundian jokes. "*Il ne vient du Morvan ni bonnes gens, ni bon vent*" runs a local expression. The winds are biting and the people reputedly austere and inward-looking. The very name Morvan is a corruption of *montagne noire* (black mountain), a reference to the dark granite slopes. The region lacks rich pastures and vineyards and relies on logging and small-scale farming. As a traditionally poor area, the Morvan is devoid of châteaux, fortified farms and Romanesque churches. Only in the south is the landscape remotely dramatic. Covering 435,000 acres (175,000 hectares), the Morvan is bounded by Avallon, Saulieu, Luzy and Corbigny. **Bas-Morvan**, the area north of Montsauche, is a plateau covered by forests and ponds. **Haut-Morvan**, climbing south, heralds the Massif Central. With fast-flowing streams, high waterfalls and alpine pastures, it is clearly mountainous. On the peaks, snow and rain fall 180 days a year. The Morvan is a sodden sponge leaking into the Cousin, Cure and Yonne rivers.

West of Saulieu is **Pierre-Qui-Vire**, a curious monastic community in the depths of the forest. In 1839 God appeared to Père Muard with the command "*Je veux que vous soyez saint.*" Muard took him at his word, establishing this Benedictine abbey in a lonely spot. The abbey takes its name from the dolmen on a rock that swivels upon the slightest touch. During the war, the abbey was a refuge for Resistance workers. One day the Gestapo burst into the refectory but the reception was so frosty that they quickly withdrew.

The monks have founded similar communities worldwide. The site is atmospheric in winter, with fir trees, silver birches and snow-covered hills. There is a big congregation for Sunday mass but for the unconverted, curiosity and forest walks justify the visit.

Prayer and penitence form the core of the community's beliefs. Given the Order's requirement for manual labour,

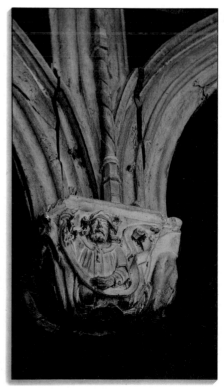

Carved corbel, Saulieu.

the 100 monks also work on their neighbouring farm. In addition, they run the renowned Zodiaque publishing house which produces books on Romanesque architecture and religion.

The books are beautifully illustrated by one privileged monk who roams France, photographing Romanesque churches for posterity. The series, *La Nuit des Temps*, follows in the footsteps of the medieval monks who laboured over illuminated manuscripts.

As to your reception, writer Robert Speaight refers to the "detached and business-like Benedictine demeanour". One can meet a monk upon request but the sombre Benedictines are more relaxed amongst male fellow Christians. Couples are occasionally welcomed on retreats. Female heretics must be content with the bookshop, chapel and the chance to buy cheese and pottery from the model farm. Few visitors leave without a Zodiaque book or a tape of Gregorian chants. But to be shown either the cloisters or the printing works, little short of a miracle is required.

Quarré-les-Tombes, the closest village to the abbey, stimulates spiritual and earthly curiosity. Encircling a severe church are 100 Merovingian tombs, most without lids. Certainly, granite was quarried nearby but opinion is divided as to whether this was a warehouse for sarcophagi or an actual necropolis. The surrounding countryside is dotted with even more ancient remains. The Forêt au Duc shelters La Roche aux Fées, a dolmen linked to druidic rites. Despite the abbey, Christianity is only skin-deep in the Morvan.

Quarré, like most of the Morvan, was a Resistance centre so is dotted with war memorials. Arms and radio transmitters arrived in British parachute drops. By the bridge over the River Cure is a *stèle* commemorating 2,000 *maquisards* who fought here in 1944. To dispel a sombre mood, Quarré offers a couple of rewarding restaurants.

As always in Burgundy, a rustic exterior belies the culinary inventiveness within. Auberge de l'Atre has a local dish for every season: wild mushrooms

A dog's dinner, Quarré-les-Tombes.

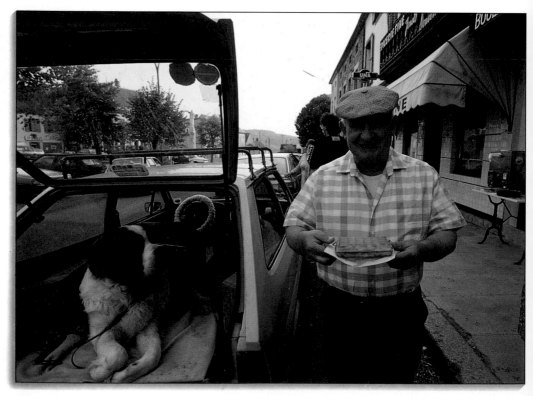

in spring; shrimps in summer; truffles and game in autumn; and *terrine de sandre en bourgogne rouge* all year round. If setting off on a hike or canoe trip, call in at La Fontaine, a *pâtisserie* with home-made flans and biscuits.

From here, it is a gentle drive south, past forests and lakes, to Mitterrand's power-base of Château-Chinon. For information on walks and wildlife, visit the Maison du Parc at **St-Brisson.** This classical mansion, built by a British architect, houses a Resistance Museum and exhibitions devoted to the **Parc Naturel du Morvan.** This is a protected zone which, according to local ecologists, is not protected enough. Between 60 and 80 percent of the Morvan is wooded. The traditional trees are oak and beeches but chestnuts are also common. But nowadays the ancient forests are losing ground to massive plantations of conifers. The fast-growing Douglas pines and miniature Christmas trees are profitable but unaesthetic and damaging to local flora and fauna.

Just south of St-Brisson is **Saut de Gouloux**, a spot that encapsulates the changing face of the Morvan. A path leads to the waterfall which, in itself, is unspectacular. A converted mill offers tacky souvenirs. However, nearby are delightful forest walks. The vegetation runs from willows beside the River Cure to daffodils and wood hyacinths in the copses or foxgloves and willow-herb in the forest clearings. Wild raspberries and bilberries grow on the higher slopes. The lush undergrowth of ferns and mosses flourishes – for now. For an original souvenir, visit a *sabotier* (clog-maker) in the hamlet of Gouloux. Alain Marchand is one of the last clog-makers and wood-carvers in the region.

The Morvan's forests have long been the main source of revenue. A harsh climate and poor soil did not favour regular farming so logging kept the region employed for six months a year. In the 16th century, Parisian landlords set up firewood companies on the Cure, Seine and Yonne rivers. In November the wood was sold at Château-Chinon fair and sent downriver in "fleets"

BURGUNDY BY BOAT

In 1787, an American tourist travelling through France penned a short note to one of his compatriots in Europe: "You should not think of returning to America without taking the tour which I have just taken." The writer was Thomas Jefferson, then American ambassador to Paris, speaking of a voyage along the Canal du Midi in southwestern France.

Jefferson's enthusiasm could easily apply to Burgundy, a region rich in navigable waterways. But while the accommodation offered today is more comfortable than Jefferson's crude packet boat, the vistas seen from the boat have changed very little through the centuries. There are still medieval villages, fields in a patchwork of green, rolling acres of cereals and corn, golden vineyards in autumn and, at each lock, the ubiquitous keeper, mistress of her domain, purveyor of foodstuffs from the garden and gossip from along the waterway.

But the most important ingredient of all is the canal that has, through the centuries,

bound these gems together. Burgundy's canal system was begun by Henri IV, linking Paris with other parts of the country. One of the earliest efforts was in 1604 in Burgundy, when work commenced on its first artificial waterway, the Briare, which connected the Seine and Loire Valleys.

Other waterways which interconnected with the Briare followed: in 1723 the Canal du Loing was opened; the Canal du Charollais appeared in 1792, and in 1838 the Canal Latéral à la Loire and the Canal de Roanne à Digoin. These five waterways form a system now known collectively as Les Canaux du Centre. The Canal de Bourgogne was started in 1775 and when it was finally completed in 1833, linked Paris to Dijon. The Yonne and Loire rivers were linked in 1785 and in 1842 the Canal du Nivernais was finally opened to traffic.

The use of waterways for recreational purposes is an innovation of the past 25 years. After World War II, when roads became the choice of transporters, lock maintenance on many of the waterways virtually halted and some rivers and canals were closed to navigation. But a hardy band of canal-boating enthusiasts prevailed, and today those canals which were begun almost 400 years ago are still navigable and form Burgundy's 620 miles (990 km) of cruising network. Most pleasurably, all the waterways are linked making it easy to go from one area to another.

Each of the waterways offers its own distinct charm: 290 miles (470 km) long, Les Canaux du Centre courses south from the Seine at St-Mammes, through the eastern Loire valley wine regions to Nevers. It connects with the Canal du Nivernais at Decize and at Digoin for the waterway to Roanne before arriving at the pilgrimage site of Paray-le-Monial. The Canal du Nivernais is considered to be the most unspoiled and beautiful, its 110-mile (175-km) length passing through a countryside of vineyards, fruit trees and châteaux.

The Burgundy Canal begins at Laroches Mignennes on the Yonne and its 150-mile (240-km) length passes some of Burgundy's most elegant châteaux, best restaurants and vineyards, and its capital city, Dijon. No matter which area you cruise, the best thing about seeing Burgundy by barge is that it's a movable feast. ∎

Quiet backwaters of the Nivernais.

steered by foresters with long poles. On the river ports of Clamécy and Vermonton the logs were bound into rough rafts and floated towards Paris. By the 19th century canals were also used and the firewood trade only died out in the 20th century. Artificial lakes and dams regulated the water flow and so helped Morvan's firewood distribution system. At logging time, the reservoirs were pumped into the rivers, swelling the water supply.

Each of the Morvan's main lakes has its own charm, from the wild Lac de Chaumeçon to the mysterious Lac de St-Agnan, hidden in the woods. **Lac des Settons** is the best-known, with all that popularity entails. Out of season, it is bleak but more Cardiff Bay than *Hôtel du Lac*. Until being dammed in the 1830s, Les Settons was a brackish peat-bog but is now a bustling summer resort. When water sports, ice-cream parlours and tourist trains begin to pall, consider a boat trip to the island on the lake.

Alternatively, escape the Swiss chalets by visiting a couple of neighbouring farms, either a *mièlerie* (honey farm) in Corancy or a *chèvrerie* (goat farm) in Ouroux-en-Morvan. It is worth returning to Les Settons for a lakeside dinner of trout, *coq au vin* or shrimps in La Morvandelle. If it is available, try *vin de noix*, a liqueur made from walnuts, red wine, sugar and brandy. *Jambon du Morvan* (home-cured ham) features on most local menus. Pork was once the only meat available throughout the year. Even today, the family pig-killing is a November and February ritual.

Lac de Pannecière, the largest lake, is enticingly rural, especially on the left bank. It feeds into the Canal du Nivernais. Here, fishermen are more in evidence than wind-surfers and sailors. To enjoy locally-caught trout, pike and pike-perch visit **Chaumard**, the village overlooking the lake. The most charming and welcoming restaurant is Les Vouas, run by an ecologist deeply committed to protecting the Morvan.

The breeding of pigs, sheep and cattle ensures that the quality of local meat is good, though beef is not as tender as on

Kayak trip.

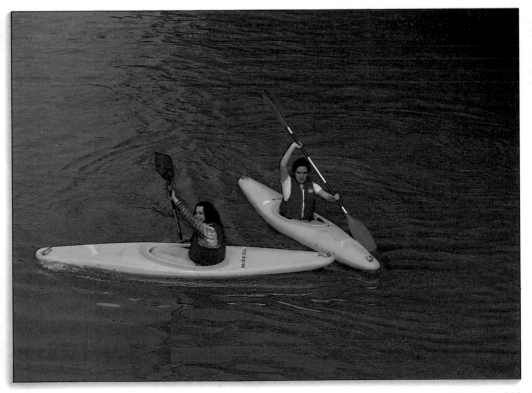

the richer Nivernais plains. In the Morvan, rye, buckwheat and potatoes are the staple fare. Traditional dishes include *crapiaux*, bacon-filled *crêpes* and *galette aux treuffes*, a pancake made with potatoes, eggs and cheese. *Meurette de l'Agnès de Civry*, made with onions, bacon and beans, is stewed with eggs and a litre of red wine. Other simple dishes are *soupe aux choux* (cabbage soup), wild mushroom omelette, and duck stuffed with chestnuts.

Before leaving Chaumard, notice the church with a Romanesque belltower and the closed village school, proof of rural depopulation. As a Resistance centre Chaumard was encircled by German soldiers in 1944 and lost most of the village in the ensuing attack. The drive up to Planchez passes several hamlets with traditional houses, including a thatched cottage. In summer, there are energetic folklore displays.

A winding road leads south to **Château-Chinon**. Its November fair was once a medieval labour exchange for farmers turned foresters. Since then,

Mitterrand has transformed his town, endowing it with worthy socialist facilities, including exceptionally ugly schools and hospitals. Despite its powerful patron, Château-Chinon is unremarkable, a medieval citadel mangled by modernity. Nonetheless, the hilly setting is appealing, with several wooded walks radiating from the ruined fortifications. The local folklore museum has just been well-restored but the star vehicle is the **Musée du Septennat**, housing the president's official gifts.

On leaving for Autun, say farewell to Mitterrand in the modest hotel that was his local home before the Elysée Palace. Au Vieux Morvan contains a couple of signed presidential photographs in the bar and, in the noted restaurant, the staff are only too happy to gossip about "Tonton". From here, a circuitous route takes in a hamlet, gorge and Gallic shrine before turning east towards Autun. **Arleuf** is a typical village tucked into the wooded mountains. Until the 20th century, traditional stone cottages were white-washed, thatched

A quiet pool near Mt Beauvais.

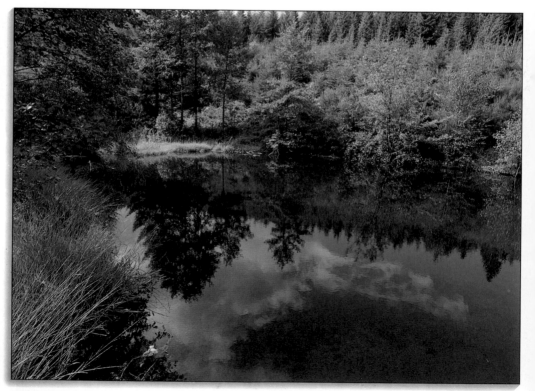

and simple, consisting of a living-room with possibly a bedroom and cellar. Attached was a barn and stables. Nowadays, granite cottages are still low-roofed but are tiled. In rough terrain, log cabins with sloping slate roofs and protective stone walls are common. The piles of firewood outside most houses reflect the triumph of the people over the landowners in Revolutionary times: the *Morvandiaux* won the right to exploit the forests without hindrance. Although personal property ownership has now filtered down to this socialist citadel, the locals still raid "their" forests for wood, mushrooms and game.

This area once boasted the region's most romantic occupation: *la galvache*. The word is a corruption of *voyage*, referring to the journeys made by carters as far afield as Flanders. Known as Morvan's cowboys, these nomadic errand boys delivered minerals, ironwork, tools and even crops. After a grand village farewell on May Day, the carters set off with loads pulled by piebald cows. They only returned for the

Anost fair on 1 December, a fair still held today, 70 years after the last cowboy hung up his boots. However, folklore groups at Château-Chinon keep alive the memory of the *galvachers* in their festivals. The atmosphere and country music faintly recalls a hot day in Nashville.

Until recently, migration was a way of life in the Morvan. Farmers and woodcutters were often away for months while thousands of peasant girls worked as maids or wet-nurses in Paris. These *nourrices morvandelles* have a lot to answer for. In the 19th century, they were prized by Parisians and, after acting as wet-nurses, stayed on as nannies and maids. Their trips back to the Morvan were an economic lifeline, also bringing city fashion and culture to a rural community. In addition, Parisian babies, both working-class orphans and children from *bourgeois* or noble families, were brought up in the Morvan. Known as *les Petits-Paris*, these children established firm ties in the region and later returned, often as owners of

South Morvan.

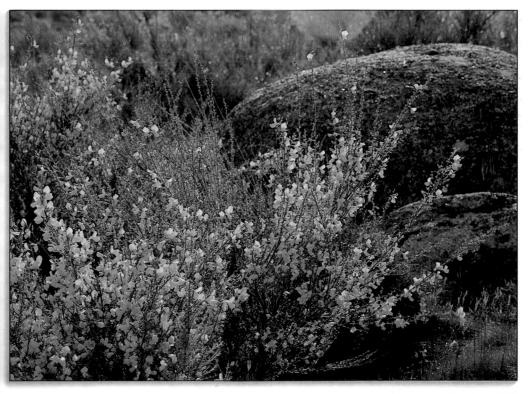

résidences secondaires. It is no surprise that a third of all houses here are second homes and, in lakeside resorts, the figure rises to 80 percent.

Just east of Arleuf lie the **Gorges de la Canche**, the most scenic valley in the Morvan. While hardly the Grand Canyon, the gorge is striking. The steep sides are covered in lindens, sycamores and witch-elms. Picturesque waterfalls tumble from the top and light plays on the mauve, brown and green rocks. A short but tortuous drive south leads to **Mont Beuvray** and the mountain once inhabited by the Gauls. A path winds through the beech forest to the summit. To bathe in a brooding Celtic atmosphere, walk up the last stretch alone.

Virtually nothing remains of **Bibracte**, the settlement controlled by the Eduens (Aedui) tribe. In 52 BC the leaders of the Gallic tribes gathered here to elect Vercingétorix as leader in a doomed attempt to stave off the Roman conquest. But the Gauls were defeated at Alésia and Bibracte was deserted on Roman orders. The demoralised farmers and artisans moved to the plains, an area more easily controlled by Rome. Augustodunum (Autun) was created to contain the warring tribes and eclipse the splendour of Bibracte. Expect few visible remains except for some ramparts, and a mysterious atmosphere. Beware of denigrating Gaul: even the sturdiest farmers become misty-eyed over folk memories of Vercingétorix's last stand.

The drive to **Autun** passes woods, streams and scattered farms. As the forests dwindle and farms seem more prosperous, defeated Gaul gives way to victorious Rome. Autun is not only the Roman heart of Burgundy but also the most Roman city north of Nîmes and Arles. As Augustodunum, it controlled the Agrippa Way, the trade route linking Lyon and Boulogne. The Roman city proffered both an olive branch and a poisoned chalice to the Gauls. *Pax romana* swept in new gods and resident legions. As a window on Rome, it commanded monumental architecture and the greatest Greek scholars.

Roman amphitheatre, Autun.

Autun is the richest yet strangest town in the region. As a cultural tool of Rome, Autun literally re-educated the Gauls, with the creation of a noted Graeco-Roman academy.

Rather like today's *Grandes Écoles*, it formed the French administrative élite for generations. Less a melting-pot than a multi-layered archaeological site, Autun offers Roman, Roman-esque, late medieval and classical moods. In the 16th century, Autun was second only to Dijon in importance, with a powerful bishopric. Even then, Autun was referred to as a fusion of Gallo-Roman and Burgundian races.

Roman Autun borders and occasion-ally overlaps the medieval city. Outside the medieval boundaries, the lunar landscape owes as much to quarrying as to the Romans. Early industrial hillocks and mounds merge with current ar-chaeological digs.

Roman architects had a gift for select-ing bold sites. In particular, **Porte d'Arroux** forms a beguiling silhouette when seen from the riverside below.

Built in the 1st century, this gateway is the most authentic, with four sculpted arcades and the Corinthian columns that inspired Cluny. **Porte St-André**, a 4th-century gateway, embodies Roman monumentality in its arcaded grandeur and stern symmetry. Designed with traffic control in mind, it has two low arches for pedestrians and two higher arches for chariots. A Roman sense of proportion is also present in the **Temple de Janus**, an isolated sanctuary to an unknown deity.

The picturesque **ramparts** trace the path of Roman walls while adjoining blind alleys incorporate Roman brick-work. Only the view is more recent: this rolling countryside was formerly dotted with temples. The ruined **Roman thea-tre** once resounded to the acclaim of 15,000 spectators. But to see Roman Autun rise from the ashes, attend Augustodunum, a summer spectacle held in the Roman theatre. Valiant Gauls, Roman legions and chariot races are presented by 600 eager citizens. Nowadays, however, Burgundian

Autun cathedral, tympanum.

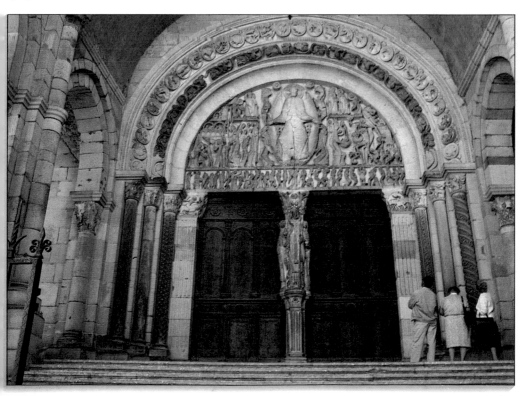

verve tends to triumph over a Roman sense of proportion.

The Romanesque **Cathedral**, built to house the relics of St Lazarus, is influenced by Cluny and Paray-le-Monial. Yet it transcends comparisons thanks to the genius of Gislebertus d'Autun, one of the greatest sculptors of the age. His tympanum is a work of soulful artistry, rivalling Vézelay. This Last Judgement presents the saved and the damned, interweaving biblical stories with fables. André Malraux described it as a "Romanesque Cézanne". Yet this masterpiece was plastered over in the 18th century and returned to its former glory only in 1948. On the lintel, giant pincers clutch the throat of a damned soul while an adulterous woman has her breasts devoured by serpents.

Abbé Denis Grivot has devoted 30 years of his life to watching over the cathedral, rescuing and deciphering the statuary. As *the* authority on Romanesque churches, Grivot is wary of expressing his preference: "Vézelay is more majestic but Autun's sculptures are remarkable, a composite canvas of the medieval mind." Many of the finest sculptures are in the chapter house; an intense Hanging of Judas, a dramatic Flight from Egypt and the wise peacock, symbol of eternal life. The sculptor's sense of fun is apparent in the portrayal of the Three Wise Men asleep in bed, too tired to take off their crowns.

Overlooking the Episcopal Palace is the **Musée Rolin**, one of the most appealing museums in Burgundy. It occupies a 15th-century *hôtel* that once belonged to Nicolas Rolin, the patron forever linked to the Hospices de Beaune. The museum reflects Autun's eclectic past, from Etruscan-style amulets to Gallo-Roman mosaics, expressive Romanesque statuary and vibrant Burgundian oil paintings. The pagan statuary, particularly the magician with a wand, springs from the same impulsion as the surreal cathedral carvings. As for the surprisingly earthy Roman mosaics, the finest is the *Taureau Marin*, an aquatic bull forming part of a tribute to Neptune. Beside it, bathed in

Quiet streets of Autun; clustered rooftops, Autun.

sunlight, is a translucent Gallo-Roman *Tête de Vénus*, carved out of marble.

The most human Romanesque statue is a frank and knowing Eve whose explicit sensuality caused her expulsion from Paradise and, in the 18th century, from the cathedral. Clutching an apple from the serpent's tree, Eve sprawls seductively, showing a gleeful lack of contrition for a fallen woman. The medieval paintings honour Burgundy's Flemish inheritance, with scenes redolent of the golden age of Bruges. But the intimacy, warm colours, expressive faces and realistic landscape belong to a Burgundian sensibility.

The cool elegance of the classical quarter contrasts with the patchwork nature of medieval Autun. Now the commercial centre, it still has a number of grand stone buildings, from an over-restored *mairie* to a baroque Jesuit church, and the Lycée Militaire, a military academy attended by Napoleon. Yet Place du Champ-de-Mars, built by Louis XIV, is a testament to the independent-minded citizens. The square is assymmetrical thanks to the locals' refusal to demolish homes; a gabled inn is a throwback to the late Middle Ages.

To appreciate the texture of Autun, revisit the cathedral. The **belltower** enjoys the most panoramic view in the region. It is worth climbing the steep, dimly-lit staircase to the top of the tower. Below stretches a panoply of glinting fish-scale roofs, intimate medieval courtyards and Roman remains. Above all, there is a realisation that the great Roman city has shrunk to its medieval frontiers, a rusty urban hub encircled by a green swathe beyond. Like an insular Tuscan hill-top town, it defies modernity.

From Autun or Château-Chinon take the D978 across the Morvan to Nevers. En route, Morvan's tiny parcels of land give way to large estates on the prairies. Unsurprisingly, Morvan's more entrepreneurial peasants flocked here after 1918. This is farmland fit for the majestic Charolais cattle and also the gateway to the **Nivernais**, a natural region with low-key charm. The flat countryside

Châtillon-en-Bazois.

stretches all the way to the sandbanks of the River Loire. **Châtillon-en-Bazois**, on the D978, spans both the River Aron and the Nivernais Canal, providing a large canal centre, overlooked by its 16th-century château. Historically, the Nivernais has the distinction of never belonging to the French crown. Even so, this ancient duchy has royal links, providing several Polish queens. This cosmopolitan duchy belonged, in turn, to Rome, Flanders, Burgundy, the Rhineland and Italy.

Nevers, the capital, reached its apogee in the 16th century. By marriage to Henriette de Clèves, Duchess of Nevers, Ludovico Gonzaga brought Italian influence to the region. In fact, Gonzaga's Renaissance Palais Ducal is often called the first Loire château. Nevers was then at the hub of north-south trade routes, a city renowned for its cattle and craftsmanship. It was thanks to the Gonzaga dynasty that Nevers developed its most prestigious industry, faïence.

By the 19th century, the pottery industry and the city had fallen into decline. Nevers recovered enough to control the regional railway network, the reason the British bombed the town in July 1944. *Les Anglais* are blamed for the damaged cathedral and gutted town centre. Yet muddled town planning and insensitive restoration are also culprits.

Nevers and the Nivernais re-joined Burgundy only in 1956 so there is no great attachment to this administrative region. Geography has compounded the historical divide: the humble Morvan separates both regions; poor east-west communications mean that Nevers has rarely sought approval from its masters in Dijon. Instead, it looks directly north to the Loire Valley and Paris or south to Clermont Ferrand and the Massif Central.

Nevers shares Dijon's traditional condescension towards the impoverished Morvan. Yet this is not translated into votes. Nevers, in keeping with the region, is a left-wing bastion run by Pierre Bérégovoy, the city's mayor and France's Prime Minister. According to

Nevers from the Loire.

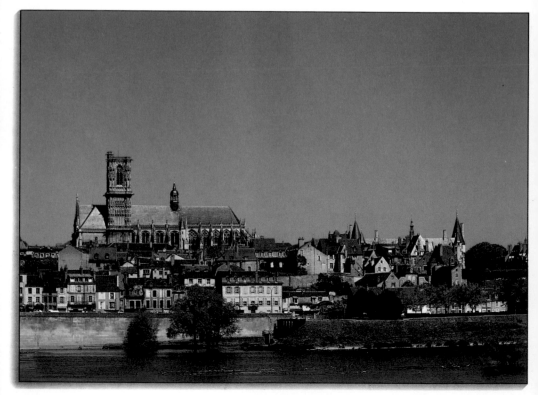

Béregovoy, Nevers's greatest asset is its *savoir-faire*, a provincial sophistication based on a mixture of past grandeur and pretension. In humdrum terms, this translates into excellent shops, hearty cuisine, lush countryside and scenic waterways. Nevers is worth visiting but Charité-sur-Loire makes a more intimate base.

Nevers is an unreconciled hotchpotch of districts. In the west, the pottery manufacturing district is shabby but intriguing. The adjacent cathedral quarter is only half-heartedly restored. The heart of the town is cold: a grandiose square overlooked by the ducal palace and town hall. The lively pedestrianised commercial quarter lies to the east. The *quartier des faïenciers*, the **pottery district**, nestles between the ramparts and the river. The **ramparts walk** is a chance to sense Nevers as it was before the British bombing. Built into the 11th-century fortifications are several well-preserved towers, of which the crenellated Porte de Croux is the finest. From the ramparts are views

of the Loire and the abbey's ruined cloisters. (From the tourist office, pick up a detailed map showing the former porcelain manufacturers.)

Follow Rue des Jacobins to the musty **cathedral quarter**, dominated by St-Cyr Cathedral. This curious church embraces every architectural style, from Romanesque to Rhineland. The profusion of turrets suggest temporal not religious power, a relic of the old dukedom. A flamboyant Gothic tower is laden with saints and griffons. Inside, a chilly atmosphere prevails, from the dark nave to the garish modern windows. More welcoming are the antiques shops clustered in the narrow alleys.

L'Esplanade, the next big square, boasts the classical Hôtel de Ville and Renaissance **Palais Ducal**. The mullioned windows and elegant lines recall the great Loire châteaux but the urban setting echoes Bruges, a city with a richer Burgundian heritage. Even on a dull day, the octagonal turrets and sculpted cherubs glisten. Depending on taste, the golden stone facade is over-

FRENCH FAIENCE

Nevers, like Sèvres, is a household name for fine chinaware. As the cradle of French faïence, it has produced pottery since the 16th century. Yet while Sèvres restricted itself to aristocratic designs, Nevers reflects the full spectrum of Burgundian tastes. In passing, faïence portrays the history of France in miniature, from the Ancien Régime to the Revolution.

Decorative flasks depict the early wine brotherhoods while statuettes of saints symbolise the Wars of Religion. The storming of the Bastille is immortalised in Revolutionary pieces and, in 1783, the first balloon ascent is celebrated in pictorial plates. Then as now, the faïence factories were on the River Loire for easy shipment of materials and pottery. The techniques were imported from Faenza, the Italian ceramics centre with similar soil. In 1566 Augustin Conrade established a French *faïencerie* with Julio Gambin from Faenza. Their elegant style became a model for later craftsmen. While the busy Faenza designs were characterised

by a horror of empty space, Nevers erred on the side of simplicity. Most pieces feature a blue wavy background, inspired by the River Loire, still a stylistic motif.

The golden age of faïence lasted from 1630 to 1730. As China opened up to the West, French potters succumbed to Orientalism. Ming vases inspired ethereal scenes of weeping willows, waterfalls, lotus flowers. Bathed in violet tints, the designs idealised court life. Yet even here Nevers was eclectic, borrowing whimsical cherry blossom scenes from Japan and a shade of deep blue from Persian silk screens. The repertoire of pieces included vases, decorative plates, screens, spice boxes and cherubs.

In the 19th century, there was competition from *porcelaine anglaise*, notably Wedgwood. Napoleon, like the people, preferred porcelain; Sèvres, Saumur and Rouen were happy to oblige. In Nevers, porcelain factories were created but to no avail: the town's future lay in functional white chinaware. Only in 1875 was there a revival of *faïence decorative*, the imaginative creations that typify the town.

Du Bout du Monde, founded in 1648, is the oldest of the *faïenceries* and is still situated by the medieval town gate. The small factory has been in the Montagnon family for five generations. In 1875 Antoine Montagnon relaunched *production artistique*, a reaction against utilitarian chinaware.

Today, Gérard Montagnon uses the same red clay amd white marl as did his 16th-century forebears. Methods are equally traditional and labour-intensive. After a year stored in a damp cellar, the clay is shaped by a potter and left to dry. The creations are then fired at 980°F (530°C), a process called biscuit after the colour of the hot clay. The glazing methods are secret: the cobalt blue sheen is the envy of rivals. The pieces are painted and decorated over the glaze before a second firing at 940°F fixes the designs.

The soft colours have a metallic base: lead and pewter make white; iron turns red, manganese violet or black, antimony yellow, and copper green. Every piece is unique: replicas of a Loire château, an antique Chinese vase, or a family heirloom. Workaday pieces may depict a city seal, a bourgeois wedding scene, a politician's portrait or a child's first communion. Now, as always, faïence is a mirror of the times. ■

Du Bout du Monde faïence workshop.

restored or a model of harmony. The **commercial district** begins on the far side of the square and combines Flemish gables and modern shop-fronts. Visitors in search of antiques, jewellery, china and chocolate could do far worse. At the end of the pedestrianised area is Nevers' loveliest church, **St-Étienne**, a fusion of Burgundian and Auvergnat Romanesque. According to Denis Grivot of Autun, the harmony of the Byzantine domes makes St-Étienne unique. Founded by a 7th-century Irish monk, the church became a Cluniac priory in the 11th century. The bee-hive domes reveal high windows and an austerity softened by the luminous sculpted capitals. By contrast, a visit to the **Couvent St-Gildard** is an unsettling spiritual experience.

The site is a homage to Saint Bernadette. The Virgin appeared 18 times in Lourdes to Bernadette Soubirous, convincing the young girl of her calling. She took her vows in 1866 and stayed in this convent until her death at the age of 35. Her body was discovered intact 30 years later and her presence still attracts 500,000 pilgrims a year, mostly Irish, Italian and Spanish. Despite a tasteless recreation of the Lourdes grotto, Bernadette's waxy face looks eerily real. She was allegedly tormented by an envious Mother Superior but rose above cruelty and sickness. With a humility tinged with resignation, she said: "The Virgin has used me like a broom. When the work is done, the broom is abandoned."

If the cloistered atmosphere is oppressive, stroll down to the **Quai des Mariners**, an old fishermen's path by the Loire. A bracing walk soon prompts thoughts of gastronomic shrines. Apart from *Charolais à la crème*, succulent beef, dishes are inspired by the Loire. Fish specialities include *carpe à la Nivernaise, friture de la Loire* and salmon cooked in local Pouilly-Fumé wine. Auberge de la Porte du Croux is the top gourmet restaurant while Les Voûtes boasts elegant cuisine in a Romanesque crypt.

Nevers is also a magnet for those with a sweet tooth. On his visit in 1862,

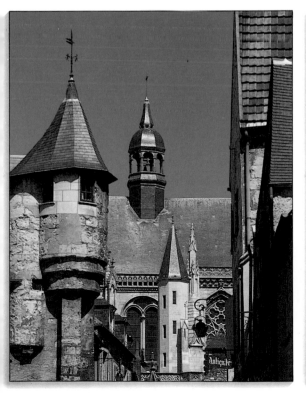

Nevers old town; Nevers shopping street.

Napoleon III fell in love with *nougatine* and ordered enough for the whole imperial court. It is available from the original maker, Confiserie Edé. *Négus* rivals *nougatine* in pedigree; in 1902 this "racist" chocolate was created to complement the skin tones of Négus, visiting Emperor of Abyssinia. The Ethiopian empire may have melted away but Négus remains in a shop akin to *One Thousand and One Nights* on acid.

The journey north is a gastronomic trail seen through a vinous haze. Although mostly grown in Burgundy, these wines are Loire *appellations*, thanks to the climate and soil. From Nevers, follow the Loire downstream to **La Charité-sur-Loire**, the most entrancing town on this stretch of river. This journey hugs the waterways and the borders, with Burgundy on the east bank and the Cher over the water. The river once carried porcelain, enamel, stone and firewood to Paris. Now, the decorative Loire runs aground on its pale sandbanks while the Canal Latéral makes do with idle pleasure barges.

Poplars and placid cattle fade into this soporific scene, a backwater in every sense. Seen from the 16th-century bridge, La Charité looks much as it did in medieval times. With the only bridge between Nevers and Gien until the 17th century, this fortified town commanded the Loire trade route. La Charité was conquered by the English in the Hundred Years' War and witnessed Joan of Arc's abortive siege. But its original fame stems from the Cluniac priory.

La Charité was one of only five priories honoured with the title of *fille aînée de Cluny*. By the 15th century it was promoted to *première fille* and, as a major Cluniac abbey, controlled 400 monasteries in England, France and Italy. After being pillaged by Protestants, the town later changed its colours to become a Protestant stronghold. La Charité's gentle decline makes it a sleepy tourist centre.

A Gothic gateway leads to **Église Notre Dame**, the priory's soul. Despite clumsy restoration, the church is Romanesque in spirit. The tympanum

Charité-sur-Loire ramparts.

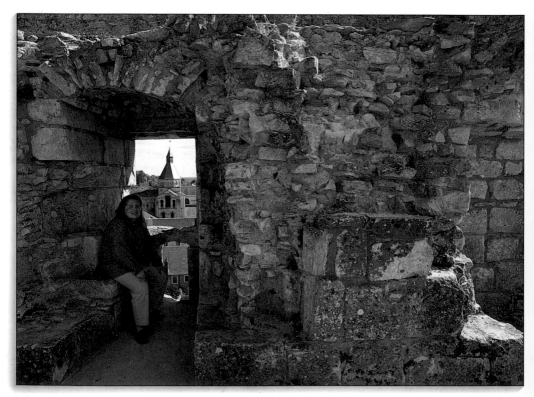

shows Christ blessing the Cluniac Order, a prelude to the airy grandeur within. The luminous transept and choir, decorated with richly-sculpted capitals, represent the confidence of Cluny's sway. Rough flagstones and vivid red and yellow stained-glass windows do not detract from the mood. Outside, the Romanesque belltower is being restored and excavations are taking place on Square des Bénédictins, behind the church. Even so, the belltower, chapter house, refectory and kitchens are partly visible.

From the front of the church, follow signs to **Promenade des Remparts**. En route, notice the converted abbey outbuildings, especially the prior's lodge and an octagonal tower. Walk up the grassy bank to the fortifications, restored after the English invasion. After climbing up to the Tour de Cuffy, cross a footbridge to the second watchtower. From here, the abbey's delicate proportions fall into place, framed by the sky and the Loire. The Grande Rue, reached by a quaint passage beside the church, is dotted with period houses. Before leaving, sip a glass of Pouilly-Fumé at the *auberge* on Place des Pêchcurs, the atmospheric church courtyard.

Pouilly-sur-Loire, the next town north, is famed for its dry white wines, introduced by the Benedictines. Until phylloxera devastated the region, vineyards stretched from here to Orléans. Today's wine estates are smaller but still slope down to the water's edge. Pouilly-Fumé and Blanc-Fumé, grown from the Sauvignon Blanc grape, are some of the best dry white wines in France. Connoisseurs can scent asparagus, nettles, caramel, roasted coffee beans and gunflint. After a *dégustation* at De Ladoucette, sample the wine with Loire fish in Le Coq Hardi, a riverside restaurant. Salmon, pike-perch or *matelote d'anguille* are natural choices.

On the other side of the Loire is **Sancerre**, Pouilly's arch-rival. Although not technically Burgundy, Sancerre is etched in the vinous landscape. At festivals, the towns' competing wine confraternities meet on the bridge over the Loire and chant: "*Eau nous divise,*

vin nous unit" (water divides us, wine unites us).

Once back in Burgundy, continue downriver to **Cosne-sur-Loire**, a busy market town overspilling its medieval ramparts and ruined château. After looking at local ceramics, stroll down to the river and walk along the *levées*, the Loire's raised banks. From here, it is only a short drive north to **La Puisaye**, the watery region celebrated by Colette. But to return to mainstream Burgundy, simply follow the Loire upstream to Decize. One scenic route explores a grand château and priory southeast of Nevers. The other side of the Canal Latéral is **Apremont-sur-Allier**, the finest château in the region. The medieval village lies on the banks of the river Allier and at its heart is the Anglo-Burgundian fortress. The château, belonging to the Schneider steel magnates, has been in the family for 300 years. The grounds are part wild and wooded, part romantically English.

St-Pierre-le-Moûtier, just south of Apremont, is a medieval walled town

St-Pierre-le-Moûtier.

built around a Benedictine priory. The French know it as Joan of Arc's last victory against the English. (Soon after the battle here in 1429, Joan was caught at Compiègne.) The atmospheric medieval towers are matched by a ruined lepers' hospital, converted mills and Renaissance houses.

The chief treasure is St-Pierre, a Romanesque church with a fine sculpted tympanum. Inside, the capitals represent vivid scenes, from admonitory griffons and biblical battles to Cluniac musical notes and dancing bears.

East of St-Pierre is **Decize**, a medieval town also noted for its Benedictine priory, perched on a rocky spur. The craggy old town centre clings to an island in the Loire. Its former defensive function is clear from the moats, circular towers and tumbledown battlements. The priory's Romanesque chapel was recently used as a cinema but is now a peaceful prelude to attractive 17th-century cloisters. Before leaving Decize, visit St-Aré, a partly Romanesque church with a remarkable double Merovingian crypt. From Decize, beat a path back to the heart of Burgundy: Paray-le-Monial and Cluny lie across the rich Charolais plains to the southeast, Dijon and the Côte d'Or further north.

When Henri Vincenot praised Burgundy as *"une civilisation lente"*, he was thinking of his homeland. Here, rivers and speech run slowly; the people appear unruffled, even placid.

Yet these were the people who fought hardest for the Resistance. Insofar as any region explains the early Burgundian heritage, the Nièvre does so. The blend of valiant Gauls, single-minded Romans and rugged Morvan peasants is the darker side of the Burgundian character. But the tough heart of the Morvan will always lose out to the hearty Burgundian wine-belt. The Nièvre suffers from depopulation, from the mountainous Morvan to the lush Loire prairies. Locals joke that even François Mitterrand has deserted them to become president in Paris.

Right, herding the goats.

DIJON

Kir and mustard are what most people associate with **Dijon** when they stop for a hurried night on their journey to the south of France or ignore it completely as they speed past. But if Dijon is often bypassed by tourists it may well be that the Dijonnais themselves are quite happy with this arrangement.

Although there is plenty of fine art and architecture to see, Dijon's appeal lies as much in its typicality. "If you wanted to choose a city to illustrate generic France, you could do much worse than Dijon," advises the travel writer Jan Morris, calling it "one of those grand old middle-sized cities of France that seem largely impervious to fashion".

Henry Miller had a less charitable opinion of Dijon, building up his short stay there as a teacher in 1932 as a humorous passage in *Tropic of Cancer* (though he and his wife, June, had enjoyed Dijon well enough when they bicycled through in the summer of 1928): "Stepping off the train I knew immediately that I had made a fatal mistake. The Lycée was a little distance from the station; I walked down the main street in the early dusk of winter, feeling my way towards my destination. A light snow was falling, the trees sparkled with frost. Passed a couple of huge, empty cafés that looked like dismal waiting-rooms. Silent, empty gloom – that's how it impressed me. A hopeless, jerk-water town where mustard is turned out in carload lots, in vats and tuns and barrels and pots and cute-looking little jars."

While there may be more to Dijon than Kir and mustard, it would be a pity to leave without sampling its famous products. Above all Dijon is a city that is serious about its food, claiming in age-old competition with Lyon to be the gastronomical capital of France.

Of all its recent visitors, the legendary American food writer M.F.K. Fisher captures best the atmosphere of Dijon and the supreme importance granted to food. In her book *Long Ago in France*, she evokes the smells, sights and tastes of Dijon in the 1930s, sampling vast cartwheel apple tarts, fresh plump snails, carefully nurtured for weeks in their crates, and eating in legendary restaurants like Racouchot's Trois Faisans, so famous for its cellar that diners would save for weeks beforehand to sample it.

Of that occasion, Fisher wrote: "I know that never since have I eaten so much... But that night the kind ghosts of Lucullus and Brillat-Savarin as as well as Rabelais and a hundred others stepped into ease our adventurous bellies and a soothe our tongues."

Touring Dijon's wonderful food shops and sampling its famous restaurants is certainly as good a way as any to theme a visit to the town and helps to leaven its grand but sometimes overwhelming architectural heritage.

More than anything apart from food, visiting Dijon means architecture and it is at the Palais des Ducs that the lightning-stop tourist coaches first unload their visitors. It is, however, essential to appreciate the history of the town before attempting to understand its role and the artistic significance of its treasures. Today Dijon, the capital of Burgundy, has a population of 150,000 and benefits as it has always done from its position as a crossroads of Europe, and an important conjunction of roads and railway routes. The coming of the railway meant major expansion for the town in the 19th century, consolidated recently by its successful lobbying for a TGV stop.

It is an important airforce base, and a centre for scientific research and higher education. A number of *Grandes Écoles* and the famous University of Burgundy contribute to Dijon's role as the cultural capital of Burgundy. The suburbs accommodate a range of industries including foods, pharmaceutical products, optical instruments, machine tools, light planes and automotive parts, but the absence of heavy industry means the area is relatively unpolluted.

Dijon indeed is very proud of its environmental progress (it even boasts the first "scenic" graveyard) and there are a number of landscaped parks just outside the town, including an artificial lake, Lac Kir, created by Canon Kir, who was mayor of the city for 22 years from 1946 to 1968. He is perhaps most famous for his now ubiquitous cocktail, a mixture of blackcurrant liqueur, a Dijon speciality, with white wine – preferably Burgundian aligoté. *Vin blanc cassis* had always been a traditional Burgundian apéritif and the mayor popularised it by serving it at official city receptions.

History: Dijon is an ancient city. It began as a Roman *castrum*, Divio, although scant evidence remains. Part of the Roman wall is visible in the crypt of St-Étienne, now the Chamber of Commerce (to see it, enquiries must be made at the Museé des Beaux Arts). There are carvings in the archaeological museum, and the limits of the original Roman town are indicated on the buildings. Dijon was at the crossroads of many trade routes, including pewter, amber and tin, and the exotic spices that were

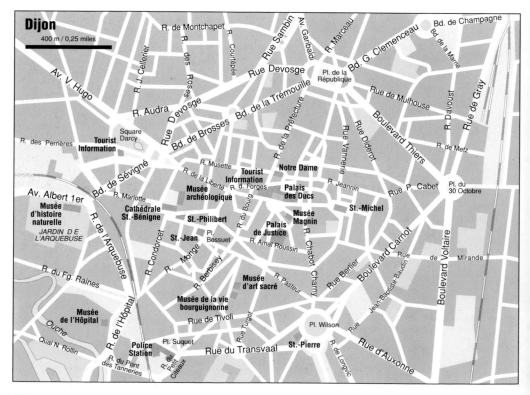

brought here resulted in the production of specialities like mustard and *pain d'épices*.

Dijon was the capital of what was the Kingdom of Burgundy in the 5th century but subsequently became part of Charlemagne's vast empire. It derived some importance at this time from the tomb of St Bénigne, who was responsible for converting Burgundy to Christianity. Pilgrims began to arrive and the Benedictines built an abbey in the 11th century; little remains of the original building but the superb Romanesque crypt of **St-Bénigne** can be visited. It is a good place to start a tour of the oldest part of Dijon and is one of the most interesting things to see there.

After St Bénigne's martyrdom, his tomb became the centre of an extraordinary cult. The original basilica was replaced by a great monastery, little of which now remains except the monks' dormitory and the crypt and Romanesque doorway of the original abbey church. The Revolutionaries who devastated so much of Dijon cannot be held responsible for all the destruction, however, since the original Romanesque abbey church, which had already been repaired several times, finally collapsed in 1272, leaving only its magnificent rotunda. Regrettably, the Revolutionaries demolished the two storeys above ground but the rubble completely filled the crypt and happily preserved it. It was rediscovered and restored 50 years later. The rotunda is of the greatest interest; built in 1002 by William of Volpiano on the ruins of a previous 6th-century church, it incorporates a mortuary chapel at its east end which dates back to the 6th century, and was originally part of the Gallo-Roman cemetery which extended over the whole area.

When this chapel was built it was above ground but, as in all old cities, the gradual accumulation of refuse over the centuries has raised the ground level and slowly buried it so that it is now completely underground. Excavation has since revealed that the foundations of the Romanesque church remain beneath the present nave, and the current

Dijon's food specialities.

entrance to the rotunda gives access to the crypt and the side aisles with their apsidal chapels and to the place where the remains of the 2nd-century sarcophagus of St Bénigne still lies.

It is a strange, dimly lit maze of closely spaced columns 1,000 years old. The rotunda forms three circles, an inner circle of eight columns, surrounded by a circle of 16 columns and, attached to the circular outer wall, a final circle of 24 columns, two of which are freestanding. Light originally streamed in from the centre which was open to the floors above, ringed with columns and surmounted by a lofty cupola. Some effort of imagination is required to understand what the original pilgrims saw, with light falling from heaven on to the colonnades.

The Gothic building which replaced the collapsed Romanesque church was begun in 1281 and completed 40 years later. It is cold, bare and featureless – built for monks, not the public and so lacking in any ostentatious display. The spire was rebuilt in 1896.

To the north of the cathedral, on the Rue Dr Maret, is the **Archaeological Museum,** housed in the dormitory of the Benedictine abbey of St-Bénigne. The 11th-century cellar, originally the refectory, has short, thick, powerful columns supporting crossed barrel-vaults. It now houses a fine collection of Gallo-Roman sculpture. The ground floor is 13th-century and two rows of slender columns hold beautiful fan vaults. This room contains the famous head of Christ by Claus Sluter originally belonging to the Well of Moses, which can be seen in the Charterhouse of Champmol. There are also two Romanesque tympana taken from the cathedral. In front of the museum is a large quiet lawn with park benches and shady trees. The buildings of the university occupy the rest of the block.

Across from St-Bénigne is the Romanesque church of **St-Philibert**, now deconsecrated and closed because the building is unsafe – sad, since it is the only example of Romanesque in the city. The spire was added in 1513 and sits somewhat uneasily, as do the unfortunate 18th-century side chapels.

It was originally intended for use by novices of the great abbey church and later became the parish church of the neighbourhood, which at that time gave on to vineyards. Excavations carried out in the transept revealed the remains of an early Christian basilica. A pizza restaurant on the south side of the Place St-Bénigne is also housed in a refurbished monastic building.

In the 12th century much of the town was destroyed by fire, and was rebuilt by the Capetian Duke Hugues III with a wall and 18 towers to encompass a much larger area, contributing to Dijon's later reputation as the city of a hundred towers. It was a prosperous period, as evidenced by the church of **Notre Dame** on the Rue de la Chouette. The street is named after the 15th-century *La Chouette*, the little owl carved on an outside pillar of the church, which is supposed to bring wisdom and happiness to those who stroke it.

Notre Dame was begun in 1230 and took only 20 years to complete. It is a **Sambin carving, Palais de Justice.**

masterpiece of 13th-century Gothic, with an amazing facade made up of three ranges of fake gargoyles and slender Italianate columns, the only one of its kind in existence. The front is topped with a mechanical clock, seized as spoils of war by Duke Philip after the Battle of Roosebeck, Flanders, in 1382. The "Jack-o-the-clock" – the Jacquemart – rang the bell alone until the 17th century when he was given a wife. Later, two children came along to help.

There is a huge open porch to the church and the arches above the three doorways were once decorated with more than 180 carved figures depicting the story of the Virgin Mary – considered to be one of the best sets of Gothic sculpture in existence. During the Revolution however, in 1794, a local pharmacist came every day with a ladder and systematically destroyed every one of them. The result is ugly and still shocking, 200 years later. Notre Dame also contains an important 12th-century black Virgin (blackened by the smoke of countless candles) and some finely preserved 13th-century stained glass.

The 14th century was really the heyday of Dijon with the rise of the Grand Dukes who established a glittering court here and made Dijon one of the most important towns of medieval Europe. The tower of Philip the Bold, the **Tour de Bar**, named after René of Anjou, Duc de Bar, its most illustrious prisoner, can still be seen, and is the oldest part of the vast ensemble of the Palais. Next to it is the beautiful 16th-century Bellegarde covered staircase.

Like his elder brother, Jean, Duc de Berry (of the *Très Riches Heures*), Philip was a great patron of the arts, commissioning illuminated manuscripts and tapestries, as well as building and furnishing many sumptuous residences in Flanders, Paris and Burgundy. Philip the Bold also built the Chartreuse de Champmol as a necropolis for his family, and commissioned the brilliant Flemish sculptor, Claus Sluter, to decorate the charterhouse chapel and his own funeral monument, now in the Musée des Beaux Arts.

Hôtel de Vogüé; Maison Millière, Rue de la Chouette.

COOKING FOR THE DUKES

The Valois dukes took food and drink so seriously that one need look no further for the origins of Dijon's reputation as a culinary capital of France. So seriously, indeed, that meals took on the aura of religious ceremonies, with hand-held torches escorting dishes to the duke's table and pointed allusions to the sacramental properties of bread and wine.

The most senior state officials had seemingly menial roles at table. The Grand Master of the Household, whose normal duties were advising on matters of justice and war, was the duke's waiter. On state occasions he led the duke into the dining-hall, a baton held high. The First Master, his immediate subordinate, tasted the duke's food for poison. The wine, too, was tested with a horn which hung by a chain from the duke's silver cup. The officer who carried the duke's pennant into battle and stayed close to him was, at meal-times, in charge of carving.

Four full-time officials, each with a staff of about 50, were responsible for food and

drink. Two of these, the *escuiers de cuisine*, were "kitchen squires" who were given an annual budget to cover the cost of meat, fish and other necessities. The *escuiers* were supervisors; the supremo in the kitchen was, unsurprisingly, the head cook.

The presiding cook commanded operations from a tall chair placed between the serving table and chimney, with a long-handled wooden ladle used equally to taste soups and sauces and to administer summary judgements in kitchen arguments. He was personally responsible for the security of the spice cabinet. When word was received that the duke wished to eat, the cook changed into clean clothes, hung a napkin over his right shoulder and went round tasting everything before it left the kitchen. If it was a very special dish, the cook might present it to the duke personally, in which case he was entitled to help himself to a drink from the sideboard and stand around to gauge the reaction and to receive compliments.

There was a strict division of labour within the kitchen. Unpaid apprentices plucked birds and cleaned fish; roasts, soups and sauces all had their respective experts. Lowest in the pecking order were boys who when not running errands kept the spits turning. One specialist, not strictly speaking a member of the kitchen staff, was the court fruiterer. By a logic which said that fruit came from flowers and flowers nourished bees, the fruiterer was responsible for the supply of wax and candles. The number of candles needed to illuminate the palace was enormous, so the fruiterer alone had a staff of eight.

Records show that the palace regularly consumed about 130,000 gallons (500,000 litres) of wine a year, and in some years double that quantity. There were many mouths to feed in the palace – about 18 aristocrats and their families were more or less permanent residents – but, even so, such quantities can only be explained by widespread court largesse. It seems a fair amount of wine was taken with meals because a chronicler notes with apparent distaste that "Wine carries in itself more greediness than any dish served." As it was thought unseemly for the duke to call out for more wine, an *eschanson* stood in front of him and forestalled any embarrassment by keeping his glass permanently topped up. ■

Banquet scene from the *Très Riches Heures du Duc de Berry*.

Philip the Good, grandson of Philip the Bold, was responsible for building a new palace in the 1430s. His vast **Ducal Kitchens** are particularly spectacular; six giant fireplaces give a good indication of the scale of cooking involved. Also extant is the tower named after him, **Tour Philippe le Bon**, which is 150 ft (46 metres) high, and gives a fine view of the burnished tile Burgundian roofs and the church spires of the old city spread below. The main body of the **Palais des Ducs et des États de Bourgogne** was built between 1450 and 1455, although various alterations and additions continued through to the 19th century, reflecting the complicated history of the building. As well as housing the art museum, it still fulfils its civil function as the Hôtel de Ville; the ground floor makes a particularly splendid marriage room and register office.

The duke's living quarters were on the first floor; the magnificent beamed ceilings and huge fireplaces of the Salle des Gardes (Guard Room) are now part of the museum. Many of the private mansions in the area surrounding the palace were also built at this time by wealthy shopkeepers and financiers.

The death of Charles the Bold ended the Valois rule and the independence of Burgundy, which reverted to the crown of France. The Palais des Ducs became the Logis du Roi. There followed troubled times; the town was ravaged by fire, the Black Death, a wine-growers' revolt and invading Swedes. It was not until the mid-17th century that Dijon regained its prosperity, when it became a thriving academic and cultural centre.

The design of the palace was substantially expanded and altered late in the 17th century by Jules Hardouin-Mansart, the architect of Versailles. It took over a century to create the vast classical ensemble we can see today. Mansart was also responsible for the **Place de la Libération,** imposing a graceful semicircle of arcading on the ramshackle medieval buildings that previously surrounded the palace. Today, sadly, the symmetry of the arcading is obscured by a busy car-park,

Facade of Palais des Ducs.

and the aforementioned tourist buses.

Most of the Palais is now given over to the **Musée des Beaux Arts,** with its vast collection of paintings, the most significant in France outside Paris; much of it acquired during the Revolution from the houses of local nobility, churches and monasteries. There are so many artworks (and so many of them undistinguished) that it would be impossible to appreciate everything. It is probably better to concentrate on selected favourites – either specific artists or periods. Look out particularly for the Dutch and Flemish masters, Vasari and works by Manet, Monet and de Staël. Sculpture is stressed, both Sluter, and Dijon-born François Rude, who was responsible for the sculptures on the Arc de Triomphe in Paris. Rude's statue of Joan of Arc graces the stairway.

No art appreciation should blind the visitor to the architectural splendours of the palais itself; in particular the Salle des Gardes, originally the Banqueting Hall, still conveys all the pomp and splendour of the dukes, themselves encased in giant mausoleums in the middle of the huge chamber, overseen by a gallery accessible by a little spiral stairway. The work of Claus Sluter can best be understood by visiting the Moses Well, but the sculptures that decorate these tombs certainly reward study. His skill lies in an amazing ability to draw real tenderness and humour, even movement, from the stone. Also worth noting in the Salles des Gardes is a fine portrait of Philip the Good by Roger van der Weyden and two magnificent carved and gilded retables.

The old town: Above all it is by wandering through the warren of small streets that surround the palace that one can best appreciate life as it was lived in Dijon. It is especially famous for its *hôtel particuliers*, splendid town houses mainly 18th-century, although in most cases it is only the facades that can be observed.

Most have little wooden doors cut into the double doors large enough to allow carriages into the courtyards and often now accommodating the cars of

Salles des Gardes, Palais des Ducs.

today's bourgeoisie. As a general rule if the door is open don't hesitate to peer inside. According to the local tourist office, if the owners objected they would lock the gates. A few places are open at certain times of year for concerts or exhibitions, and for the Dijon Music Festival in June, or the Theatre festival in July and August, since many of the concerts and performances take place in the courtyards.

Although these great houses, evidence of Dijon's past grandeur, are scattered all over the city, it would be a mistake to think that there was much contact between the nobility and the common people. The only reason the rich did not build a smart new neighbourhood of their own was that it was safer to remain within the city walls.

They had to buy up a number of humble dwellings until they had enough land to demolish and build a grand house of their own; this is the reason that some of the ground plans are so oddly shaped. Seeing these great mansions, it is hard not to feel a sympathy for the common people whose work enabled the bourgeoisie to live in luxury and to understand the blind rage of the revolutionaries and the terrible damage they inflicted. The **Rue des Forges** behind the palais was, until the 18th century, the main street of Dijon, named after the goldsmiths, jewellers and knife-makers who had their workshops there. It is now pedestrianised with a series of medieval and Renaissance facades.

The tourist office is here, housed in the **Hôtel Chambellan** at number 34, an astonishing piece of flamboyant Gothic with a stone spiral staircase and wooden galleries round the inner courtyard. The **Maison Milsand** at number 38 was built in 1561 and has an extravagant facade of stone decorations by the celebrated Hugues Sambin, a pupil of Leonardo da Vinci.

Next door, the famous **Hôtel Aubriot**, though originally dating from the late 13th century, was entirely rebuilt in 1908. It has a superb glazed tile roof, best seen from the Rue du Bourg.

The Rue des Forges ends at the **Place**

Tomb carving in Palais des Ducs.

François Rude, a lively square with many outdoor cafés and a charming fountain of a wine-grower crushing grapes in a tub. There is a children's merry-go-round there in the summer months. The 17th-century **Hôtel Lantin** on the charmingly named **Rue des Bons Enfants,** houses the **Magnin Museum**, which has a collection of paintings but is worth visiting mainly for its period furniture, giving a very good idea of the elegant life lived in 17th-century Dijon.

Around the corner, the **Palais de Justice**, the former Burgundian Parliament, should be visited. On your way in, look at the doors which were made by Hugues Sambin (actually these are a copy, the originals are in the Fine Arts Museum). Four pairs of columns support a Renaissance porch, but only the central part of the building is 16th-century. Inside is a vast lobby with a fine panelled ceiling. Several of the rooms are open including the richly decorated Chambre Dorée.

The **Municipal Library** on Rue de l'École de Droit, is housed in a 16th-century college. Its 17th-century chapel is now the reading room. Among the treasures are 12th-century illuminated manuscripts from the Abbey of Cîteaux. You pass the much altered gatehouse to the old Abbey of St-Étienne as you enter the **Place du Théâtre**. Actually on the Place is the abbey church, now used as the Chamber of Commerce.

The wide **Rue Vaillant** leads to the **Église St-Michel**, a strange piece of flamboyant Gothic on Place St-Michel. The church was built over 200 years, beginning in the 15th century. It has an odd front, with a porch extending beyond the main facade. The porch, much older than the towers which rise above it, is famous for its long frieze of foliage and grotesque decorations on all three doorways, which miraculously survived the Revolution.

From here you can follow the **Rue Vannerie**, which extends north all the way to **Place de la République**. Houses of note include the 18th-century man-

Maison des Cariatides.

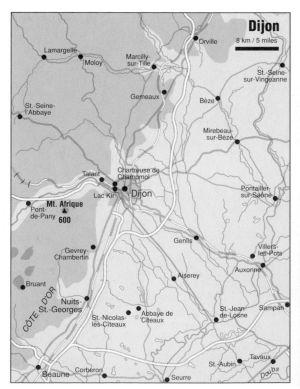

sion at number 41, and a watchtower built by the ubiquitous Hugues Sambin. A particular highlight on Rue Chaudronnerie is the 17th-century **Maison des Cariatides** at number 28, a beautiful stone house with 10 caryatids framing the windows. The ground floor arches were originally open.

The **Rue Verrerie** is famous for its concentration of half-timbered houses and wood carvings. Numbers 8, 10 and 12 were originally one 15th-century mansion and there is a *pietà* over the door. Number 21 has some good carving, including lion heads and Burgundy cabbages (*choux bourguignons*), a local decorative speciality. Numbers 27 and 29 comprise the 17th-century **Hôtel de St-Seine**.

This section of the old quarter has many important buildings: the **Hôtel de Vogüé** at 8 Rue de la Chouette is a fine 17th-century mansion, built by Hugues Sambin in 1614 for Étienne Bouhier, the first president of the parliament, and has sculpture by Sambin in its inner courtyard. Note the geometric coloured tiles on the roof, a style introduced from Flanders. Though the courtyard seems symmetrical, the building in fact occupies an odd-shaped site and is very cleverly planned to look bigger than it really is. The doorway is Renaissance. Next door is the **Maison Millière,** a superb example of a 15th-century half-timbered shop, decorated with animals on the roof.

The **Rue de la Liberté** is today the main shopping street of Dijon, extending to the Place Darcy. It has many elegant clothes and shoe shops, and is also the place to find Dijon's gourmet specialites. Here at number 32 is the famous **Grey-Poupon Mustard** shop, with a wide selection of different flavoured mustards, and charming reproduction porcelain mustard jars. At number 16 is **Mulot et Petitjean**, the source for Dijon's *pain d'épices* – spiced breads and cakes in every imaginable form. The only thing Dijon lacks, most surprisingly, are many decent wine shops. Beaune is a much better place to buy and taste regional wines.

Hôtel Chambellan, Rue des Forges; half-timbered houses in old town.

MUSTARD

The dukes of Burgundy were in the habit of sending their visitors off with a parting gift of a barrel of mustard. In the light of such noble largesse it is not surprising that the name Dijon has become almost synonymous with mustard. The word itself derives from the Latin, *must,* which refers to *verjus,* the juice of the newly pressed grapes which are mixed with the seeds to make the condiment. Thus the plant was named after the preparation.

Mustard has been around for a long time. It was very popular with both the Greeks and Romans, who enjoyed it served with roast meat, and it was praised lavishly by Pliny. Because Dijon was on the European spice route, exotic ingredients became familiar to its citizens, resulting in the popularity of mustard and also *pain d'épices,* the spicy gingerbread for which Dijon is also famous.

The first recorded mention of mustard in Burgundy was in 1336, when the incumbent duke, Eudes III, gave a banquet in honour of the king of France, Philip VI. According

to the account book, they consumed 66 gallons of mustard on that particular occasion. And Louis XI of France apparently never travelled anywhere without his own personal pot of mustard.

In 1390 regulations about the quality of mustard were first established, but it was not until 1630 that the guild of mustard-makers was founded in Dijon. In those days mustard was often made at home and mustard-mills were in common use. All the ingredients – mustard, vinegar and salt – were easily available; mustard seed from the Saône Valley, vinegar a by-product of wine, and salt from the Jura mountains. Mustard could be bought fresh like bread from special mustard shops, and townsfolk would bring their own pots to be filled every day. At first only vinegar was used, but in 1756, Jean Naigeon, a Dijon mustard-maker, first substituted *verjus,* the juice of grapes still green at harvest-time, for vinegar. It is the *verjus* which distinguishes Dijon mustard, and it was this combination which has given Dijon mustard its particular taste and reputation.

Today mustard is no longer grown in Burgundy and 95 percent of the seeds are imported from Canada, the USA and Hungary. The term Dijon really refers to the manufacturing process rather than the origin of the ingredients but nevertheless Dijon continues to produce about 70 percent of France's mustard. The production process is simple; the seeds are pressed and then steeped in *verjus,* or in slightly fermented wine. Then the mixture is crushed; to create a smooth mustard the resulting paste is centrifugally separated to remove the hulls. For a coarse, grainier mustard the hulls are left in. The darker the mustard seed, the more powerful the mustard.

Today Dijon mustard comes in a wide variety of flavours: tarragon, green pepper, green herbs, shallots. Remember that when cooking with mustard, it loses its sharpness when heated so it is important to add it only towards the end of cooking. Although mustard will not go off, it does lose its pungency once exposed to air, so it is best to buy and use it in small containers (the small reusable glass tumblers sold in supermarkets are ideal). Mustard is of course also famous for its medicinal benefits; from stimulating the appetite to curing headaches, fever and asthma. ∎

Place Darcy is full of cafés and restaurants and the **Jardin Darcy** provides an elegant resting place in the middle of the city, with tall mature trees, fountains and swans.

But it is still food which dominates life in Dijon; some of Dijon's legendary restaurants remain, such as the Trois Faisans, and new legends are rapidly being established, notably the Restaurant Jean-Pierre Billoux on Place Darcy, next to the Hôtel de la Cloche.

During November the Foire Internationale Gastronomique takes over the town, an event described by M.F.K. Fisher as "injected with a mysterious supercharge of medieval pomp and Madison-Avenue-via-Paris commercialism". A food event no visitor should miss is the market which takes place three times a week in Les Halles – Friday, Saturday and Tuesday. The great wooden rafters of the market hall echo with the sound of market traders purveying their produce: brightly coloured vegetables, plump sausages, and all the fine ripe cheeses of the region.

Fisher recalls the bustle of market days long past, "a kind of whispering pattering rush of women's feet, all pointed one way", and when they returned with "the crooked curls of green beans and squashes, the bruised outer leaves of lettuces, stiff yellow chicken legs... I saw that the women were tired but full of a kind of peace, too."

Chartreuse de Champmol: All that remains of Philip the Bold's monastery, after the ravages of the Revolution, is a chapel doorway and the famous Well of Moses by Claus Sluter, and these are now located, bizarrely, within the grounds of a mental hospital. (Considering the priceless value of the sculpture it is extraordinary that it is exhibited without any security and only rudimentary protection from the elements.) It is about a mile to the west of the Dijon railway station, and not easy to find, though there are signs if you follow them carefully.

The effort is worth it, however. The well is not really a well, but a huge monument illustrating the theme of the

Sluter's carving, Well of Moses, Champmol; statue of Claus Sluter.

Spring of Life. It stood in the middle of the monastery cloisters, originally crowned by a Calvary group, but this was broken by accident – before the Revolution. The lower part of the monument was surrounded by water, and between the water and the heavens are six prophets, each carrying a scroll of prophecy. The carving is exquisite, the stone looks so lifelike it is almost warm, and the folds of the garments are remarkably tactile. Sluter is particularly famous for his deep-cut carving.

Environs of Dijon: Apart from the obvious attractions of the Côte d'Or enumerated elsewhere, the countryside around Dijon offers a number of pleasant drives, quiet retreats and interesting architectural highlights; there are no spectacular sights for the hard-pressed tourist to include but instead the opportunity for a gentle ramble through variegated countryside, small villages and little market towns. Heading out of Dijon to the north, perhaps after a visit to the Well of Moses, is the little village of **Talant.** It is high on a hill overlooking

Dijon and Lac Kir and the wooded slopes of Combe la Serpent, a 320-acre (130-hectare) spread of national park, close to the city centre. The view is a good way to get a picture of the evolution of the old city of Dijon and the rapid recent new development evidenced by the tower blocks which surround the old quarter. The 13th-century church at Talant has a rather kitsch rusticated chapel and a good collection of saints, most of them 16th-century, including a Virgin and Child.

If you continue along the N71 you will arrive at **St-Seine-l'Abbaye;** although the Sources de la Seine is actually quite nearby, the town is, somewhat confusingly, named for the saint not the river. It is worth stopping to see the church, which is all that remains of what was once a very important monastery. It looks impressively battered from the outside, but has many interesting features within. The west entrance is at the top of a steep incline with houses either side and appears very imposing. The top two storeys of the south tower no longer

Beaumont Château near Fontaine-Française.

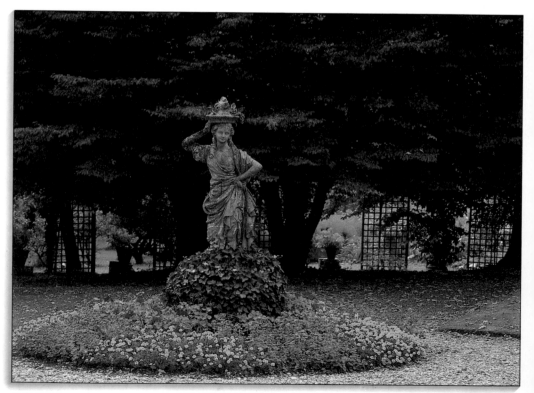

exist and the entrance, set back in an open porch, has also sustained damage. Enter through a tiny old doorway, less than 5 ft (1.5 metres) tall, cut into one of the huge wooden doors. Inside there is a fine life-sized skeleton tomb cover of Jean de Chaudenay-Blaisy in the north transept. The choir has a wall separating it from the transepts, the outsides of which have been covered with fabulous 16th-century frescoes – biblical scenes presented in several dozen panels like a medieval comic-strip, and still very rich in colour, show the legends of St Seine and the Tree of Jesse.

From St-Seinc-l'Abbaye follow the D16 skirting the forest of Is-sur-Tille on to **Lamargelle, Is-sur-Tille** and **Til-Châtel,** where there is an interesting Romanesque church. It is a quiet, almost empty landscape suffering from the effects of rural depopulation; for the visitor there is plenty of opportunity for quiet hikes through beautiful forest-land. **Lux** has a 16th-century château but it is not open to the public; it should be noted in general that many historic buildings are open for only a few hours a week at certain times of year so strenuous efforts must be made if you wish to be sure of access. A better plan is merely to potter and visit what happens to be open; serendipity often compensates for missing the established tourist trail.

Further to the northeast of Dijon, **Bèze** is a charming place to visit even if you are not interested in the gloomy mysteries of underground caves and rivers. The village itself has the remains of ramparts, a fortified church and several old buildings on the central square.

If you follow the signs to the Sources and grotto out of the village, walk along the side of the River Bèze, a deceptively mature-looking river which comes to a sudden beginning. Its waters run shallow and clear over flowing reeds between the houses, with here and there a little boat bobbing beside a back gate straight onto the river. It really doesn't matter which side you walk along because the river begins here, its wide mature flow springing up as if fully formed from mother earth. You can

Source of Bèze River.

walk right round the end which is protected by a curved stone balustrade, and watch the waters bubble up in the pool, all overhung with chestnut trees and willows. Just above is the entrance to the grotto where underground river boat rides are possible during the summer.

Further along the D960 is the forest and town of **Fontaine-Française**. The château, which incorporates the walls of the original medieval fortress, was once a famous literary salon, and has some fine Regency furniture and tapestries. **Rosières** is another château worth a detour mainly for the splendid work of restoration which is still taking place. Only the donjon remains of the original 14th-century fortress. The nearby town of **Mirebeau** merits a visit for the 12th-century church of St-Pierre.

To the southeast on the pretty Vingeannes river is the Château of **Talmay** with its original 13th-century tower. The main building is classical 18th-century with formal French gardens and Renaissance interior. The tower provides an excellent view, and it is nearby that poor Brunhilde was apparently tortured to death.

Over to the east of Dijon, **Auxonne,** a comfortable-sized market town on the Saône river, has a number of interesting features. Military connections dominate, evidenced by the statue of the young Napoleon in the main square. He was garrisoned here from 1788 to 1789 and there is a Napoleonic museum in the château. The Arsenal building has two fine stone gateways with cannons carved above the arches, a siege cannon and an artillery cannon. The gateways also lead to a particularly splendid market hall with vast wooden beams.

The church of Notre Dame has a 12th-century Romanesque tower, a nave in the Burgundian Gothic style and a Virgin attributed to Claus Sluter. Steep roofs are characteristic of the town and often have two storeys of dormer windows piercing the slates. Beyond Auxonne, the Côte d'Or and its very particular attractions beckon insistently. They should not be resisted.

Right, Dijon market.

THE CÔTE D'OR AND CHALONNAIS

The eminent French historian Fernand Braudel said he thought the Côte d'Or vineyards were the most beautiful in the world. But he added coyly, as if aware that there were several stronger candidates when it came to traditional aesthetic criteria (the terraced vineyards of the Mosel or Hermitage, for instance): "The pleasure of the eye can be combined with certain other pleasures."

When considered objectively, that is to say without interference from the resonance of the name **Côte d'Or** ("Golden Slope") or the glory of its wines, this narrow strip of land where soil, microclimate, vine and human skills combine so magically, is nothing special to look at. Stendhal was probably a bit severe when he wrote in 1837: "Were it not for its admirable wines, I would find nothing in the world as ugly as this celebrated Côte d'Or." But he had a point.

The drive south from Dijon to Santenay via Beaune, along the Route des Vins, takes one through a vast expanse of well-kempt vines that is barely interrupted by hedge or tree or wall. To the left the vineyards are almost flat; to the right they rise – quite steeply until you reach Nuits-St-Georges, then more gently – to a wooded ridge some 350 ft (100 metres) above the road. Vines run right up to the walls of the occasional wine-growers' houses that dot the landscape, for not a scrap of valuable soil – predominantly a reddish-ochre colour (hence the name Côte d'Or) – can be wasted. For the same reason, villages tuck in their skirts.

Yet driving through this rather featureless landscape causes the pulse to quicken: every 2 or 3 miles a sign heaves into view bearing the name of a village of worldwide renown, a commune often pregnant with historical and literary associations, a name excruciatingly evocative of wines once drunk or,

Preceding pages: ballooning over the Côte d'Or. **Right**, grape-harvesting.

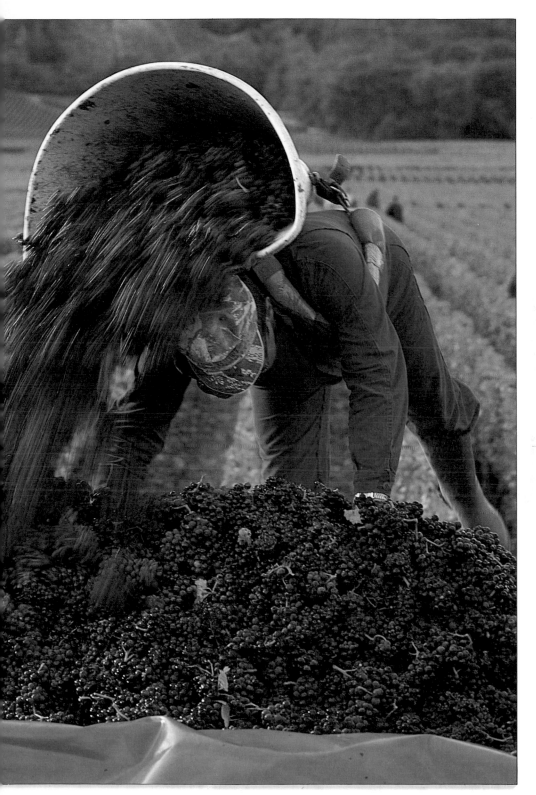

alas, only dreamt of. Gevrey-Chambertin, Chambolle-Musigny, Vosne-Romanée, Nuits-St-Georges, Aloxe-Corton, Pommard, Volnay, Meursault, Puligny-Montrachet, Chassagne-Montrachet: the mind reels as the great names of Burgundy all succeed each other over a distance of less than 30 miles (50 km).

Côte de Nuits: The first leg of the journey from Dijon consists of the **Côte de Nuits**, an area which runs to a point just south of Nuits-St-Georges and produces mainly red wines. Still within the suburbs of Dijon but an appropriate beginning to a wine tour, is the great 13th-century wine cellar, the *Cuverie des ducs de Bourgogne*, at **Chenôve**. Within are the massive 13th-century wine presses, which continued to function until 1924. The first village with an *appellation communale* is **Marsannay**, which includes some vineyards in the suburbs of Dijon itself. Until World War II, Marsannay supplied Dijon with gallons of cheap Gamay and made virtually the only Burgundy rosé. Some years ago it started to produce classier reds and whites, which earned it an *appellation* in 1987.

Next comes **Fixin**, one of the lesser-known Burgundy *appellations* to contain *premiers crus* (the "x" in Fixin, as in other Burgundy place names, is pronounced "ss"). It produces an earthy red reminiscent of the wine of its more famous neighbour to the south, **Gevrey-Chambertin**, but with less breeding. Fixin village contains a curiosity worth visiting, the Parc Noisot and its little museum. Claude Noisot, one of Napoleon's captains, had a sculpture of *Napoleon Awakening* placed well up the hill in the grounds of his château in 1847 – and had himself buried opposite it. In 1847 Gevrey was the first Côte d'Or village to suffix the name of a famous vineyard located on its territory, in this case Chambertin, to its own. This was understandable, as the nine *grands crus* in the Chambertin constellation, which produce deeply coloured, wonderfully intense red wines, were already celebrated. The best-known *grands*

Clos des Langres, Côte d'Or wine sale.

crus, apart from Chambertin itself, is Clos de Bèze, thought to be the oldest named vineyard in Côte d'Or, apparently planted in the mid-6th century by the monks of the Abbaye de Bèze.

Chambertin is one of the most famous Côte d'Or names, partly because Napoleon made it his everyday drinking wine after his doctors had recommended it. Sacriligiously perhaps, to the modern mind, he watered it down. He took it on numerous campaigns, to Egypt, Germany, Spain and Moscow. After his victory at Elchingen, he repaired for the night at Ober-Falheim, where his Chambertin, among other things, was stolen. He is said to have remarked cheerfully that he had never before had to go without his Chambertin, "not even in the midst of the sands of Egypt".

Chambertin was also much loved by Thomas Jefferson, the German writer and composer Ernst Hoffmann (author of *The Tales of Hoffman*, who called it "the true poetic wine"), and Alexandre Dumas (Athos in *The Three Musketeers* says that nothing makes the future seem so rosy as looking through a glass of Chambertin). But none of the three, as we shall see, was short-sighted enough to restrict his appreciation of Burgundy to Chambertin alone.

Next on the road south comes the pretty village of **Morey-St-Denis**. Although not a very well-known name, it has no fewer than five *grands crus* on its territory which produce, depending on their altitude, robust or delicate reds of great elegance that many rate more highly than those of its much more illustrious neighbour to the north. One of them, Clos de Tart, has a particularly long history. Cistercian nuns of the Abbaye de Notre Dame de Tart bought the vineyard in the late 12th century and husbanded it for 600 years without interruption until the Revolution.

Just south of Morey-St-Denis is **Chambolle-Musigny**, another attractive and unspoilt village. Its vineyards sweep majestically up towards limestone crags. This is significant because the soil's high limestone content gives its two remarkably subtle red *grands*

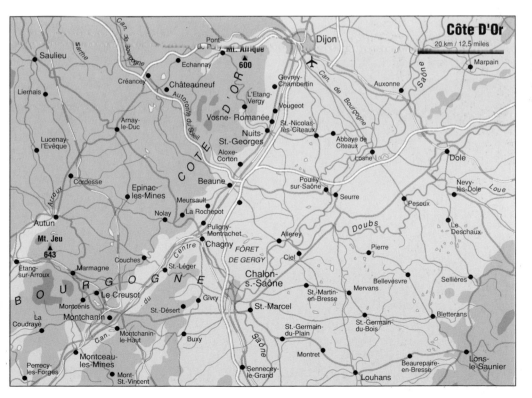

crus, an additional *goût du terroir.*

Moving from Chambolle-Musigny down the slope to **Clos de Vougeot** is rather like stepping out of a chamber music concert into the blare and razzmatazz of an American political convention. All the ingredients are there: smooth organisation, selection, ruthlessness, complication. Each year thousands of tourists are shepherded round the Château du Clos de Vougeot as the highlight of their tour of Côte d'Or. People with the right connections are able to wangle an invitation to rub shoulders with the glitterati at the banquet held in the château on the third Saturday in November, the day before the famous charity auction at Hospices de Beaune.

The château is the headquarters of the hard-headed Confrérie des Chevaliers du Tastevin, a guild whose members are mainly *négociants* and growers, with a sprinkling of VIPs who have been persuaded to lend their names in return for plenty of free Burgundy. The Confrérie had lofty ambitions when it was founded in 1934, likening itself not only to the Cistercian community that had created the vineyard but to a smaller-scale version of the League of Nations, it saw its role as one of spreading the good word throughout the world and encouraging peaceful relations. In fact the Confrérie acts as Burgundy's advertising agency and watchdog rolled into one. It has even prevented, through the courts, any use of the word *tastevin* or even its alternative spelling *tâtevin* on the label of any wine other than its own.

But what about the *grand cru* Clos de Vougeot itself (called Clos Vougeot on some bottles), arguably Côte d'Or's most celebrated red wine? Its 125 acres (50 hectares) are divided up among some 70 owners, some of whom possess handkerchief-sized parcels. This makes for enormous variation in quality. At its best, Clos de Vougeot is a full-bodied wine with a remarkably lingering aftertaste. The small amounts of grapes produced by the tiny parcels are difficult to vinify separately, so they are sometimes pressed and fermented along with **Harvesting in all weathers, Gevrey-Chambertin.**

grapes from other vineyards. A quantity of wine equivalent to the quantity of Clos de Vougeot the owner is authorised to produce is then drawn off the resulting blend and, allegedly, sold as Clos de Vougeot.

The history of Clos de Vougeot is more interesting than its wine. The vineyard was founded by Cistercian monks from the nearby Abbaye de Cîteaux in the 12th century. In 1371 one of the monks sent 30 barrels of their wine to Pope Gregory XI in Avignon, then seat of the papacy. The Pope duly rewarded his benefactor by making him a cardinal four years later. Not surprisingly, Petrarch claimed in 1366 that the popes so loved Clos de Vougeot they were reluctant to move to Rome, where they would be deprived of that "Olympian nectar".

The château, a fairly unremarkable building lent majesty by being marooned in an ocean of vines, was built in 1551 by Dom Jean Loysier, the 48th abbot of Cîteaux. The massive grape press used by the monks can still be seen in the winery. The châteaux and vineyards remained in Cistercian hands until 1790, when they were confiscated on behalf of the state by a junior army officer called Napoleon Bonaparte.

Vineyards such as Clos de Vougeot attract legends like flies. Stendhal was told by a fellow traveller in Côte d'Or that General Bisson, en route to join the Rhine army with his troops, told them to halt in front of the vineyard and present arms. According to other sources, his gesture was repeated by Marshal de Saxe, General Galliffet and Marshal Mac-Mahon. Others again claim that no such military posturings ever took place at Clos de Vougeot.

To get to Clos de Vougeot from their base at the **Abbaye de Cîteaux**, to the east of Côte d'Or, the Cistercians had to travel some 8 miles (13 km) across a then marshy plain. So they built a fortress near the vineyard, at Gilly-les-Cîteaux. It was there that they stored their wines. When the building was destroyed during the Thirty Years' War, they replaced it with a finely propor-

Côte d'Or grape-picking.

tioned château in which they entertained lavishly. The Château de Gilly is now a luxury hotel. The Abbaye de Cîteaux was founded in 1098. It is a stark and desolate place, vast in its proportions but, following the ravages of the Revolution, incomplete and lacking in harmony. Nothing remains of the 12th-century church, and most of the buildings that have survived are not open to visitors.

There is, however, a little shop where books, postcards and the excellent (and rare) cheese, Cîteaux, can be bought. Anyone unaware that the monks made cheese would quickly be enlightened, on entering the shop, by the rich smell within. Interested flies, as well as tourists, slip through the door, but the monk behind the counter is very expert with a fly-swatter.

The austere, frugal Cistercian community is a very different universe from that of **Vosne-Romanée**, whose church now houses the magnificent wood carvings from the former chapel of the Abbaye de Cîteaux. This sleek little village, which lies between Clos de Vougeot and Nuits-St-Georges, oozes wealth, albeit discreetly. It includes on its limited territory no fewer than eight *grands crus* (Grande Rue was elevated to that status in 1992), several of which rank among the very finest red Burgundies: earthy, spicy and breathtakingly refined Romanée-Conti, with its never-ending aftertaste, deep-flavoured La Tâche, and velvety Richebourg.

Some of these wines are not only horrendously expensive but virtually unobtainable: Romanée-Conti, which is pricier than any other Burgundy except Montrachet, comes from a vineyard only slightly larger than two football pitches and cannot possibly meet demand with its curmudgeonly average production of 6,000 bottles a year. A parcel of its neighbouring *grand cru*, Romanée-St-Vivant, is believed to have sold for nearly 10 million francs an acre in 1990.

The qualities of Romanée-Conti did not escape the beady eye – or should one say quivering tastebuds? – of popes or **Pernand-Vergelesses.**

kings. It is alleged that, like Clos de Vougeot, the wine militated against the papacy moving from Avignon to Rome in the 14th century: Pope Urbain V is said to have been distraught at the idea of being deprived of his supplies. After operating on Louis XIV, doctors recommended he should drink Romanée-Conti. The king remarked that an illness which allowed him to discover a wine like that was a "gift from heaven".

If Vosne-Romanée is the princess of Burgundy villages, **Nuits-St-Georges** is the ugly duckling. It gives its name to the Côte de Nuits, the name taken from the village of Nuits, which then became Nuits-St-George; although it has no *grands crus* on its territory, it naturally acts as the commercial nerve centre for its wines. So one cannot really complain about its industrial sprawl, unsightly warehouses and bleak railway sidings. But it is sad that such a renowned and prosperous place should feel the need to deck itself out with vulgar buntings while allowing some of its public buildings to fall into disrepair. Its late 13th-century Église St-Symphorien is worth visiting, though, as is the small archaeological museum devoted to locally excavated Gallo-Roman and Merovingian objects.

One great fan of Nuits-St-Georges wine was Ernst Hoffmann. He loved to visit the cellar of his friend Kunz, where they indulged their taste for Nuits wine (it was not yet called Nuits-St-Georges). They made a point of doing so at night (because of the name *nuit*), sometimes sitting astride either end of the barrel and "drinking in no ordinary fashion". Another fan of the wine was the UK politician Ernest Bevin. When asked what he dined on each evening at the House of Commons restaurant, he alarmed his questioner by replying: "Steak and 'newts'." He did not, however, say whether he had ever tried the combination "steak and Beaune".

Côte de Beaune: The town of Beaune gives its name to the second section of Côte d'Or vineyards, **Côte de Beaune**, which produces roughly equal quantities of whites and reds. The area begins

Nuits-St-Georges, wine harvest.

HOSPICES DE BEAUNE

The annual Vente des Vins des Hospices de Beaune in November, which claims to be the world's biggest charity sale, is to the Burgundy wine trade what the spring collections are to the fashion business: both establish the year's trends and, in the case of wine, its prices.

The Hospices sale became a major event due to its bursar in the mid-19th century, Joseph Pétasse, who displayed considerable business acumen in the best tradition of the *négociants* of Beaune. The Hospices' vintages of 1847, 1848 and 1849 sold badly, and the cellars of the Hôtel-Dieu were consequently overflowing with wine. Pétasse travelled round France, Belgium, Holland and Germany and managed to sell off the Hospices' stocks. On his return he told the administrators: "We have established our clientele and our wines are well-known." The Hospices auction was started up again in 1859 and has never looked back.

Wealth in Burgundy has always been synonymous with wine, and when people

decided to leave some of their worldly goods to the Hospices, out of gratitude or in the hope of bettering their chances in the afterlife, those goods often took the form of vineyards. The first donation of nearly an acre (0.35 hectare) in Corton was made by Jehannette Dubois in 1471, 28 years after the founding of the Hôtel-Dieu. The establishment acquired the plural name Hospices de Beaune as hospitals in other communes (and the vineyards they owned) were added to it. By the mid-18th century, the hospitals of Pommard, Volnay and Meursault had swelled the vineyards belonging to the Hospices to about 75 acres (30 hectares).

Today, the Hospices' total area of vineyards is about 130 acres (53 hectares). The value of the wines they produce has soared in value thanks to Pétasse's energy in the 19th century and the marketing skills of the Confrérie des Chevaliers du Tastevin, which in 1934, when it was formed, organised a three-day jamboree, Les Trois Glorieuses, around the annual auction.

Day One begins with a banquet in the Château of Clos de Vougeot; on Day Two comes the serious business of the auction, which, like the banquet, is traditionally held by candlelight. Day Three takes place at La Paulée in Meursault. Most of the diners in this case are growers, who bring along bottles of their finest vintages. La Paulée is rounded off by a literary award.

So much for the folklore. The Hospices auction does serve a serious purpose. The prices paid for the various *cuvées* (which are named after their donors, not the vineyards they come from) are generally inflated – it is after all a charity sale for the Hospices – but they do give an indication of how Burgundy prices are going to move in a given year. The quality of the actual wines is another matter. There is a scramble to produce wines that are presentable by the third week in November, when they will be tasted from the barrel by prospective buyers.

There is no guarantee that the way the wine is treated, during its primary fermentation before the sale, or afterwards, during the cellaring and bottling at the *négociants*, will be up to standard. There is undeniable pageantry, suspense and excitement at the annual Hospices de Beaune auction. But, as with so much else in Burgundy, all that glisters is not gold. ∎

just north of Beaune, at Aloxe-Corton, and gets off to a majestic start with the red and white Corton and the white Corton-Charlemagne, which at its best can rival the queen of white Burgundies, Montrachet. These big, powerful and long-lived wines are produced on the free-standing hill of Corton, which provides a wide range of exposures and altitudes. Ownership is extremely fragmented: there is one tiny parcel which is one and a half times the size of a squash court and produces only about four cases of wine. Past, and bigger, owners have included Charlemagne, Henri II and Charles le Téméraire.

Voltaire did not own any vineyards in Corton but adored the wine. In 1759 (the year *Candide* was published), he revealed an endearing vice in a letter he wrote from Ferney to his supplier of Corton, Le Bault: "The older I get, Sir, the more highly do I value your kindnesses. Your good wine is becoming a necessity to me. I give quite good Beaujolais to my guests from Geneva, but I drink Burgundy in secret."

Tucked away in a valley behind the hill of Corton are the Romanesque church and narrow streets of **Pernand-Vergelesses**, a pretty little village which gives its name to a little-known wine which, for that reason, is often good value. Similar wine – described in a 17th-century inscription as "nourishing, theological and disease-preventing" – is produced, round a bend in the valley, by **Savigny-lès-Beaune**, which huddles beneath the A6 motorway. Despite its sprawl of modern villas (it is now virtually a suburb of Beaune), the village has an interesting church and château worth visiting.

After such a long succession of vineyards and villages, it makes a pleasant change to enter a real town like **Beaune**. Its tiny centre – a mere half mile in diameter – has hardly changed physically down the years: a circular boulevard runs round its former ramparts, many of which still stand. Within, there is a dense maze of narrow old streets.

But don't imagine that you can escape the all-pervasive wine culture:

Hôtel-Dieu interior; Salles de Pôvres.

every other shop peddles if not wine, then books on wine, cellar equipment or wine glasses and fancy table accessories; every other café or restaurant proclaims its loyalty to the vinous tradition. The big Beaune *négociants*, who have called the tune in the Burgundy wine trade since the beginning of the 18th century, lure tourists – some 400,000 a year visit Beaune – into their often spectacularly honeycombed old cellars with offers of free tastings. Free they may be, but what comes out of the bottle may unfortunately bear little relation to what the label advertises.

Beaune exudes such affluence today that it is hard to picture the massacres, disease and famine suffered by its past inhabitants as the town was fought over by warring noblemen or blighted by the plague. It was in that context that Beaune was endowed with what is by far its most interesting building, the **Hôtel-Dieu**. This charity hospital was erected in the mid-15th century by Nicolas Rolin, chancellor of Burgundy and one of the wealthiest men of his time, to care for the poor and the sick. His motive, as was often the case at the time, was a desire for prestige. Louis XI, the man who brought down the Duchy of Burgundy, was to remark acidly: "It was only right that he who had made so many men poor during his lifetime should prepare an asylum for them before his death."

From the outside the Hôtel-Dieu has a forbidding, semi-fortified appearance (note the massive knocker on its door, which depicts a salamander about to pounce on a fly). One is therefore unprepared for the Flemish-influenced riot of patterned roof tiles and dainty dormer windows that meets the eye as one walks into the main courtyard. The interior includes the spectacular vaulted Salle des Pôvres (*sic*), which is lined with curtained beds and has a chapel at one end. The beds are now empty – the Hôtel-Dieu functioned as a hospital right up to 1971 – but other rooms evoking everyday life, such as the kitchen and pharmacy, contain rather spooky models of the Soeurs Hospital-

Beaune market.

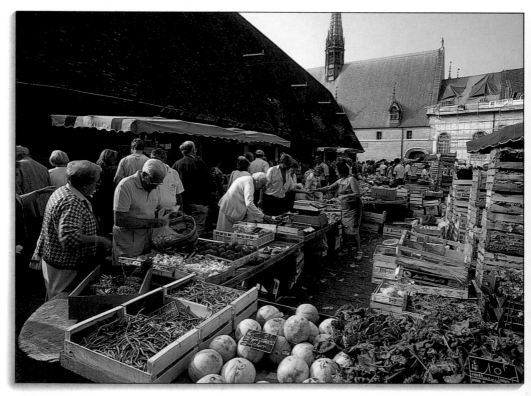

ières. The highlight of a visit to the Hôtel-Dieu is the splendid nine-panelled altarpiece, *The Last Judgement,* by the 15th-century Flemish painter Roger van der Weyden.

No other sights in Beaune can compete with the Hôtel-Dieu – Eugène Viollet-le-Duc, restorer of Vézelay and Notre Dame de Paris, said that it was so beautiful it made him want to fall ill. But it is also worth taking in the **Collégiale Notre Dame**. Despite its handsome 14th-century porch and delightful Renaissance side chapel, this church is basically Romanesque, to wit its sculpted capitals, which include a particularly dramatic "Stoning of St Stephen".

The **Musée des Beaux-Arts** also deserves a visit. It is mainly devoted to work by local artists such as the 19th-century painter Félix Ziem, whose landscapes are reminiscent of Turner's. The same building houses the **Musée Étienne-Jules Marey**. Marey, another local man, was one of the pioneers of chronophotography, which paved the way for the invention of the cinema.

Naturally Beaune also has a **Musée du Vin de Bourgogne**, which throws interesting light on such questions as soil and wine-making techniques. Just outside the town, in a motorway rest area, there is another instructive museum, the **Archéodrome**, which evokes Burgundian dwellings and daily life from the Stone Age to the Gallo-Roman period, mainly through the use of reconstructions. In the little town of **Seurre** to the east, can be seen a smaller version of Beaune's Hôtel-Dieu with the same communal arrangement for the sick. There is also a 14th-century church and a number of wooden houses.

Beaune is not just a town but an excellent fruity Burgundy *appellation* of great finesse. Erasmus said he wished he had lived in France instead of the Low Countries, "not to command armies there, but to drink Beaune wine". In the 16th century many Huguenots moved in the other direction, fleeing to the Netherlands and even today Beaune is a favourite tipple of the Dutch.

Erasmus did not just drink Beaune,

A successful shopping trip.

but also had a soft spot for its celebrated neighbour Pommard. When charged with drinking it on a fast day, he retorted that, while his heart was Catholic, for a wine like Pommard his stomach was Reformed. In recent years, suspicions of fraud have hung over Pommard. The mass of consumers in red Burgundy-importing countries have always tended to go for long-lasting wines with plenty of tannin. Pommard filled the bill. Despite the considerable size of its vineyards, mounting popularity meant there was never enough of the wine to go round, so it often ended up being blended with another. This unfortunately gave Pommard a bad name among serious Burgundy drinkers – which was unfair, for at its best it is an attractively sturdy wine which goes particularly well with game.

Perhaps in an attempt to improve its image, the village of **Pommard** has planted flowers everywhere, scrubbed its houses and paved its streets. The result is picture-postcard prettiness. Its close neighbour **Volnay** is more de-mure, though it has more historical associations to boast about. In 1328 its suave and fragrant red wine was served at the coronation of Philippe de Valois, who owned the vineyard Les Cailles du Roi (now the *premier cru* Les Caillerets). Pope Gregory XI liked Volnay (as well as Romanée-Conti), which he said was "much more agreeable than the thick beverages produced by Roman vines". One of the first things Louis XI did when Burgundy fell into his hands after the death of Charles le Téméraire was to get the whole 1477 Volnay vintage despatched to his château near Tours. And Louis XIV was a great fan too – but that is no surprise.

The red wine of Monthelie (also spelled Monthélie), down the road, is the poor man's Volnay – which means that it is still pretty satisfactory. The village of **Monthelie**, with a 12th-century church, is attractive and remains unspoilt.

Wedged in the deep valley that leads up to St-Romain, **Auxey-Duresses** is another picturesque village that keeps

View of Santenay.

itself to itself. Its church has a fine 16th-century triptych. Before *appellation contrôlée* was introduced (and sometimes, fraudulently, afterwards), its red and white wines were sold as Volnay and Meursault respectively. Nowadays, because it is so little known, it is one of the best buys in Côte d'Or.

The same could be said of **St-Romain**, whose red and white wines are full of character even though they come from vineyards whose altitude (1,000–1,300 ft/300–400 metres) precludes true greatness. The recently excavated ruins of its castle, built on a rocky spur at one end of the upper part of this quiet village, offer a splendid view of the circus of cliffs on the other side of the valley. Down the hill, in the *mairie*, local archaeological finds are on show.

Compared with the calm of St-Romain, the very large and proudly affluent village of **Meursault** seems a hive of activity. It is here that the last of the Trois Glorieuses, a banquet called La Paulée, which culminates with the award of a book prize, is held the day after the Hospices de Beaune sale. Following donations down the years, the Hospices now own large tracts of Meursault vineyards. The village used to have its own hospital, but its patients were transferred to the Hospices de Beaune in the year 1766.

The soft, round and complex white wine of Meursault took Jefferson's fancy when he did a tour of Côte d'Or vineyards in 1787, and two years later he ordered 250 bottles of its *premier cru*, Gouttes d'Or, telling his supplier it was his favourite. A wine-imbibing French prelate, Cardinal Bernis, who was French ambassador in Rome under Louis XV, even went so far as to use nothing but Meursault (from a good year) as altar wine. When surprise was expressed at his practice, he replied quite unabashed: "I wouldn't want our Lord to see me wincing while I take communion."

An almost uninterrupted expanse of vines, with not a building in sight, awaits you as you drive the few miles from Meursault to **Puligny-Mon-**

A deserved tipple.

trachet and from Puligny-Montrachet to **Chassagne-Montrachet**. These last two villages boast a total of five white *grands crus*, two of whose vineyards they share, including Côte d'Or's most celebrated and most ferociously expensive white wine, Montrachet. Elegant, with a haunting bouquet, it is a wine that has been treated to every superlative. Alexandre Dumas said one should drink it kneeling and bare-headed. Recently some Montrachets have been reported to be below par and unworthy of such a great *appellation*. Nemesis rather than human error may be responsible: some vines have been affected by an incurable virus known as fan-leaf – it has been called "the Aids of Montrachet" – which results in inferior wine.

The refined, if lightweight, red and white wines from the village of St-Aubin are produced by vineyards almost as high up as those of St-Romain. Within the commune lies the charming hamlet of **Gamay**, which has a medieval castle and a partly 10th-century church. It gave its name to the grape variety that Philippe le Hardi banned from Burgundy in the 14th century, describing it as a "a very evil and treacherous plant which produces a very great abundance of wine".

The last of the great Côte de Beaune *appellations*, a forceful, mostly red wine that ages well, is produced by the village of **Santenay**, which has a bustling atmosphere not found elsewhere in Côte d'Or villages, no doubt because it doubles up as a busy spa complete with a turn-of-the-century casino. Spectacular views over the vineyards are to be had from its 13th-century wooden-porched church of St-Jean, tucked under cliffs high above the village. If the building is open, do not miss the lively statues of saints within.

Côte Chalonnaise: The area south of Santenay marks the start of the **Côte Chalonnaise** *appellation régionale*. Here, the concentration of Romanesque village churches that reaches its flabbergasting apogee in the area west of Tournus begins to build up. There are four *appellations communales* in the

Chalon-sur-Saône from the river.

Chalonnais, strung out along or near the road south towards Cluny (D981): Rully, Mercurey and Givry, whose reds and whites rival, at their best, the lesser *appellations* of Côte d'Or; and Montagny, an aromatic white.

Rully, with its impressive 12th-century stronghold and abundance of very old houses, is a congenial village well worth visiting. The once fortified village of **Givry** was, like Rully, devastated by the plague in 1348 and sacked more than once. It is now a quietly prosperous, spacious little town with several old fountains and two fine 18th-century buildings, its *mairie* and its majestically proportioned church, which has no fewer than six cupolas. Just west of Givry is some delightful rolling countryside where vineyards are interspersed with small hedge-lined fields growing other crops. There are Romanesque churches worth visiting in the sleepy villages of **Mellecey** (which also contains Philippe le Hardi's country residence, the Château de Germolles), **St-Jean-de-Vaux**, **Châtel-Moron** and **Jambles** (note the unusual emblem of a crowing cockerel on the village war memorial).

A good place to sample local wines (some of which come from vineyards in Jambles) in relaxed surroundings, either on their own or with Burgundian cuisine, is the reasonably priced Maison des Vins de la Côte Chalonnaise in **Chalon-sur-Saône**. The city also boasts a tip-top restaurant that is very good value for money, Le Moulin de Martorey, housed in a delightful former water mill that is about to be engulfed by Chalon's urban sprawl.

Because of its strategic location on the River Saône at the point where it meets the Dijon-Lyon land corridor, Chalon has always been a busy trading city. Its two annual fur fairs are the relics of major medieval fairs. Tin from Cornwall in England used to be loaded on boats there and taken down the river to the Mediterranean. Stendhal noted in 1837: "Chalon seems to me full of activity, youth and life. It is maritime activity, a foretaste of Marseille."

Cathedral cloisters, Chalon.

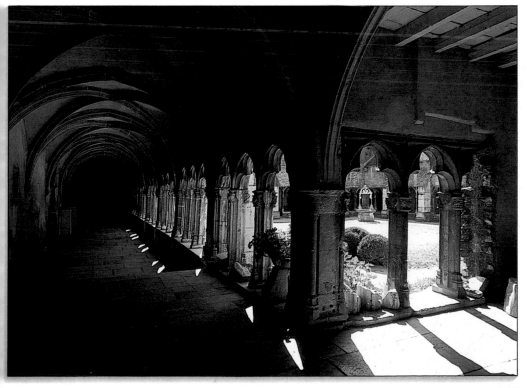

Worth seeing in Chalon are the **Musée Denon** (a good archaeological section, 17th to 19th-century Dutch and French painting, handsome 18th-century Burgundian furniture), the former Cathedral of St-Vincent (partly Romanesque), the **Musée Nicéphore-Niepce** (Niepce, who was born in Chalon, was one of the inventors of photography) and the **Roseraie St-Nicolas** (a collection of 25,000 roses).

West to Le Creusot: The **Canal du Centre** runs like an umbilical cord from Chalon to Montchanin, a few miles from Le Creusot. Once an important industrial town, **Le Creusot** is now a quiet, clean backwater. It first began to expand in the 18th century, when Marie-Antoinette transferred her glassworks there and built the elegant **Château de la Verrerie** in 1787. Its two conical glass-making furnaces (now converted into a theatre and exhibition hall) stand incongruously in the courtyard, as though they had descended from outer space.

The château was bought in 1836 by Eugène and Adolphe Schneider. They exploited the local presence of coal and iron ore and founded an integrated industrial complex that manufactured locomotives, bridges, armour-plating and so on. Within a few years Schneider became France's biggest industrial company, partly through a shrewd reliance on paternalism: it provided its workers with medical care (in 1905 infant mortality in Le Creusot was the lowest in France) and housed them in neat little bungalows complete with gardens. Some of these in the 1865 Villedieu housing estate below the château's extensive grounds have survived the demolition squads. The massive, 68-ft (21-metre) high power hammer invented by a Schneider engineer has been placed at one of Le Creusot's crossroads as a monument to its former industrial glory. The history of Le Creusot is intelligently illustrated by the Ecomusée in the Château de la Verrerie.

As it expanded, Le Creusot hoovered up manpower from the surrounding countryside, much of which became

Sully Château; "Burgundy's Fontaine-bleau".

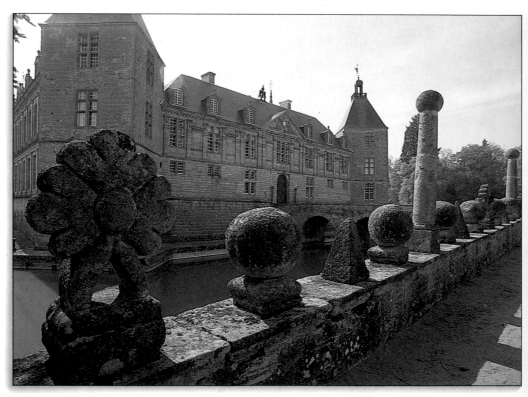

depopulated. The long-strung-out village of Couches not only helped to swell the ranks of Schneider's workers but provided plonk to assuage their thirst. It now makes more upmarket wine that qualifies for the Bourgogne *appellation*. This village, which was important in the Middle Ages, has several features of interest: the 13th-century Château de Marguerite de Bourgogne, the Templars' house, the Tour Guérin with a roof of patterned tiles (now a gîte), the 12th-century Tour Bajole, once a monastery and now a restaurant, and, outside the village, a group of five large menhirs.

To the north lies **Nolay**, a compact little town with a 14th-century covered market. Those interested in Renaissance architecture should strike out westwards to the moated **Château de Sully**, a remarkably harmonious building set in extensive grounds and described by Madame de Sévigné as "Burgundy's Fontainebleau". Just east of Nolay is the village of **La Rochepot**, which has a delightful 12th-century church, with a 16th-century triptych and several Romanesque capitals. Perched above it is the heavily restored 15th-century Château de La Rochepot.

The area north of Nolay marks the beginning of the other face of Côte d'Or – its little-known hinterland, which is as wild and romantic as the vineyard side is trim and materialistic. Near Nolay is the **Bout du Monde**, a valley that runs past Vauchignon between spectacular cliffs up to a dead end and a waterfall. Farther north, around **Bouilland**, **Bruant** and **Arcenant**, country lanes lined with wild angelica twist and turn beneath beetling crags. On the plateau above, patches have been snipped out of the dense forest to make huge and curiously bleak wheat fields.

Narrow, round-bottomed, sinuous valleys (*combes*) that look like giant bobsleigh runs sweep down to Gevrey-Chambertin, Chambolle-Musigny, Nuits-St-Georges and Beaune, slicing through the limestone of the Côte d'Or ridge; the most magical of these is the tiny **Combe Demange** that careers down from **Clavoillon**.

La Verrerie Château, Le Creusot.

The hinterland is dotted with peaceful untouristy villages: **Reulle-Vergy**, which has an interesting little folk museum; **Arcenant**, a centre of blackcurrant growing (blackcurrants replaced some vines when Phylloxera hit Côte d'Or; **Dijon** subsequently became famous for its cassis, and **Canon Kir** launched his immensely popular apéritif); and **Bouilland**, which has remained totally unspoilt despite the presence there of one of Côte d'Or's finest restaurants, the Auberge du Vieux Moulin. A much larger village, and a pleasant backwater in which to stay, is **Bligny-sur-Ouche**. Perhaps in memory of the fact that it was already a large seigneury in Charlemagne's time, it has a touchingly grand and outsized 19th-century *mairie*, built at a time when the village was a major centre of weaving (in the older streets, note the large openings to the cellars where the weavers worked). Its church, half-Romanesque, half-15th-century, once formed part of the stronghold razed by Louis XI because Bligny had remained loyal to Marguerite de Bourgogne.

One of the most compelling religious buildings in Côte d'Or is the tiny ruined **Abbaye de Ste-Marguerite**, near Bouilland. Founded in the 11th century by the lords of Vergy, it huddles among trees near the top of a high and inaccessible little valley. It evokes more strongly than many grander and better preserved monasteries what life must have been like for the monks of a small abbey in the perilous Middle Ages. Did they, one wonders, have such a marked predilection for the wines of Burgundy as their Cistercian brothers on the plain or later prelates and popes?

The papal connection with Côte d'Or did not die when the papacy returned to Rome in 1377. In 1951, for instance, Angelo Roncalli (papal nuncio to France and Pope Jean XXIII-to-be) was persuaded to ascend the Montagne de Beaune, a hill just outside the town, and bless the vines stretched out before him. Did the already thrice-blessed Côte d'Or really need a further benediction?

Left, La Rochepot.

SOUTHERN BURGUNDY

Southern Burgundy, most of which is within the Saône-et-Loire *département*, is still wine country, but once the hills of the Mâconnais are left behind other elements of the Burgundian tapestry predominate. To the west cows; the rich farmland of the Charolais is home to the famous milk-white cattle. To the east chickens; the flat plains of the Bresse accommodate such fine fowl they have their own *appellation contrôlée* and the dedicated can follow chicken trails across the country.

But most of all this area is distinguished by its Romanesque architecture; the grand abbeys of Cluny, Paray-le-Monial and Tournus are only rivalled by the sheer number of exquisite little churches to be discovered. It provides an extraordinary opportunity for surveying an entire period of architecture and its development from the simplest barrel vault to the soaring naves of the abbey churches. Anyone with a particular interest might choose to follow a route dictated by architectural chronology rather than geographical logic.

There is much else to see and many distractions of a more venal nature. This is not dramatic countryside although there is a distinct thrill in seeing an entire hillside of soon to be harvested vines, but it is almost always pretty and often very beautiful in a soft, mellow, almost English way. Apart from the occasional limestone crag, the contours are rounded and soft. And, however quiet and sleepy the countryside, it is never remote, never primitive. This is land that has, after all, been civilised and cultivated for centuries, by monks above all, dedicated to more than prayer, drawing the very best wine and produce from the land.

The Bresse: To the east the Burgundian Bresse (in the great regional reorganisation of 1790 the Bresse was

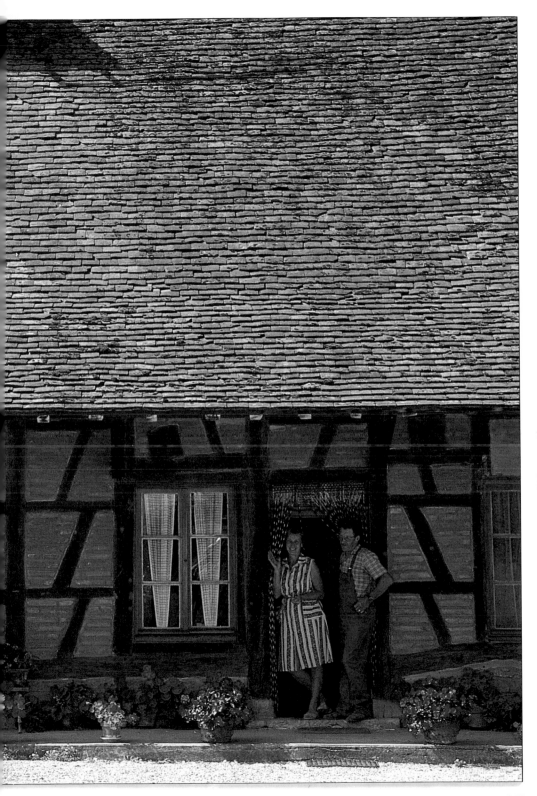

divided between three different *départements*) is distinctly different from the rest of Burgundy but well worth exploring. **Louhans** in particular has a very fine market (every Monday) where the local produce can be seen at its best, particularly a huge amount of very live livestock including the superb white-feathered Bresse chickens, fed on maize and milk; and many different breeds of rabbits. It is a pleasant town best explored when the market has closed for the day – when everyone has headed off for lunch in the many small brasseries.

The arcaded central street is part 14th-century, and is famous for its Hôtel-Dieu with its 18th-century dispensary and fine collection of pottery and glass. The Bresse is also known for its unusual "Saracen" chimneys; elaborate central chimneys like miniature Romanesque belltowers, originally above fireplaces in the middle of the room with a large hood to take away the smoke. (Saracen seems to have been a label used indiscriminately for anything of foreign origin.)

Villages such as **Romenay** and **St-Trivier-de-Courtes** have some of the best examples, and at St-Trivier-de-Courtes there is a farm open to the public which has its original fireplace intact, with its open hood and "ancestors' bench" tucked against the wall.

Local Bresse architecture still predominates, low half-timbered houses with overhanging roofs of curved tiles, where corn cobs and huge bunches of red peppers are hung to dry. Considerable effort has been made to preserve local traditions and a series of Ecomuseums in various locations throughout the region specialise in different aspects of Bresse life; for example, agriculture, forestry, chair-making, tile production and bread-making.

Tournus makes an ideal base for visiting the Chalonnais and Mâconnais vineyards. Its superb abbey – for some the most beautiful in Burgundy, where there is plenty of competition – predates Cluny and thus makes an excellent introduction to the Romanesque trail. The old town has dozens of secret alleys, buildings set with curious gables and corbels, old shop fronts and mansions, a wealth of antique shops, and enough cafés and restaurants to make life very pleasant. Restaurant Greuze, presided over by Jean Ducloux, offers typical Burgundian dishes such as *quenelle de brochet*, Charolais beef *entrecôte* and local Mâcon and Beaujolais wines. Also worth trying are local *chèvre* cheeses, *boutons de culotte*.

The **Abbaye St-Philibert** merits an extended visit because there is so much to see, including the bones of St Philibert himself (616–685). The best way to approach is by the west gate. Two imposing 10th-century towers (with 11th and 12th-century additions) mark the abbey precincts, and from here the church has a distinct military look of tremendous strength with arrow slits and high thick walls, designed more for repelling invaders than welcoming pilgrims. This is not surprising considering the events leading to its construction: in 836 the monks of St-Philibert-de-Noirmoutiers fled before the Nor-

man invaders, taking with them the bones of their saint. They tried to settle near Angers, on the Loire, but the Normans swept all before them. The monks tried again in Messay, then in 871 reached St-Pourçain in the Auvergne. Four years later, Charles the Bold offered them the Abbey of St-Valérien at Tournus which they accepted. However, though they were safe from the invaders from the north, they had not reckoned with danger from the east and in 937 the Hungarians sacked the town and destroyed the abbey.

They quickly rebuilt, but in 1006 the building was again destroyed, this time by fire. They were a determined band, however, consecrating the present church only 13 years later. It was built before Cluny and always managed to remain independent of its powerful neighbour. You enter at the narthex, almost 1,000 years old and the most ancient part of the abbey, an anteroom crowded with huge pillars supporting the massive weight of the towers and floor above.

Tournus from River Saône.

The narthex has its own chapel of St-Michel, on the second storey, which is of tremendous height with views up into the two towers, and can be reached by the stairway just inside the entrance. It is worth the climb for the aerial view of the nave and its magnificent black and white banded vaulting.

As you enter the nave, note the wall painting above the north entrance. From here the sight of the side aisles of unbroken columns is stunning. It is worth taking binoculars to view the superb capitals, the best of which are at the crossing in the nave. Most are very primitive carvings of strange mythical beasts and goblins.

The choir is a joy. The five apsidial chapels are all square with zigzag brickwork. In the lady chapel are the celebrated relics of St Philibert in a gold case: his thigh bones and elbows there for all to see. Be sure to visit the crypt, with its deep well and a series of slender columns supporting the choir with decorative capitals carved with foliage.

To the south of the church there is only a small surviving section of cloister but it is very calm and peaceful. It is reached from the Chauffoir, where the monks warmed their hands and their inks. Capitals taken from the belltower are exhibited here, and there are two beautiful carved figures representing St Philibert and St Valérien.

The abbey is in the northern part of the old town, famous for its historic houses. The **Rue de la République** runs the length of the town, beginning at the tourist office in the wooden frame house, Logis de la Tête Noir, dating from the 14th century, and the rest of the street ranges from 14th-century to 16th-century buildings. Note particularly the Logis de la Piguette at number 67; the buildings and arcades flanking the Place Hôtel de Ville; the 15th-century arcaded Hôtel Jean Magnon; the 17th-century turreted Hôtel de l'Escargot at number 72 and the Hôtel Delaval with 13th to 16th-century features.

At the southernmost end of the street is **Ste-Madeleine**, a 12th-century church built on the site of a Roman

Stone carving in St-Philibert; church of St-Pierre, Brancion.

castrum, with a fine doorway and square tower. A stroll down the facing Rue de la Friperie brings you to the old Rue du Quatre Septembre and the Maisons des Chapelains de la Madeleine, four 16th-century buildings. The Hôtel-Dieu has a wonderful 17th-century pharmacy.

Perhaps it is the river that gives Tournus its special timeless quality. The Saône is very wide at this point, with only one bridge crossing it in the town. A series of quiet *quais* run next to the water, used by walkers and fishermen.There is a road along by the river, but unlike Mâcon, it has not been turned into a urban throughway; the Quai de Verdun is a quiet, tree-lined boulevard, with car parking beneath the shady trees and the occasional café. Boats can be taken from the Quai du Midi to Chalon-sur-Saône and Mâcon, and also for river trips returning to Tournus.

The Mâconnais hills: Heading southwest towards Cluny, the route takes you through the gentle hills, verdant valleys and forests of the Mâconnais. These roads are off the main tourist route and can be very quiet. Approaching Cluny, it is possible to imagine the experience of earlier pilgrims as they arrived at the crest of a wooded hill to view their sacred objective for the first time.

But head first for **Brancion**, perched on a col overlooking two ravines. It is a charming little town within 14th-century ramparts entered through an ancient gateway. The keep and the Tour de Beaufort remain of the ruined 10th-century fortress, and there are many well-restored medieval houses. There is an especially splendid 15th-century wooden raftered market hall. At the highest point of the town is the little church of St-Pierre, also beautifully restored with a series of exquisitely coloured 14th-century frescoes. From its terrace is a breathtaking view over the surrounding countryside, and here in June the feast of St John is celebrated with a huge bonfire visible for miles.

Wine-lovers reluctant to leave the Mâconnais hills may wish to divert to the little village of **Chardonnay**, which

Chapaize, church of St-Martin.

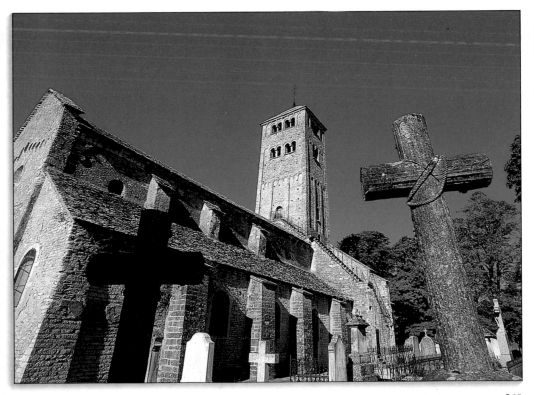

gave its name to probably the most famous grape in the world, known from California to Australia, and responsible for all the best white wine in Burgundy. As in most villages in wine country the grapes occupy all of the valuable land, growing right up to the sides of the houses and the road. A large wine producer occupies pride of place in the village square.

Returning to the ecclesiastical trail, **Chapaize** has a very beautiful church, its lovely Lombardic square tower visible through a veil of trees as you approach. St-Martin is early 11th-century and carefully restored, all that remains of the priory founded by the Benedictine monks from Chalon. It is a fine composition of volumes and forms, very stark and simple, with walls, huge columns and ceiling all in the same warm yellow-ochre limestone so that you feel as if you are inside a great sculpture. The aisles end in charming little apsidial chapels rebuilt in the 13th century and the whole building has a very pleasing unity.

There are a number of fine châteaux to see in this region; **Sercy**, near **St-Gengoux-le-National**, has an extraordinary mixture of architectural styles including five distinctly different towers. **Cormatin,** on the D981, is a magnificent Renaissance château, built on the site of a 13th-century fortress founded by the du Blé family, and particularly famous for its richly painted 17th-century interiors.

Although nothing of the original building remains, when the moat was drained recently evidence of the corner towers was discovered. It was rebuilt by Antoine du Blé, Baron d'Uxelles, at the beginning of the 17th century. The interiors were painted for his son, Jacques, by Parisian artists; walls and ceilings are completely covered in panel paintings and gilding to extraordinary effect, completed by period furniture. Also noteworthy are the kitchens and the arched stone staircase, one of the earliest of its kind.

In 1896 Raoul Gunzbourg, director of the Monte-Carlo opera, bought the cha-

Cormatin, painted ceiling.

teau and entertained, in sumptuous style, stars like Dame Nellie Melba, Caruso and Sarah Bernhardt. Then the building fell into disrepair and was bought in 1980 by private owners who have dedicated themselves to its restoration and use as an arts centre.

Beyond the moat, and its imperious black swans, the restored gardens are lovely, with a long avenue of lime trees, particularly favoured by the poet Lamartine, who was a frequent visitor to the château – so frequent indeed that Jacques's daughter, the Comtesse de Pierreclos, bore him a son. Ornamental topiary, parterres and a charming wrought-iron dovecote complete the picture of a formal Renaissance garden.

A few miles further along the D981 is **Taizé**, a small village world-famous for its international religous community visited by thousands of young people every year. Its proximity to the now defunct Cluny is supremely apposite. The community has built and filled to the rafters its own large modern church but the exquisite little Romanesque vil-

lage church nearby makes a pleasing contrast; very dark, lit only by a modern stained-glass window, and empty of chairs, just a few wooden kneeling stools on the bare stone floor.

The Romanesque trail: Cluny itself feels like a town with something missing: a vast empty space around which all the streets and buildings arrange themselves. The great abbey, once the largest building in Christendom, no longer exists but the small town which grew up around it is still there, and has expanded into the ruins.

Rues Lamartine, Mèrciere and Filaterie were all built against the massive southern enclosure wall of the abbey, with many of the old houses propped against it. The Rue Porte-de-Paris follows the north and east walls of the abbey, both ending in watchtowers, the Tour Ronde and the Tour Fabry.

The whole town was originally enclosed by fortifications and of its eight gateways, two remain: the 12th-century Porte Ste-Odile on the Promenade du Fouettin, a wide boulevard, flanked by

Cormatin panelling.

TAIZÉ

"**A**h Taizé, that little springtime!" So Pope John XXIII described this ecumenical monastic community which has grown to become one of the most influential places of pilgrimage in contemporary Christianity. He always kept in regular contact with the founder of the community and subsequent popes have visited it in person, such is its importance.

It is appropriate that this should happen here, in the shadow of the once-famous but now long-dead Cluny. Every year tens of thousands of young people from all religious backgrounds visit Taizé to participate in its simple life and inspirational worship.

Founded by a Swiss pastor, Roger Schutz, when he came to the almost deserted village of Taizé in 1940, the community began as a hiding place for members of the Resistance and those escaping Nazi persecution, particularly Jews. Brother Roger, as he is known, believed that taking his Christianity seriously meant that he had to live among those who were suffering and not in neutral

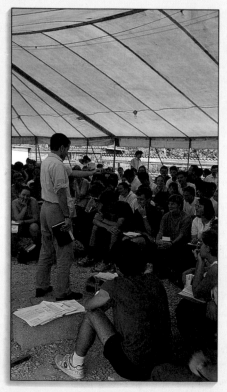

Switzerland. But in 1944 the Gestapo visited Taizé and he was forced to flee to Geneva. He returned after the Liberation of France, accompanied by friends from Geneva. On Easter day 1949 the first seven brothers made a commitment to live together in celibate community life, working to relieve suffering and to bring reconciliation between Christians. In 1962, having out-grown the tiny village church, they built the Church of the Reconciliation, which now stands centrally on the hill at Taizé.

Today there are over 90 brothers from all denominations, 30 of whom live in small "fraternities" in poor parts of the world. Both there and at Taizé they accept no gifts, surviving on what they earn by their work. This includes delightful earthenware pottery, art-work and books, all of which are sold at Taizé.

There is not a great deal to see at Taizé; it is rather a place to be experienced. At the top of the steep hill to the village is the tiny Romanesque village church, its dark interior sparsely lit with candles. The atmosphere is intense with the prayer of a few figures kneeling in the dim light. The little village occasionally feels swamped by the torrent of visitors which can sometimes amount to as many as 6,000 in one week.

The young pilgrims come from all over Europe, staying for a week at a time in simple barracks and tents, many of them returning year after year. Everyone joins in the daily life of the community, doing the chores, attending Bible studies and worship three times a day.

At the heart of it are the "worships" which take place daily, morning, lunchtime and evening. The community church is huge but even so during the summer people often spill into adjoining tents.

It is always kept dark, the only light coming from stained-glass windows and hundreds of tiny candles. Everyone sits on the floor around the altar in silence, interspersed with meditative chants and Bible readings in several different languages. These gatherings also take place in cities throughout Europe, encouraging young people to work for peace and reconciliation. It is in this way that Taizé exerts its influence, not in the building of daughter communities as Cluny once did, but in the inspiration of its worship throughout the world. ■

Taizé at prayer.

lime trees, created by filling in the moat, and the Porte St-Mayeul opening onto the old road to Charolles.

Sadly the great central space of Cluny is now impossible to enter without paying for a 75-minute guided tour of the few fragments of the abbey that the 18th and 19th-century burghers of the town inadvertently left standing. The classic octagonal tower, of the south transept, with its two tiers of arcades, copied all across France, appears tantalisingly over high walls and locked gates. It is all that remains of the massive church which dominated the entire region and influenced building all over Europe.

The destruction of the abbey was not the work of a mob as is often thought; even a mob crazed with anger could not demolish a building of such great size. It took the Revolutionary army a whole week just to burn the archives. The mob did break a few statues, but it was left to the town government to destroy it totally. After the Revolution it became town property and was divided up into four lots with a road driven right through the centre of the nave to show the division. The church was bought at auction by Batonard of Mâcon, who, despite the protests of Paris and antiquarians worldwide, set up a quarry there from 1798 to 1823, selling off the dressed stones as building materials. It took more than 70 explosions to topple the 700-year-old walls.

Less than a tenth of the building remains: one of the transepts and a few column bases, around which Cluny now bases its tourist industry. Should you stay in the Hôtel de Bourgogne you will not have to look far to see the abbey – you will be sleeping right on top of it. The hotel's geranium-festooned windows follow the course of the columns of the north aisle of the nave. (One column has been excavated beneath the hotel and the base of it sits in a little cave hollowed out of the hotel wall.)

Throughout Cluny there are reminders of what lies hidden or destroyed. The whole quarter by Rue des Tanneries is in ruins, but hopefully awaiting restoration. In Rue Filaterie opposite, is the

Cluny, view of south tower.

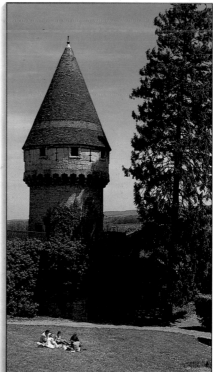

15th-century Hospice St-Blaise, which took in poor travellers and pilgrims in the Middle Ages. It has a Gothic doorway and window lintel which have aged to a beautiful brown patina. Not everything has been ruined, however; Rue Lamartine has a number of fine Romanesque buildings with arcaded windows. There is a 12th-century house on Rue de la République and the Hôtel des Monnaies on Rue d'Avril.

The parish church of **Notre Dame** is worth a visit. Built shortly after 1100, it was enlarged and altered so that it is now largely Gothic in character. The original floor level has been revealed in the northwest corner of the nave, showing a well head and the base of the pillars, giving a good indication of its original proportions. Each arm of the transept has a beautiful rose window with ten branches. Note also the superb 17th-century woodwork. The tympanum and the narthex were destroyed during the Revolution, though parts of the springing arches remain either side of the battered 13th-century front door with its mutilated statues of Moses and Aaron. The outside walls of the nave can also be seen, thanks to the bombardment of 1944 which destroyed the houses built against it. In front of the west door is the charming Place Notre Dame with an 18th-century fountain and the 13th-century Maison des Griffons, named after its carved capitals.

The great barn-like volume of **St-Marcel-de-Cluny** is also interesting, with no columns or even chairs to clutter up the space. There is a 13th-century baptismal font at the entrance but most remarkable is the slender three storey Romanesque octagonal belltower 138 ft (42 metres) high.

Struggle the 120 steps to the top of the 11th-century **Tour de Fromage** in the abbey walls for the excellent view. The ground floor houses the tourist information office. The abbey palaces are both standing though by no means complete. The palace of John of Bourbon was built in 1460 and now houses the Ochier Museum. It originally extended by means of a fortified pavilion to the pal-

Adam and Eve capital, Cluny; interior of south tower, Cluny.

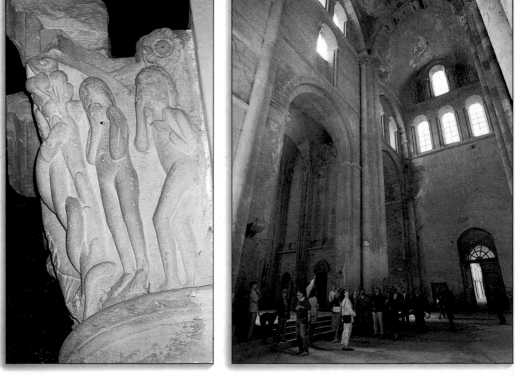

274

ace of John of Amboise, built in 1500 and connected to the main gate and watchtower. Gate and pavilion were both demolished during the Revolution but the main body of the Amboise Palace remains, now the Hôtel de Ville.

The fantastic flamboyant Gothic carving on its facade is in the then fashionable Italian manner, which looks as if it was assembled as booty from other people's palaces (like the front of St Mark's in Venice.) It looks out over one of the abbey lawns – open to the public and a good picnic spot. To the immediate west of the church are the abbey gates, battered but still standing. Through here passed popes and kings.

On Rue Lamartine, the 11th-century **Tour de Moulin**, the Mill Tower, rises over the steep rooftops. It has been well-restored after considerable bomb damage in World War II. Through the basement flows the stream which used to work the abbey mill, and adjoining the building is the 12th-century abbey grain store (which can be seen only as part of the abbey tour).

It is well worth visiting **Berzé-la-Ville** at this point to view the magnificent paintings, executed by the same painters as at Cluny. The **Chapelle aux Moines** is a small estate, clinging to a rock jutting out over the Saône plain, which came under the control of Cluny in 1093. It was one of 30 such farms, with attached chapels, that supplied the abbey of Cluny with food. St Hugues, then engaged in expanding Cluny, loved the place and used it as his private retreat. But it was during the time of Ponce de Melgueil, St Hugues's successor, that a team of artists were sent from the Cluny workshop to paint the interior. The entrance is unassuming, down a dark tunnel and through a farmyard, but on entering you are confronted with a truly amazing spectacle. The entire east end of the chapel is a mass of brilliant colours. After St-Savin, this is the most important collection of Romanesque paintings in France. The luminous colours and eastern technique indicate Oriental inspiration. The painted murals owe a tremendous

Berzé-la-Ville apse painting.

amount to mosaic work and the "golden gloom" of Byzantium. There are five colours in all, red, ochre, blue, gold, and violet, obtained by a red wash over blue.

A huge Christ figure dominates the half dome of the apse, surrounded by his apostles and deacons. Below the windows are a group of Byzantine-looking saints – identities unknown. The paintings are lit by a typical Cluniac arrangement of three windows in an arcade around the apse with two blind arches filled with paintings. The apsidial arch originally had a round light above it, now closed, the crossing had two windows, one above each other on either side, and finally the nave arch, where it rises above the apse, has a top window. The chapel was bought after World War II by the great Romaneseque scholar, Joan Evans, and presented to the Academy of Mâcon in 1947.

The village of Berzé also has a little church, later in date, with a square tower and there are remnants of much older houses to be detected. Nearby the castle at **Berzé-le-Châtel** is like driving straight into the Duc de Berry's book of hours with vineyards planted right up the steep incline to the castle walls. It is a proper castle with the remains of a drawbridge, machicolations for pouring horrible things down on unwelcome visitors, and an ancient crooked gatehouse with two powerful towers of its own. A small formal garden with topiary and stone statues connects the two parts of the château and is the only part open to the public.

There is a beautiful drive to the east of Cluny to the archaeological site at **Azé** where there is a network of caves and an underground river, and a museum with a collection of local paleolithic remains.

Rich pastures: To the west are the **Charolais** hills, prime agricultural country, a carefully stitched patchwork of little fields divided by dry stone walls or carefully trimmed hedges dotted with *étangs*, pools of water glittering in the green-gold light. Small brown farms nestle into the folds of accommodating hills and valleys moulded by centuries of human labour. Almost every field has

Berzé-le-Chatel.

a couple of huge white Charolais cows with their short necks and long curved horns, ruminating comfortably, surrounded especially on damp mornings by the plump *champignons* that will eventually join them in an authentic *boeuf bourguignon*.

It is a region reminiscent of the Cotswolds in England 50 years ago: every hedgerow abuzz with small birds and in the autumn, thick with blackberries, rose-hips and haws. Autumn shows its most fruitful aspect: fields full of plump corn, kitchen gardens with burgeoning fruit trees, bulging red pumpkins and clumps of tied crysanthemums, golden, purple and pink.

The Butte de Suin is an excellent orientation point on the route to Charolles, whether you stick to the main Route Nationale or preferably wander along the narrow but always well-maintained country roads that dictate a slower and more appropriate pace for this deeply rural landscape.

Suin is a tiny hamlet near the top of Suin hill, one of the mystical buttes of Charolais, which has panoramic views of rolling hills, forests and vineyards. There are two small towers, one of which is an orientation platform from which you can see a sum total of 52 belltowers. The Romanesque tower of Suin church has unusual arcading, and the fields around the church, with their 360° views, are ideal picnic spots. To the north are a number of small villages with particularly fine Romanesque churches. In the tiny village of **St-Vincent-des-Prés** the church is a bijou version of Cluny II, built between 1030 and 1063; six huge cylinders support its barrel vault at the east end and below the tower, carved fleur-de-lys and leaves pattern the remaining west end capitals, and the apse has small fragments of the original wall paintings.

Nearby **Massy** is a classic example of the Romanesque churches found in southern Burgundy but, like so many, it has suffered some interference. In this instance there is a false ceiling which almost halves the height of the nave, and a lot of gilt and hideous statuary. It is

Prime pastureland of Charolais.

better seen from outside; the strong tower with its wonderful naïve but powerful zigzag work; the gravestones in the tiny churchyard huddled right up to the church walls; a manor house looming protectively over the church and, if you're lucky, a red squirrel scuttling down the lane.

Charolles itself is a small, sleepy, country town with tractors in the main street and very little tourism. The ruins of the château dominate the town from a bluff, approached via Rue Baudinot, a steep cobbled thoroughfare leading up through the old quarter to the stone gateway of the château.

Despite its sleepiness Charolles has had a chequered history. It was dependent on the dukes of Burgundy, four of whom held the title of Count of Charolais. Originally Charolles was independent of the king of France though it was owned at different times, through marriage or purchase, by both the house of Bourbon and the house of Armagnac. From the 13th century until the French Revolution in was also owned at various times by the kings of France, Spain and Austria.

Just inside the castle gateway, to the right, is a rusticated round tower, the 14th-century Tour de Diamants, the old town prison, so named because the stones are cut with facets. Inside the château there is little left except the 15th-century ivy-covered tower of Charles the Bold. This has remarkable woodwork on the fourth floor which is designed like a wheel with interlocking spokes. Most of the watchtowers have been levelled: pink dahlias grow in the base of one and a 1916 cannon has been placed in another for children to play on. A potager grows between the inner and outer walls of the ramparts. The terrace area has been laid out in formal flowerbeds and gives a pleasant view over the town.

Halfway down the hill, at 25 Rue Baudinot, is **L'ancien couvent des Clarisses**, a 16th-century building now used as a tourist information centre and exhibition hall. Ste Marguerite Marie Alacoque, who was born in nearby

Charolles canals.

Verosvres, lived for several years in the convent and made her first communion there in 1656. She was the founder of the cult of the Sacred Heart of Jesus (to which the local neo-Romanesque edifice is dedicated, as is Sacré Coeur in Paris). The convent roof is made of chestnut in the shape of an inverted boat and there is a good spiral stone staircase.

The slow-moving Arcone divides and flows through the town in a series of attractive algae-covered canals, meandering down the middle of a block then disappearing beneath a house, to reappear in someone's backyard, its banks and footbridges overhung with flowers. There are more than 30 bridges in the town which is sometimes known, at least in travel brochures, as "the Venice Charolaise". There is a regular market here every Wednesday and apart from the fine local beef, specialities include Charolais cheese, a long cylinder which can be made from goat's or cow's milk.

Cow culture and churches: Cow country continues south into the **Brionnais**, a quiet rural landscape of small farms and tiny villages with probably the best pastureland in France. The local domestic architecture is unpretentious, with outside staircases and wooden porches sheltering chickens and hung with drying corn. The Romanesque churches of this area are, however, superb. Though usually small, they are often exquisitely decorated with fine carvings and sculpture, a surprising development in such a backwater, due of course to the influence of Cluny. There are so many to see that a *Circuit des Églises Romanes* has been mapped out by the local tourist authority.

But first, to experience contemporary cow culture to the full, consider an early morning trip to the cattle market in **St-Christophe-en-Brionnais** held every Thursday. It starts at 5am and you really need to be there by about 8am to see any action. It claims to be the biggest weekly market in France and, for such a small place, this is no mean feat. Everywhere are huge, double-parked cattle trucks, the bellowing of cows and bulls, and throngs of red-faced farmers, all

Charolais cattle.

with flat peaked caps, wellingtons and sturdy sticks. There is a powerful reek of ammonia and rich slurry underfoot from the thousands of cattle gathered in the covered market, tethered to railings, or in the holding yard where 50 trucks at a time can unload straight into the pens. The farmers prod and pull the cattle, earnestly discussing their finer points. By 9am the enormous market café is lost in a cloud of steam and smoke, its tables packed with rows of peak-capped farmers, each with a bottle of red wine and huge baguettes of sausage and salami.

Before embarking on the Romanesque trail of the Brionnais, **La Clayette**, where Potain cranes are made, is worth a slight detour to the east. In the middle of town is a very fine castle set on a lake, which reflects its lovely mansard roof, round turreted towers and drawbridge. It is private, but is opened on 1 June every year for visitors to pick lily-of-the-valley, considered to be lucky. Its outbuildings house a popular vintage car museum.

You can wander at will through the Brionnais looking at Romanesque churches and never see them all, so the following examples are only edited highlights. The church at **Vareilles** to the west of La Clayette, has an apse lit by three fine Romanesque windows with a blind arch either side in the manner of Cluny. Unfortunately, a nasty false ceiling has been erected in the nave, destroying its proportions. The high square tower is its pride and joy with two storeys of boldly cut arcading, contrasting nicely with the solid cylinder of the apse. The village also has some charming buildings, a typical shuttered Brionnais house with curved tiled roof, a wooden house with an open upstairs porch, and an old house which uses the original columns from the nave of the church to make a gallery.

The exterior of **St-Laurent-en-Brionnais,** just to the south, is very attractive; thick tiles on the apse and chapels look like clam shells piled on top of each other. The tower is very tall, rising three storeys above the nave. **St-**

St-Julien-de-Jonzy tympanum.

Maurice, a tiny hamlet just outside Châteauneauf, has a lovely little ruined 12th-century Romanesque church. All that remains is the square tower and semi-circular apse set in its old churchyard but this has been made into a room used for exhibitions and though the walls have massive cracks and the floor is simply gravel, the ancient structure is charming. Two miles west on the D8, at **Ligny-en-Brionnais,** are the 11th-century remains of the Abbey of St-Ligard, home of Peter the Hermit, who preached the first crusade. Going east, the D8 crosses the river Sornin to **Châteauneuf** over a Roman bridge.

St-Julien-de-Jonzy is a small hamlet dominated by the square tower of its Romanesque church, in an old churchyard overlooking open countryside and the Beaujolais mountains. The tympanum and lintel were cut from the same huge block of sandstone by an anonymous master and feature a wonderful carving of the Last Supper with everybody's feet sticking out from under a carefully modelled tablecloth. All but two of the heads were knocked off during the Revolution but the work is still very impressive. Just inside the porch, to the left of the main door, is a cow's head capital, appropriately enough, staring quizzically at the visitor. The uplifiting sense of light and space inside is caused by a tall clerestory level filled with plain glass.

One of the most charming features in the 11th-century church at **Iguerande** is the Cyclops playing the pipes of Pan who stares, with his one central eye, down from the first pillar on the left as you enter. There are many other fine carved capitals featuring foliage and geometric designs, some of them still painted in their original colours, and a medieval wall-painting extending right over the crossing and around the apse. The interior proportions of the church are very pure and simple with delightful semi-circular apsidial chapels either side of the apse in the correct Cluniac manner. Outside, don't miss the carved cornice corbels on the chevet which feature dogs, monkeys and horses.

La Clayette.

Semur-en-Brionnais is especially beguiling; a once fortified town, with part of its ramparts still remaining and an arched town gate leading to grassy footpaths and fields. The castle is small but very impressive, with flocks of black birds swooping round its squat 9th-century keep. This was the birthplace of St Hugues, the famous abbot of Cluny, and a geneology of his family, the house of Semur, is on display. The two towers were used as a prison in the 18th century and still have prisoners' graffiti on the walls, and a game carved on the window-sill of a lookout slit, by the soldiers of the watch. Steep stone steps, almost 1,000 years old and very narrow, lead to the secret dungeon and an 18-ft (5-metre) deep pit which has been luridly lit with green light.

Outside the castle is a square of shady lime trees, and a wonderful old-fashioned café, with a big fire in winter, home-made blackberry conserves served with bread and coffee, wood beamed ceiling, simple wooden tables and an importunate cat. The unmistak-able aroma of Gauloises intensifies when farmers from the cattle market at St-Christophe stop on Thursday mornings for a late breakfast of wine and soup. Outside the café is a water pump with a huge iron handle that could have been made by Miró or Calder.

The church of St-Hilaire is a beautiful and celebrated example of Cluniac architecture, in particular its octagonal belfry with two storeys of Romanesque arcading, one of the best in the region. The view from the east end is remarkable with the flat planes of the tower contrasting with the semi-circles of the apse. There are tympani over both north and west doors. The interior has triforum arcading and an overhanging gallery at the west end supported by superb corbelling. This gallery is thought to be a copy of an original in the Chapel of St Michael in the abbey church of Cluny.

The church has plenty of breathing space and stands in a wide square surrounded by sympathetic architecture with plenty of turrets and towers, in-

Anzy-le-Duc fresco ceiling.

cluding the former priory and the18th-century Hôtel de Ville.

The late 11th-century church at **Anzy-le-Duc,** once part of an important priory, is considered to be one of the finest in the Brionnais, with a three-storey Romanesque tower and particularly well preserved capitals. Its famous tympanum can now be seen in the museum at Paray-le-Monial. It is very similar to Vézelay and allows us to see how Vézelay looked before the addition of its Gothic buttresses.

Sacred Heart: Paray-le-Monial, which is at this point only a few miles to the north, is an essential element in the Romanesque jigsaw puzzle. The twinning of Paray with Wells is appropriate – both towns have the same quiet, bourgeois confidence, seemingly exempt from world events, their lives dominated by the giant churches at their centre, their rivers slow-moving and their population unhurried.

Paray-le-Monial is famous as the centre of the worship of the Sacred Heart, a cult which was started by Marguerite-Marie Alacoque, born in nearby Verosvres. As a nun in Paray, she had a divine revelation to worship the Sacred Heart of Jesus. After her beatification in 1864, the church of Sacré Coeur was built in Paris, and yearly pilgrimages to Paray have taken place ever since, establishing the town as a very important religious centre.

To get an idea of how Cluny III must have looked, visit the basilica of Paray-le-Monial (**Basilique du Sacré Coeur**) first. It was begun at the end of the 11th century and completed by 1109. It is in a beautiful setting, its impressive facade of golden stone facing the river bank and removed from whatever hustle and bustle Paray can muster.

Paray shows how daring the Romanesque Burgundian church builders could be. To get light into the church they built a very high nave, 71 ft (22 metres), crowned by a pointed barrel vault. This exerted less downward thrust than a round barrel so did not need the usual supporting vaults above the aisles to buttress it. Without the galleries above the vaults they could build

clerestory windows and illuminate the nave directly from outside. Fluted pilasters with Corinthian capitals line the nave arcade and classical details have been taken from Roman buildings such as the Roman gateway in Autun.

The glory of Paray is in the lighting of its east end. The nave terminates in a vertical wall with three lights directly over the choir which has nine clerestory windows of its own on a lower level. The ambulatory has two storeys of windows and each radiating chapel has three windows. Thus light enters the east end on four levels of elevation and in four different planes of space, a remarkable achievement for the time. Cluny III was very similar, only on a larger scale with more chapels.

The nave of Paray was not completed; only three bays join the crossing to the narthex with its two great towers, but the awkward joining of the nave to the narthex, coupled with the fact that the west door is not quite aligned to the present altar, suggest that the builders intended to demolish the 11th-century

Anzy-le-Duc capital carving.

towers and narthex, and continue their new nave to a point much closer to the river. The result is a strange, squeezed appearance from the west, with the towers frankly too close to each other, whereas the east end is expansive and confident. The towers are the oldest part of the present church, predating it by about 100 years, but they have suffered extensive rebuilding. The narthex which they house is on two floors, as in Tournus – a Burgundian speciality.

The central tower is mock Romanesque, built in the 1860s to replace an unsympathetic 18th-century dome. The community of monks the abbey was originally built to accommodate was never more than 25 strong – its huge scale was for the glory of God, not man. However, it is providentially suitable for receiving the great crowds of Sacred Heart pilgrims who flock here every year. The **Hiéron Museum**, part of the basilica complex, houses the beautifully carved 12th-century tympanum from Anzy-le-Duc, rescued during the Revolution.

There are other fine buildings to see in Paray: the marvellous 16th-century Renaissance **Hôtel de Ville**, formerly the private mansion of Pierre Joyet who contructed it in 1525–28. The elaborate carved facade is festooned with medallions and emblems, niches, carved figures and many *coquilles St Jacques*. Note the pair of faux dormer windows on the third floor which do not actually pierce the steep roof: their top windows open to the roof tiles instead of attic rooms. Two doors to the right is a building with a remarkable row of medieval windows, each in a different style. Across from this group is the finely proportioned **Tour St Nicolas,** which is a deconsecrated church.

The old quarter of town is pretty in a restrained way, particularly the Place de la Boucherie, with low buildings set at attractive angles on wide airy streets, window boxes and newly restored fronts. In front of the church the Bourbince flows between quiet riverbanks shaded by planched trees, with ducks and swans calmly floating by.

The Central Canal passes close to Paray and local industrial production includes sandstone paving and tiles. To the north is **Montceau-les-Mines**, an industrial town which developed due to the coal mined locally. The best view of this area is to be had from the small town of **Gourdon** which overlooks Montceau-les-Mines, Le Cruesot and out as far as the Morvan.

But in Paray, we have now almost reached the Loire, and the D79 follows it for some time, making a very pleasant drive onto **Digoin**, an important pottery centre and the hub of a network of canals with a canal-bridge linking the Saône and the Loire.

A little further on is **Bourbon-Lancy** with its thermal baths and medieval buildings; it is quiet, the approach shaded by huge chestnut trees, and there are good views from the old town, high on its hill. But these are digressions from the more essential aspects of Burgundy, and, surfeited with Romanesque, it is time to return to its other main attraction; the wine country of Mâcon and Beaujolais.

Left, Cluny, south tower. **Right**, Paray-le-Monial; modelled on Cluny.

MÂCON AND BEAUJOLAIS

The red pantile roofs of Mâcon herald the south, the landscape becomes more rugged as the hills of Beaujolais beckon and only the most dedicated oenophile would regret exchanging the dullard contours of the Côte d'Or for more challenging vistas. Nor is the wine a poor substitute; both in Mâcon and in Beaujolais it is affordable, a realistic accompaniment to a picnic lunch rather than the revered travel objective.

Apart from the splendid monument at Brou, and a sprinkling of churches and châteaux, this region is not especially rich in architecture, and can be enjoyed most of all for its judicious combination of good wine and beautiful country. Lamartine is its spokesman; he was born here in the tiny village of Milly-Lamartine (and his legacy is fully exploited) and adored this land, writing innumerable poems singing praises to its beauty. "My eye finds a friend in all this horizon; / every tree has its history and each stone a name."

To the north, between Mâcon and Tournus, are the Mâconnais hills where most of the Mâconnais *appellation* is grown. About a third of this wine is red or rosé, based on the Gamay or Pinot Noir grape and two-thirds are white, grown from the Chardonnay grape. The main *appellations* are Mâcon Rouge, Mâcon-Villages Blanc, Pouilly-Fuissé and Saint Véran. The latter two, considered the best of the Mâcon wines, are grown on the chalky hills to the south of Mâcon itself.

The town of **Mâcon**, though an important wine centre, and a pleasant enough base for visiting the region, is not a particularly compelling tourist attraction. As the most southerly of the Burgundy towns it looks more towards Lyon than Dijon, and has always been an important regional crossroads, linking Paris with the south and looking east towards Switzerland. It was established

Preceding pages: Jarnaux Château, Beaujolais. **Left**, Mâcon, Quai Lamartine.

as a port by the Romans, though its history can be traced right back to prehistoric times, and the river has always been its *raison d'être*, with trade as its mainstay. At this point the Saône is about as wide as the Thames in London, sluggish and slow-moving; Julius Caesar observed that it was so slow he could not tell which way it was moving. There is a river walk from one end of the town to the other and at either end it widens out, with poplars and willows lining the banks. Upstream the Saône provides a wide enough basin to accommodate the French Rowing Championships. Along Quai Lamartine and Quai Jean Jaurès are terrace cafés and restaurants with a good view of the river.

The northern part of the old town of Mâcon is built over a steep hill on the west bank of the river. Sadly, many of the old over-hanging houses in the area have been demolished, and what remain are dwarfed by massive 1960s-style government buildings.

Mâcon was one of the centres of early Protestantism, and was the scene of fierce fighting during the Wars of Religion. During the French Revolution the Mâconnais took anti-clericalism to heart and did a thorough job, destroying all 14 of their Romanesque churches. Only a few fragments of the cathedral church of **St-Vincent** remain, looking as if they have suffered from a great conflagration, which they have. Any visitor coming to Burgundy in search of the beauties of the Romanesque will thus be disappointed in Mâcon. In the 1860s the citizens even had to construct a neo-Romanesque parish church, the Église St-Pierre, to cater for their own needs.

In the battered remains of St-Vincent there is a small museum of Romanesque artefacts salvaged from the rubble – mainly capitals and fragments of pillars. The tympanum is largely intact and has many interesting carved figures, otherwise all that remains of the church are the narthex, the two hexagonal towers and the portion of the nave beneath.

But churches are not everything: there is the beautiful **Place des Herbes**, where the vegetable market shelters beneath

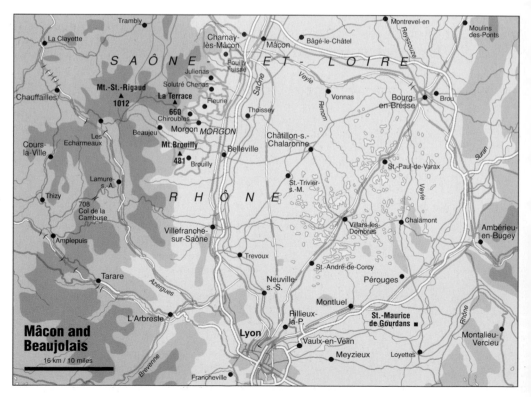

Mâcon and Beaujolais

16 km / 10 miles

two rows of leafy, shade, trees. Here on the corner of the market and the rue Dombey is the amazing **Maison de Bois**: a three-storey, 15th-century wooden house covered in the kind of elaborate carving you would normally expect to find adorning the interior; here be dragons, birds, unicorns and griffons. Monkeys and human figures pull faces and parade naked overhead. In *La revendeuse de Mâcon*, the Goncourt brothers described the building as "a large wooden sideboard that the people of Mâcon can only sneak a glance at", due to the risqué figures on the walls. The Maison de Bois now houses a reasonably priced café and makes a good place to sit and get the feel of the town.

A little further along the Rue Carnot, one of the busiest shopping streets of the town, is the **L'Ancien Hospice de la Charité**, designed and built in 1752–62 by Soufflot as a hospital and now an old people's home. The oval chapel of St-Vincent-de-Paul was designed to link directly with the hospital, to allow the sick to attend church services without

having to move to the ground floor. To the right of the front door is a swivel-gate, one of the few remaining in France. It consists of a barrel built into the wall to allow desperate parents to abandon new-born babies without being seen. The child was placed in the barrel which was then swivelled to face inside. When the bell was rung the nuns ran immediately to collect the baby.

The **Musée des Ursulines** on the Rue des Ursulines is the municipal museum, housed in a 17th-century convent building. It has mainly Flemish and French paintings and porcelain, and is worth visiting for its local history material and the collection includes a particularly good exhibition on the excavations at nearby Solutré, as well as examples of local pottery, wine-growing tools and Bresse furniture.

It is in Mâcon that the Lamartine trail begins; the **Hôtel d'Ozenay** at 15 Rue Lamartine is his old family house, and in the 17th-century Hôtel Senecé is housed the **Musée Lamartine**, with a collection of literary and political docu-

Risqué carvings on Maison des Bois.

ments relating to the poet. On the way out of Mâcon to the north, on Avenue de Lattre de Tassigny, is a new cultural centre and theatre complex, and also the **Maison des Vins**, which provides an opportunity for tasting regional wine and food; look out for a wide variety of local *saucisson*, and the famously pungent *chèvre de Mâcon*. Each May, Mâcon holds a national wine fair with hundreds of different wines.

Although it's not technically in Burgundy, it would be a pity to be so close and not visit **Bourg-en-Bresse**. Head out of Mâcon to the east across the 14th-century St-Laurent bridge – a good place to get a general view of Mâcon over the river. This is Bresse country again with its busy market gardens and low wood and red brick houses hugging the earth. Bourg (pronounced Bourk if you want to sound like the locals) is the centre of this rich agricultural region, well-known for its cattle and poultry, best seen on market days and at the annual fair.

The town is most famous, however, for the church and monastery at **Brou**,

though you would hardly know it should you try and find directions; it is advisable to visit Brou (to the southeast) before entering the town itself, since once within the central traffic zone it is poorly signposted. (Brou is also situated on a major crossroads and if you miss the turning it can take considerable effort to retrace your steps.) However, the effort is worth it.

A sacred promise: Brou was built by Margaret of Austria to fulfil a vow made by her mother-in-law, Margaret of Bourbon, who promised to rebuild the existing small priory at Brou if her husband, Philip, Count of Bresse, recovered from a hunting accident. She unfortunately died before she could fulfil her promise and Margaret of Austria, her daughter-in-law, initiated the construction in 1506.

As the daughter of Emperor Maximilian, she had been a particularly unfortunate pawn in the politics of the time and by the time she was 24 had been widowed twice. She became regent of Flanders and Franche-Comté, and was a highly respected and cultured

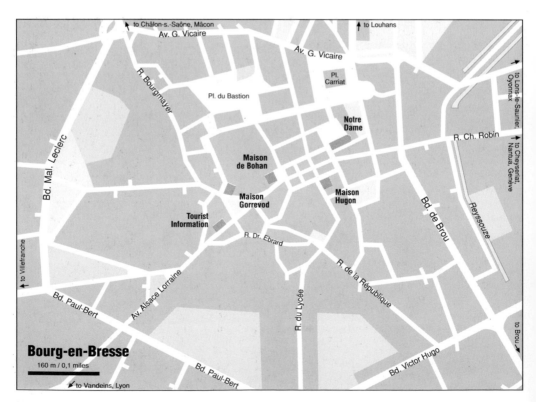

ruler. In fulfilling the sacred promise of the earlier Margaret she hoped to avoid further disaster. She left Bourg-en-Bresse to live in Malines, near Brussels, from where she oversaw the plans, but died of an infected foot in 1530, and never saw the completion of the building. The monastery and church (now deconsecrated) which houses the tombs of Margaret, her husband Philibert, and Margaret of Bourbon, was designed and built by Louis Van Boghem, a Flemish mason. The church is a fine example of flamboyant Gothic with superb carving on the facade. Within, the light from the clerestory brilliantly illuminates the soaring nave and double aisles. Note in particular the superb carving of the choir stalls and the detail of the misericords, the brilliant colours of the original stained-glass windows, and the finely carved rood screen.

In the centre of the choir and the two chapels to the side, are the tombs themselves, extraordinary monuments, richly carved, the three effigies sculpted from huge blocks of white Carrara marble, transported all the way from Italy. Margaret's effigy even shows the gangrenous foot which caused her death.

The monastery to the side of the church has three fine cloisters, a world apart from the traffic which surrounds the building. The kitchen cloisters are the oldest, the remains of the former 14th-century priory. Above the vaulted great cloisters are the monks' dormitories which now house a museum of paintings, including a portrait of Margaret of Austria by Bernard van Orley, and works by Breughl, Gustave Doré and Millet. There is also a collection of Bresse furniture and tapestries. Perhaps most pleasing about the entire ensemble at Brou (apart from the fact that it miraculously survived the Revolution) is the way it has retained its original purpose as a monument – a glorious testimony both to its founder and the many skilled artists that she employed.

Bourg-en-Bresse is a surprising town; despite its agricultural base, it feels very elegant, with luxury shops, well-dressed people and an almost Parisian ambience

Brou, misericord carving; Brou sculptures on St Philibert's tomb.

LAMARTINE

Burgundy's greatest native writer, Alphonse de Lamartine (1790–1869), is revered in France as one of the greatest poets of the French Romantic movement, second only to Victor Hugo; every schoolchild studies his work. Being a somewhat humourless and high-flown figure, he was very far from the stereotype of a jolly, bibulous, down-to-earth Burgundian. But he did have a warm feeling for his homeland, the hills west of Mâcon, as is clear from many of his poems.

He was born in Mâcon, into a family of landowning minor aristocrats who owned several manor houses in the villages to its west. Here he spent much of his time, when he was not working elsewhere as a diplomat or Paris politician. Just as Rousseau influenced Wordsworth, so the bard of Grasmere in turn had an impact on Lamartine; and the significance that the French poet attached to his early environment, and to its deep effect on his character, has strong Wordsworthian echoes. In one long poem, telling of the

moon and stars, the billowing grassland, the herds on the hillsides, he says: "All these speak to me a most intimate language… these old memories that sleep deep within us, that a landscape preserves for…" Those lines are from *Milly ou la terre natale*, about the village of Milly where he spent much of his childhood ("Here is the rustic bench where my father sat"). Here is the family's old stone house, where he later wrote the first of his *Méditations* and recalled "the sweet and melancholy voices of the little frogs that sing on summer evenings".

Nearer Mâcon, just north of the N79, the handsome ochre-coloured château of Monceau was one of Lamartine's favourite homes in his middle years: here this lover of pomp lived in extravagant style as a country squire, sometimes plagued by creditors. Neither this château nor the house at Milly is open to visitors; nor is the 17th-century manor at Pierreclos, south of Milly, home of the woman who was his inspiration for Laurence in his epic poem *Jocelyn*. In Mâcon itself, his home from 1805 to 1820 still stands, at 15 Rue Lamartine, and the nearby Hôtel Senecé contains a museum of his souvenirs.

The Château of St-Point, west of Milly, *can* be visited. The poet received it from his father as a wedding gift in 1820, and he lived there often. It contains his bed, writing-desk and other mementoes. In the little church are two paintings by his English wife, Anna Eliza Birch, and in its chapel are his tomb and hers. In the garden, you can still see the stone bench under the lime-trees where he wrote many of the *Méditations*, and the oak-tree under which he wrote *Jocelyn*.

All this is authentic. But a notice by the pond in the park states "Le Lac" which is misleading, for Lamartine's best-known poem, *Le Lac*, is actually about the large and lovely Lac du Bourget, in the alpine foothills of Savoy, where in 1816 the young poet met the wife of a Paris doctor, Julie, and fell romantically in love. She suffered from a lung complaint, and died in Paris before she could return to meet him the next year. Just before her death, he sat on a hill above the lake and wrote his famous poem: *O temps, suspend ton vol! et vous, heures propices, suspendez votre cours!*… (O time, suspend your flight! and you, propitious hours, suspend your course!). ■

to its streets and cafés. Don't miss, for example, Le Français, an old-style brasserie with aspidistras and velvet banquettes, tall mirrored columns and brown nicotine stained ceiling. The comfortable plumpness of its patrons attests to their consumption of large quantities of rich local dairy produce. The old buildings of the town, clustered round the Gothic church of Notre Dame, have been recently and very well restored; look out for fine Renaissance mansions and 15th-century half-timbered houses like the Maison du Bois on the corner of Rue l'Espagne and Rue du Palais, the double-jettied Maison Hugon on the Rue Gambetta and the wooden buildings on the Place des Bons Enfants.

West of Mâcon: After this detour, head west again to complete a tour of the southernmost part of Burgundy. Leaving Mâcon on the N79 in the direction of Cluny, there is what is now the suburb of **Charnay-les-Mâcon**. Continue further, over the autoroute, and the 11th-century church of Charnay can be found, away from the road, in the middle of a wide village green, originally the graveyard. Over the years the church has been embellished with four side chapels, a narthex and an inappropriate glazed tiled dome added to the tower. Beneath it all, however, remains a beautifully proportioned Romanesque building; the hexagonal tower rises from a square base against which is set the semi-circular apse. It is built from golden brown stone and was well restored in 1970 with the exception of the new stained-glass windows, which resemble disco lighting and make the interior too dark.

There is a small museum on the floor above the triple arches of the narthex; unfortunately, it is difficult to see very much because of the dim light, but the view of the nave is good.

In the chapel housing the font, protected by a 17th-century oak screen, the legendary Claude Brosse is buried. He was an enterprising local wine-grower, a giant of a man, who decided to take his wine to Paris in the hope of selling it to a great lord.

The journey took him 33 days; his

Pierreclos Château.

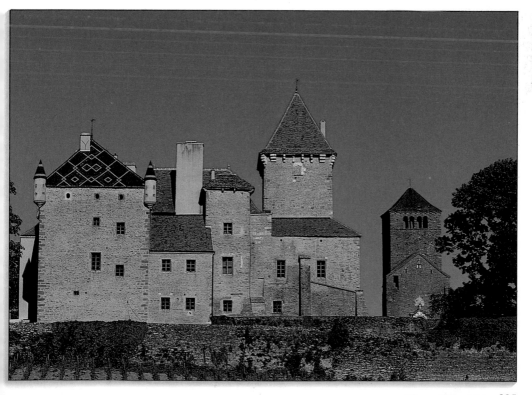

two oxen pulling a wagon groaning with two hogsheads of his best wine. In Versailles, Brosse attended mass where his great size attracted the attention of the Sun King. Brought before Louis XIV, Brosse, a simple country man unencumbered by elaborate court etiquette, happily explained his plan. Charmed, the king tasted his wine and pronounced it far superior to the Suresnes and Beaugency normally drunk at court. The assembled nobility placed orders and the wines of Mâcon assumed the prestigious position that they hold today.

The church is the centrepiece of a pleasant rural ensemble of village houses, all in the same warm ochre stone, with a glorious view out over the golden vineyards of Pouilly-Fuissé.

The Lamartine Trail: A dedicated fan could spend a pleasant day touring the "circuit Lamartinien" and indeed it is a good a way as any to structure a visit to the area. Getting lost is certainly not a problem since every possible Lamartine connection has been diligently labelled.

South of the N79 is the tiny village of **Milly-Lamartine**, where the poet spent much of his childhood, and which inspired his early work. Sadly, Lamartine had to sell the house here 10 years before his death in order to pay off some of his debts. It is beautiful in the formal French sense: symmetrical and flanked by low outbuildings. The two cedar of Lebanon trees, planted when Lamartine returned from the East more than 170 years ago are still there, now mature and beautiful. The building is clearly identified, but is private. A statue of the poet stands at the top of the village overlooking the vineyards.

The Château of **Pierreclos,** residence of the woman who inspired the heroine, Laurence, in Lamartine's epic poem, *Jocelyn*, is also private, but worth visiting for its wonderful site among the vineyards which come right up to its walls. It is a very attractive, classic 17th-century château with steep roofs and towers, one of which has coloured glazed tiles which catch the sun.

But probably the most authentic place to visit is the Château of **St-Point**, a

The Rock of Solutré.

little further to the west. Lamartine loved it and is buried with his wife in the little chapel. In the château his study, salon and bedroom are open, with many mementoes, portraits and letters exhibited.

By now the great Rock of **Solutré** will be a familiar sight, its great craggy outline dominating the gentle slopes of the Pouilly-Fuissé vineyards which surround it, shadowed by the smaller rock of **Vergisson** close by. This great limestone outcrop is also a famous archaeological site; since excavation began in 1866 the discoveries made there of bones and flints have helped establish the chronology of the Palaeolithic era. It was a hunting site for over 25,000 years; the bones of horses and reindeer are scattered over more than 2 acres (0.8 hectares) to a depth of 3 feet (1 metre).

However, the idea that the horses were actually driven over the cliff by their hunters has recently been discredited, and its now thought that they were slaughtered at the foot of the great rock. A fine archaeological museum has recently been established, built under-

ground at the site. There is a path to the excavation site and on to the summit from which there are splendid views of the Saône Valley and on a clear day all the way to the Alps.

Solutré has achieved a more recent fame, due to a vow made by President Mitterrand while he was a prisoner of war in Germany, that he would climb the rock at Solutré every Whit Sunday. Actually, according to the mayor of Fuissé, Georges Burrier, the climb itself is a myth, "He often comes by helicopter for a photo-opportunity." For lesser mortals, an excellent place to view Solutré is from the heights of **Grange du Bois**, a little village on the D31 which has terrific views right across the vineyards. The village itself is bisected by the boundary between the *départements* of Saône-et-Loire and the Rhône.

Circumscribed by the vine: Pouilly-Fuissé is the most highly regarded of the Mâcon wines, grown on 1,730 acres (700 hectares) divided between the villages of Pouilly, Fuissé, Solutré, Vergisson and Chaintré. It is a dry

Golden vineyards of Pouilly-Fuissé.

golden-green wine, a colour which often seems to suffuse the land itself, and it is particularly pleasing to drink *in situ*. Local restaurants plan their menus to complement the wine, and a good (expensive) Pouilly-Fuissé inevitably seems just the right choice.

Fuissé is typical of these wine villages, utterly dominated and circumscribed by the vines which grow right up to the village walls, indeed right up to the walls of the village church and the small château of Fuissé. The roads actually seem to get narrower, encroached by vines planted as tightly as possible in every available pocket of space.

The local architecture – ochrecoloured stone walls and pale terracotta tiled roofs – has a distinctly southern aspect, and worth noting are some of the fine houses of the *vignerons* with their verandahs and stone colonnades. Mayor Georges Burrier is a wine-maker, as was his father before him; he explains that the area which is permitted to call itself Pouilly-Fuissé is strictly controlled. Every scrap of available land is cultivated, "No-one is ever allowed to build on wine land," emphasises Burrier.

St-Véran is close in quality to Pouilly-Fuissé, and the vineyards are situated to the north and south of Vergisson and Fuissé. In the north the *appellation* includes the villages of Davayé and Prissé, and in the south Chânes, Chasselas, Leynes, St-Amour and St-Vérand, which gave its name to the *appellation*. There are two other small *appellations*, still within the Mâcon area, **Pouilly-Loché** and **Pouilly-Vinzelles**, again producing wines very similar to Pouilly-Fuissé.

The Beaujolais Trail: From here on we have entered the **Beaujolais**, whose vines merge imperceptibly, to anyone other than a Mâcon wine-maker. Following a wine trail through France is perhaps a dangerous thing to do since once on a southern track there is wine everywhere and no particular reason to stop. Still, no wine-lover visiting Burgundy would wish to resist the temptation to add northern Beaujolais to the route, and it is officially considered (at least by Dijon) to be part of Burgundy.

Harvesting Beaujolais.

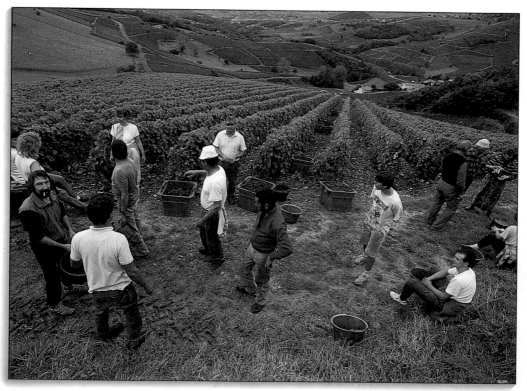

Once in Beaujolais, there is an encouraging proliferation of *vente directe* signs and *dégustations*; the casual visitor is welcomed rather more warmly to the *caveaux* than in the rest of Burgundy. That said, it is still generally assumed that you will buy wine if you are tasting, even if it is only one bottle.

The fame of Beaujolais Nouveau means that more than half today's crop is turned into *primeur* wine, made to be drunk young, and many people are thus less familiar with the fine wines of Beaujolais; a brief tour of the main *appellation* villages is the best possible way to acquaint oneself better. Nearly all Beaujolais wine is grown from the Gamay Noir à Jus Blanc, and this grape produces the best wine; the *crus* and Villages of the Haut Beaujolais, about a third of the total Beaujolais production.

While Beaujolais is not of course comparable to the serious Burgundies, the lighter quality of its *crus* has a distinct appeal to today's market. Hachette's *Les Vins de France* describes it thus: "Beaujolais has the colour of rubies,

The Gamay grape.

tinged with violet. The bouquet suggests fruit and flowers and is lively, fresh, sprightly and straightforward." The wine writer Hugh Johnson confesses he finds it difficult to distinguish between most of the various *grand crus*, but adds that they all have one thing in common, "a sheer joyful smooth drinkableness which balks analysis". Needless to say, Beaujolais has inspired more poetic tributes; for example, "When one drinks Beaujolais, one wishes one had a neck as long as a swan's, to make the pleasure last longer."

What is certain is that for a wine tourist with a limited budget they provide a good opportunity to sample and buy a range of delicious and dependable wines without breaking the bank or building one's own wine cellar. You will often be served local *saucisson* to accompany the wine, especially *rosettes*, traditionally served with the wine of the same year, and *saucisson au vin*, a coarse sausage cooked, naturally, in Beaujolais. The landscape too makes a refreshing change with its wooded hills and cultivated valleys. If approaching from the Charolais to the west, it is interesting to experience the change in the rural landscape, from rich pastureland dotted with turreted farmhouses and small discreet châteaux, up to the rounded hills of the Beaujolais vineyards with sheep and goats on the upland slopes, and little brown stone hamlets huddled within the folds of the mountains.

Beaujolais stretches for 30 miles (50 km) or so towards Lyon to the west of the Saône river. Beaujeu, once the capital, gave its name to the region but was replaced in 1514 by Villefranche-sur-Saône, which is on the boundary dividing Beaujolais into two distinct geological zones. The northern area is granite rock and the vines are grown on the hillsides. To the south limestone predominates, a golden stone, known as *pierre dorée,* which seems to give a permanently warm glow to this lovely landscape. Here the Beaujolais vineyards mingle with pine and chestnut forests on the upper slopes, and there are gentle meadows full of cows in the valleys. Wine-growing in the area since the 10th century has left a legacy of small châteaux, and the wine-making technique has contributed to a particular style of architecture; the living quarters are built over the caves and grain storehouses, with access from an exterior staircase and verandah. Often the wine is fermented on the upper floor and then poured straight into the cellar vats.

Here we are most concerned with seeking out the 10 Beaujolais *crus,* all of which are in the northern region, easily accessible from Burgundy. The *crus* consist of St-Amour, Juliénas, Moulin-à-Vent, Chénas, Fleurie, Chiroubles, Morgon, Brouilly and Côte de Brouilly, and finally Régnié, which was added only in 1988. A route which takes in some or all of these villages can be followed comfortably in a day, allowing for frequent stops and restrained *dégustations.*

The small town of **Juliénas**, which forms part of the Juliénas appellation, is entirely typical of the region in its devotion to wine; growers selling directly to

Terracotta rooftops herald the south.

the public, shops selling local wines, as well as corkscrews, bottles in every conceivable size and other cellar equipment. Tastings are enthusiastically conducted and even the old church, replaced by a larger one, is now used as the *caveau*, the Cellier de la Vieille Église. The château of Juliénas also has famous cellars, and the château of Bois de la Salle, a former 17th-century priory is now used by the Cave cooperative. Look out for the 16th-century Maison de la Dîme, the tithe house, with its double row of arcading.

The local restaurant Coq au Vin is famous for its own special recipe for *Coq au Vin* and other local dishes, and Juliénas wine owes much of its fame to journalists on the satirical newspaper *Le Canard Enchaîné* in the 1930s. Local wine merchant, Victor Peyret, (also responsible for founding the Cellier) was a friend of the cartoonist, Henri Monnier, and often visited the Paris offices equipped with bottles of his wine, which were enthusiastically drunk and subsequently celebrated in print.

St-Amour is slightly to the north, right on the border between Mâcon and Beaujolais. It is named after a Roman soldier, St Amateur, who founded a monastery here overlooking the Saône. The *appellation* was the most recent (1946) until Regnié in 1988.

To the south it is a short drive through the hillside vineyards to **Chénas**, named originally for its oak trees, most of which have long ago been chopped down and replaced by vines. It is the smallest of the *crus* but one of the best for keeping and was known as far back as the 17th century when it was served to Louis XIII. It has been charmingly described as "a bunch of flowers in a velvet basket". Chénas has the distinction of two *grand crus* on its territory, its own and the grapes that go to make Moulin-à-Vent. A brief detour will bring you to the famous **Moulin-à-Vent**, the name given to the combined *cru* of Chénas and the nearby village of **Romanèche-Thorins**. It is the oldest *cru* in the Beaujolais, fixed in 1924, and claims, *"la grace d'un beaujolais et le prestige d'un*

BEAUJOLAIS NOUVEAU

One of the wine trade's most spectacular marketing successes of recent years has been Beaujolais Nouveau. Its arrival in shops, bars and restaurants each year has become an "event" on the calendar. The third Thursday in November is now synonymous with the scramble to get the infant wine to Paris, London, Tokyo and other world capitals. Publicity gimmicks to promote Beaujolais Nouveau (also known as Beaujolais Primeur) have included, over the years, delivery by sports or vintage cars, microlight, elephant and rickshaw.

Enthusiasts are prepared to pay the equivalent of the cost of a bottle of Montrachet for the privilege of being the first to sample the year's vintage, whether in Beaune or at Tokyo airport. Producers and *négociants* naturally adore it; a whole year's vintage can be shifted within a matter of weeks. It is not surprising that an ever greater proportion — now about two-thirds — of all Beaujolais and Beaujolais Villages (but not the *crus*) is now marketed as Beaujolais Nouveau, and that

many other regions and countries have hopped on to the Nouveau bandwagon.

Yet often the brew offered to customers is overpriced and disappointing. A dark purplish liquid with only a hint of the characteristically Gamay nose, it hits the tastebuds like a sledgehammer, rasps the oesophagus like a breadknife and produces an instant headache. As for its taste, "bubble gum and synthetic banana" (Paul Levy) would in most cases be a fair description.

A far cry indeed from the original Beaujolais Nouveau which, until discovered by Parisians after the last war, was little known outside the cafés of Lyon. Regarded as a *petit vin bourru* (a churlish little wine), it had an alcoholic content of only 9.5°–11° and a wonderfully fruity nose. It was usually served straight from the barrel, from which the carbon dioxide still being given off by the wine could escape.

Now that Beaujolais Nouveau is no longer consumed only on the spot, fermentation of the wine has to be brought to a halt before it is bottled, otherwise there is a danger that corks may start popping unasked. But no wine naturally ceases to be active by the third week in November, just six weeks or so after the harvest. So steps are taken to ensure that it behaves itself in the bottle: in addition to the usual practice of adding sulphur dioxide to kill bacteria and unwanted yeasts, producers bombard the wine with ultra-violet rays and pasteurise it at 185°F (85°C). The traditional wine-maker's technique for clearing wine is fining or filtration, but this takes too long, so Beaujolais Nouveau is subjected to the equally efficient, but brutal, processes of centrifugation or freezing or both. Even supposing that Beaujolais Nouveau escapes this treatment, the chances of its tasting as it did in the prewar cafés of Lyon are very slender. This is simply because it is not the same wine. The massive increase in demand has resulted in the familiar old syndrome of vineyard extension and increased yields.

Fortunately, there are still some who supply discriminating bars and restaurants in Beaujolais and Lyon with the genuine product, a light-coloured wine low in alcohol and high in fruitiness, served very cool, but not chilled, direct from the barrel. It's a marvellous accompaniment to hearty, unpretentious food. ∎

bourgogne". Hugh Johnson says it is the one Beaujolais that really stands apart, and he recalls drinking it with a perfectly complementary meal of *volaille de Bresse aux morilles* and *crêpes Parmentier* (potato flour pancakes.)

The windmill itself, three centuries old and no longer working, is built on a rocky promontory with a panoramic view of vines as far as the eye can see, right across the Saône Valley. There are tasting cellars either side of the road from the path which leads to it.

The most famous son of **Romanèche-Thorins** is Benoît Raclet, a *vigneron* who in the 1830s saved the Beaujolais vineyards from the pyralid moth blight. The vines were continually devastated, until one day Raclet noticed that the vine which grew where the maid threw out the dirty water from the house, was flourishing. Raclet decided to try watering his vines with boiling water to great success. Scalding or *échaudage* then became common practice. Today the Musée Raclet exhibits the wide, and often eccentric, variety of containers which were used for this essential labour, as well as furniture and domestic objects from the 19th century. To the east of the village is the zoo, a 25-acre (10-hectare) park full of birds and animals roaming free; the main purpose of the centre is in breeding different species, but a leisure park caters to visitors.

Perhaps because of its delightful name, **Fleurie** is often described as the most "feminine" Beaujolais; it is appropriate then that it has been enthusiastically promoted by one Marguerite Chabert, famous for her passionate devotion to the wine, and the first woman head of a wine cooperative in France. The Chapel of the Madonna, built in 1875, stands in protection over the vineyards.

The cave cooperative in the middle of the village, built in the 1930s, still retains its original lettering, and there are plenty of *vente-directe* outlets as well as two very welcome restaurants. Here you would do well to try the local culinary speciality, *andouillettes au Fleurie*, naturally accompanied by the local wine.

Head west through the mountains to

Corcelles
Château.

Chiroubles, where there is a bust in the village square in memory of Victor Pulliat, famous for saving the vines from Phylloxera in the 1880s, by the use of American vine stocks. From here if you continue along the mountain road to the Terrasse des Chiroubles, you will be rewarded by a magnificent view of the vineyards. A little further on, at **Fut d'Avenas**, an orientation point gives an excellent panorama of the region. The tiny village of **Avenas** has a 12th-century Romanesque church, noted for its exquisitely carved marble altar.

Once up in these beautiful mountains you may wish to follow the quiet winding roads down to Beaujeu; otherwise to complete the Beaujolais *cru* trail head back towards **Villié-Morgon** along the D18. In the village the *caveau* can be found in the middle of a delightful little park which has animal pens for deer and chickens. It was the first tasting *caveau* in the area and can be found in the spacious cellar of the 18th-century château. Morgon is a rich wine, and considered one of the best of the *crus* for ageing. Nearby the **Château de Pizay** is famous for its topiary gardens and its *cuvage*. The **Château de Corcelles,** close to the N6, has medieval buildings and a Renaissance courtyard, and a guard room now used as a *caveau*. The château was painted by Utrillo, who once lived nearby with his mother, the painter Suzanne Valadon.

Regnié, between Morgon and Brouilly, is the most recent *cru* appellation. The village of **Regnié-Durette** is distinguished by its 19th-century church with two towers and the Domaine de la Grange Charton, built in 1820 with dwellings for *vignerons* on the upper floor with typical outside staircases, entwined by vines. It still belongs to the Hospices de Beaujeu, and its huge *cuvages* store all the local wine.

The Regnié vines flank the road from Belleville-sur-Saône to Beaujeu, along the Ardières valley, once the old wine route to Paris. Just to the south are the *appellations* of **Brouilly** and **Côtes de Brouilly**, the largest of the *crus*, dominated by the rounded hill of Mont de

Beaujeu street; Beaujeu rooftops.

Brouilly. At the summit of the hill, which affords good views over the Saône and south towards Lyon, is a small chapel, Notre Dame du Raisin, built in 1857. The hill is the site of an annual celebration by *Les Amis de Brouilly*, which appears to consist mainly of drinking as much Beaujolais as possible and still being able to get back down the slope.

In fact, Beaujolais is distinguished by the passion with which it is celebrated and the quantity in which it is drunk. Not just drunk either – a favourite snack is *tartines au vin*, toasted bread soaked in Beaujolais and sprinkled with sugar.

The Brouilly *appellation* includes the communes of Odenas, St-Lager, Charentay, Cercié, Quincié and St-Étienne-la-Varenne, but, strangely, there is no actual village of Brouilly. At **St-Lager** is a tasting cellar for both Brouilly and Côtes-de-Brouilly. From here you can follow a *route des vins* which includes a number of châteaux, including the 17th century **La Chaize**, to the west of Odenas, built from plans by Mansart, with huge gardens designed by Le Nôtre.

It is most famous, however, for having the largest wine cellar in Beaujolais. One notable scion of the family was Père La Chaize, Louis XIV's confessor, after whom the famous Paris cemetery is named.

Ancient capitals: Beaujeu itself is charming, strung out along the Ardières valley, overlooked by vineyards on the steep hillsides. It is now just a small town with little evidence of its importance in the Middle Ages when it was ruled by the Lords of Beaujeu and held a commanding position on the trade route between the Rhône and the Loire. However, the Hospices de Beaujeu continues to hold its wine auction as it has done since the 12th century. Worth a visit, in the town square, is the Romanesque church of St-Nicolas, with its 12th-century rounded apse and square tower. Across from the church is the 15th-century Maison de Pays de Beaujolais, a beautiful wooden Renaissance building, with overhanging eaves and very old windows; it holds tastings and sales of local produce including wine,

Villefranche-sur-Saône market.

honey and cheese. The whole group surrounding the church is very attractive including the town hall, behind which there is a small park beside the river. The Musée Marius-Audin has a large collection devoted to regional crafts and traditions, particularly wine-making, and a doll museum. Best of all, perhaps, is the main street which looks as if time has stood still for 60 years since most of the shop fronts retain their wonderful '30s facades. Beaujeu is a good base for walkers, and many footpaths have been established through the vineyards and forests which surround it.

Villefranche-sur-Saône today merits a visit as the wine capital of the region; it is full of small cafés, rather like Lyon, where Beaujolais is drunk from the traditional *pots*. Its residents are known as *Caladois*, after the paving stones, *calades*, in front of the church of Notre Dame des Marais, which is distinguished by its oddly assymetrical frontage, Romanesque belltower and 15th-century flamboyant Gothic facade, donated by Anne de Beaujeu, daughter of Louis XI and patron of Villefranche, who made Villefranche capital of the Beaujolais in 1514. (She paid for it by fining the people of Trévoux who were caught counterfeiting coins.) The Rue Nationale has a number of fine 16th and 17th-century houses, tall and Italianate with beautifully restored facades and courtyards. From Villefranche either return to Mâcon or continue the eternal wine trail on to the south of Beaujolais, to Lyon, and beyond.

Gabriel Chevalier, author of *Clochemerle*, and perhaps more responsible than anyone else for the image of a typical Beaujolais village, summarises the people of Beaujolais thus: "They offer their hearts in the palms of one hand… the hand, that is, that does not hold a glass." But his description of Beaujolais wine is as good a general tribute to wine as any: "The more you drink of it, the more delightful you find your wife, the more loyal your friends, the rosier your future and the more bearable mankind."

Left, **Burgundy vineyards.**

TRAVEL TIPS

GETTING THERE

BY AIR

Air France (*see Useful Addresses, page 364*) is the main agent for flights to France. Direct flights go to Dijon airport from London Stansted; also to Lyon, just south of the region, from Heathrow (Air France has a fly-drive option on this route). Geneva airport gives easy access to southern Burgundy.

Air France operates a rail package with flights available from 12 airports around the UK (not Heathrow) to Paris, then onward by train to Dijon, Nevers or Mâcon via Paris Gare de Lyon.

Travellers from America and other countries can get direct flights to Paris, Lyon and Geneva, although a charter flight to London, then onward from there may work out cheaper. Nouvelles Frontières offer some of the most competitive fares on both scheduled and charter flights to Paris and London from the US and Canada. Availability of charter flights is variable; details from their offices at:
London: 11 Blenheim Street, London W1. Tel: 071-629 7772.
New York: 12 East 33rd Street, New York NY. Tel: 212-779 0600.
Montreal: 800 Boulevard de Maisonneuve Est, Montreal, Quebec H2L 4M7. Tel: 514-288 4800.

Other low-price charter flights can be obtained through "bucket shops"; check the national press or *The European* newspaper for offers.

Students and young people can normally obtain discounted charter fares through specialist travel agencies in their own countries.

In the UK try Campus Travel, tel: 071-730 3402 for your nearest branch. Campus is part of the international group USIT, whose main US address is the New York Student Centre, William Sloane House YMCA, 356 West 34th Street, New York NY 10001, Tel: 239-4247 695 5024.

BY SEA

Several ferry services operate from the UK, Eire and the Channel Islands to the northern ports of France. All of them carry cars as well as foot passengers. Hovercraft crossings are fast, but more dependent on good weather than the ferries. The new Seacat catamaran service offers the quickest crossing but, like the hovercraft, can carry only a limited number of cars. The port of Calais offers the fastest access by motorway to the region; other good alternatives are Boulogne and Dunkerque.

Brittany Ferries: sail from Portsmouth to St-Malo, Portsmouth to Caen, Cork (Eire) to Roscoff, and a cheaper Les Routiers service from Poole to Cherbourg (summer only). Details from The Brittany Centre, Wharf Road, Portsmouth PO2 8RU. Tel: 0705-827 701, or from Millbay Docks, Plymouth PL1 3EW. Tel: 0752-221 321.

Hoverspeed: operates hovercraft from Dover to Calais and Boulogne (crossing time approx. 30 minutes). The new Seacat catamaran started on the same route in June 1991. Details of all services from Hoverspeed Ltd, Marine Parade, Dover CT17 9TG. Tel: 0304-240 101. Central Reservations: Maybrook House, Queens Gardens, Dover CT12 9UQ. Tel: 0304-240 241.

North Sea Ferries: connect travellers from the north of England and Scotland to France, via their Hull-Zeebrugge route. Situated 35 miles (55 km) from the French border, Zeebrugge gives relatively good access to the region. The overnight services offer entertainment and a five-course dinner and breakfast are included in the fare. Contact the company at King George Dock, Hedon Road, Hull HU9 5QA. Tel: 0482-795 141.

P&O European Ferries: operate the short sea routes from Dover to Calais and Boulogne, as well as Portsmouth to Le Havre and Cherbourg. Fares and schedules from P & O, Channel House, Channel View Road, Dover CT16 3BR. Tel: 0304-203 388.

Sally Line: ferries use the smaller ports of Ramsgate and Dunkerque. Details from 81 Piccadilly, London W1V 9HF. Tel: 071-409 2240; for reservations: Argyle Centre, York Street, Ramsgate, Kent CT11 9DS. Tel: 0843-595 522.

Sealink: Stena Line ferries operate from Dover to Calais (the fastest shipping route at 90 minutes), Folkestone-Boulogne and Newhaven-Dieppe. Details and reservations for all services are available from Sealink UK Ltd., Charter House, Park Street, Ashford, Kent TN24 8EX. Tel: 0233-647 047. Personal bookings can be made at Sealink Stena Line Travel Centre, Victoria Station, London SW1.

Irish Ferries: sail to Normandy with a year-round service from Rosslare to Le Havre and Cherbourg, and ferries in July and August, once a week to Le Havre from Cork. Contact them at 2/4 Merrion Row, Dublin 2. Tel: 610 511.

Emeraude Lines: runs a ferry from Jersey in the Channel Islands to St-Malo, daily or twice daily in season, and less frequently the rest of the year. Information from Albert Quay, St Helier, Jersey, C.I. Tel: 0534-74458; New Jetty, White Rock, St Peter Port, Guernsey, C.I. Tel: 0481-711414; Gare Maritime du Naye, 35400 St-Malo. Tel: 99.40.48.40.

BY TRAIN

For visitors travelling from Paris, the train is a fast, efficient way to reach the region, especially with the high-speed express trains (TGV) – the journey time to Dijon, for instance, is 1 hour 36 minutes. All services leave from Paris-Gare de Lyon; the principal destinations in the region are Dijon, Mâcon, Nevers, Beaune and Chalon-sur-Saône. Car and bicycle hire is available at most main stations – as a package with your rail ticket if you prefer (*see French Railways, below*).

Tickets may be booked for through journeys from the UK, including ferry travel, from any British Rail station; BR travel centres can supply details of continental services, or contact British Rail European Enquiries, Victoria Station, London SW1. Tel: 071-834 2345. Some passengers can obtain discounted fares, eg., people under 26 qualify for up to 30 percent discount on single or return tickets booked through Eurotrain who also sell a "France Vacances" pass which offers four days' travel in any 15 (or nine days within one month) for around £65 and £110 respectively. Tel: 071-730 3402 for details. Holders of a senior citizen's rail pass can pay an extra £5 for a Rail Europe card which then entitles them to 50 percent reduction on fares; a Family Rail Europe card is available for £5 for family groups of a minimum of three and maximum of eight people, which can be used to purchase cheaper tickets. Details of all these tickets can be obtained from British Rail European Enquiries, as above. Similar tickets are available for other foreign visitors to France, but they have to be purchased before leaving your home country.

Information and reservations for all the above services are available from French Railways Ltd, French Railways House, 179 Piccadilly, London W1V 0BA, tel: 071-499 2153; Frenchrail Inc., 226–230, Westchester Avenue, White Plains, NY 10604; and 1500 Stanley Street, Suite 436 Montreal, Quebec H3A IR3, tel: 514-288 8255. In Australia and New Zealand details are available from Thomas Cook offices. SNCF has a central reservation office in Paris, tel: 1-45.65.60.60 and a telephone information service in English on 1-45.82.08.41.

Most French railway stations accept payment by Visa and Amex.

BY COACH

Eurolines European coach services operate overnight services from London (Victoria) to Dijon. There are weekly departures in winter, twice-weekly in spring and autumn and daily (except Sunday) in summer. The ticket includes the ferry crossing (via Dover) and National Express coaches have connections with the London departures from most major towns in the UK. For details contact: Eurolines UK, 52 Grosvenor Gardens, Victoria, London SW1W 0AU. Tel: 071-730 8235.

BY CAR

The A6 motorway from Paris takes you right through the centre of the region via Auxerre and Beaune down to Mâcon. It connects with the A31 to Dijon at Beaune. From the northern coast, take the A26 motorway from Calais to Châlons-sur-Marne (due to be extended to Troyes); from there the N77 takes you on to Auxerre, or alternatively, follow the N67 to Chaumont, then the N19 and N74 to Dijon. If speed is not of the essence and you intend to make the drive part of your holiday, follow the green holiday route signs to your distination – these form part of a national network of *bison futé* routes to avoid traffic congestion at peak periods. You will discover parts of France you never knew existed and are more likely to arrive relaxed. The first weekend in August and the public holiday on the 15th are usually the worst times to travel, so avoid them if you can. For further details about driving in France, *see Getting Around* (page 316).

Travel Essentials

VISAS & PASSPORTS

All visitors to France need a valid passport; in addition visitors from the USA, Canada, Australia and New Zealand (anywhere outside the EC), require a current visa. These are available from the French consulate in your country and last for either 90 days or 3 years, and are valid from the date of issue. If you intend to stay in France for more than 90 days at any one time, then a *carte de séjour* must be obtained (again from the French consulate) – this also applies to EC members.

MONEY MATTERS

The Franc is divided into 100 centimes – a 5-centime piece being the smallest coin and the F500 note the highest denomination bill.

Banks displaying the "Change" sign will change foreign currency and, in general, at the best rates (you will need to produce your passport in any transaction). If possible avoid hotel or other independent bureaux which may charge a high commission. Credit cards are widely accepted, but Visa is by far the most common and can now be used in hypermarkets and many supermarkets. Access (Mastercharge/Eurocard) and American Express are also accepted in some establishments. Eurocheques, used in conjunction with a cheque card, drawn directly on your own bank account, can be used just like a cheque in the UK and are commonly accepted. Apply for these, or if you prefer, travellers' cheques, from your own bank, allowing a couple of weeks before your departure.

ANIMAL QUARANTINE

It is not advisable to take animals to France from the UK because of the six months' quarantine required by the British authorities on your return. However, if you do wish to take a pet you need to have either a vaccination certificate for rabies, or a certificate to show that your country has been free of the disease for three years. No animal under three months of age may be taken into the country. For further information, contact the French consulate in your country.

CUSTOMS

All personal effects may be imported without formality (including bicycles and sports equipment). It is forbidden to bring into the country any narcotics, pirated books, weapons and alcoholic liquors which do not conform to French legislation. Certain items (e.g., alcoholic drinks, tobacco, perfume) are limited as to the amount you may take in or out, and these amounts vary for those coming from the EC, other European countries or outside Europe. The public often seem confused about exactly how many bottles of wine they are allowed to take home from France; the confusion is perhaps due in part to the fact that you are allowed to take more if it is bought actually in France, rather than from a duty-free shop on the boat or at the airport. The current allowances are shown below, with the amounts allowable from duty-free shops shown in brackets; these may change after the creation of the European single market at the end of 1992. If in doubt, check with HM Customs and Excise, Dorset House, Stamford Street, London SE1 9PS. Tel: 071-928 0533 or your local Customs and Excise office.

CUSTOMS ALLOWANCES

1.5 litres (1 litre) of spirits, strong liqueurs, over 22 percent vol.
　　OR
3 litres (2 litres) sparkling or fortified wines, certain liqueurs or still table wine.
　　PLUS
5 litres (2 litres) still table wine.

GETTING ACQUAINTED

GOVERNMENT & ECONOMY

The region enjoyed early prosperity due to its position as a major crossroads for trade routes. It continued to thrive after the Roman invasion, as can be seen from the well-preserved remains. Later, around the 10th century, Burgundy came under the powerful influence of the abbey established at Cluny and its satellites.

The Burgundians experienced a revival of their fortunes under the great dukes of Burgundy (the House of Valois), the first of whom, Philip the Bold, ruled the region from 1364 for 40 years. The Duchy of Burgundy then extended much further than the present region, encompassing what was later to become Belgium and Holland. It was Philip who brought the artists from Flanders that gave much of the local architecture its particular decorative style.

The last duke, Charles, who died in 1477, was largely responsible for the fall of the Duchy, when most of Burgundy's territory was added to the French kingdom. He continually antagonised King Louis XI, so after the duke's death, the king added most of the territory to his kingdom, except for a small area which Charles's daughter Mary took with her to the House of Hapsburg on her marriage to the Emperor Maximilian I.

Although nominally part of France, Burgundy largely retained its independence until the reign of Napoleon I. In recent history France has been ruled by a very centralised form of government, but under the socialists (1981–86) the Paris-appointed *préfets* lost much of their power as the individual *départements* (or counties) gained their own directly elected assemblies for the first time, giving them far more financial and administrative autonomy. Each *département* still has a *préfet*, but the role is now much more advisory. The *préfecture* is based in the county town of each *département*: Bourg-en-Bresse in Ain, Dijon in Côte d'Or, Nevers in Nièvre, Lyon in Rhône, Mâcon in Saône-et-Loire and Auxerre in Yonne. These offices handle most matters concerned with the social welfare of their citizens.

Each French *département* has a number which is used as a handy reference for administrative purposes, for example it forms the first two digits of the postcode in any address and the last two figures on vehicle licence plates. The *département* numbers for Burgundy are as follows: Ain – 01, Côte d'Or – 21,

Nièvre – 58, Rhône – 69, Saône-et-Loire – 71, Yonne – 89.

Each *département* is divided into a number of disparately-sized communes whose district councils control a town, village or group of villages under the direction of the local mayor. Communes are responsible for most local planning and environmental matters. Decisions relating to tourism and culture are mostly dealt with at regional level, while the state still controls education, the health service and security.

Without a doubt, wine is the principal product of the region, with just over 1,500 acres (610 hectares) of vineyards, mostly in the east of the region. Agriculture too is very important, with the Charolais cattle being the pride of the local farmers. The Bresse poultry, bred in the south of the region have the rare distinction of carrying an *appellation contrôlée*.

In the west, the Morvan has its own industry, mostly related to forestry, including sawmills, the production of charcoal, Christmas trees and quality furniture.

Other good sources of income for the region are stone quarrying (much of Paris is built with the white stone of Burgundy), and the allied manufacture of cement; as well as ceramics, in particular decorative tiles and pottery.

GEOGRAPHY & CLIMATE

Still dominated by agriculture, much of the region is cultivated; to the east it is fairly flat with fields devoted to such crops as maize and sunflowers. To the south it becomes hillier, with the gentle slopes providing the *côtes* for the vines to grow on.

The west of Burgundy is much more attractive scenically with the vast Morvan park offering all-year-round colour, low mountains, lakes and streams. The waterways too, are very much a part of the regional landscape; some 745 miles (1,200 km) of rivers and canals make up a network which has added much to Burgundy's prosperity in the past and now provides a wide range of leisure possibilities.

Burgundy enjoys a pleasant climate which varies with the seasons. Summer can be very hot with occasional showers, while winter is cold, but not damp. Autumn is often recommended as the best time for visitors when it is bright and sunny, but not too hot for touring. However, early morning mists may put a damper on some sightseeing. In the Morvan, where the altitude climbs to over 1,970 ft (600 metres), expect mountain conditions.

TIME ZONES

For most of the year, France is one hour ahead of Greenwich Mean Time, so if it is noon in London, it is 1pm in Dijon, and 7am in Washington.

LANGUAGE

Standard French is spoken in the region. The local accents should not cause any problems of understanding for anyone with a reasonable grasp of the language. Harsh sounds tend to be softened – Auxerre, for example, becomes Ausserre. Most people are very willing to try and communicate with visitors whose French is limited.

WEIGHTS & MEASURES

The metric system is used in France for all weights and measures, although you may encounter old-fashioned terms such as *livre* (roughly 1 lb weight – 500 grams) still used by small shop-keepers.

For quick and easy conversion remember that 1 inch is roughly 2.5 cm, 1 metre roughly equivalent to a yard, 4 oz is just over 100 grammes and a kilo is just over 2 lbs. As a kilometre is 5/8 of a mile, a handy reckoning whilst travelling is to remember that 80 km = 50 miles, thus 40 km = 25 miles. Accurate conversions are given below:

Weight:

3.5 oz	=	100 grammes (g)
1.1 lb	=	500 grammes
2.2 lb	=	1 kilo (kg)

Length:

0.39 inch	=	1 centimetre (cm)
1.094 yard	=	1 metre (m)
0.62 mile	=	1 kilometre (km)

Liquid:

2.113 pints	= 1 litre (l)
0.22 Imp gallon; 0.26 US gallon	= 1 litre
2.2 Imp gallons; 2.6 US gallons	= 10 litres

Temperature:

Temperatures are always given in celsius (centigrade). For conversion to fahrenheit, see below:

0° C	=	2° F
10° C	=	50° F
15° C	=	59° F
20° C	=	68° F
25° C	=	77° F
30° C	=	86° F

ELECTRICITY

Electric current is generally 220/230 volts, but still 110 in a few areas. Current alternates at 50 cycles, not 60 as in the US, so Americans will need a transformer for shavers, irons, hairdryers etc., which also solves the problem of outlet prong shapes.

BUSINESS HOURS & PUBLIC HOLIDAYS

Office workers normally start early – 8.30am is not uncommon – but often stay at their desks until 6pm or later. This is partly to make up for the long lunch hours (from noon or 12.30 for two hours) which are still traditional in banks, shops and other public offices. Many companies are beginning to change to shorter lunchbreaks as employees appreciate the advantages of getting home earlier in the evening.

A list of major public holidays is given below. It is common practice, if a public holiday falls on a Thursday or Tuesday, for French business to *faire le pont* (literally, bridge the gap) and have the Friday or Monday as a holiday too. Details of closures should be posted outside banks etc. a few days before the event but it is easy to be caught out, especially on Assumption Day in August, which is not a holiday in the UK.

New Year's Day (1 January); **Easter Monday** (but not Good Friday); **Labour Day** (Monday closest to 1 May); **Ascension Day**; **8 May** to commemorate the end of World War I; **Whit Monday** (Pentecost); **Bastille Day** (14 July); **Assumption Day** (15 August); **All Saints' Day** – Toussaint (1 November); **Armistice Day** (11 November); **Christmas Day** (25 December), but not Boxing Day (26 December).

Banks are normally open 8.30am–noon and 1.30pm–5pm, Monday–Friday.

COMMUNICATIONS

POSTAL SERVICES

Post Offices: *Postes* or PTTs are generally open Monday–Friday 9am–noon and 2–5pm, Saturday 9am–noon (opening hours are posted outside). Inside major post offices, individual counters are marked for different requirements – if you just need stamps, go to the window marked *Timbres*. If you need to send an urgent letter overseas, ask for it to be sent *par exprès*, or through the Chronopost system which is faster, but very expensive.

For a small fee, you can arrange for mail to be kept *poste restante* at any post office, addressed to Poste Restante, Poste Centrale (for main post office), then the town post code and name, eg. 21000 Dijon. A passport is required when collecting mail.

Stamps are often available at tobacconists (*tabacs*) and other shops selling postcards and greetings cards. Letters within France and most of the EC go for FF2.50 for up to 20g, FF3.40 for airmail to Ireland, the US and Canada.

Telegrams can be sent during post office hours or by telephone (24-hours); to send a telegram in English dial 16-1 42.33.21.11.

Telex, **Minitel** information service (useful for directory enquiries) and **fax** facilities are available at the main post office in most major towns.

Many post offices have coin-in-slot **photocopying** machines.

TELEPHONE

The French telephone system has undergone a drastic overhaul in the past 20 years, and after being one of the worst in the world is now one of the best. That is not to say that you can be guaranteed to find telephone boxes (*cabines publiques*) that are always operational, but most are. Telephone numbers have been rationalised to eight figures, given in sets of two, eg. 99.44.63.21. The only codes necessary are for dialling into or out of Paris (put 16.1 before the rest of the number) or overseas.

International calls can be made from most public booths, but it is often easier to use a booth in a post office – ask at the counter to use the phone, then go back to settle the bill – but you have no record of the cost of the call until the end.

Coin-operated phones take most coins and card phones are now very common and simple to use. It is worth purchasing a phone card (*une télécarte* – currently FF40 or FF96) if you are likely to need to use a public call box, as many are being converted to take cards and in some towns are far more numerous now than coin-operated ones. Cards are available from post offices, stationers, railway stations, some cafés and *tabacs*.

If you use a phone (not a public call box) in a café, shop or restaurant you are likely to be surcharged. Some hotels and cafés now have computerised public telephones whereby the caller receives a printed statement of the details of his call on payment of the bill at the bar – a useful asset for people travelling on business.

To make an international call, lift the receiver, insert the money (if necessary), dial 19, wait for the tone to change, then dial the country code (*see below*), followed by the area code (omitting any initial 0) and the number.

International dialling codes:

Australia	61
Canada	1
Ireland	353
UK	44
USA	1

Useful numbers:
operator services 13; directory enquiries 12

Note that numbers will be given in pairs of figures, unless you ask for them to be given *chiffre par chiffre* (singly).

Some main post offices in France have now replaced their traditional telephone directories with the computerised Minitel system. Members of the public can use this free of charge to look up any number in the country. The instructions (in French) are fairly simple to understand, and you simply tap in the name of the town, *département* and person (or company) whose number you seek for it to be displayed on the small screen, connected to the telephone. It can also be used in the same way as *Yellow Pages* to find, for example, all the dry cleaners listed in a particular town.

If you need to make a phone call in rural areas, or small villages with no public phone, look out for the blue plaque saying *téléphone publique* on private houses. This means the owner is officially required to allow you to use the phone and charge the normal amount for the call.

You cannot reverse charges (call collect) within France but you can to countries which will accept such calls. Go through the operator and ask to make a PCV *(pay-say-vay)* call. Telephone calls can only be received at call boxes displaying the blue bell sign.

To take advantage of cheap rates, use the telephone weekdays between 10.30pm and 8am and at weekends after 2pm on Saturday when you will have 50 percent more time for your money.

THE MEDIA

Regional newspapers, such as *Le Progrès*, *Le Bien Public*, *Les Dépêches* and *Le Courrier*, contain national and international as well as local news, and have a far higher standing in France than their counterparts in the UK and are often read in preference to the national dailies such as *Le Monde*, *Libération* and *Le Figaro*. British and American dailies, notably *The Times* and the *International Herald Tribune*, are also available in major towns and cities.

Television viewers in the region can receive the two main national channels: TF1 (commercial) and Antenne 2 (state-owned but largely financed by advertising); as well as FR3 which offers regional programmes. French houses are also beginning to be defaced by satellite dishes at about the same rate as their British counterparts. Cable TV provides access to BBC channels.

France Inter is the main national radio station (1892m long wave), it broadcasts English-language news twice a day in summer (generally 9am and 4pm). There is fairly good reception of BBC Radio 4, particularly in the north of the region.

EMERGENCIES

SECURITY & CRIME

Sensible precautions regarding personal possessions are always necessary. Theft and other crime exists here as elsewhere but it is not a serious problem as far as tourists to the region are concerned. Drivers should follow the rules of the road and always drive sensibly. Heavy on-the-spot fines are given for traffic offences, such as speeding, and drivers can be stopped and breathalysed during spot checks. Police are fairly visible on the main roads of France during the summer months.

To report a crime or loss of belongings, visit the local *gendarmerie* or *commisariat de police*. Telephone numbers are given at the front of local directories, or in an emergency dial 17. If you lose a passport, report first to the police, then to the nearest consulate (*see Useful Addresses*). If you are detained by the police for any reason, ask to telephone the nearest consulate for a member of the staff to come to your assistance.

HEALTH CARE

Before leaving for France, check with the Department of Health that you qualify for subsidised treatment under the EC (most British nationals do) and acquire from them the form E111. Alternatively, arrange private medical insurance, as should all non-EC citizens. The E111 does not cover the full cost of any treatment so you may find it worthwhile to take out private insurance too. The International Association for Medical Assistance to Travellers (IAMAT) is a non profit-making organisation which anyone can join, free of charge (although a donation is welcome). Benefits include a membership card, entitling the bearer to services at fixed IAMAT rates by participating physicians, and a Traveller Clinical Record, a passport-sized record completed by the member's own doctor prior to travel. A directory of English-speaking doctors, belonging to IAMAT, and on call 24 hours a day, is published for members' use.

IAMAT offices:
USA: 736 Center Street, Lewiston NY 14092. Tel: 716-754 4883.
Canada: 1287 St Claire Avenue W.,Toronto M6E 1B9, tel: 416-652 0137; 40 Regal Road, Guelph. Ontario N1K 1B5, tel: 519-836 0102.

New Zealand: PO Box 5049, Christchurch 5.
Switzerland: 57 Voirets, 1212 Grand-Lancy, Geneva.

For minor ailments it may be worth consulting a pharmacy (recognisable by its green cross sign), who have wider "prescribing" powers than chemists in the UK or US. They are also helpful in cases of snake or insect bites and for identifying fungi!

If you need to see a doctor, expect to pay around FF80 for a simple consultation, plus a pharmacist's fee for whatever prescription is issued. The doctor will provide a *feuille des soins* which you need to keep to claim back the majority of the cost (around 75 percent) under the EC agreement. You have to attach to the *feuille* the little sticker (*vignette*) from any medicine prescribed to enable you to claim for that too. Refunds have to be obtained from the local *Caisse Primaire* (ask the doctor or pharmacist for the address).

In cases of medical emergency, either dial 15 for an ambulance or call the Service d'Aide Médicale d'Urgence (SAMU) which exists in most large towns and cities – numbers are given at the front of telephone directories.

The standard of treatment in French hospitals is generally high, and you should be able to find someone who speaks English to help you. Show the hospital doctor or authorities your E111 and you will be billed (once you are back home usually), for approximately 25 percent of the cost of treatment.

GETTING AROUND

MAPS

A first essential in touring any part of France is a good map. The Institute Géographique National is the French equivalent of the British Ordnance Survey and their maps are excellent; those covering the region are listed below:

Red Series (1:250,000, 1 cm to 2.5 km) sheet No. 108 covers the whole region at a good scale for touring.

Green Series (1:100,000, 1 cm to 1 km) are more detailed, local maps – sheet Nos. 28, 29, 36 and 37 cover most of the region, although you may need Nos. 21 and 22 for the extreme north and west of the region and No. 43 for southern Saône-et-Loire and Beaujolais.

There is also a special map No. 306 at the same scale as the *Green Series* covering the Morvan regional park.

Also available from **IGN** are the highly detailed 1:50,000 and 1:25,000 scales, which are ideal for walkers (*see the Ramblers section, page 320*). For planning your route, IGN 901 covers the whole of France at a scale of 1 cm to 10 km and is regularly updated.

The **Michelin** regional maps are published at a scale of 1:200,000 (1 cm to 2 km); the whole of Burgundy is covered in two sheets – No. 238 for the west and 245 for the east and centre, and on four more detailed sheets at the same scale, Nos. 65, 66 (north), 69 and 70 (south).

Michelin also publish town plans, as do Blay, but local tourist offices often give away their own town plans free of charge. Michelin's Route Planning Map 911 shows motorways and alternative routes and other travel advice.

Stockists in London are Stanfords International Map Centre, 12–14 Long Acre, Covent Garden WC2, tel: 071-836 1321; The Travel Bookshop, 13 Blenheim Crescent, London W11 2EE, tel: 071-229 5260; and The European Bookshop, 4 Regent Place, London W1R 6BH, tel: 071-734 5259.

Compass Books, Freepost, Dereham, Norfolk NR19 1TE, tel: 0362-691 623, offer a mail order service (seven-day, money-back guarantee) and carry a wide range of maps and guides for the region and the whole of France. IGN maps are also available by mail order from the IGN sole agent in the UK, Robertson-McCarta, 17 Angel Gate, City Road, London EC1V 2PT, tel: 071-278 8276. Please note that their shop in London is now closed. In France, most good bookshops should have a range of maps, but they can often be bought more cheaply in hypermarkets or service stations.

DOMESTIC TRAVEL

Car hire is expensive (*see Driving*), but bikes are fairly readily available. Most railway stations have them for hire at around FF50 per day and they do not necessarily have to be returned to the same station. Bikes can be carried free of charge on buses and some trains (Autotrains); on other, faster services you will have to pay. Travelling by a combination of bike and bus or train can be an excellent way of touring, and relieves you of some of the legwork.

BY BUS

Details of routes and timetables are generally available free of charge either from bus stations (*gare routière*) which are often situated close to rail stations, or from tourist offices.

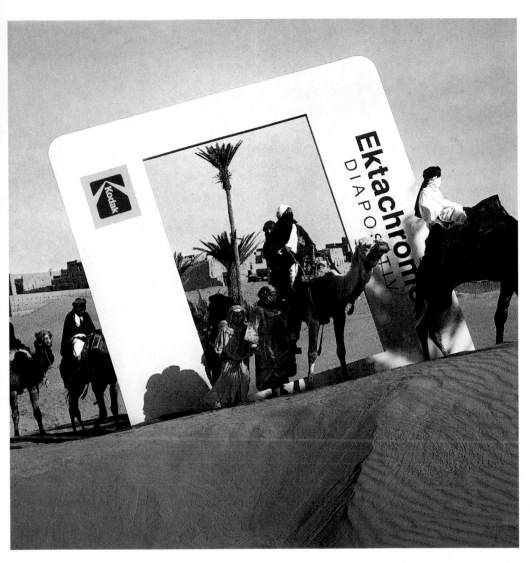

THE COLOUR OF LIFE.

A holiday may last just a week or so, but the memories of those happy, colourful days will last forever, because together you and Kodak Ektachrome films will capture, as large as life, the wondrous sights, the breathtaking scenery and the magical moments. For you to relive over and over again.

The Kodak Ektachrome range of slide films offers a choice of light source, speed and colour rendition and features extremely fine grain, very high sharpness and high resolving power.

Take home the real colour of life with Kodak Ektachrome films.

LIKE THIS?

OR LIKE THIS?

A KODAK FUN PANORAMIC CAMERA BROADENS YOUR VIEW

The holiday you and your camera have been looking forward to all year; and a stunning panoramic view appears. "Fabulous", you think to yourself, "must take that one".

Unfortunately, your lens is just not wide enough. And three-in-a-row is a poor substitute.

That's when you take out your pocket-size, 'single use' Kodak Fun Panoramic Camera. A film and a camera, all in one, and it works miracles. You won't need to focus, you don't need special lenses. Just aim, click

and... it's all yours. The total picture.

You take twelve panoramic pictures with one Kodak Fun Panoramic Camera. Then put the camera in for developing and printing.

Each print is 25 by 9 centimetres. Excellent depth of field. True Kodak Gold colours.

The Kodak Fun Panoramic Camera itself goes back to the factory, to be recycled. So that others too can capture one of those spectacular phoooooooooootoooooooooooos.

BY TRAIN

Information on services is available from stations (gare SNCF). The region is well served by trains north-south en route to or from Paris; getting across the region east to west by train is not so easy. If you intend to travel extensively by train it may be worth obtaining one of the rail passes available before leaving home (*see Getting There*). These tickets can be used on any journey, otherwise individual tickets need to be purchased, but check on any discounts available, e.g., the *Carte Couple* for married couples travelling together on off-peak services. Children under four years travel free, from four to 12 for half-fare. All tickets purchased at French stations have to be put through the orange machines at the stations to validate them before boarding the train. These are marked *compostez votre billet*.

BY CAR

Even if you have never driven abroad before, it doesn't take long to get used to driving on the right, but take extra care when crossing the road, for instance, to use a service station, it is very easy to come out and automatically drive on the left – especially if there's no other traffic around. British, US, Canadian and Australian licences are all valid in France and you should always carry your car's registration document and valid insurance (third party is the absolute minimum, but a green card – available from your insurance company – is strongly recommended).

Additional insurance cover, which can include a get-you-home service, is offered by a number of organisations including the British and American Automobile Associations and Europ-Assistance, in the UK: 252 High Street, Croydon CR0 1NF, tel: 081-680 1234; in the US: Europ Assistance World-wide Services Inc., 1133 15th Street, Suite 400, Washington DC 20005, tel: 202-347 7113.

RULES OF THE ROAD

The use of seat belts (front and rear if fitted) and crash helmets for motorcyclists is compulsory. Children under 10 are not permitted to ride in the front seat unless the car has no rear seat.
Priorité à la Droite: An important rule to remember is that priority on French roads is always given to vehicles approaching from the right, except where otherwise indicated. In practice, on main roads the major road will normally have priority, with traffic being halted on minor approach roads with one of the following signs:
STOP
Cédez le passage – give way
Vous n'avez pas la priorité – you do not have right of way
Passage protégé – no right of way

Particular care should be taken in towns, where you may wrongly assume you are on the major road, and in rural areas where there may not be any road markings (watch out for farm vehicles).

The French recently changed the rules concerning roundabouts – in theory drivers already on the roundabout now have priority over those entering it, but beware; some drivers still insist that priority belongs to the drivers entering a roundabout.

SPEED LIMITS

Speed limits are as follows: 130 kph (80 mph) on toll motorways; 68 mph (110 kph) on other motorways and dual carriageways; 56 mph (90 kph) on other roads except in towns where the limit is 30 mph (50 kph). There is also a *minimum* speed limit of 50 mph (80 kph) on the outside lane of motorways during daylight with good visibility and on level ground.

Speed limits are reduced in **wet weather** as follows: toll motorways: 68 mph (110 kph), dual carriageways: 62 mph (100 kph), other roads: 50 mph (80 kph).

On-the-spot **fines** can be levied for speeding; on toll roads, the time is printed on the ticket you take at your entry point and can thus be checked and a fine imposed on exit. Nearly all motorways (auto-routes) are toll roads, so you will need to have some cash with you (especially small change) if you intend to use them, although toll booths will accept payment now by Visa and Mastercard.

Autoroutes are designated "A" roads and national highways "N" roads. "D" roads are usually well maintained, while "C" or local roads may not always be so.

You must carry a red triangle to place 50 metres (165 ft) behind the car in case of a **breakdown or accident**. In an accident or emergency, call the police (dial 17) or use the free emergency telephones (every 1 mile/2 km) on motorways. It is useful to carry an European Accident Statement Form (obtainable from your insurance company) which will simplify matters in the case of an accident.

Unleaded petrol (*essence sans plomb*) is now widely available in France. If in doubt, a map showing the location of filling stations is available from main tourist offices.

For information about current **road conditions**, telephone the Inter Service Route line on 1-48.94.33.33 (this is a recorded anouncement in French and not always terribly clear).

CAR HIRE

As previously mentioned, hiring a car is an expensive business in France, partly because of the high VAT (TVA) rate – 33 percent on luxury items. Some fly/drive deals work out reasonably well if you're going for only a short visit. French Railways offer a good deal on their combined train/car rental bookings. Weekly rates often work out better than a daily hire and it can be cheaper to arrange hire in the UK or US before leaving for France. Offices of the major car hire companies in the region are listed below:

AVIS

Central reservation office: tel: 1-46.06.68.68.
Auxerre: 3 Rue Paul Doumer, 89000. Tel: 86.46.83.47; fax: 86.46.03.54.
Beaune: Rue Jules Ferry, 21200. Tel: 80.22.87.88.
Bourg-en-Bresse: 3 Boulevard St-Nicolas, 01000. Tel: 74.22.29.58.
Chalon-sur-Saône: 34 Avenue Victor Hugo, 71000. Tel: 85.48.30.52.
Châtillon-sur-Seine: Rance Gilbert, 9 Rue du Docteur Robert, 21400. Tel: 80.91.00.54.
Cosne-sur-Loire: Route de Cours, 58200. Tel: 86.26.64.28.
Le Creusot: Station Total, 12 rte Expresse, 71210 Torsy. Tel: 85.55.04.53.
Dijon: 5 Avenue Foch, 21000. Tel: 80.43.60.76.
Mâcon: 23 Avenue Edouard-Herriot, 7100. Tel: 85.38.68.75.
Montceau-les-Mines: Station Total, 22 Avenue Roger Salengro, 71300. Tel: 85.58.18.64.
Nevers: 5 Rue de la Passière, 58000. Tel: 86.57.51.03.
Sens: 7 Rue du Général Leclerc, 89100. Tel: 86.95.27.29.
Villefranche-sur-Saône: 83 Rue Pierre Berthier, 69400. Tel: 74.68.08.43.

BUDGET

Central reservation office: tel: 1-46.86.65.65.
Beaune: Service Location Galmard, 18 Boulevard Jules Ferry, 21200. Tel: 80.22.29.20.
Bourg-en-Bresse: 11 Rue Pierre Semard, 01000. Tel: 74.21.44.66.
Chalon-sur-Saône: 122 Avenue de Paris, 71100. Tel: 85.41.88.00.
Digoin: Route Roanne, 71600 Varennes-Saint-Germain. Tel: 85.53.18.50.
Joigny: 35 Quai du Général Leclerc, 89300. Tel: 86.62.42.42.
Louhans: Route de Lons, 71500. Tel: 85.75.22.01.
Mâcon: 73 Route Bioux, 71000. Tel: 85.29.04.11.
Sens: 1 Route de Voulx, 89100. Tel: 86.65.00.00.

EUROPCAR

Central reservation office: tel: 1-46.09.92.21.
Autun: Hamelin SA, 3 Grande Rue Marchaux, 71400. Tel: 85.52.13.31.
Auxerre: 9 Avenue Gambetta, 89000. Tel: 86.46.99.08.
Avallon: Auto Location, 28 Rue de Lyon, 89200. Tel: 86.34.38.10.
Bourg-en-Bresse: 34 Avenue Alphonse Baudin, 01000. Tel: 74.21.50.98.
Chalon-sur-Saône: 31 Rue du 11 novembre, 71100. Tel: 85.48.50.52.

Le Creusot: Hamelin SA, 9 Rue de la Verrerie, 71200. Tel: 85.55.18.95.
Dijon: Loca Bourgogne, 47 Rue Guillaume Tell, 21000. Tel: 80.43.28.44.
Joigny: 31–33 Avenue Jean Hemery, Route de Migennes, 89300. Tel: 86.62.22.00.
Mâcon: 35 Rue Lacretelle, 71000. Tel: 85.38.00.19.
Montceau-les-Mines: Hamelin SA, 19 Rue Jules Guesde, 71300. Tel: 85.57.33.35.
Nevers: 41 faubourg de Paris, 58000. Tel: 86.59.02.32.
Sens: Societé Senonaise de Location, carrefour Ste Colombe, 89100. Tel: 86.64.18.66.
Villefranche-sur-Saône: 504 Boulevard Louis Blanc, 69400. Tel: 74.68.49.87.

HERTZ

Central reservation office: tel: 1-30.45.65.65.
Auxerre: 36 Avenue de la Fournelle, 89000. Tel: 86.46.57.30.
Beaune: SA Ruivo, 7 Avenue du 8 Septembre, 21200. Tel: 80.24.75.20.
Bourg-en-Bresse: 36 Avenue Alphonse Baudin, 01000. Tel: 74.21.16.30.
Chalon-sur-Saône: 2 Avenue Boucicaut, 71100. Tel: 85.43.08.88.
Cosne-sur-Loire: Garage Boyer, 84 Avenue du 85ème, 58200. Tel: 86.26.65.07.
Le Creusot: Station Shell, 75 Route de Montcenis, 71200. Tel: 85.55.56.00.
Dijon: ARNO, 18 bis Avenue Foch, 21000. Tel: 80.43.55.22.
Mâcon: 77 Rue Victor Hugo, 71000. Tel: 85.38.63.22.
Montceau-les-Mines: 35 Rue de la République, 71300. Tel: 85.57.07.99.
Nevers: Place de la Gare, 58000. Tel: 86.57.22.96.
Sens: Station Shell, Boulevard de Verdun, 89100. Tel: 86.65.00.11.
Villefranche-sur-Saône: 1568 Route Frans, 69400. Tel: 74.60.02.36.

ROUTES

Following a tourist circuit or *route* is a sure way of getting to see the major sites of a region. Tourist offices will help with suggestions; but probably the most important is the **Route des Ducs de Bourgogne** which covers much of the region from Auxerre and Châtillon-sur-Seine in the north, down to Chalon-sur-Saône in the southeast. It takes in many of the important ducal châteaux such as Ancy-le-Franc, Bussy-Rabutin and Tanlay, as well as some important religious buildings like the Abbaye de Fontenay.

In the far northeast of the region around Auxerre you can follow the **Route Historique des Trésors de La Puisaye** which includes the churches of La Ferté-Loupière and Toucy as well as some important secular buildings such as the Châteaux de St-Fargeau and La Bussière.

Part of the **Route Historique Buissonière**, which goes from Paris right down to Lyon, can be traced through Burgundy, on a direct north-west-south-east axis from Auxerre to Paray-le-Monial, taking in the sites at Vézelay, and Château-Chinon, among others on the way.

Details of all the above routes are available from the Caisse Nationale des Monuments Historiques et des Sites, 62 Rue Saint-Antoine, 75004 Paris, tel: 1-42.74.22.22; and the Demeure Historique, 57 Quai de la Tournelle, 75005 Paris, tel: 1-43.29.02.86.

INLAND WATERWAYS

Possibly one of the most popular ways of discovering Burgundy is on board a narrowboat or one of the other craft that can be hired on the region's many navigable canals and rivers. Situated at the watershed of France's three great rivers, the Seine, Loire and the Rhône, served by a network of canals and complemented by the rivers Saône, Yonne and Seille, Burgundy offers almost 745 miles (1,200 km) of waterways, now barely used by commercial traffic. The Canal du Centre is the only one which still has any significant amount of business traffic, but not enough to disturb its tranquil scenery.

The Canal de Bourgogne is the longest, connecting the River Yonne in the north to the Saône in the south. It also boasts the greatest number of locks. Devotees of canal architecture will wish to incorporate into their trip the aqueduct at Briare. This remarkable edifice, whose foundations were laid by the engineer Eiffel's company, was built in 1896 to connect the Briare and the Loire lateral canals. A masterpiece of engineering, 2,180 ft (664 metres) long and now mainly used by pleasure boats, it was built to enable freight to be carried all the way from the Channel to the Mediterranean. The Briare canal itself was built by Sully in the early 17th century and served as a prototype for all France's later canal-building.

There are several options available for holidays afloat. Small boats for just two people or narrowboats accommodating 12 can be hired from several operators; these are fully equipped for self-catering. Boats can be hired for a weekend or longer and even if you have never navigated before, you will feel confident after a minimum of instruction (foreigners require no permit or licence).

Several companies in the UK offer "package" holidays afloat including travel arrangements. A selection is given below:
Abercrombie and Kent Ltd, Sloane Square House, Holbein Place, London SW1W 8NS.
Tel: 071-730 9600.
Blakes Holidays, Wroxham, Norwich NR12 8DH.
Tel: 0603-784131; fax: 0603-782871.
Crown Blue Line, 8 Ber Street, Norwich, Norfolk NR1 3EJ. Tel: 0603-630513; fax: 0603-664298.
French Country Cruises, Andrew Brock Travel Ltd, Barley Mow Workspace, 10 Barley Mow Passage,

Chiswick, London W4 4PH. Tel: 081-995 3642; fax 081-742 1066.
Hoseasons Holidays Abroad, Sunway House, Lowestoft NR32 3LT. Tel: 0502-500555; fax 0502-500532.
Slipaway Holidays, Phyllis House, 2 Sompting Road, Worthing, West Sussex BN14 9EP. Tel: 0900-821000 or dial-a-brochure on 0900-214211; fax: 0903-203157.

Agencies in the United States include:
Abercrombie and Kent Ltd, 1420 Kinsington Road, Oak Brook, Illinois 60521-2106.
Tel: 800-323 7308.
French Country Waterways, PO Box 2195, Duxbury, Massachusetts 02331. Tel: 800-222 1236.

If you prefer to book direct in France, try the Service Loisirs Accueil in the individual *départements* (*see Useful Addresses*) or contact one of the following companies (this is just a selection of the many operators):
Bateaux de Bourgogne, SRLA Yonne, 3–4 Quai de la République, 89000 Auxerre. Tel: 86.52.18.99.
Burgundy Cruisers SA, 8 Route Nationale, 89460 Cravant-Accolay. Tel: 86.81.54.55.
SARL Navigation, Port de Plaisance, BP4, 71160 Digoin. Tel: 85.85.29.19.
Blue Line Bourgogne, La Gare d'Eau, Saint-Usage, 21170 Saint-Jean-Losne. Tel: 80.29.12.86.
Crown Cruisers, Port de la Jonction, 58300 Decize. Tel: 86.25.46.64.
Locaboat Plaisance, Quai du Port-au-Bois, 89300 Joigny. Tel: 86.91.72.72.

For those who prefer to travel in style, and whose idea of a holiday is to be pampered, and not have to do the navigating, opening of locks and the catering, then a cruise on a *péniche-hôtel* may be the answer. It is not surprising that these are becoming quite a popular option as the cuisine on these hotel barges is invariably excellent. There are about 10 such boats operating in Burgundy with a capacity of between six and 24 persons. Prices range from around FF5,000 to FF15,000 per week, depending on the boat and season. Prices include full board and excursions. Information is available from the regional tourist office; a selection of the operators is given below:
Aquarelle, Port de Plaisance, Quai Saint-Martin, 89000 Auxerre. Tel: 86.46.96.77.
La Belle Aventure, 89000 Auxerre. Tel: 86.81.44.77.
Navigation et Technique, Port du Canal, 21370 Plombières-lès-Dijon. Tel: 80.45.44.60.
Péniches-Hôtels de France, 21140 Villeneuve-sous-Charigny. Tel: 80.97.21.27.

If you are navigating for yourself, a map or guide to the waterway is essential. These are often provided as part of a package deal, otherwise you will need to take your own. Crown Blue Line produce large format map-guides for their own clients, which are now available to the general public; their titles for Burgundy are CBL2 Bourgogne-Franche-Comté and CBL3 Loire Nivernais. ECM map-guides are well-produced strip maps with all navigation aids, boating serives and tourist information. There are several titles for the Burgundy region. Vagnon map-guides are also very good, with some colour photography. All these, and a selection of general publications about French waterways, are available by mail order from Compass Books (address in the *Maps* section of *Getting Around*).

For details of short trips on the waterways, see the *Excursions* section of *Things to Do*; for rowing and canoeing and activity holidays of this type, consult the *Sports* section.

RAMBLERS

There are countless opportunities for exploring the region by foot – perhaps the most obvious is the unspoiled Morvan regional park right at the heart of Burgundy. The **Tour du Morvan**, taking in most of the major lakes, is an ideal circuit of around 135 miles (220 km). Alternatively, you can follow the GR13 footpath from Auxerre to Autun. All the main footpaths in France form part of the national network of long distance footpaths (**Sentiers de Grandes Randonnées** or GR). The major footpaths in the region outside the Morvan are the GR7 in the east of the region, passing near Dijon and continuing on to Cluny; part of the GR2 from Châtillon-sur-Seine to Dijon; and the GR3 which follows the path of the Loire along the western edge of the region, taking in Nevers. Another suggested tour in the north is the **Tour de La Puisaye** – in author Colette's country.

The French Ramblers' Association, Fédération Française de la Randonnée Pédestre (FFRP) based at 8 Avenue Marceau, 75008 Paris, tel: 1-17.23.62.32., publishes *Topoguides* (guidebooks incorporating IGN 1:50,000 scale maps) to all France's footpaths but they are available only in French. Titles available for Burgundy include Nos. 032 Tour de Morvan, 022 Tour de La Puisaye, 352 Sentier de la Loire (covering the GR3), 125 Sentier Île de France-Bourgogne for the GR13, No. 201 Sentier de la Seine et de l'Yonne for the GR2 and 710 Sentier Vosges-Pyrénées which covers the GR7. These guides are available in good bookshops in the region, or in the UK try Stanfords (*see Maps*). A good basic guide for serious walkers is Rob Hunter's book *Walking in France*, published by Oxford Illustrated Press. The IGN Blue series maps at a scale of 1:25,000 are ideal for walkers, and sheet No. 306 Morvan Regional Park, although less detailed, is also useful. (*See Maps*, for stockists.)

Each *département* has its own ramblers' organisation which arranges a variety of activities throughout the year: guided walks taking a day, a weekend or more, as well as walks with a particular theme –

flora or wildlife, for example. For more information, contact the Comité Départemental de la Randonnée Pédestre at the following addresses:

Côte d'Or: Hôtel du Département, BP 1601, 21035 Dijon Cedex. Tel: 80.63.66.00.

Nièvre: 3 Rue du Sort, 58000 Nevers. Tel: 86.36.37.01.

Saône-et-Loire: Mairie, 71460 St-Gengoux-le-National. Tel: 85.92.61.67.

Yonne: Maison des Sports, 12 Boulevard Galliéni, 89000 Auxerre.

All these groups come under the regional umbrella of the Association Bourguignonne de Randonnée (ABOURA), Conseil Régional, BP 1602, 21035 Dijon Cedex. Tel: 80.50.10.20.

Other useful addresses for walkers are as follows:

Parc Naturel du Morvan, Maison du Parc, St-Brisson, 58230 Montsauche. Tel: 86.78.70.16.

FFRP/Comité National des Sentiers de Grande Randonnée, Délégation Départementale, (M. M. Dunel), Tour Bagatelle, Appt 63, 56 Rue des Perrières, 21000 Dijon.

Various walking holidays with accommodation either in hotels or under canvas are available. Some are organised through package tour operators in the UK, others can be booked through the French tourist offices and other local organisations. The Service Loisirs Accueil in both Nièvre and Côte d'Or (*see Useful Addresses*) offer walking holidays, and a selection of other operators are:

Les Quatre Chemins, 25, Rue aux Raz, 71400 Autun. Tel: 85.52.07.91. Walking and other activity holidays in the Morvan.

La Peurtantaine, École du Bourg, 71550 Anost. Tel: 85.82.77.74. Discover the natural environment of the Morvan.

Horizon Aventure, 5 Place Jacques Prévert, 21000 Dijon. Tel: 80.30.38.64.

La Billebaude, Suin, 71220 Saint-Bonnet-de-Joux. Tel: 85.24.76.59.

Clés de France, 13 Rue St-Louis, 78100 St-Germain-en-Laye. Tel: 1-30.61.23.23. The national organisation for holidays in France's regional parks.

Ramblers Holidays, Box 43, Welwyn Garden City, Herts AL8 6PQ. Tel: 0707-331133. Holidays based in Beaune.

HITCHHIKING

With sensible precautions, hitchhiking can be an interesting and inexpensive way to see France. Would-be hitchhikers may be discouraged by the difficulty of getting a lift out of the Channel ports, so it may be worth taking a bus or train for the first leg of your journey. Hitching is forbidden on motorways, but you can wait on slip roads or at toll booths. Allostop is a nationwide organisation which aims to connect hikers with drivers (you pay a registration fee and a contribution towards the petrol). Tel: 1-42.46.00.66.

WHERE TO STAY

HOTELS

Hotels are plentiful in the main towns of the region and along the main highways, but are rather thinner on the ground in the more rural areas such as the Morvan. All hotels in France conform to national standards and carry star-ratings, set down by the Ministry of Tourism, according to their degree of comfort and amenities. Prices (which are charged per room, rather than per person) range from as little as FF90 for a double room in an unclassified hotel (i.e., its standards are not sufficient to warrant a single star (☆), but is likely to be clean, cheap and cheerful), to FF550 for the cheapest double room in a ☆☆☆☆ luxury hotel.

Hotels are required to show their menus outside the hotel and details of room prices should be visible either outside or in reception, as well as on the back of bedroom doors. It is possible for a hotel to have a ☆ rating, with a ☆☆ restaurant. This is ideal if you are on a budget and more interested in food than fading wallpaper or eccentric plumbing.

When booking a room you should normally be taken to see it; if it doesn't suit you, ask to be shown another (this may sound odd advice, but rooms can vary enormously within the same building). Prices are charged per room; supplements may be charged for an additional bed or a cot (*lit bébé*). You may be asked when booking if you wish to dine, particularly if the hotel is busy – preference should not but may in fact be given to hungry customers as there is not a lot of profit in letting rooms alone. Also the simple request *on peut dîner ici ce soir?* will confirm that the hotel's restaurant is open (many are closed out of season on Sunday or Monday evenings).

Lists of hotels in the region can be obtained from the French Government Tourist office in your country or from tourist offices in the region. It is also worth buying from the Tourist Office in London the *Logis et Auberges de France* guide. This is an invaluable guide to a very good and reasonably priced network of family-run hotels who aim to offer a friendly welcome and good local cuisine. The guide can be bought in France but is much more expensive there. It can be used to book hotels before travelling (for the central reservation office in Paris, tel: 1-45.84.83.84).

Some tourist offices will make hotel bookings for you for a small fee (usually around FF15).

Another useful chain is Minotels France Accueil, based at 85 Rue du Dessous-des-Berges, 75013 Paris. Tel: 1-45.83.04.22. This group of good quality hotels also has a booking offices overseas:
UK: France Accueil, 10 Salisbury Hollow, Edington, Westbury, Wilts BA13 4PF. Tel: 0380-830125; or Minotels Great Britain, 5 Kings Road, Cleveleys, Lancs FY5 1BY. Tel: 0253-866266; fax: 0253-866251.
USA: Minotels Europe, 683 South Collier Boulevard, Marco Island, Florida 33037. Tel: 813-394 3384 (toll free – 800 336 4668); fax: 813-394 3384. **Canada**: Tours Chanteclerc, 65 Rue de Brésoles, Montreal, Québec H2Y 1V7. Tel: 514-845 1236; fax: 514-845 5794.

If you are not restricted by a budget and wish to stay at the very best hotels in the region, try those in the Relais et Châteaux chain. These are usually converted castles, manor houses and even abbeys, run by their owners and offering high standards of décor and cuisine. A complete list is available from the French Government Tourist Office or Relais et Châteaux, 9 Avenue Marceau, 75116 Paris. Tel: 1-47.23.41.42.

Another particularly good local chain is Charme Hôtel, around 10 ☆☆ and ☆☆☆ hotels on the route from Paris–Lyon. For a full list, contact Mme A. Procureur, Présidente Charme Hôtel, Hôtel Terminus, Bourg-en-Bresse. Tel: 74.21.01.21; fax 74.21.36.47.

Many hotels can be booked through the Sesamtel system in France; in Britain, this is possible through Prestel *7760 followed by the hotel code number, given in the listing as S.

The following list is by no means comprehensive, but gives a selection of recommended hotels in the region, at various prices.

Star ratings are given thus ☆; CC: means credit cards. Prices are given for double rooms.

YONNE

ARCY-SUR-CURE

Hôtel des Grottes ☆, on the RN6, 89270. Tel: 86.81.91.47. Small hotel on the main road, with its own garden, convenient for visitors to the famous caves. CC: Visa, Mastercard. Rooms: FF110–180; Menus: FF65–140. Closed: Wednesdays out of season and 20 December–25 January.

AUXERRE

Hôtel Les Clairions ☆☆, Avenue Worms, 89000. Tel: 86.46.85.64; fax: 86.48.16.38; S890BRUY. Member of both the Logis and Charme Hôtel chains on the RN6, 1 mile (2 km) from the town centre; facilities include a swimming-pool and tennis court in the garden. Has rooms suitable for the disabled.

CC: Amex, Diners, Visa, Mastercard. Rooms: FF270–290; Menus: FF100–180.

Hôtel Normandie ☆☆, Boulevard Vauban, 89000. Tel: 86.52.57.80; fax: 86.51.54.33. An attractive hotel with a small garden, close to the town centre. CC: Amex, Diners, Visa, Mastercard. Rooms: FF240–280.

Hôtel de la Porte de Paris ☆, 5 Rue St-Germain, 89000. Tel: 86.46.90.09; S8900PORT. A modest hotel; only 2 of its rooms have private bathrooms. CC: Amex. Rooms: FF110–180.

AVALLON

Le Moulin des Ruats ☆☆☆, Vallée du Cousin, 89200. Tel: 86.34.07.14; fax: 86.31.65.47. Hotel in a converted watermill with river terrace, offering innovative menus. CC: Diners, Visa, Mastercard. Rooms: FF280–580; Menus: FF150–350. Closed: Monday evening out of season; 15 November–15 December and 15 January–15 February.

Le Relais Fleuri ☆☆☆, Route Saulieu (RN6), 89200 Avallon. Tel: 86.34.02.85; fax: 86.34.09.98; S8920RELA. Comfortable hotel, just off the motorway, with a garden, swimming-pool and tennis court. Some rooms accessible for the disabled. CC: Amex, Diners, Visa, Mastercard. Rooms: FF300–390; Menus: FF120–160.

Hôtel Au Bon Accueil ☆, 4 Rue de l'Hôpital, 89200 Avallon. Tel: 86.34.09.33. Modest hotel (only one room has private bathroom). Rooms: FF105–195; Menus: FF42–105. Closed: Sunday.

CHABLIS

Hostellerie des Clos ☆☆, 18 Rue Jules Rathier, 89800 Chablis. Tel: 86.42.10.63; fax: 86.42.17.11; S8980CLOS. A Logis de France hotel with pleasant rooms overlooking the garden, offering local cuisine (restaurant holds a Michelin star, but quality can be variable). CC: Visa, Mastercard. Rooms: FF230–520; Menus: FF150–370. Closed: 10 December–10 January, plus Wednesday, and Thursday lunchtime out of season.

JOIGNY

Hôtel à la Côte Saint-Jacques ☆☆☆☆, 14 Faubourg de Paris. Tel: 86.62.09.70; fax: 86.91.49.70.; S8930COTE. Ultimate luxury in a Relais et Châteaux hôtel; its superb restaurant is across the road. CC: Amex, Diners, Visa, Mastercard. Rooms: FF600–2,450; Menus: FF360–520. Closed: January.

Relais Paris-Nice ☆, rond-point de la Résistance. Tel: 86.62.06.72. Logis hotel for those on a more limited budget. Rooms: FF130–190.

MAILLY-LE-CHATEAU

Hôtel le Castel ☆☆, Place de l'Église, 89660. Tel: 86.81.43.06; fax: 86.81.49.26. Small, family-run hotel and restaurant with a pleasant garden. CC: Visa, Mastercard. Rooms: FF220–280; Menus: FF70–170. Closed: Wednesdays and from 15 November–15 March.

MONTBARD

Hôtel de l'Écu ☆☆☆, 7 Rue August-Carré, 21500. Tel: 80.92.11.66; S2150LECU. A characterful old house, close to the Burgundy Canal, with two restaurants; member of the France Accueil chain. CC: Amex, Diners, Visa, Mastercard. Rooms: FF250–380; Menus: FF95–360.

ST-FARGEAU

Le Relais du Château ☆☆, Promenade du Grillon, 89170. Tel: 86.74.01.75; S8917RELA. Moderately-priced, family-run Logis. CC: Amex, Visa, Mastercard. Rooms: FF180–220.

ST-PERE-SOUS-VEZELAY

Hôtel l'Espérance ☆☆☆☆, 89450 St-Père-sous-Vézelay. Tel: 86.33.20.45; fax: 86.33.26.15. In a delightful setting; some rooms are in a converted mill. Imaginative food. CC: Amex, Diners, Visa, Mastercard. Rooms: FF500–900; Menus: FF290 (weekdays only), or FF540–750. Closed: January; restaurant closed Tuesday and Wednesday lunch.

Hôtel la Renommée ☆, on the RN6, 89450. Tel: 86.33.21.34. By contrast, a small hotel for those on a budget. Rooms: FF150–220. Closed: Wednesday and November.

SEMUR-EN-AUXOIS

Hôtel de la Côte d'Or ☆☆, 3 Place Gaveau, 21140. Tel: 80.97.03.13. Logis de France hotel. CC: Amex, Visa, Mastercard. Rooms: FF180–230; Menus: FF68–170. Closed: Wednesdays and from 15 November–27 December.

SENS

Hôtel de Paris et de la Poste ☆☆☆, 97 Rue de la République, 89100. Tel: 86.65.17.43; fax: 86.64.48.45; S8910PARI. Good quality hotel and charming restaurant (meals may be taken on the terrace). CC: Amex, Diners, Visa, Mastercard. Rooms: FF350–520: Menus: FF166–300.

La Croix-Blanche ☆☆, 9 Rue Victor Guichard, 89100. Tel: 86.64.00.02; S8910CROI. Family-run Logis de France hotel with a garden. CC: None. Rooms: FF112–243; Menus: FF70–160.

TONNERRE

Hôtel l'Abbaye St-Michel ✩✩✩✩, Montée de St-Michel. Tel: 86.55.05.99; fax: 86.55.00.10. Very modern rooms in an old building; excellent restaurant. CC: Amex, Diners, Visa, Mastercard. Rooms: FF700–1,000; Menus: FF290–500. Closed: 1 January–8 February.

VEZELAY

Résidence Hôtel le Pontot ✩✩✩, Place du Pontot, 89450. Tel: 86.33.24.40. Small, quiet hotel with its own garden, but no restaurant. CC: Amex, Diners, Visa, Mastercard. Rooms: FF500–850. Closed: 12 November–28 March.

Relais du Morvan ✩, Place du Champ-de-Foire, 89450. Tel: 86.33.25.33. Small family-run hotel. Rooms: FF122–230.

MORVAN & NIEVRE

AUTUN

Hôtel St-Louis, 6 Rue de l'Arbalète, 71400. Tel: 85.52.21.03. Attractive old coaching inn, member of the France Accueil chain. CC: Amex, Diners, Visa, Mastercard. Rooms: FF100–320; Menus: FF85–200. Closed: 22 December–28 January.

Hôtel les Ursulines, 14 Rue de Rivault, 71400. Tel: 85.52.68.00; fax: 85.86.23.07. The priciest hotel in town, but worth it for the restaurant and the views. CC: Amex, Diners, Visa, Mastercard. Rooms: FF350–510; Menus: FF140–240.

Hôtel de France, Place de la Gare, 71400. Tel: 85.52.14.00; S7140FRAN. More modest Logis de France. CC: Amex. Rooms: FF116–126. Closed: Sunday.

CHATEAU-CHINON

Hostellerie l'Oustalet ✩, Route de Lormes, 58120. Tel: 86.85.15.57. Low-budget hotel and restaurant. Rooms: FF65–190; Menus: FF50–90.

COSNE-SUR-LOIRE

Auberge du Vieux Relais ✩✩, 11 Rue St-Aignan, 58200. Tel: 86.28.20.21. Family-run hotel which is small, but all rooms have private bathrooms. Meals can be taken on the terrace. CC: Amex, Diners, Visa, Mastercard. Rooms: FF200–280; Menus: FF90–280. Closed: Friday evening and Saturday morning out of season.

DECIZE

Hôtel les Capucines ✩✩, St Thibault, 58300. Tel: 86.25.04.12; fax: 86.25.10.17. Modest hotel, set in its own garden. CC: Amex, Diners. Rooms: FF100–180; Menus: FF50–120.

LORMES

Hôtel Perreau ✩✩, 8 Rue d'Avallon, 58140. Tel: 86.22.53.21. Logis de France hotel. Rooms: FF240; Menus: FF80–200. Closed: Sunday evening and Monday out of season, and February.

MAGNY-COURS

Hôtel la Renaissance ✩✩✩, Le Bourg, 58470. Tel: 86.58.10.40; fax: 86.21.22.60; S5847RENA. Quiet country auberge, offering a mix of traditional and more original cooking. CC: Amex, Visa, Mastercard. Rooms: FF450–500; Menus: F200–430. Closed: Sunday evening and Monday, and February.

NEVERS

Château de la Rocherie ✩✩, on the RN7, 58000. Tel: 86.38.07.21. Small château in a quiet setting, back from the main road; good food. CC: Amex, Diners, Visa, Mastercard. Rooms: FF160–300; Menus: FF95–225. Closed: Sunday.

Hostellerie la Folie, Route des Saulaies, 58000. Tel: 86.57.05.31; fax: 86.57.66.99. This comfortable family-run hotel has its own garden, swimming-pool and tennis court. CC: Visa, Mastercard. Rooms: FF200–270; Menus: FF65–135. Closed: 16 December–5 January.

SAULIEU

Résidence La Côte d'Or ✩✩✩✩, 2 Rue d'Argentine, 21210. Tel: 80.64.07.66; fax: 80.64.08.92. Relais et Château hotel with comfortable rooms — some fairly simple, others very luxurious with prices to match. Superb cuisine. CC: Amex, Diners, Visa, Mastercard. Rooms: FF260–1,800; Menus: FF290–570. Closed: 19 November–22 December.

Hôtel de la Poste ✩✩✩, 1 Rue Grillot, 21210. Tel: 80.64.05.67; fax: 80.64.10.82. Logis de France in a 17th-century post house; innovative cooking, served in a sumptuously decorated dining-room. CC: Amex, Diners, Visa, Mastercard. Rooms: FF160–395; Menus: FF128–298.

Hotel la Renaissance ✩, 7 Rue Grillot, 21210. Tel: 80.64.08.72. Moderately priced hotel and restaurant, set in its own garden. CC: Amex. Rooms: FF95–180; Menus: FF60–120. Closed: Monday evening and Tuesday, also 5 January–5 February.

DIJON & COTE D'OR

BEAUNE

Hôtel le Cep ✩✩✩✩, 27 Rue Maufoux, 21200. Tel: 80.22.35.48; fax: 80.22.76.80. Absolute luxury in a beautiful building. CC: Amex, Diners, Visa, Mastercard. Rooms: FF550–850.

Hôtel Central ☆☆☆, 2 Rue Victor Millot, 21200. Tel: 80.24.77.24. Popular with tourists for its central position; comfortable with a good restaurant. CC: Visa, Mastercard. Rooms: FF400–450; Menus: FF125–320. Closed: in Janaury and Wednesdays from November–end March.

Hôtel le Home ☆☆, 138 Route de Dijon, 21200. Tel: 80.22.16.43. An elegant hotel with a very pleasant garden. CC: Amex, Visa, Mastercard. Rooms: FF245–420.

CHALON-SUR-SAONE

Hôtel St-Georges ☆☆☆, 32 Avenue Jean Jaurès, 71100. Tel: 85.48.27.05; fax: 85.93.23.88; S711CSTGE. Convenient for the station; comfortable rooms and a fine restaurant. CC: Amex, Diners, Visa, Mastercard. Rooms: FF250–400; Menus: 110–380.

Hôtel St-Jean, 24 Quai Gambetta, 71100. Tel: 85.48.45.65. Inexpensive hotel by the river. CC: Visa, Mastercard. Rooms: FF200–220.

COUCHES

Hôtel des Trois Maures ☆☆, Place de la République, 71490. Tel: 85.49.63.93. Modest, family-run Logis de France hotel and restaurant with its own garden. CC: Amex. Rooms: FF120–210; Menus: FF67–155. Closed: Monday out of season and February.

DIJON

Hôtel Urbis Central ☆☆, 3 Place Grangier, 21000. Tel: 80.30.44.00; fax: 80.30.77.12; S2100CENT. Recently modernised rooms (some suitable for disabled visitors) in an old house in a very central location. Good restaurant. CC: Amex, Diners, Visa, Mastercard. Rooms: FF290–310; Menus: FF150.

Hôtel le Jacquemart ☆☆, 32 Rue Verrerie, 21000. Tel: 80.73.39.74; fax: 80.73.20.99. In the old quarter: very inviting and friendly. CC: Visa, Mastercard. Rooms: FF248–285.

Hôtel du Palais ☆☆, 23 Rue du Palais, 21000. Tel: 80.67.16.26. Good for travellers on a limited budget, nonetheless pleasant and comfortable. CC: Visa. Rooms: F180–240. Closed: 24 December–1 January.

Hôtel Pullman la Cloche ☆☆☆☆, 14 Place Darcy, 21000. Tel: 80.30.12.32; fax: 80.30.04.15. One of Dijon's most prestigious hotels with excellent regional menu. CC: Amex, Diners, Visa, Mastercard. Rooms: FF550–1,200; Menus: FF240 (weekdays only)–FF450.

DRACY-LE-FORT

Hôtel le Dracy ☆☆☆, 71640 Dracy-le-Fort. Tel: 85.87.81.81; fax: 85.87.95.12; S7164DRAC. Comfortable hotel, set in its own grounds (where meals may be taken) with a swimming-pool and tennis court. Some rooms accessible to the disabled. CC:

Amex, Diners, Visa, Mastercard. Rooms: FF320; Menus: FF90–180.

GEVREY-CHAMBERTIN

Hôtel les Grands Crus ☆☆☆, Route des Grands Crus, 21220. Tel: 80.34.34.15; fax: 80.51.89.07. Stands in a quiet spot with a lovely garden, surrounded by the famous vineyards. CC: Visa, Mastercard. Rooms: FF285–360. Closed: 1 December–25 February.

NUITS-ST-GEORGES

Hostellerie la Gentilhommière ☆☆☆, Vallée de la Serrée, 21700. Tel: 80.61.12.06; fax: 80.61.30.33. Modern but pleasant and comfortable hotel with a separate restaurant in a former hunting lodge (good food). CC: Amex, Diners, Visa, Mastercard. Rooms: FF300; Menus FF160–220. Closed: 31 December–20 January.

ST-GERMAIN-DU-PLAIN

Hôtel le Château, le Bourg, 71370. Tel: 85.47.38.13. Convenient for Chalon, this luxurious mansion stands in quiet grounds. CC: Amex, Diners, Visa, Mastercard. Rooms: FF650–850. Closed: 5–15 March and 19–29 November.

Hôtel de la Poste, Rue de la Poste, 71370. Tel: 85.47.31.56. Small, moderately priced hotel, without a restaurant, just outside Chalon. CC: Visa, Mastercard. Rooms: FF135–300.

SAONE-ET-LOIRE & BEAUJOLAIS

BOURBON-LANCY

Grand Hôtel ☆☆☆, Place d'Aligre, 71140. Tel: 85.89.08.87. Traditional, quiet hotel in a spa town. CC: Visa, Mastercard. Rooms: FF82–220. Closed: 11 October–9 April.

BOURG-EN-BRESSE

Hôtel de France, 19 Place Bernard, 01000. Tel: 74.45.29.11; fax: 74.23.69.96. Old style hotel in a central square. CC: Amex, Diners, Visa, Mastercard. Rooms: FF180–330.

Hôtel Terminus, 19 Rue A. Baudin, 01000. Tel: 74.21.01.21; fax: 74.21.36.47. This comfortable hotel, is set in lovely grounds, convenient for the station; and a member of the local Charme Hôtel chain. CC: Amex, Diners, Visa, Mastercard. Rooms: FF245–330.

CHERVINGES

Château de Chervinges, Chervinges, 69400 Villefranche-sur-Saône. Tel: 74.65.29.76. Fine 18th-century mansion just outside Villefranche; facilities

THE KODAK GOLD GUIDE TO BETTER PICTURES.

Good photography is not difficult. Use these practical hints and Kodak Gold II Film: then notice the improvement.

Move in close. Get close enough to capture only the important elements.

Frame your Pictures. Look out for natural frames such as archways or tree branches to add an interesting foreground. Frames help create a sensation of depth and direct attention into the picture.

One centre of interest. Ensure you have one focus of interest and avoid distracting features that can confuse the viewer.

Use leading lines. Leading lines direct attention to your subject i.e. – a stream, a fence, a pathway; or the less obvious such as light beams or shadows.

Maintain activity. Pictures are more appealing if the subject is involved in some natural action.

Keep within the flash range. Ensure subject is within flash range for your camera (generally 4 metres). With groups make sure everyone is the same distance from the camera to receive the same amount of light.

Check the light direction. People tend to squint in bright direct light. Light from the side creates highlights and shadows that reveal texture and help to show the shapes of the subject. If shooting into direct sunlight fill-in flash can be effective to light the subject from the front.

CHOOSING YOUR KODAK GOLD II FILM.

Choosing the correct speed of colour print film for the type of photographs you will be taking is essential to achieve the best colourful results.

Basically the more intricate your needs in terms of capturing speed or low-light situations the higher speed film you require.

Kodak Gold II 100. Use in bright outdoor light or indoors with electronic flash. Fine grain, ideal for enlargements and close-ups. Ideal for beaches, snow scenes and posed shots.

Kodak Gold II 200. A multipurpose film for general lighting conditions and slow to moderate action. Recommended for automatic 35mm cameras. Ideal for walks, bike rides and parties.

Kodak Gold II 400. Provides the best colour accuracy as well as the richest, most saturated colours of any 400 speed film. Outstanding flash-taking capabilities for low-light and fast-action situations; excellent exposure latitude. Ideal for outdoor or well-lit indoor sports, stage shows or sunsets.

APA INSIGHT GUIDES

ARE Going Places:

Asia & Pacific

East Asia
South Asia
South East Asian Wildlife
South East Asia
★ Marine Life
Australia
Great Barrier Reef
Melbourne
★★ Sydney
★ Bhutan
Burma/Myanmar
China
Beijing
India
Calcutta
Delhi, Jaipur, Agra
India's Western Himalaya
Indian Wildlife
★ New Delhi
Rajasthan
South India
Indonesia
★★ Bali
★ Bali Bird Walks
Java
★ Jakarta
★ Yogyakarta
Korea
Japan
Tokyo
Malaysia
★ Kuala Lumpur
★ Malacca
★ Penang
★★ Nepal
Kathmandu
Kathmandu Bikes & Hikes
New Zealand
Pakistan
Philippines
★ Sikkim
★★ Singapore
Sri Lanka
Taiwan

Thailand
★★ Bangkok
★ Chiang Mai
★ Phuket
★ Tibet
Turkey
★★ Istanbul
Turkish Coast
★ Turquoise Coast
Vietnam

Africa

East African Wildlife
South Africa
Egypt
Cairo
The Nile
Israel
Jerusalem
Kenya
Morocco
Namibia
The Gambia & Senegal
Tunisia
Yemen

Europe

Austria
★★ Vienna
Belgium
Brussels
Channel Islands
Continental Europe
Cyprus
Czechoslovakia
★★ Prague
Denmark
Eastern Europe
Finland
France
★★ Alsace
★★ Brittany
★★ Cote d'Azur
★★ Loire Valley
★★ Paris

Provence
Germany
★★ Berlin
Cologne
Düsseldorf
Frankfurt
Hamburg
★★ Munich
The Rhine
Great Britain
Edinburg
Glasgow
★★ Ireland
★★ London
Oxford
Scotland
Wales
Greece
★★ Athens
★★ Crete
★ Rhodes
Greek Islands
Hungary
★★ Budapest
Iceland
Italy
Florence
★★ Rome
★★ Sardinia
★★ Tuscany
Umbria
★★ Venice
Netherlands
Amsterdam
Norway
Poland
Portugal
★ Lisbon
Madeira
Spain
★★ Barcelona
★ Costa Blanca
★ Costa Brava
★ Costa del Sol/Marbella
Catalonia

Gran Canaria
★ Ibiza
Madrid
Mallorca & Ibiza
★ Mallorca
★ Seville
Southern Spain
Tenerife
Sweden
Switzerland
(Ex) USSR
Moscow
St. Petersburg
Waterways of Europe
Yugoslavia
★ Yugoslavia's Adriatic
Coast

The Americas

Bermuda
Canada
Montreal
Caribbean
Bahamas
Barbados
Jamaica
Trinidad & Tobago
Puerto Rico
Costa Rica
Mexico
Mexico City
South America
Argentina
Amazon Wildlife
Brazil
Buenos Aires
Chile
Ecuador
Peru
Rio

USA/Crossing America
Alaska
American Southwest
Boston
California
Chicago
Florida
Hawaii
Los Angeles
Miami
Native America
New England
New Orleans
★★ New York City
New York State
Northern California
Pacific Northwest
★★ San Francisco
Southern California
Texas
The Rockies
Washington D.C.

★★ Also available as
Insight Pocket Guide

★ Available as Insight
Pocket Guide only

INSIGHT *pocket* GUIDES

Ci VEDREMO PRESTO!

See You Soon! In Italy

include a swimming-pool and tennis court. CC: Amex, Diners, Visa, Mastercard. Rooms: FF650–950. Closed: Sunday and Monday out of season and the whole of January/February.

CLUNY

Hôtel de Bourgogne ✩✩✩, Place de l'Abbaye, 71250. Tel: 85.59.00.58; fax: 85.59.03.73. Quiet, friendly hotel, with a good restaurant. CC: Amex, Diners, Visa, Mastercard. Rooms: FF390–800; Menus: FF110–380. Closed: Tuesday and January.
Hôtel de l'Abbaye ✩✩, Avenue de la Gare, 71250. Tel: 85.59.11.14. Logis de France hotel. Rooms: FF135–230; Menus: FF85–130. Closed: Sunday evening out of season and December/January.

LOUHANS

Hostellerie du Cheval Rouge, 5 Rue d'Alsace, 71500. Tel: 85.75.21.42. Family-run hotel and restaurant. CC: Visa, Mastercard. Rooms: FF250; Menus: FF75–170. Closed: Sunday evening and Monday; 2–10 January and 15–25 June.
Auberge de St-Usage, 71500. Tel: 85.72.10.95. Small, inexpensive hotel and restaurant, set in its own garden. CC: Amex. Rooms: FF68–185; menus: FF38–180. Closed: Friday evening out of season and 15 January–15 February.

MACON

Hôtel Terminus ✩✩, 91 Rue Victor Hugo, 71000. Tel: 85.39.17.11; fax: 85.38.02.75; S7100FRAN. Comfortable hotel and restaurant with private swimming-pool and garden. CC: Amex, Diners, Visa, Mastercard. Rooms: FF252–270: Menus: FF75–145.
Grand Hôtel de Bourgogne ✩✩, 6 Rue Victor Hugo, 71000. Tel: 85.38.36.57; fax: 85.38.65.92. Centrally located hotel and restaurant, part of the Interhôtel chain. CC: Amex, Diners, Visa, Mastercard. Rooms: FF226–312; Menus: FF74–210.
Hôtel du Nord ✩✩, 313 Quai Jean Jaurès, 71000. Tel: 85.38.08.68; fax: 85.39.01.92. This moderately priced hotel is located by the river. It does not have a restaurant. CC: Amex, Visa, Mastercard. Rooms: FF110–220. Closed: Sunday out of season and 20–30 November.

PARAY-LE-MONIAL

Hostellerie des Trois Pigeons, 2 Rue Dargaud, 71600. Tel: 85.51.03.77; fax: 85.81.58.59; S7160HOPI. Hotel set in its own garden, with some rooms suitable for disabled visitors. CC Amex, Mastercard. Rooms: FF95–220; Menus: FF90–220. Closed: January/February.
Hôtel aux Vendanges de Bourgogne ✩✩, 5 Rue Denis Papin, 71600. Tel: 85.81.13.43. Family-run Logis de France hotel and restaurant. CC: Visa,

Mastercard. Rooms: FF110–220; Menus FF58–125. Closed: Sunday evening out of season.

REPLONGES

Hôtel la Huchette, on the RN79, 01750 Mâcon. Tel: 85.31.03.55; fax: 85.31.10.24. This elegant country hotel with swimming-pool in lovely grounds is located on the main road, just outside Mâcon. CC: Amex, Diners, Visa, Mastercard. Rooms: FF480–600. Closed: Monday out of season and 10 November–16 December.

TOURNUS

Hôtel de Greuze ✩✩✩✩, 5–6 Place de l'Abbaye, 71700. Tel: 85.40.77.77; fax: 85.40.77.23; S7170GREU. Fine old hotel overlooking the abbey. CC: Amex, Diners, Visa, Mastercard. Rooms: FF740–1,150.
Hôtel le Rempart, 2–4 Avenue Gambetta, 71700. Tel: 85.51.10.56; fax: 85.40.77.22; S2170REMP. Fine old hotel near the abbey with some rooms suitable for disabled visitors. Excellent restaurant offering regional dishes. CC: Amex, Diners. Rooms: FF320–950; Menus: FF155–400.
Nouvel Hôtel ✩, 1 bis, Avenue des Alpes, 71700. Tel: 85.51.04.25. Very small, modest hotel and restaurant for those with a limited budget. Rooms: FF95–130; Menus: FF68–130.

VILLEFRANCHE-SUR-SAONE

Hôtel Plaisance, 96 Avenue de la Libération, 69652. Tel: 74.65.33.52. Comfortable (air-conditioned) and well-kept "France Accueil" hotel. CC: Amex, Diners, Visa, Mastercard. Rooms: FF325–330; Menus FF80–250 Closed: 24 December–2 January.
Hôtel Newport, Avenue de l'Europe, Z.I., 69652. Tel: 74.68.75.59. Hotel and restaurant set in pleasant grounds – meals may be taken outside. CC: Amex, Visa, Mastercard. Rooms: FF225–250; Menus: FF68–190. Closed: 23–31 December.

BED & BREAKFAST

There is a good choice of bed and breakfast accommodation in the region in private houses (often on working farms) whose owners are members of the Fédération Nationale des Gîtes Ruraux de France. This means that the accommodation is inspected by a local representative of the Fédération to ensure that standards are maintained in accordance with its "star" rating (which in fact is shown by ears of corn on a scale of one to four). The majority of these *chambres d'hôtes* are in the country or small villages. They can be booked for an overnight stop or a longer stay. Breakfast is included in the price (from around FF100 for one person, FF150 for a couple) and evening meals – usually

325

made with local produce and extremely good value – are often available.

Staying with a family in this way provides an ideal opportunity really to get to know the local area and its people. A brochure of all recognised *Gîtes-Chambres d'hôtes* is available from the regional tourist office; lists for individual *départements* are available from the local offices of the Fédération, and some are bookable through the Gîtes de France office in London (for all these addresses, *see Self-Catering*).

B & B Abroad, offer a straightforward bed and breakfast service which can include ferry bookings if desired. They will book accommodation in the region and overnight stops en route. Contact: 5 Worlds End Lane, Green St. Green, Orpington, Kent BR6 6AA. Tel: 0689-855538.

Café-Couette is a Paris-based organisation offering B & B, or as they call it, *Hébergement chez l'habitant*. Contact them at 8 Rue de l'Isly, 75008 Paris. Tel: 1-42.94.92.00.

For B & B on a slightly grander scale, try **Château Accueil**. This is a group of owners of private châteaux who offer luxury accommodation and usually evening meals in their own homes. There are four Burgundian châteaux in the current brochure which can be booked in the UK through Château Welcome, PO Box 66, 94 Bell Street, Henley on Thames RG9 1XS, tel: 0491-578803; or in Canada through Tours Chanteclerc, 65 Rue de Brésoles, Montréal, Québec H2Y 1V7, tel: 514-845 1236, and at 100 Adelaide Street West, Toronto, Ontario M11 1S3, tel: 416-867 1595.

If you do not wish to book anything in advance, just look out for signs along the road (usually in the country) offering *chambres d'hôtes*. You will be taking pot luck, but you may be delighted by the simple farm food and accommodation on offer.

SELF-CATERING

France has what is probably the best network of self-catering holiday cottages anywhere in Europe. The Fédération des Gîtes Ruraux de France was set up over 30 years ago with the aim of restoring rural properties (by means of offering grants to owners) on the condition that these properties would then be let as cheap holiday homes for the less well-heeled town and city dwellers. These *gîtes* (literally, a place to lay one's head) have now become extremely popular with the British as an inexpensive way of enjoying a rural holiday in France. The properties range from very simple farm cottages to grand manor houses and even the odd château.

The properties are all inspected by the Relais Départemental des Gîtes Ruraux de France (the county office of the national federation) and given an *épi* (ear of corn) classification. The *gîtes* are completely self-catering (in many cases expect to supply your own bed linen), but most have owners living nearby who will tell you where to buy local

produce (and if on a farm, often provide it). One salutary note – many of these cottages are on farms, and as such, are surrounded by wildlife, so if you are squeamish about the odd mouse in the kitchen, stay in a hotel! Having said that, the properties should be, and generally are, kept clean and in good order.

Many *gîtes* are rather off the beaten track and a car, or at least a bicycle, is usually essential. Bicycles can often be hired locally or sometimes from *gîte* owners. Car hire is expensive, but some fly/drive packages still make this a relatively inexpensive way to visit the region, as *gîtes* can cost as little as FF1,000 per week for the whole house. *Gîtes* can get heavily booked in high season, so start the process in the New Year. If you wish to deal directly with France, the Relais Départemental will send you a list of all the *gîtes* in their *département*. Alternatively, you can book through the London booking office: Gîtes de France, 178 Picadilly, WIV 9DB. Tel: 071 493 3480. For a £3 membership you have the choice of over 130 *gîtes* in the region.

Relais des Gîtes Ruraux (départemental **offices**):
Ain: 1 Place Clémenceau, 01000 Bourg-en-Bresse Cedex. Tel: 74,23.61.96.
Côte d'Or: 14 Rue de la Préfecture, 21000 Dijon. Tel: 80.50.15.60.
Nièvre: Service Réservation Loisirs Acceuil, 3 Rue du Sort, 5800 Nevers. Tel: 86.59.14.22; fax: 86.36.36.63.
Rhône: 146, Rue Pierre Corneille, 69426 Lyon cedex 3. Tel: 72.60.44.49.
Saône-et-Loire: Chambre d'Agriculture, 14 bis Rue Guynemer, 89015 Auxerre Cedex. Tel: 86.46.47.48. Or Service Réservation Loisirs Accueil, 1–2 Quai de la République, 89000 Auxerre. Tel: 86.51.12.05.
Yonne: Service de Réservation Loisirs Accueil de L'Yonne, 1–2 Quai de la République, 89000 Auxerre. Tel: 86.51.12.05; fax: 86.51.68.47.

The main ferry companies also offer *gîte* holidays in association with the Gîtes de France office in London – apply to the ferry companies for their brochures. Many other tour operators and private individuals also offer self-catering accommodation, ranging from a simple farm cottage to an apartment in a luxurious château. Sometimes these properties are official *gîtes* and so have to conform to the Féderation's standards, but others are not subject to any form of inspection at all. Try the private advertisements in the national press.

A selection of UK-based companies, who will usually handle your travel arrangements as part of the package, are listed below:
Blakes Holidays, Wroxham, Norwich NR12 8DH. Tel: 0603-784131; fax 0603-782871.
Hoseasons Holidays Abroad, Sunway House, Lowestoft NR32 3LT. Tel: 0502-500555; fax: 0502-500532.
Jet Tours & French Travel Service, 69 Boston Manor Road, Brentford, Middlesex TW8 9JQ. Tel: 081-750 4266; fax 081-750 4269.

Vacances en Campagne, Bignor, nr Pulborough, W. Sussex RH20 1QD. Tel: 07987-433; fax 07987-343. The company has overseas agents in the US and Canada (contact Sussex office for addresses).

CAMPING

There is a good choice of campsites in the region, many of them situated near lakes or rivers. The Comité Régional du Tourisme (*see Useful Addresses*) produces a list of all recognised sites, with details of star-rating and facilities. As with other types of holiday accommodation, the sites can get booked up in high season, so do consider advance booking. Members of the Camping Club or Camping and Caravanning Club of Great Britain may make use of their booking services. The Michelin Camping/Caravanning Guide lists sites which accept (or insist on) pre-booking. The Camping Service at 69 Westbourne Grove, London W2 4UJ, tel: 071-792 1944, can book sites either from their own brochure of ✩✩✩ and ✩✩✩✩ sites or any and will also book ferries.

A camping *carnet* is useful (some sites will not accept a booking without one). It is available in the UK to members of the AA, RAC or the Camping Clubs mentioned above; or for £5 from the GB Car Club, PO Box 11, Romsey, Hants. SO5 8XX.

Campsites, like hotels, have official classifications from P (minimal comfort, water points, showers and sinks) to ✩✩✩✩ luxury sites with more space to each pitch, and offer above-average facilities, often including a restaurant or takeway food, games areas and swimming-pools. The majority of sites nationwide are two-star. Average prices are around FF12 per person per night at a P site, to around FF22 at a ✩✩✩✩ site.

If you really like to get back to nature, and are unimpressed by the modern trappings of hot water and electric power, look out for camp-sites designated *Aire naturelle de camping* where facilities will be absolutely minimal and prices to match. These have a maximum of 25 pitches so offer the opportunity to stay away from some of the more commercial sites (which can be huge).

The FFCC Guide (*see below*) lists over 2,000 such sites nationwide.

Some farms offer "official" sites too under the auspices of the Fédération Nationale des Gîtes Ruraux (*see Self-Catering*) – these are designated *Camping à la ferme*; again facilities are usually limited but farmers are allowed to have only six pitches and if you are lucky you will get to know and enjoy the farm life and some of its produce.

Another option, currently becoming popular on some sites, are wooden huts which are rather more attractive than caravans, but offer the same sort of facilities. For details of sites and rentals contact: Huttes de France, tel: 73.34.18.48.

Packaged camping holidays are now very popular with British holidaymakers and ideal for other overseas visitors too, as all the camping paraphernalia is provided on the site – you only have to take your personal luggage. Many companies now offer this type of holiday, mostly with ferry travel included in the all-in price. Like other package tours, the companies have couriers on the sites to help with any problems. It is interesting to note that where such companies have taken over sections of existing sites, that facilities have improved to meet the demands of their customers and so benefit all campers. Many companies offer good opportunities for sports and leisure, such as wind-surfing or surfing; often the equipment, and sometimes instruction too is covered by the cost of the package. Be warned, though, that some of the sites are very large, so might not suit those who wish to get away from it all.

A selection of the package operators is listed below, for others check the Sunday press.

Canvas Holidays, Bull Plain, Hertford, Herts. SG14 1DY. Tel: 0992-553535. Pioneers in the field; offer a nanny service.

Eurocamp, Edmundson House, Tatton Street, Knutsford, Cheshire WA16 6BG. Tel: 0565-633844 for ready erected tents and caravans or 0565-755399 for campers with own equipment.

Carefree Camping, 126 Hempstead Road, King's Langley, Herts WD4 8AL. Tel: 0923-261311. Free holidays for under-14s and children's couriers on most sites.

French Life, 26 Church Road, Horsforth, Leeds LS18 5LG. Tel: 0532-390077; fax 0532-584211. Offer a "multicentre" deal.

Keycamp Holidays, Ellerman House, 92–96 Lind Road, Sutton SM1 4PL. Tel: 081 661 1836.

Sunsites, 30 Princess Street, Knutsford, Cheshire WA16 6BN. Tel: 0565 55644.

CAMPER VAN HIRE

Camper vans can be hired locally in the region from the following companies:

Hertz SA Ruivo, 7 Avenue du 8 Septembre, 21200 Beaune. Tel: 80.24.75.20. **Hertz Arno**, 18bis Avenue Foch, 21000 Dijon. Tel: 80.43.55.22.

Bourgogne Évasion, Garage Moderne SA, 156 Avenue de la République, BP 30, 71210 Montchanin. Tel: 85.78.52.11.

Bidaut Caravanes, Route de Dijon, 39100 Sampans. Tel: 84.82.09.50; fax: 84.82.60.32.

Useful Publications and Addresses: *The French Federation of Camping and Caravanning Guide (FFCC)*, lists 11,300 sites nationwide, and also shows which have facilities for disabled campers. Available from Springdene, Shepherd's Way, Fairlight, E. Sussex TN35 4BB. Price £7.95.
Michelin Green Guide – Camping/Caravanning France. Very informative and also lists sites with facilities for the disabled. Published annually in March, £5.95.

Camping and Caravanning Club, 11 Lower Grosvenor Place, London SW1.

Caravan Club, East Grinstead House, East Grinstead, Sussex RH19 1UA.

YOUTH HOSTELS

Holders of accredited Youth Hostel Association cards may stay in any French hostels which are in fact run by two separate organisations; Fédération Unie des Auberges de Jeunesse (FUAJ), 27 Rue Pajol, 75018 Paris, tel: 1-42.41.59.00, which is affiliated to the International Youth Hostel Federation, and the Ligue Française pour les Auberges de Jeunesse (LFAJ), 38 Boulevard Raspail, 75007 Paris, tel: 1-45.48.69.84. Expect to pay around FF60 per night.

The British YHA publishes the International Youth Hostel Handbook, Vol I (revised each March), which includes all the hostels in the region, price £5.99 by post from Youth Hostel Association, 14 Southampton Street, London WC2E 7H7. Tel: 071-836 8541. They also handle membership queries, tel: 071-836 1036.

In the USA apply to the American Youth Hostels Inc, PO Box 37613, Dept. USA, Washington DC 20013/7613. Tel: 202-783 6161.

Gîtes d'Etapes offer hostel accommodation and are popular with ramblers, climbers and horse riders (some offer stabling). All official gîtes d'étapes come under the auspices of the Relais Départementaux des Gîtes Ruraux (for addresses see Self-Catering). These are a popular form of cheap accommodation particularly in the national parks. Prices are similar to youth hostels – around FF50 per night for basic accommodation, but up to FF110 or more in the more luxurious establishments which may be on farms offering riding facilities and/or stabling. You do not have to be a member of any organisation to use them.

Other hostel accommodation is available in Côte d'Or in Maisons d'Amies at Francheville, tel: 80.35.05.11; and at Semur-en-Auxois, tel: 80.97.10.22. Cluny-Séjour at Rue Porte de Paris, 71250 Cluny offers 76 beds for individuals, families and groups, tel: 85.59.08.83.

FOOD DIGEST

RESTAURANTS

Burgundy is renowned for its cuisine and the following list includes its most famous restaurants and recommends a selection of less expensive establishments which are very good value. Many are within hotels so we indicate where accommodation is also available. Booking is always advisable.

YONNE

JOIGNY

La Côte Saint-Jacques, 14 Faubourg de Paris. Tel: 86.62.09.70. For pure luxury and some of the most exciting food around, such as the *croustillant de pieds de porc, tourteau et pâtés fraîches au basilic* (pig's feet with crab, pasta and basil). There's exquisite traditional cooking, too: *boeuf bourguignon* and homemade blood sausage with silky mashed potatoes. Menus: FF300 (weekday lunch) and 620. À la carte FF700. Closed: 6 January–6 February. CC: Visa, Amex, Diners. Accommodation available.

AUXERRE

Restaurant Jean-Luc Barnabet, 14 Quai de la République. Tel: 86.51.68.88. The menu in this former coaching inn features several luxuries as well as more down-to-earth fare: warm foie gras in pastry with cabbage, sea bass with oysters, and *pièce de boeuf au gamay d'Irancy* (a lighter version of *boeuf bourguignon*). Menus: FF160 and 230. À la carte FF350. Closed: Sunday dinner, Monday, last week in December, and first week in January. CC: Visa, Eurocard.

Le Jardin Gourmand, 56 Boulevard Vauban. Tel: 86.51.53.52. Pierre Boussereau changes his menu seven times a year, and always produces imaginative and zesty food. Good examples include rabbit with honey and rosemary, poached chicken with mushroom and celery risotto, and spicy pears in puff pastry. Menus: FF130, 180, and 260. À la carte: FF350. Closed: Monday (except July and August) and December. CC: Visa, Eurocard.

CHEVANNES

La Chamaille, 4 Route de Boiloup. Tel: 86.41.24.80. In a thoroughly romantic spot in the French countryside, a creative chef makes good use of local Burgundian products: e.g., *pithiviers de pigeon au fumet d'Irancy* (squab with Irancy wine sauce and puff pastry). Menus: FF150, 248. À la carte FF320. Closed: Monday, Tuesday, and mid-January to mid-February. CC: Visa, Amex, Diners. Accommodation available.

CHABLIS

Hôstellerie des Clos, 18 Rue Jules Rathier. Tel: 86.42.10.63. Michel Vignaud's contemporary menu is expertly tuned to the seasons and the surrounding Burgundy landscape. In autumn, for example, there's wild squab paired with quince, veal kidneys with verjuice and grapes, and oysters in Chablis wine sauce. Closed: Thursday lunch and Wednesday (October to June), and mid-December to mid-January. Menus: FF155, 270, and 380. À la carte FF350. CC: Visa. Accommodation available.

Au Vrai Chablis, Place du Marché. Tel: 86.42.11.43. This village bistrot, complete with zinc-covered bar, is a fine place for sampling Burgundy's sturdy cooking – snails, eggs in red wine sauce, andouillette, and, of course, the local Chablis, here served by the glass. Menus: FF72 and 180 (daily). À la carte FF100. Closed: December–February. CC: Visa, Amex, Eurocard.

VINCELOTTES

Auberge les Tilleuls, tel: 86.42.22.13. An unassuming spot for homemade terrines, *coq au vin d'Irancy*, ham in Chablis sauce as well as seasonal dishes. Menus: FF98 (except Saturday dinner and holidays), 168, and 200. À la carte FF250. Closed: Wednesday dinner and Thursday (October–Easter), and last week in December to last week in February. CC: Visa, Eurocard. Accommodation available.

NITRY

La Beursaudière, Chemin de Ronde. Tel: 86.33.62.51. At this folkloric institution, energetic waitresses in regional costume serve up platters of wonderful Burgundy soul food: eggs in red wine sauce, rabbit baked in the bread oven, and melting Époisses cheese on country bread. Menus: FF69, 135, 180, and 250. À la carte FF250. Open: daily. Last dinner orders taken at 10pm. CC: Visa, Amex.

THE HEARTLAND

VEZELAY

L'Espérance, St-Père-sous-Vézelay. Tel: 86.33.20.45. Marc Meneau delivers some of the best food in the Burgundy countryside, drawing on the finest local ingredients. A light-filled dining room and terrace in summer set the stage for his contemporary dishes: e.g., *ambroisie de volaille* and *turbot rôti au jus de viande* (turbot in rich meat juices). Menus: FF300 (except Sunday and holidays), 580, and 780 (daily). À la carte FF700. Closed: Wednesday lunch, Tuesday, and January to mid-February. Last dinner orders taken at 10pm. CC: Visa, Amex, Diners. Accommodation available.

AVALLON

Moulin des Ruats, Vallée du Cousin. Tel: 86.34.07.14. A secluded, enchanting spot – especially in summer when tables are set up outside, by the stream – for contemporary dishes such as *fricassée d'escargots en soupe de champignons* (snails with mushroom sauce) and banana tart with ginger. Menus: FF150 and 180 (weekday lunch), 220 and 320 (evening). À la carte FF400. Closed: Monday (off season) and November to mid-February. CC: Visa, Diners. Accommodation available.

STE-MAGNANCE

La Chènevotte, Route Nationale 6. Tel: 86.33.14.79. The Luciani family runs this homely, flower-filled restaurant, offering heirloom recipes: *terrine maison*, *escargots de Bourgogne*, and duck with cider. Menus: FF98 (lunch) and 132. À la carte FF150. Closed: Wednesday dinner and Thursday. Last dinner orders taken 10.30pm. CC: Visa.

EPOISSES

Ferme-Auberge La Garande, Jeux-lès-Bard. Tel: 80.96.74.51. Near the village of Époisses, which gives its name to the pungent Burgundian cheese washed with the local *marc de Bourgogne*, Robert and Jacqueline Charlut welcome guests to their country auberge, serving products from the farm. This is the place to sample *oeufs en meurette* (poached eggs in red wine), farm-raised poultry and lamb, and, of course, Époisses cheese. Menus: FF80 and 100. À la carte FF150. Open: Saturday dinner, Sunday lunch, and holiday lunch. Closed: mid-December to March. Last dinner orders taken 8.30pm. Reservations required. No credit cards.

SEMUR-EN-AUXOIS

Café-Restaurant des Minimes, 39 Rue de Vaux. Tel: 80.97.26.86. Try this savvy village bistrot for a good salad, leek or onion tart, and a Burgundy standby like *boeuf bourguignon* or *oeufs en meurette*. Closed: Tuesday dinner and Wednesday. Last dinner orders taken 10.30pm. Menus: FF57 (lunch) and 89 (dinner). À la carte FF80. CC: Visa.

FLAVIGNY-SUR-OZERAIN

La Grange des Quatre Heures Soupatoires, Place de l'Église. Tel: 80.96.20.62. Marie-Françoise Couthier prepares generous farm cooking in this converted barn-restaurant, run by a farmers' coop. Among the offerings on one four-course menu are two terrines and several choices of tarts, roast chicken or chicken simmered with vegetables, rabbit stew, a seasonal vegetable, cheese, dessert, wine, and coffee – all for 80 francs. Menus: FF80 and 85. Closed: Monday and October–July. Open: Easter and Easter Monday, 1 and 8 May, Pentecost and Pentecost Monday, and the last Sunday in October. No credit cards.

VITTEAUX

La Rochefontaine, Ste-Colombe-en-Auxois. Tel: 80.49.60.12. "We've got no freezers here," explains Madame Aubertin. Based on her list of reservations for each meal, this farmer's wife makes up a single, special menu and sets aside just so many fresh chickens and goat's-milk cheeses for her guests. Ask what's on the menu when booking. Menu: FF100. Open: weekends. Closed: January and February. Reservations required. No credit cards.

NIEVRE

QUARRE-LES-TOMBES

Auberge de l'Atre, Les Lavaults. Tel: 86.32.20.79. In an old stone house in the Parc Régional du Morvan, Francis Salamolard cooks with the park's bounty: trout from fast-flowing rivers, with wild herbs, Charolais beef with forest mushrooms, tarts packed with the fruit of low-bush blueberries. Menus: FF95 (weekdays), 168, and 245. À la carte FF300. Closed: Tuesday dinner and Wednesday (off season), last week in November, first week in December, and February. CC: Visa, Amex, Diners. **Auberge des Brizards**, Les Brizards. Tel: 86.32.20.12. Francine and Jérôme Besancenot's old-time auberge, set alongside a stream in the Morvan forest, this makes a peaceful retreat and the perfect spot to sample regional fare: *crapiaud de blé noir* (a local pancake), blood sausage, and *civet de canard au sang* (duck stew thickened with blood). Menus: FF100 (weekdays except holidays) and 300. À la carte FF200. Closed: January–early February. Last dinner orders taken 10.30pm. CC: Visa, Amex. Accommodation available.

SINCEY-LES-ROUVRAY

Ferme-Auberge de la Mothe, tel: 80.64.71.13. This unusual, 15th-century château-farm offers a generous set menu with down-home food: local cured ham, quiche, roast leg of lamb, lemon chicken, farm cheeses, chocolate charlotte. Menu: FF110. Open: weekends and holidays. Closed: Christmas–Easter. No credit cards.

PRECY-SOUS-THIL

Ferme-Auberge de la Morvandelle, Fontangy. Tel: 80.84.33.32. Jean-Charles and Marie-Claude Prommer raise Charolais cattle for a living, but at the weekend they open their farmhouse to hungry eaters with a yearning for grandmother's cooking: terrines, chicken with tarragon, guinea fowl and cabbage, rabbit in mustard sauce, and homemade tarts. Menus: FF85 and 89. Open: for lunch weekends mid-April to mid-January. Reservations required. No credit cards.

SAULIEU

La Côte d'Or, 2 Rue d'Argentine. Tel: 80.64.07.66. This landmark to French gastronomy (the legendary Alexandre Dumaine was chef here) is today one of France's most luxurious hotel-restaurants. Bernard Loiseau's food is stark but satisfying: e.g. *panaché d'abats de veau à la purée de truffes* (veal escalope and sweetbreads served with the best mashed potatoes). Menus: FF390 (lunch) and 690 (daily). À la carte FF700. Closed: Tuesday lunch and Monday (November–April), first two weeks in March, last week in November, and three weeks in December. CC: Visa, Amex. Accommodation available.

POUILLY-EN-AUXOIS

Ferme-Auberge de Laneau, Arconey. Tel: 80.84.11.18. A good farm address to know, where you can enjoy an authentic home-cooked meal. Françoise Doret's copious *potée bourguignonne* (pork and vegetable stew) is a must. Menus: FF55 and 90. Closed: Monday. Last dinner orders taken 8pm. No credit cards. Accommodation available.

ARNAY-LE-DUC

Chez Camille, 1 Place E.-Herriot. Tel: 80.90.01.30. Down the road from the Maison Régionale des Arts de la Table, a museum dedicated to the art of eating, is Chez Camille, a solid, old-fashioned hotel-restaurant. Here, in an enclosed garden, Armand Poinsot offers classic cooking from the Burgundian repertoire: *jambon persillé à l'Aligoté* (parsleyed ham), *rissoles d'escargots aux pâtes fraîches et aux champignons* (snails with fresh pasta and mushrooms), and *truffière de charolais*, prepared with Burgundy's fine beef. Menus: FF168, 250, and 310. À la carte FF280. Open: daily. CC: Visa, Amex, Diners. Accommodation available.

AUTUN

Le Chalet Bleu, 3 Rue Jeannin. Tel: 85.86.27.30. In this small-town restaurant, Philippe Bouché prepares imaginative cuisine with strong regional roots at prices to applaud. Even the 110-franc menu offers plenty of choice, including eggs in red wine sauce with Burgundy snails, and hare served with wine-poached pears and a celery mousse. Menus: FF75 (weekdays only), 110, 140, and 175. À la carte FF150. Closed: Monday dinner, Tuesday, and the last two weeks in February. CC: Visa, Amex, Diners.

DIJON

Restaurant Jean-Pierre Billoux, 14 Place Darcy. Tel: 80.30.11.00. Jean-Pierre Billoux's elegant cooking includes: *terrine de pigeonneau à l'ail* (squab terrine with garlic), *blanc de pintade au foie de canard et aux cèpes* (guinea fowl with duck liver and wild mushrooms) as well as several Burgundy classics. Menus: FF220 (weekday lunch), 260 (weekday dinner), 480 (weekend lunch and dinner). À la carte FF450. Closed: Sunday dinner, Monday, last week in February, first week in March, and two weeks in August. CC: Visa, Amex. Accommodation available (Hôtel de la Cloche).

Restaurant Thibert, 10 Place Wilson. Tel: 80.67.74.64. For wonderful upscale dining, try Jean-Paul Thibert's *petits choux verts farcis aux escargots* (cabbage stuffed with snails) and *assiette de lapin* (confit of rabbit leg with squid and celery, roast saddle of rabbit, and stuffed cabbage rolls). Menus: FF115 (except Saturday dinner and holidays), 195, 250, 300, and 380. À la carte 400. Closed: Monday lunch, Sunday, and three weeks in August. CC: Visa.

Le Chabrot, 36 Rue Monge. Tel: 80.30.69.61. Christian Bouy's wine bar-restaurant specialises in salmon (the menu lists no fewer than 15 salmon dishes), but you can also try hearty regional favourites, including the rare consommé *chabrot* (doused with red wine), and wine by the glass. Menus: FF69 and 92 (dinner). À la carte FF180. Closed: Monday lunch and Sunday. Last dinner orders taken 10.30pm. CC: Visa.

Coum' Chez Eux, 68 Rue Jean-Jacques Rousseau. Tel: 80.73.56.87. A friendly, funky spot (the menu is in comic-strip form) for a simple omelette or a daily special from the Morvan: ham hock and lentils, *la potée morvandelle* (pork and vegetable stew), *boeuf gros sel* (boiled beef), and *lapin sauté morvandiotte* (rabbit stew). À la carte FF110. Closed: Sunday and mid-July to mid-August. Last dinner orders taken 10.30pm. CC: Visa, Amex, Diners.

COTE D'OR

MARSANNAY-LA-COTE

Les Gourmets, 8 Rue du Puits-de-Têt. Tel: 80.52.16.32. This is the place local vintners take their clients, where Burgundy wines are flattered by the creative dishes of Joël Perreaut: *tarte fine au saumon fumé* (smoked salmon tart) and *daube de lapin en lasagne* (rabbit with fresh pasta). Menus:

FF165 (weekday lunch), 210, 340, and 450. À la carte 300. Closed: Sunday dinner, Monday, and January. CC: Visa, Amex.

FIXIN

Chez Jeannette, 7 Rue Noisot. Tel: 80.52.45.49. Set in a hamlet amongst Burgundy vineyards, this modest hotel-restaurant offers classic regional specialities – *jambon persillé, coq au vin*, snails – and wonderful local cheeses. Menus: FF75, 135, and 300. À la carte 195. Closed: Thursday and 24 November–7 January. CC: Visa, Amex, Diners, Eurocard. Accommodation available.

GEVREY-CHAMBERTIN

Rôtisserie du Chambertin, Rue du Chambertin. Tel: 80.34.33.20. A Burgundy landmark with inspired regional cooking: carp with sorrel sauce, a lighter version of *coq au vin*, and frogs' legs with parsley sauce. Menus: FF260, 330, and 410. À la carte FF350. Closed: Sunday dinner, Monday, February and first week in August. CC: Visa, Eurocard.

TERNANT

La Ferme de Rolle, Hameau de Rolle. Tel: 80.59.50.39. At their rural bistrot near Gevrey-Chambertin, Didier and Martine Chevalier serve up all the Burgundian favourites: e.g., *salade à la gratinée d'Époisses*, snails, *coq au vin*, and pears in red wine. Note that on Sundays food is served all day long from noon–8pm, 10pm in summer. Menus: FF75, 85, and 98 daily. À la carte FF120. Closed: Tuesday, Wednesday, and mid-December to mid-January. CC: Visa, Amex, Eurocard.

BOUILLAND

Le Vieux Moulin, tel: 80.21.51.16. The young Jean-Pierre Silva finds inspiration for his eclectic, sophisticated food both within the classic Burgundian repertoire and beyond it: *estouffade de jeunes poireaux, jambonnette de grenouille en meurette* (leeks and frogs' legs in red wine sauce) and *turbot aux épices* with *compôte d'oignons* (turbot with spices and onion jam). Menus: FF190 (lunch), 300, and 430 (daily). À la carte FF400. Closed: Thursday lunch, Wednesday (except holidays), and mid-December to late January. CC: Visa, Eurocard. Accommodation available.

CHOREY-LES-BEAUNE

Le Bareuzai, Route Nationale 74. Tel: 80.22.02.90. A rock-solid Burgundy address for the regional classics: *jambon persillé, oeufs en meurette*, snails, wine-poached pears. Menus: FF134 and 280. À la carte FF250. Closed: January and the first week in February. CC: Visa, Amex, Diners.

CHAGNY

Lameloise, 36 Place d'Armes. Tel: 85.87.08.85. At Lameloise, one of Burgundy's finest tables, you can still taste perfect *haute cuisine bourguignonne*, including *raviolis d'escargots de Bourgogne dans leur bouillon d'ail doux* (snail ravioli in garlic-infused broth) and *pigeon de Bresse en vessie et ses pâtes fraîches au foie gras* (poached squab with fresh pasta and foie gras). Menus: FF350 and 500. À la carte FF500. Closed: Wednesday, Thursday lunch, the last week in December to the third week in January, and 19 May. Reservations recommended. CC: Visa, Amex, Eurocard. Accommodation available.

CHALON-SUR-SAONE

Le Moulin de Martorey, Saint-Rémy. Tel: 85.48.12.98. Jean-Pierre Gillot redefines the Burgundy classics and invents new ones with such dishes as snails in red wine with deep-fried oyster mushrooms, rabbit sausage and fillet with verjuice sauce, and *fondant au Guyaquil et pralin feuilleté* (rich chocolate with praline). Menus: FF170, 235, and 365. À la carte FF300. Closed: Sunday dinner, Monday, the last two weeks in February, and the last two weeks in August. CC: Visa, Eurocard.

LE MACONNAIS

SENNECEY-LE-GRAND

Ferme-Auberge de Malo, Etrigny. Tel: 85.92.21.47. For a Burgundian snack of *charcuterie* or an omelette and a glass of wine, try this heartwarming auberge. If you order ahead, Jacqueline Goujon will also prepare more substantial fare such as a simple roast chicken (or in cream sauce), *civet de porc* (pork stew), and peaches in Aligoté wine. Menus: FF80 and 120. À la carte FF55 to 80. Closed: Wednesday (July and August). Open: Saturday dinner and Sunday 11 November–Easter. Last dinner orders taken 8pm, 8.30pm July and August. No credit cards.

MONTPONT-EN-BRESSE

Les Plattières, Ste-Croix-en-Bresse. Tel: 85.74.80.74. On a typical half-timbered Bresse farmstead, sample homemade pâté and light cheese tart, or ring ahead and settle into a serious meal featuring René Perrin's Bresse chicken. Menus: FF50, 65, 80, and 100. À la carte from FF50 to 120. Closed: Monday. Last lunch orders taken 1pm. No credit cards. Accommodation available.

VERNOUX

Ferme-Auberge du Colombier, tel: 74.30.72.00. Catherine Debourg sets a superb table with *salade bressane* (warm chicken liver salad), chicken in cream sauce, *gratin dauphinois*, and *tarte bressane* (cream

and sugar tart hot from the bread oven), while the star ingredients – chickens and turkeys – scratch in the barnyard. Note that competition for a table here can be fierce, so book ahead. Menu: FF88. Closed: Tuesday dinner, Wednesday, and dinner October to mid-March (except Saturday). No credit cards.

MACON

Restaurant Laurent Couturier, 70 Rue de Lyon. Tel: 85.38.16.16. Laurent Couturier, a rising star on the local horizon, takes simple ingredients, herbs and spices, and transforms them into inventive dishes: e.g., roast duck with turnips and sesame seeds – at modest prices. Menus: FF105 (weekday lunch), 155, 200, and 320 (daily). À la carte 300 F. Closed: Saturday lunch, Sunday, and August. CC: Visa. Reservations recommended.

LA CLAYETTE

Ferme-Auberge de Lavaux, Châtenay-sous-Dun. Tel: 85.28.08.48. At this restored farmhouse, feast on *poulet à la crème* (chicken in cream sauce), *canard aux olives* (duck with olives, in April and October) and the *gâteau de foies de volaille* (chicken liver mousse). Menus: FF80 and 90. Closed: Tuesday and All Soul's Day to Easter. No credit cards. Accommodation available.

CHATEAUNEUF

La Fontaine, tel: 85.26.26.87. Don't miss the remarkable talents of Yves Jury on display in this excellent value village restaurant. His intelligent, earthy food exemplifies the best of contemporary French cooking: fricassee of snails, artichokes and cabbage, oxtail with marrow and white beans, and rich chocolate cake with licorice custard sauce. Menus: FF98 (except Sunday and holidays), 140, 170, and 240. À la carte FF250. Closed: Tuesday dinner, Wednesday, and the first two weeks in February. CC: Visa, Eurocard.

MAILLY

La Maillerotte, tel: 85.84.00.50. While Annik Costa watches over the dining-room at this simple inn, Dominique Costa tends to the stove, preparing the renowned local Charolais beef. Menus: FF105, 140, 150, and 185. À la carte FF140. Closed: Tuesday and the first two weeks in January. CC: Visa, Amex, Diners, Eurocard. Accommodation available.

BEAUJOLAIS

MEZERIAT

Les Bessières, tel: 74.30.24.24. A cosy hotel-restaurant with authentic regional specialities. On a summer's day, reserve a garden table and sample sautéed frogs' legs with herbs, carp with chervil (both from local ponds), Bresse chicken in cream sauce, and homespun desserts. Menus: FF130 and 170. À la carte FF220. Closed: Monday and Tuesday (except July and August), and January. CC: Visa. Accommodation available.

VONNAS

Restaurant Georges Blanc, tel: 74.50.08.80. For an outstanding dining experience with attentive service, a comfortable setting, and brilliant food: *crêpe parmentière au saumon et caviar* and Bresse chicken with garlic and *foie gras*. Menus: FF410 and 620. À la carte FF550. Closed: Wednesday and Thursday (except mid-June to mid-September – open Thursday dinner), January, and the first week in February. CC: Visa, Amex, Diners. Reservations recommended. Accommodation available.

L'Ancienne Auberge, Place du Marché. Tel: 74.50.11.13. Georges Blanc's bistrot annexe with modish, soothing bistrot fare: homemade sausage with lentils in Beaujolais, sautéed frogs' legs, *crème brûlée*. Menus: FF110, 150, and 200. À la carte FF190. Closed: Sunday dinner, Monday, and January. Last dinner orders taken 10pm. CC: Visa, Amex. Reservations recommended.

BOURG-EN-BRESSE

Le Français, 7 Avenue Alsace-Lorraine. Tel: 74.22.55.14. and 74.22.47.02. A cavernous, turn-of-the-century brasserie with a pleasantly tacky décor and a 90-franc menu, studded with such regional specialities as the local rosette sausage and Bresse chicken – worth the extra 20 francs. Menus: FF90, 160, and 190. À la carte FF180. Closed: Saturday lunch, Sunday, the last three weeks in August, and the last week in December. CC: Visa, Amex, Eurocard.

MONTMERLE-SUR-SAONE

Hôtel-Restaurant du Rivage, 12 Rue du Pont. Tel: 74.69.33.92. With tables set out under shady trees and an inviting 80-franc menu, this family-run establishment makes a pleasant stop for local *charcuterie*, *petite friture* (tiny fried fish), and sweetened fresh cheese with cream. Menus: FF80, 170, 190, 210, and 250. À la carte FF200. Closed: Monday (October–June), Monday lunch (June–October), and mid-November to mid-December. CC: Visa, Amex, Eurocard. Accommodation available.

CHENAS

Restaurant Robin, Les Deschamps. Tel: 85.36.72.67. For classic regional cooking, reserve a garden table here in summer. Try the andouillette sausage with chervil butter, gratin of crayfish (*écrevisses*), and

Bresse chicken, the famed local poultry. Menus: FF190, 240, 290, and 340 daily. À la carte FF300. Closed: dinner Sunday, Monday, Tuesday, and Thursday; Wednesday; and mid-February to mid-March. Credit cards: Visa, Amex, Diners, Eurocard.

FLEURIE

Auberge du Cep, Place de l'Église. Tel: 74.04.10.77. Here you'll feast on some of the best of the region's fare including andouillette sausage braised in Beaujolais, Bresse chicken with cream and morels, crayfish *en ragoût*. Menus: FF290, 340, 390, 440, and 550. À la carte FF400. Closed: Sunday dinner, Monday, and mid-December to mid-January. CC: Visa, Amex.

TARARE

Restaurant Jean Brouilly, 3 ter Rue de Paris. Tel: 74.63.24.56. A *maison bourgeoise* set in a park on the edge of town, for modern food with a regional twist: perch-pike and lobster *pauchouse*, a variation of the local fish stew, and *filet de sole au vin de Brouilly*. Menus: FF140, 200, 260, and 330. À la carte FF320. Closed: Sunday, Monday, two weeks in January, and one week in August. CC: Visa, Amex, Diners.

WINE

THE BURGUNDY APPELLATION

The area known as Greater Burgundy (Grande Bourgogne) officially includes: Chablis and the Auxerrois, Côte de Nuits and Côte de Beaune (which together make up Côte d'Or), the Chalonnais, the Mâconnais and Beaujolais. Roughly half its total annual output of about 2.5 million hectolitres (330 million bottles) consists of Beaujolais. Greater Burgundy is not a major wine-producing region in volume terms, accounting for a bare 10 percent of total French production.

For convenience's sake, Greater Burgundy is usually divided into two categories, which are treated separately: Burgundy (all *appellations* except Beaujolais) and Beaujolais.

BURGUNDY

The *appellations* (in ascending order of quality) are:

Appellation régionale

Wine from vineyards that qualify for the Burgundy *appellation*. It accounts for 52 percent of total Burgundy production. There are two types of *appellation régionale*:

Wine made from a specific grape variety or varieties: Bourgogne: (red) Pinot Noir; (white) Chardonnay. Bourgogne Grand Ordinaire (BGO): (red) Gamay;

(white) Chardonnay and Aligoté.

Bourgogne Passe-Tout-Grains: (red) Gamay and Pinot Noir.

Bourgogne Aligoté: (white) Aligoté.

Crémant de Bourgogne: (white) Chardonnay and Aligoté.

There also exist rosé versions of Bourgogne, BGO, Bourgogne Passe-Tout-Grains and Crémant de Bourgogne. These are made with various blends of the grape varieties permitted for the whites and reds.

Wine made in a specific Burgundy area:

These wines include: Petit Chablis, Bourgogne Côtes d'Auxerre, Bourgogne Irancy, Bourgogne Hautes-Côtes de Nuits, Bourgogne Hautes-Côtes de Beaune, Bourgogne Côte Chalonnaise, Bourgogne Aligoté de Bouzeron, Mâcon, Mâcon-Supérieur and Mâcon-Villages. Principal grape varieties permitted: Pinot Noir, Chardonnay.

Appellation communale

Wine from 35 specific communes. It accounts for 35 percent of total Burgundy production. Any wine with the mention "*villages*" after its name is an *appellation communale*, with the notable and confusing exception of Mâcon-Villages (an *appellation régionale*).

Ex.: Chablis, Gevrey-Chambertin, Givry, Côte de Beaune-Villages (a blend of wines from various Côte de Beaune communes entitled to the *appellation communale*).

Principal grape varieties permitted: Pinot Noir, Chardonnay.

Appellation premier cru

Wine from over 400 specially classified vineyards (or *climats*) located in certain *appellations communales*. The name of the vineyard usually appears on the label. It accounts for 10 percent of total Burgundy production.

Ex.: Chablis Premier Cru Fourchaume, Fixin Premier Cru Les Arvelets, Rully Premier Cru Margotey.

Principal grape varieties permitted: Pinot Noir, Chardonnay.

Appellation grand cru

Wine from Burgundy's finest vineyards (or *climats*) located in a handful of *appellations communales*. It accounts for 3 percent of total Burgundy production. Because of the prestige of the vineyards, the *appellation grand cru* mentions only the name of the vineyard, not the commune(s) in which it is located, except in the case of Chablis.

Ex.: Chablis Grand Cru Vaudésir, Montrachet, Romanée-Conti.

Principal grape varieties permitted: Pinot Noir, Chardonnay.

List of grands crus:

Grand cru		Commune(s)
Chablis:		
Les Clos	white	Chablis
Vaudésir	white	Chablis
Valmur	white	Chablis
Blanchot	white	Chablis
Preuses	white	Chablis
Grenouille	white	Chablis
Bougros	white	Chablis
Côte de Nuits:		
Chambertin	red	Gevrey-Chambertin
Chambertin-Clos-de-Bèze	red	Gevrey-Chambertin
Latricières-Chambertin	red	Gevrey-Chambertin
Charmes-Chambertin	red	Gevrey-Chambertin
Mazoyères-Chambertin	red	Gevrey-Chambertin
Mazis-Chambertin	red	Gevrey-Chambertin
Ruchottes-Chambertin	red	Gevrey-Chambertin
Chapelle-Chambertin	red	Gevrey-Chambertin
Griotte-Chambertin	red	Gevrey-Chambertin
Clos de la Roche	red	Morey-St-Denis
Clos St-Denis	red	Morey-St-Denis
Clos des Lambrays	red	Morey-St-Denis
Clos de Tart	red	Morey-St-Denis
Bonnes-Mares	red	Morey-St-Denis, Chambolle-Musigny
Musigny	red	Chambolle-Musigny
Clos de Vougeot	red	Vougeot
Grands-Echezeaux	red	Flagey-Echezeaux
Echezeaux	red	Flagey-Echezeaux
Richebourg	red	Vosne-Romanée
Romanée-St-Vivant	red	Vosne-Romanée
Romanée-Conti	red	Vosne-Romanée
Grande Rue	red	Vosne-Romanée
La Romanée	red	Vosne-Romanée
La Tâche	red	Vosne-Romanée
Côte de Beaune:		
Corton	red	Aloxe-Corton, Ladoix-Serrigny
Corton-Charlemagne	white	Aloxe-Corton, Ladoix-Serrigny, Pernand-Vergelesses
Montrachet	white	Puligny-Montrachet, Chassagne-Montrachet
Chevalier-Montrachet	white	Puligny-Montrachet
Bâtard-Montrachet	white	Puligny-Montrachet, Chassagne-Montrachet
Bienvenues-Bâtard-Montrachet	white	Puligny-Montrachet
Criôts-Bâtard-Montrachet	white	Chassagne-Montrachet

BEAUJOLAIS ·

Beaujolais is a red wine made from a single grape variety, Gamay. The *appellations* (in ascending order of quality) are:

Beaujolais

Wine from any vineyard that qualifies for the Beaujolais *appellation*. It accounts for about half of total Beaujolais production, and three quarters of Beaujolais Nouveau.

Beaujolais-Villages

Wine from 39 specific communes. It accounts for about a quarter of total Beaujolais production, and one quarter of Beaujolais Nouveau.

Crus

Wine from the 10 named Beaujolais growths, which are:
Brouilly, Chénas, Chiroubles, Côte de Brouilly, Fleurie, Juliénas, Morgon, Moulin-à-Vent, Régnié and St-Amour. The *crus* account for about a quarter of total Beaujolais production. None is sold as Beaujolais Nouveau.

Ideal temperatures for drinking Burgundy:
Superior white Burgundy: 58°–60°F (14.5°C–15.5°C)
Ordinary white Burgundy: 48°F–50°F (9°C–10°C)
Red Burgundy: 58°F–61°F (14.5°C–16°C)
Beaujolais: 53°F–56°F (11.5°C–13.5°C)

GLOSSARY OF WINE TERMS

AOC	Appellation d'origine contrôlée. Guarantee of origin of wine.
cave	wine cellar.
caveau	wine cellar open to public.
cave coopérative	collectively run wine-making enterprise.
chaptalisation	adding sugar to increase fermentation and alcoholic strength.
climat	Small section of vineyard with its own geological and climatic conditions.
cru	a specific vineyard.
cuve	wine vat.
dégustation	wine tasting.
fining	clarifying the wine.
INAO	Institut National des Appellations d'Origine organisation controlling the AOC system.
maceration	soaking and separating the grapes.
must	grape juice before fermentation.
négociant	term used mainly in Burgundy for shipper or wine merchant who buys wine in bulk for storage and re-sale.
Phylloxera	aphid which destroyed many French vineyards in 19th century.

primeur	wine ready for early drinking, particularly Beaujolais.
tastevin	shallow silver cup used for tasting.
vendange	grape harvest.
vigneron	wine grower.
vignoble	vineyard.
vin de garde	wine for maturing.

(Source: *The Wines and Vineyards of France*. Viking)

WINE TASTING

Many cellars are open to the public for tours, tastings and sale of wine. The following organisations disseminate information about wines and viticulture, organise courses and produce lists of cellars open to the public:
Fédération Interprofessionelle des Vins de Bourgogne, 12 Boulevard Bretonnière, 21200 Beaune. Tel: 80.22.21.35; also at 389 Avenue de Lattre de Tassigny, 71000 Mâcon. Tel: 85.38.20.15.
Commission de Promotion des Vins de Pouilly, 1 Rue de Paris, 58150 Pouilly-sur-Loire. Tel: 86.39.00.34.
La Maison des Vins de la Côte Chalonnaise, Promenade Ste-Marie, 71100 Chalon-sur-Saône. Tel: 85.41.64.00.
La Maison Mâconnaise des Vins, Avenue de Lattre de Tassigny, 71000 Mâcon. Tel: 85.38.36.70.
La Maison des Hautes-Côtes, Marey-les-Fussey, 21700 Nuits-St-Georges. Tel: 80.62.91.29.
Union Interprofessionnelle des Vins du Beaujolais, 210 Boulevard Vermorel, 69400 Villefranche-sur-Saône. Tel: 74.65.45.55.

Some tourist organisations in the region offer wine tours and holiday courses, mostly lasting a weekend. Some of the possibilities are listed below; for more information, contact the professional bodies or tourist offices and Loisirs Accueil services in the *départements* (*see Useful Addresses*).
L'Ambassade du Vin, La Chaussière, 21420 Pernand Vergelesses. Tel: 80.21.53.72; fax: 80.21.51.10. Intensive introduction to the wines of Côte de Nuits and Côte de Beaune and regional gastronomy. Also tours of vineyards and weekend courses in wine-tasting with professional experts. (English spoken).
Domaine Comtesse de Loisy, 28 Rue du Général de Gaulle, 21700 Nuits-St-Georges. Tel: 80.61.02.72; fax: 80.22.52.27. Madame la Comtesse, holder of a diploma in oenology, invites you to her ancestral home for courses in wine-tasting and an introduction to the wines of Burgundy.
Bureau Interprofessionelle des Vins de Bourgogne (*see address above*). Courses for those with a professional interest in the wine trade.

The following UK tour operators offer holidays for **wine-lovers**:
Ablaster & Clarke Wine Tours, 104 Church Road, Steep, Petersfield, Hants GU32 2DD. Tel: 0730-

66883; fax: 0730-68620. Short holidays (4 nights), based in a 3-star hotel in Beaune, touring the vineyards led by an acknowledged British authority on the wines of the region; also individual tours arranged.

World Wine Tours, Drayton St Leonard, Wallingford, Oxon OX10 7BH. Tel: 0865-891919; fax 891337. Tours for all, led by a senior wine expert, specialising in the small, but highly rated domaines. Accommodation in 3-star or château hotels.

Blackheath Wine Trails, 13 Blackheath Village, London SE3 9LA. Tel: 081-463 0012. Conducted tours of the vineyards for small groups.

Hide-a-Way Holidays, The Hide-a-Way, Lampagny, Gigny-sur-Saône, 71240 Sennecey-le-Grand. Tel: 85.44.71.27. Or in England contact Mr & Mrs K Deeming, Greenbank, Penrith Road, Keswick, Cumbria CA12 4LJ. Tel: 07687-72522. The Deemings invite you for a week's stay at their renovated country cottage; three days are devoted to touring the vineyards, including a comprehensive programme of tastings, with themselves as guides.

Travel Formula, C4 Imperial Business Estate, Gravesend, Kent DA11 0DL. Tel: 0474-335180; fax 0474-536912. Not for the purist, maybe; this outfit organises holidays for entrants in the annual Beaujolais run – the race to the UK with the new season's wine in November. Various trips available.

Listed below is a selection of wine cellars open to the public for tours, tastings and sales. Some require appointments to be made, but many are open to visitors at most reasonable times. Some offer free visits and tastings, others make a charge (from around FF15–40 per person).

CHABLIS

Cave William Fèvre, 8 Rue Jules Rathier, 89800. Tel: 86.42.12.06. Visits, by appointment, to one of the most important Chablis estates. Reservations: Mme Brédèche. Closed: Sunday afternoon and Monday.

Domaine Vocoret, 40 Route d'Auxerre, 89800. Tel: 86.42.12.53; fax: 86.42.10.39. By appointment only (by letter or fax); open Monday–Saturday.

La Chablisienne, 6 Boulevard Pasteur, 89800. Tel: 86.42.11.24.

AUXERRE

Caves de la Sica du Vignoble Auxerrois, 89530 Bailly. Tel: 86.53.34.00; fax: 86.53.80.94. The company's cellars are in huge underground quarries; visit includes tasting of Burgundy wines including Crémant de Bourgogne. By appointment only (15 days' notice required).

Caves de Saint-Bris, 10 Rue de l'Église, St-Bris-le-Vineux. Tel: 86.53.87.93. Open: daily.

Regine et Gérard Borgnat, 1 Rue de l'Église, Escolives-Ste-Camille. Tel: 86.53.35.28.

DIJON

Caves de l'Espace Grévin, 13b Avenue Albert 1er, 21000. Tel: 80.42.03.03; fax: 80.41.76.37. Tastings in the cellars beneath the city's new waxworks museum. Open: daily 1 June–31 December.

Caveau de la Porte Guillaume, Place Darcy (Hôtel du Nord), 21000. Tel: 80.30.58.58; fax: 80.30.61.26. Open: every afternoon except from 24 December–10 January.

COTE D'OR

AUXEY-DURESSES

Jean-Pierre Diconne, 21190. Tel: 80.21.25.60.

BEAUNE

Cave des Hautes-Côtes, Route de Pommard, 21200. Tel: 80.24.63.12. Open: Monday–Saturday.

Cave des Cordeliers, 6 Rue de l'Hôtel-Dieu, 21200. Tel: 80.22.14.25; fax: 80.22.28.19. Tastings in a Franciscan friars' convent. Open: daily.

La Halle aux Vins, Cave de Bourgogne, 28 Rue Sylvestre Chauvelot, 21200. Tel: 80.22.18.34. Open: daily. Closed: Sundays October–March.

La Reine Pédauque, 2 Faubourg St-Nicolas, 21200. Tel: 80.22.23.11; fax: 80.26.42.00. Exhibition cellar of the main vintages of Burgundy.

Marché aux Vins, Rue Nicolas Rollin, 21200. Tel: 80.22.27.69. Wine-tasting cellar in front of the Hospices. Open: daily. Closed: 15 December–15 January.

Patriarche Père et Fils, 7 Rue du Collège, 21200. Tel: 80.22.23.20. Boasts the largest cellars in Burgundy.

BUXY

Cave des Vignerons de Buxy, 71390. Tel: 85.92.03.03.

FIXIN

Vincent et Denis Berthaut, 21220. Tel: 80.52.45.48.

GEVREY-CHAMBERTIN

Charles Mortet, 21220. Tel: 80.34.10.05.

GIVRY

Domaine Ragot, 71640. Tel: 85.44.38.84.

MERCUREY

Yves de Launay, 71640. Tel: 85.45.13.92.

MEURSAULT

Château de Meursault, 21190. Tel: 80.21.22.98. A few miles from Beaune; fine 19th-century cellars where you can try the wines produced on the estate.
Yves Boyer-Mertenot, 21190. Tel: 80.21.26.25.

MONTHELIE

Château de Monthélie, 21190. Tel: 80.21.23.32.

MOREY-ST-DENIS

Jean Raphet, 21220. Tel: 80.34.31.67.

NUIT-ST-GEORGES

Cave Moillard-Grivot, 21700 . Tel: 80.61.03.34; fax: 80.61.28.13. On the RN 74. Open: Monday–Friday (weekends and bank holidays by appointment).
Morin Père et Fils, 9 Quai Fleury, 21700. Tel: 80.61.19.51; fax: 80.62.37.38. Visits to an 18th-century cellar. Open: daily.

PERNAND-VERGELESSES

R. Denis Père et Fils, 21420. Tel: 80.21.50.91.

PULIGNY-MONTRACHET

Gérard Chavy, 21190. Tel: 80.21.31.47.

SANTENAY

Domaine de la Buissière, 21590. Tel: 80.20.61.79.

VOLNAY

Domaine Michel Lafarge, 21190. Tel: 80.21.61.61.

VOSNE-ROMANEE

Pascal Chevigny, 21700. Tel: 80.61.17.42.

VOUGEOT

La Grande Cave, RN74, 21640. Tel: 80.62.87.13; fax: 80.61.28.08. Tasting of "grands vins" in these fine ancient cellars. Open: daily.

MACON & BEAUJOLAIS

MACON

Le Cellier des Cordeliers, Rue Dufour, 71000. Tel: 85.38.91.05. A wide range of wines can be sampled in this 17th-century cellar. Open: Tuesday–Saturday and Sunday morning.
Caveau de dégustation St-Pierre, 71260 Lugny. Tel: 85.33.20.27. Mâcon and a range of other

Burgundy wines. Visits by appointment only; open weekends from March–December and daily in July and August (except Wednesday).
Le Cuvier des Amis, "Les Plantes", 71960 Davaye. Tel: 85.35.83.65. Selection of Beaujolais and Burgundy wines. Open: daily (by prior request on Sunday).
Caveau de Pouilly-Fuissé, 71960 Solutré-Pouilly. Tel: 85.35.83.83. Reservation requested five days in advance (apply to Mme Odile Prudent). Open: daily March–December.
Henri Perrusset, 71700 Farges-les-Mâcon. Tel: 85.40.51.88.

POUILLY-FUISSE

Catherine et Pascal Rollet, 71960 Solutré-Pouilly. Tel. 85.35.81.51.

SAINT-VERAN

Caveau de dégustation du cru, Relais Beaujolais-Mâconnais. Visits by appointment only (two weeks' notice required). Apply to M Tissier, Union des Producteurs du Cru St-Véran, 71570 Leynes. Tel: 85.35.10.31.

BEAUJOLAIS

Caveau des Deux Clochers de Régnié-Durette, 69430 Beaujeu. Tel: 74.04.38.33. At the heart of Beaujolais; open daily, except Wednesday, May–November.
Georges Duboeuf, La Gare, 71570 Romanèche-Thorins. Tel: 85.35.51.13.

LOIRE

POUILLY

Cave coopérative de Pouilly, caveau de dégustation, 39 Avenue de la Tuilerie, 58150 Pouilly-sur-Loire. Tel: 86.39.10.99.
Landrat et Guyollot, 58150 St-Andelain. Tel: 86.39.11.83. Visits free if buying; by appointment only (one week's notice required).

SANCERRE

La Châtelaine, 18 Rue St-Martin. Tel: 48.54.21.50.

Most of the above give commented tours. Driving along the wine routes of Burgundy you will also be beckoned by road signs inviting visits to cellars for simple tastings with a view to sales.

The locals will tell you that no decent Burgundy should be drunk until it is at least 4 years old. And beware; it is rare to find a bargain in Burgundy. Even in the hypermarkets you are unlikely to find a drinkable Burgundy for under FF40 or FF50.

Things to Do

PLACES OF INTEREST

The listing below covers a variety of different activities: technical visits, parks and gardens, miniature railways and so forth. Some of the suggested venues are quite particular to the region and are well worth seeking out.

All the places listed are open daily, morning and afternoon (not including public holidays) except where otherwise specified. Most close for a long lunchbreak – noon or 12.30 until 2 or 2.30pm. Expect to pay an entrance fee at most venues.

A list of museums and art galleries, historic buildings (including churches) and archaeological sites are given under the heading of *Culture Plus*, whilst a listing of wine cellars open to the public is given in the *Wine* section.

Most of the major towns in the region offer guided tours – enquire at the Office de Tourisme or Syndicat d'Initiative. The main sights are listed here.

YONNE

ARCY-SUR-CURE

Les Grottes, a network of vast caves with remarkable limestone concretions which can be explored by following a half-mile (900-metre) underground walk (easily accessible to the elderly or disabled). Picnic area. Open: daily mid March–mid November. Tel: 86.40.90.63.

AVALLON

Two **glassworking** studios are open to the public. For further information, contact: Michel Desarce, Vallée du Cousin, 89200. Tel: 86.34.10.14.

CHABLIS

Maison de la Vigne et du Vin, Syndicat d'Initiative, 28 Rue Auxerroise. Tel: 86.42.42.22. Offers a permanent exhibition about wine-making in the area. Also a video and wine-tasting. Open: daily, except Wednesday and Thursday in December.

CHAMOUX

Cardo-Land, tel: 86.33.28.33. A most unusual site. In a wooded park, 4 miles (7 km) from Vézelay, the sculptor Cardo has created an imaginary prehistoric world of life-sized creatures from the sea and land. See also the museum of prehistory and paleontology and the decorated cave. Open: daily June–August; September–October and April–May open at weekends, public and school holidays.

ROGNY-LES-SEPT-ECLUSES

This village is almost worth a visit for its name! The *sept écluses* are seven locks on the Briare canal, built at the beginning of the 17th-century by the engineer Cosnier, and in use from 1642 until 1880. They now stand as a testimony to the engineering skills of that time.

ST-AMAND-EN-PUISAYE

The area of La Puisaye is renowned for its **pottery**, and there are several studios which welcome visitors. In many the traditional methods, which are particular to the area, are still employed; most also have shops where their works are for sale. There is no entry charge at any of the studios.
Daniel Auger, Faubourg des Poteries, 58310. Tel: 86.39.66.52.
Michel Dumont, Route de Cosne, 58310. Tel: 86.39.71.08.
Mallet Fils, Route de Cosne, 58310. Tel: 86.39.60.80.

ST-FARGEAU

La Ferme du Château, in the shadow of the imposing château this farm, typical of the region, gives glimpses of rural life at the turn of the century. Regular attractions and sale of local produce on Sunday afternoons. Open: daily. Tel: 86.74.03.76. Visit too the **Parc naturel de Boutissaint**, a natural wild-life reserve with deer etc. roaming freely. Open: daily 8am–8pm. Tel: 86.74.71.28.

ST-PERE-SOUS-VEZELAY

In a village of beautiful old stone houses is the Atelier de Saboterie, one of the last working clog-makers of the region. Visit the studio and watch a demonstration. Free entry, but by reservation, in writing only. Contact: M Doré, Sabotier, 89450. Tel: 86.33.26.03.

ST-SAUVEUR-EN-PUISAY

Birthplace of the author Colette which appears in her novels under the name of Montigny-en-Frenois.

NIEVRE

ALLIGNY-EN-MORVAN

Studio in the Morvan Regional Park where you can see weaving, wood sculpting and other local crafts. Information from S. Bourgeac, tel: 86.76.13.29.

CORBIGNY

Visit the studio of a cabinet and furniture maker in the Morvan Park, M J. Dufour, Rue Lavoignat. Tel: 86.20.15.68.

CORRANCY

Les Ruchers du Morvan, visit and tastings offered at a centre of honey production in the Morvan Park. Information from D. and J. J. Coppin, Le Port de l'Homme, Corrancy, 58120 Château-Chinon. Tel: 86.78.02.43.

DONZY

Moulin de Maupertuis, an old mill and ecomuseum open to the public, daily except Tuesday, from mid June–mid September, weekends only mid April–mid June and mid September–mid October. Tel: 86.39.39.46.

DOMPIERRE-LES-ORMES

Arboretum of Pézanin, an extensive park displaying a mixture of local and exotic trees. Two signposted walks (lasting 40 and 90 minutes), plus a botanical walk with information panels. Signposted from Dompierre.

FOURS

It is possible to visit the town's glassworks and studios any weekday. Free entry. For more information contact: Créations Bourdon, tel: 86.50.20.22.

GUERIGNY

Forges Royales de la Chaussade, discover the region's industrial archaeology at this former royal blacksmith's which used to produce chains and anchors for the navy and steam engines. Open: July–mid September, except Tuesday. Tel: 86.37.31.98.

LORMES

Studio and exhibition of a stained glassworker in the Morvan Park, C. Leclerc, Richâteau, 58140. Tel: 86.22.50.73.

MAGNY-COURS

The ultra-modern **motor racing circuit** near Nevers is open to the public, free of charge, by appointment. Research is carried out here for the car industry. Training sessions are available on Renault or Porsche cars. For information: tel: 86.21.20.74.

ST-BENIN-DES-BOIS

A producer of foie gras welcomes visitors to see the methods of production and for tastings. Open: all year. Contact: M Ortynski, Les Chaumes de Ligny, 58330. Tel: 86.58.20.48.

ST-BRISSON

Herbularium, situated in the Morvan Regional Park (by the Maison du Parc), this botanical garden displays some 160 plants with explanatory notes. Open: daily; free entry. Tel: 86.78.70.16. Also on the site is the Museum of Wartime Resistance (*see Museum listings*).

TAMNAY-EN-BAZOIS

FUKO workshop, studio in the Morvan Park where craftworkers work with the wool and mohair from their own goats. Tel: 86.84.06.44.

COTE D'OR

ARNY-LE-DUC

Maison Régionale des Arts de la Table, Anciens Hospices St-Pierre, 15 Rue St-Jacques. Tel: 80.90.11.59. Something for the gourmand – an exhibition about regional food and cooking methods, as well as tastings of local products. Open: daily April–October, 10am–6.30pm.
The studio of a **local potter** who has the appropriate name of Gérald Pott, is open to the public every day from 10am until 7pm. Information from M Pott, Chassenay, 21230 Arnay-le-Duc, tel: 80.90.18.20.

ARNEY-SOUS-VITTEAUX

Zoo de l'Auxois, tel: 80.49.64.01. There are 3,000 animals on view at this park which also has adults' and childrens' amusements, a restaurant and lakeside picnic spot, beach, skating rink and mini-golf. Open: daily 10am–late.

BEZE

Visit the caves and take a boat ride along the underground river. Superb illuminations. Open: daily May–September, weekends only in April. Tel: 80.75.31.33.

BUFFON

Buffon Forges, tel: 80.89.40.30. An 18th-century "model factory", built by the Count of Buffon, with most of its buildings still intact: an excellent example of the industrial heritage of the region. Audiovisual exhibition of the traditional iron and steel works of northern Burgundy. Open: every afternoon June–September, plus Wednesday–Friday mornings in July and August.

CHENOVE

The 18th-century wine presses of the dukes of Burgundy are some of the oldest in existence. They have been restored to working order and can be visited. Open: every afternoon from mid-June to September, other times by appointment only. Tel: 80.52.51.30.

CUSSIGNY

The château boasts a beautiful 18th-century garden with bowers and arbours. Open: daily 15 July–31 August. Tel: 80.62.98.28.

DIJON

The region's capital has much to offer its visitors. When you have taken in as much culture as you can cope with, head for the **Parc Récréatif de la Toison d'Or** which has amusements for old and young alike, including a flume ride, a giant labyrinth, merry-go-rounds, children's park, and a audiovisual spectacle of the story of the dukes of Burgundy. Restaurants. Open: daily May–September. The entrance fee also admits each person for 90 minutes to the adjoining **water park**, the Aquacenter Les Cyclades, which offers a wave pool, water slides, river rapids, jacuzzis and a solarium. Closed: January, otherwise open daily. BP 236, Rue de Colchide, 21000. Tel: 80.74.16.16.
Jardin Botanique, founded in 1771, and now composed of two parts: the School of Botany with its large plots exhibiting around 3,500 species, and the Arboretum which has a section devoted to medicinal plants. On the same site, housing the Natural History Museum, is the splendid Jardin de l'Arquebuse. 1 Avenue Albert Premier. Tel: 80.43.46.39.
Cassis Lejay-Lagoute, the cellars and modern plant where cassis (blackcurrant) liqueur is made, are open to the public (tastings included). Enquire at the Syndicat d'Initiative in the town or at the company at 19 Rue Ledru-Rollin, BP 278, 21007 Dijon Cedex. Tel: 80.72.4172. It is also possible to visit the **Amora mustard factory** which has its own museum. One month's notice is normally required. More information from the Syndicate d'Initiative, tel: 80.30.35.39.

GRISELLES

Miellerie Prévost, manufacturer of hives and honey offers visits with slides to the general public, and tastings. Free entry on request. Tel: 80.81.46.80.

LAMARGELLE

Le Moulin, a working mill, open for the public to observe vegetable oil being pressed. Open: daily except Monday mid June–mid September. Tel: 80.35.15.06.

MENESSAIRE

Maison du Seigle, an exhibition devoted to rye-growing, including articles made from rye straw. Also available are details of a rye-trail to follow (3 miles/5 km). Open: daily except Tuesday, mid April–September. Town Hall, tel: 80.64.28.65.

POUILLY-EN-AUXOIS

A town remarkable for the fact that the Burgundy canal flows underneath it, by means of a 2-mile (3.3-km) tunnel. There are several lakes and reservoirs in the locality which feed the canal; also worth a visit are the rocks at nearby Baume-la-Roche.

QUETIGNY

Parc Aquatique de Quetigny, Société Cap Vert, Rue du Cap Vert, 21800. Tel: 80.46.14.44. A health centre and water park where amenities include two wave pools, three jacuzzis, river rapids and indoor amusements such as a bowling alley, billiards and squash. Hotel on site. Open: daily from 10am–10pm.

ST-GERMAIN

A green and pleasant place which is the source of the River Seine. Also of note is the statue of the Goddess Sequena.

ST-JEAN-DE-LOSNE

An old fortified port on the River Saône and the end of the Burgundy Canal. Celebrates in June le Pardon des Mariniers – a two-week festival.

VAUCHIGNON

A remarkable natural site, with a fantastic waterfall.

SAONE-ET-LOIRE

AZE

Les Grottes, tel: 85.33.32.23. Two caves open to the public – one is prehistoric and a very rare example of its type, the other boasts an underground river.

Accessible to all (no stairs). Collections of weapons, tools, etc. as well as evidence of ancient cavern animals can be seen in the archaeological museum on the site. Open: daily Easter–September, Sundays only in October.

BLANZY

The machines and galleries of the old mine have been rebuilt and opened to the public with an exhibition "Mine and Men" telling the story of the life and work of miners since the industry began. Open: Saturday and Sunday afternoons May–September (but every afternoon July–August). Information from Mme Lotte, 20 Rue Paul Valéry, 71450. Tel: 85.58.40.02.

BOURBON-LANCY

Bourbon-Expo, Rue du Docteur Pain. The Puzenat factory, which revolutionised agricultural machinery at the beginning of the 20th century, but closed in 1956, is now a permanent exhibition of agricultural tools and equipment.

CHAUFFAILLES

There is a permanent **motor show** at 35 Rue du 8 mai. Tel: 85.84.60.30. On display and for sale are 300 sports, luxury and collector's cars. Open: daily Closed: weekends July–August. Dedicated motor fans will also want to visit the **Automobile Museum** at nearby La Clayette (*see Museums listing*).

CLUNY

Haras National, tel: 85.59.07.85. The main reason for visiting Cluny is its remarkable Romanesque architecture (*see Culture Plus*). However, it also houses one of France's national stud farms which is open daily to visitors 9am–7pm, free of charge. Demonstrations take place from 15 August–15 February.

LE CREUSOT

A **notable industrial town**, although not unattractive. Its heavy industry is celebrated in the huge power hammer (built 1840), at the entrance to the town, which despite its size (68 ft/21 metres high and weighing 1,300 tons), was accurate enough to cork a bottle without breaking it. Guided visits available. Visit too the charming 70-acre (28 hectare) **park** in the town centre and the **Castle** (former glassworks).

LOUHANS

Hôtel-Dieu et Apothicairerie, the apothecary in the 17th-century former hospital boasts rare chinaware, including 16th-century vases and blown glass still

containing its original substances. Louhans itself is a very attractive town which boasts one of the longest arcaded streets in the country; there is a Bresse poultry market on Mondays. Open: daily, except Tuesday; afternoons only September–June. For information: tel: M Cotte, 85.75.54.32.

LUCENAY-L'EVEQUE

Les Miels Fleurs du Morvan, a centre for the production of honey in the Morvan Park. Information from A. and M. Hersant, tel: 85.82.63.79.

MONTCEAU-LES-MINES

Guided visits of the industrial sites and mining towns of the area are avilable, free of charge, but must be booked two or three weeks in advance with the Syndicat d'Initiative, 1 Place de l'Hôtel de Ville. Tel: 85.57.38.51.

PARAY-LE-MONIAL

The city attracts many pilgrims and one of its more unusual sites is the **Diorama** in the park behind the Basilica. Here painted statues in 21 settings relate the story of St-Margaret-Mary and the history of the city. Open: daily Easter–October (afternoons only Easter–31 May and mid September–31 October). Tel: 85.88.85.80.

AIN

BOURG-EN-BRESSE

Bouvent leisure park, all kinds of leisure and sporting activities, including water sports.

CEYZERIAT

Pretty village nestling in the foothills of Revermont, with remarkable natural sites – the Cuiron rock and Vallière waterfalls.

MEILLONAS

Several craftworkers here welcome visitors to their studios (preferably by prior appointment). Aldo Priore, Route de Viriat, tel: 74.51.34.62 – cabinet maker, produces furniture in traditional Bresse style. Mme Nicole Reverdiau, tel: 74.51.34.06 is a potter producing local faience while at the Atelier "Fol Avril", Rue de l'Église, tel: 74.51.34.62 you can watch local artists painting on wood.

MONTREVEL-EN-BRESSE

La Ferme du Sougey, a large working farm, open to the public, at the heart of the Bresse poultry region. The farmhouse with its remarkable fireplace may also be visited. Tel: 74.25.47.12.

ST-TRIVIER-DE-COURTES

La Ferme de la Forêt, Courtes, a beautiful 17th-century farmhouse, well-restored and now functioning as a museum. Open: daily mid June–mid September, also Sundays between Easter and October. Tel: 74.30.71.89.

VILLARS-LES-DOMBES

Parc Départemental des Oiseaux, on the RN 83, a bird sanctuary with some 350 species, including water birds such as pelicans and non-flying varieties like the emu. Snack bar and children's play area, also a miniature train which runs from April–October. Tel: 74.98.05.90.

EXCURSIONS ·

BOAT TRIPS

With its vast network of canals and splendid lakes (particularly in the Morvan Regional Park) there are many opportunities for spending some time on the water. For holidays afloat, *see Getting Around*. It you want to be master of your own boat for just a day contact the companies below:

Locadif, Gissey-sur-Ouche, 21410 Pont de Pany. Tel: 80.49.04.76.

Navigation et Technique, Port du Canal, 21370 Plombières-lès-Dijon. Tel: 80.45.44.60.

France Cruisers, Rue Armand Thibaut, 21600 Longvic. Tel: 80.67.53.05.

Other companies offer a day's cruising, with meals on board, for around FF300 per person. For more information contact the tourist offices or Service Loisirs Accueil (*see Useful Addresses*) or try the following:

Continentale de Croisières Françaises, 9 Rue Jean Renaud, 21000 Dijon. Tel: 80.30.49.20; fax: 80.30.27.01. Cruising the Burgundy canal, departing from Dijon.

Grands Bateaux de la Saône, 28 Quai de Verdun, 71700 Tournus. Tel: 84.25.49.30. Cruising the River Saône, departing from Tournus.

Shorter cruises are also available, lasting an hour or maybe half a day. Some have restaurants on board, or at least a bar. Most of these do not have to be booked and ply their trade by canals and lakesides. A selection of operators is given below:

Navigation et Technique, Port du Canal, 21370 Plombières-lès Dijon. Tel: 80.45.44.60. Depart Dijon, cruise the Burgundy Canal.

Tourisaône, 1 Place d'Armes, 21170 St-Jean-de-Losne. Tel: 80.39.22.61. Various trips on the Saône, leaving from St-Jean-de-Losne.

J. Mari-Gadrey, Lac des Settons, 58230 Montsauche-les-Settons. Tel: 86.84.52.09. Short cruise on the Settons Lake in the Morvan Regional Park, leaving from Les Terrasses restaurant. Bateaux-Mouches "Morvan" depart from the left bank of the Settons Lake, near the barrage. For information and booking contact Entreprise Bosset, tel: 86.84.52.81. Other boats leave from the right bank; information from Camping de la Plage du Midi, 58230 Montsauche-les-Settons. Tel: 86.84.51.97.

NF Navigation, BP 342, 89006 Auxerre Cedex. Tel: 86.52.60.60. On the Nivernais Canal, departs from Auxerre.

Croisières de Bourgogne, Bragny-sur-Saône, 71350 Verdun-sur-le Doubs. Tel: 85.91.58.17. A luxury boat leaving from Chalon-sur-Saône.

SNC, Les Canalous, BP 63, 71160 Digoin. Tel: 85.88.51.34. Departures from Digoin on the Lateral, Centre and Roanne-Digoin canals.

TOURIST TRAINS

Little tourist trains offer a good means of seeing the local countryside at a slower pace than by express. They are ideal for family outings, particularly if they give children the chance to ride on a real steam train.

The **Ouche Valley railway** runs a steam train on the former "fisherman's" track from Dijon to Bligny. Trains leave Bligny-sur-Ouche station (first train 2.30pm). The trip lasts 45 minutes. Information and booking: ARVO, Gare, 21360, Bligny-sur-Ouche. Tel: 80.22.86.35.

From **Plombières-lès-Dijon**, you can take a round trip on a diesel train, known as the "**petit train de la Côte d'Or**". It follows the River Ouche and the Burgundy Canal. Trip lasts 90 minutes and is available 18 March–22 November. Information and booking: M Gaugué, Rue d'Échirey, Bellefond, 21490 Ruffey-lès-Échirey. Tel: 80.23.83.75.

There are two lines running in the **Morvan Regional Park**, "Le Furet de Morvan" (information from CFTA, tel: 86.57.09.06); and "L'Cagouille" which runs between Cercy-la-Tour and Clamecy; information from Association Morvan Bazois. Tel: 86.84.11.17.

The "**Petit train de Massangis**" follows disused rail tracks for 3 miles (5 km) through the countryside. The trip takes 45 minutes. Information and booking: ATPVM, Chemin des Fossés, 89440 L'Isle-sur-Serein. Tel: 86.33.81.20.

Explore the **Puisaye area** on the special tourist train which connects with mainline trains to Paris and Nevers. Its complete route is 48 miles (78 km) from Montargis in Loiret to St-Sauveur in Yonne. Information and booking: Chemin de Fer Touristique de la Puisaye, Avenue de la Gare, 89130 Toucy. Tel: 86.44.05.58.

IN THE AIR

There is a surprisingly large number of companies offering balloon trips in the area; some even offer ballooning holidays. Here are a few suggestions.

Air Escargot, Remigny, 71150 Chagny. Tel: 85.87.12.30. One hour trips or hotel packages.

Air Aventure, Château Laborde, 21200 Meursanges. Tel: 80.26.63.30; fax: 80.26.69.20. Mostly luxury holiday breaks of four days, but also introductory flights arranged. Information and booking also direct in the US from: Bombard Balloon Adventures, 6727 Curran Street, McLean, Virginia 22101-6006. Tel: 703-448 9407 or toll free 800-862 8537; fax 703-883 0985.

L'Escapade, BP 14, 89000 St-Georges-sur-Baulche. Tel: 86.48.26.40. One-hour balloon trips with champagne send-off.

L'Aéroclub de Bourgogne, 71100 Chalon-sur-Saône. Tel: 85.41.82.64. Balloon trips and flights in light aircraft.

HORSE-DRAWN CARRIAGES

Some riding centres offer trips, lasting an hour or more, in carriages or traps. Full day trips often include meals in the price. You may have to have a minimum number to make up a party. Some trips can be booked by the Service Reservation Loisirs Accueil (*see Useful Addresses*); a selection is given below:

Centre Équestre, 89120 Chevillon. Tel: 86.73.12.05. For groups of eight minimum; one hour excursions. Also courses and lessons available.

Ferme Équestre des Grilles, 89170 St-Fargeau. Tel: 86.74.12.11. Full day, including gastronomic meal, costs around FF300 per person (eight people per carriage).

Écuries de l'Arbressey, Route de Ruffey, 21850 St-Apollinaire. Tel: 80.47.56.76. Trips lasting around 90 minutes, also hire of carriages for weekends.

Centre Équestre de la Barotte, Les Mauritaines, 21120 Is-sur-Tille. Tel: 80.91.07.55. Excursions and hire of carriages.

Centre Équestre le Galopin, Rue de Tissage, 21470 Brazey-en-Plaine. Tel: 80.29.88.59. Discover the Saône Valley in the old style.

COACH TRIPS

Let someone else do the driving and you can take in all the scenery and sights. Day or half-day trips are widely available to major tourist sights, usually with a guide. For more information contact local bus stations or tourist offices. If being shepherded in groups is not your style, then you can take a guided taxi tour. Contact: Central Taxi Radio Dijon, Cour de la Gare, 21000 Dijon. Tel: 80.41.41.12.

CULTURE PLUS

Rich is an adjective that is often used to describe Burgundy and it is certainly rich in its cultural heritage. It has come under the influence of many civilisations through the centuries: the Romans and Greeks, the early Christians, and this is now reflected in the sumptuous collections in its many museums and art galleries. All its famous sons (and daughters) – Canon Kir, Vauban, Larousse and Colette – are celebrated, mostly at their birthplaces.

MUSEUMS & ART GALLERIES

There is a huge number of museums to choose from, ranging from the sparkling new Musée Grevin in Dijon, to simple local collections in Town Halls around the region. Here we list some of the best and some of the most unusual.

Most museums charge an entrance fee; for those that are state-owned expect to pay between FF10 and FF25 (half-price on Sundays). Reductions are usually given for children, senior citizens and students – on production of a valid card. Those listed here are open every day, mornings and afternoons (except public holidays), unless otherwise specified. Remember, most close for a long lunch from noon or 12.30 to around 2.30pm.

YONNE

ANCY-LE-FRANC

Musée de l'Automobile et de l'Hippomobile, cars and horse-drawn carriages exhibited in the grounds of the Renaissance château. Open: April–November. Information: M de Menton, Château d'Ancy-le-Franc, 89160 Ancy-le-Franc. Tel: 86.75.12.41.

AUXERRE

Musée Leblanc-Duvernoy, 3 Place du Coche-d'Eau. Important collections regional porcelain and Puisaye earthenware; also Beauvais tapestries and various furniture all set in a grand 18th-century house. Open: every afternoon, except Tuesday. Ticket includes entry to the crypts of St-Germain Abbey (*see Archaeology and Architecture*). Tel: 86.51.09.74. Nearby is the Musée du Coche-d'Eau, Place du Coche-d'Eau. In a beautiful 16th-century house, it specialises in temporary exhibitions on different

themes: archaeology, porcelain, popular art, etc.
Open: every afternoon, except Tuesday. Free entry.
Tel: 86.51.09.74.

Conservatoire de la Nature Paul-Bert, 5 Boulevard
Vauban. Local natural history: fossils, prehistoric
exhibits, fauna, etc. Open: daily (weekends afternoons only). Free entry. Tel: 86.51.51.64.

AVALLON

Musée de l'Avallonnais, Place de la Collégiale.
Collections include local archaeological finds, particularly around Arcy-sur-Cure, Gallo-Roman statues and mosaics and more recent works of art. Open:
mid June–October. Closed: Tuesday.

LADUZ

Musée Rural des Arts Populaires. Vast collection of
tools, plus local crafts and toys of the 19th and 20th
century. Open: daily June–end September; weekends
only Easter–May and October. Tel: 86.73.70.08.

NOYERS-SUR-SEREIN

Donation Yankel. Museum of naive art, including
modern collections. Open: weekends Easter–November, daily from June–September in the afternoons.
Information from the town hall: tel: 86.55.83.72.

POURRAIN-LES-VERNES

Musée de la Guerre 1939–45, Atelier Sontrop, Les
Vernes, 89240 Pourrain. The work of a former pilot
and Dutch Resistance fighter: a moving memorial to
the Resistance; plus rare armoured vehicles, and
workshops where Sontrop restores Jaguars and Rolls
Royces. Tel: 86.41.13.27.

ST-LEGER-VAUBAN

Maison Vauban. An exhibition on the life and works
of Vauban, marshall of France and one of the
country's most notable figures, who was born in the
town in 1633. Open: daily June–mid September. Tel:
86.22.25.54.

SENS

Musée, Place de la Cathédrale (entrance via the
Palais Synodal). A new museum in the former
Archbishop's Palace, which now houses all the major
local collections. Next door is the treasure house (Le
Trésor) which is one of the richest in France Open:
daily, except Tuesdays. Closed: Monday, Thursday
and Friday mornings October–May. Free entry on
Wednesdays. Tel: 86.64.15.27 (curator).

VILLIERS-ST-BENOIT

Musée d'Art Régional. Set in a faithful representation of an 18th-century Burgundian home are
collections of regional sculpture, porcelain and
earthenware. Closed: Tuesdays and from 15 December–31 January. Tel: 86.45.73.05.

NIEVRE

CHATEAU-CHINON

Musée du Septennat, 6 Rue du Château. Unusual
museum, showing the collection of gifts received by
President Mitterrand, since 1981. Open: daily May–
September. Tel: 86.57.80.90., ext: 418.

CLAMECY

Musée d'Art et d'Histoire Romain Rolland. Dedicated to the life and work of the French writer, plus
other collections of paintings, archaeology and
exhibits about log-rafting in the 19th-century.
Closed: Tuesday and also Sundays from November–
Easter. Tel: 86.27.17.99.

COSNE-SUR-LOIRE

Musée Municipal, Place de la Résistance. Devoted
to the River Loire, its history and future. Also some
fine arts and ethnography. Open: July–mid September, or by appointment at other times.

DONZY

Ecomusée de la Meunerie, Moulin de Maupertuis.
Ecomuseum housed in an old mill; regular exhibitions. Open: July–end September, daily except
Tuesday; other times by appointment. Information
from APSMM, Rue André Audinet. Tel: 86.39.39.46.

LA MACHINE

Musée de la Mine, 1 Avenue de la République.
Reconstruction of the mines, galleries, engine rooms,
etc. The life and work of the miners, mineralogical
and paleontological collections. Open: mid-June to
mid-September, except Tuesday, otherwise just Sunday afternoons or by appointment. Closed: November–March. Tel: 86.50.91.08.

NEVERS

Musée Municipal. Porcelain, glassware, paintings
and sculptures. Closed: Tuesday. Free entry. Tel:
86.57.35.31, ext.385.

ST BRISSON

Musée de la Résistance en Morvan, Maison du Parc Naturel Régional du Morvan. Dedicated to the local activities of the *maquis*, the Resistance movement of World War II. Open: every afternoon, July–mid September. Tel: 86.78.70.16.

COTE D'OR

BEAUNE

Musée du Vin de Bourgogne, Rue d'Enfer. At the heart of the wine-making region, it is fitting that this museum should be found in the splendid former mansion of the dukes of Burgundy. Twelve rooms are devoted to viticulture, from the type of local soil to displays of Bacchanalian art, including a tapestry by Lurçat. Closed: Tuesdays November–April.
Visit too the **Maison des Confréries**, 20 Rue du Faubourg Madeleine. This newly-opened museum of the European Brotherhoods of wine also offers wine-tastings, shops and banqueting suites. Tel: 80.24.05.05.

CHATILLON-SUR-SEINE

Musée Archéologique, 7 Rue du Bourg. A fine 16th-century building housing one of the most important collections in the region, including the Vix treasure (remarkable 5 ft 3-inch/1.64-metre high urn). Closed: Mondays, except from mid June–mid September. Tel: 80.91.24.67 (town hall).

FIXIN

Musée Noisot. Set in Noisot Park, reminders of the Napoleonic era, including sculptures of F. Rude: *Le Reveil de Napoléon*. Open: afternoons Wednesday, Thursday, Saturday and Sunday, April to mid-October. Tel: 80.52.45.62.

DIJON

Musée des Beaux Arts, Place de la Ste-Chapelle. The region's most important museum is housed in the Philippe le Bon Tower of the former Ducal Palace. Its varied collections include the tombs of Philip the Bold and John the Fearless; sculptures, ceramics, medieval weaponry and European paintings. The terraced tower itself offers panoramic views over the city. Closed: Tuesdays. Tel: 80.74.52.70.
Musée d'Art Sacré, 15 Rue Ste-Anne. Collections of liturgical objects (12th–19th centuries) from France and other countries, plus 19th-century chasubles, copes, etc. The museum is responsible also for preserving and displaying *objets d'art* from churches in the *département*. Closed: Tuesday. Tel: 80.30.06.44.
Musée Grévin de Bourgogne, 13 Avenue Albert 1er. The city's newest museum (opened June 1990), depicting the region's history by means of 17 waxworks tableaux, starting with the 6th century BC. Tel: 80.42.03.03.
Musée de la Vie Bourguignonne Perrin de Puycousin, 17 Rue Ste-Anne. Scenes from everyday life in old Burgundy; reconstructed 19th-century shops and workshops; vast collections of ethnographical items and costumes. Also temporary exhibitions. Closed: Tuesday. Tel: 80.30.65.91.
Musée Archéologique, 5 Rue du Docteur Maret. In the main wing of the former Benedictine Abbey of St-Bénigne, it offers a chronolgical panorama of man's presence in the region from prehistoric times to the Middle Ages, including remarkable Bronze Age finds such as the Blanot Treasure. Closed: Tuesday. Tel: 80.30.88.54.
Musée d'Histoire Naturelle, 1 Avenue Albert 1er. Situated in the Arquebuse gardens, geology and fauna of the region, plus a vivarium where live animals, both regional and exotic, can be observed. Open: afternoons only (except Tuesday). Tel: 80.41.61.08.

The Dijon tourist office offers a ticket (around FF13) which gives entry to most of its major museums (not including the Musée Grévin or Natural History Museum), without further payment.

NUITS-ST-GEORGES

Musée Archéologique, Rue Camille-Rodier. Gallo-Roman furniture from the Bolards excavations (visits to the site possible on request), plus furniture discovered in the Merovingian necropolis of Argilly, and other local exhibits. Open: May–September daily except Tuesday. Tel: 80.61.12.54 (town hall).

REULLE-VERGY

Musée des Arts et Traditions des Hautes-Côtes. A history of the life and times of the people working the vineyards of the area. Also a **nature trail**. Open: every afternoon July–mid September, otherwise weekends only or by appointment. Tel: 80.61.42.93.

SAULIEU

Musée François Pompon, Parvis de la Basilique. Works of the animal sculptor, Pompon, plus archaeology, geology and local history of the Morvan area. Closed: Tuesdays and Sunday afternoons. Tel: 80.64.09.22 (town hall).

SAVIGNY-LES-BEAUNE

Part of the castle has been made into a **motor-bike museum**, with 200 models from 1903–1960; see too the showroom of 15 Abarth cars and an **Aircraft Museum**, with the French Mirage III jet. Closed: 15–31 December. Tel: 80.21.55.03.

SEURRE

Ecomusée du Val de Saône, Rue Bossuet. Set in the 16th-century home of the Bossuet family, dedicated to the natural heritage of the Saône Valley. Open: daily June–September; weekend afternoons only in May. Tel: 80.21.15.92 (town hall).

SAONE-ET-LOIRE

AUTUN

Musée Rolin, 3 Rue des Bancs. Collections include Roman mosaics, 12th-century sculpture of Eve and 19th-century paintings. Closed: Tuesdays. Tel: 85.52.09.76.

Musée Lapidaire, 10 Rue St-Nicolas. Gallo-Roman architecture. Open: daily mid April–September; otherwise closed on Tuesdays and all of February. Tel: 85.52.35.71.

Musée d'Histoire Naturelle, 14 Rue St-Antoine. Exhibition of Burgundy's natural environment, flora and fauna. Closed: Monday and Tuesday and in the mornings October–July. Tel: 85.52.09.15.

Musée Verger Tarin, 7 Rue Sous-Chantre. Shows the interior of a Burgundian house as it would have been in 1845 with all its furniture, decoration and household utensils intact. Closed: Tuesdays, Sunday mornings and the month of October. Tel: 85.52.09.76.

AZE

Musée Archéologique. On the site of its famous caves, the museum has a huge collections of bones, weapons, tools, coins, etc. from prehistoric to medieval times. Open: daily, Easter–September; Sundays only in October. Tel: 85.33.32.23.

BOURBON-LANCY

Musée St-Nazaire. Modern art collections and temporary exhibitions in a disused 11th-century Romanesque church; also pottery, porcelain and paintings from earlier periods. Open: July and August Tuesday, Thursday–Sunday afternoons. Tel: 85.89.23.23.

CHALON-SUR-SAONE

Musée Denon, Place de l'Hôtel de Ville. Diverse collections ranging from archaeological exhibits, an important Bronze Age collection, popular arts and crafts of southern Burgundy and transport on the waterways. Closed: Tuesdays. Tel: 85.48.01.70., ext: 4237.

Musée Nicéphore Niepce, 28 Quai des Messageries. Named after the father of photography, this museum claims to be the best photographic museum in Europe, with an outstanding collection of cameras, the first colour photos ever taken and contemporary exhibitions. Closed: Tuesdays. Tel: 85.48.41.98.

CHAROLLES

Musée René Davoine. Modern sculptures from all media. Open: Easter–end October. Closed: Tuesdays. Information from the tourist office, tel: 85.24.05.95.

LA CLAYETTE

Musée de l'Automobile, Château La Clayette. Over 100 cars can be viewed in the outbuildings of the château. Tel: 85.28.22.07.

CLUNY

Musée Ochier, Palais Jean de Bourbon. Plans and models of the town and abbey; plus paintings, furniture and other works of art. Free entry. Tel: 85.59.23.97.

LE CREUSOT

Ecomusée, Château de la Verrerie. Devoted to the life and times of the urban communities of Le Creusot and Montceau-les-Mines. Tel: 85.55.01.11.

CRUZILLE

Domaine des Vignes du Maynes, museum of rural and Burgundian crafts and tools, in the old vineyards of the Cluny monks. Closed: during grape-picking season. Free entry. Tel: 85.33.20.15.

CUISEAUX

Part of the **Ecomusée de la Bresse Bourguignonne**, which has several branches devoted to different subjects, between Beaune and Bourg-en-Bresse. This branch celebrates wine and viticulture. Open: after-noons May–September. Tel: 85.76.27.16 (main museum at Château de Pierre).

DICY

La Fabuloserie. A very unusual museum where Alain Bourbonnais exhibits the works of modern fringe artists, and stages spontaneous happenings. Open: daily July and August; other times at weekends and public holidays only. Tel: 86.63.64.21.

ECUISSES

La Maison du Canal, by the 9th lock gate of the Canal du Centre. Devoted to the history and development of the canal. Open: July–October Tuesday–Saturday. Tel: 85.78.92.56.

LA GRANDE VERRIERE

Mineral Museum of the Morvan, Les Vernottes, 71990 La Grande Verrière. Exhibition and sales of Morvan minerals (fluorite, crystalline rocks and gems); also exhibits from the Auvergne, Pyrenees and South America. Open: afternoons, July–end September; other times by appointment. Tel: 85.82.51.01.

LOUHANS

A branch of the **Ecomusée de la Bresse Bourguignonne** at 29 Rue des Dodanes. This branch shows the life of a newspaper, *L'Indépendant*, and is the major French museum on the newspaper printing industry. Open: afternoons, except Tuesday, May–September. Tel: 85.76.27.16 (the main museum at Château de Pierre).

MACON

Musée Lamartine, Hôtel Sennecé, Rue Sigorgne. Documents concerning the life and work of the poet Lamartine, plus furniture, tapestries, paintings and other objets d'art. Closed: Tuesdays and Sunday mornings, also the months of January and February. Free entry. Tel: 85.38.96.19.

Musée des Ursulines, 5 Rue des Ursulines. Collections from prehistoric and Gallo-Roman times, also medieval art, furniture and popular arts. Closed: Tuesdays and Sunday mornings. Tel: 85.38.18.84.

MARCIGNY

Musée de la Tour du Moulin. Collections of ceramics; six rooms in an original 15th-century tower; note the splendid chestnut roof timbers. Open: afternoons March–November (mornings too, July and August). Tel: 85.25.37.05.

MONTBARD

Montbard is the **birthplace** (1707) of naturalist and author, **Georges-Louis Leclerc**, Count of Buffon. A museum of his life and works is housed in the former stables of the family house. Open: May–October, daily except Tuesday.

There is also a **Fine Arts Museum** in the former chapel of the Buffon institution, Rue Piron and an **Archaeological Museum** in Buffon's Park. Both open: April–October, daily except Tuesday (Fine Arts Museum afternoons only). Tel: 80.92.01.34.

MONTCEAU-LES-MINES

There are some remarkable sights and interesting museums in this industrial town, but many are only open by appointment. For information about the **Musée de l'Ecole Primaire** (restored school rooms in a working primary school), the **Mining Museum** and the **Fossil Museum**, enquire at the Tourist Information Office, 1 Place de l'Hôtel de Ville. Tel: 85.57.38.51.

PARAY-LE-MONIAL

Musée d'Art Sacrée, "Le Hiéron", 28 Rue de la Paix. Appropriately enough, in a place of pilgrimage, this museum has a major collection of religious works, including the 12th-century tympanum from the priory of Anzy-le-Duc. Recent renovations may affect opening hours. Tel: 85.88.85.80.

Musée de la Faïence Charolaise, Prieuré Bénédictin, Avenue Jean-Paul II. A fine collection of porcelain dating from 1836 to the present day. Also exhibition of moulds and tools, plus drawing and documents. 20 March–20 October, daily except Tuesday. Tel: 85.88.83.07.

Musée de l'Insigne et de la Médaille, 7 Rue Billet. A private collection of military insignia, heraldry, civil, religious and military medals; plus a medal workshop with tools. Open: daily March–end December, except Mondays. Tel: 85.88.83.08.

PIERRE-DE-BRESSE

Ecomusée de la Bresse Bourguignonne, Château de Pierre. The main departments of the ecomuseum are in the château and its remarkable ensemble of 17th-century buildings, others are scattered around the region. Exhibits on the natural environment, archaeology and history of the region. In the grounds are works of the British sculptor, David Nash. Open: every afternoon. Tel: 85.76.27.16.

RANCY

A branch of the **Ecomusée de la Bresse Bourguignonne** (*see above*), dedicated to the craft of chair-making and cane work. Open: Sunday afternoons, May–September. Tel: 85.76.27.15 (Château de Pierre).

ROMENAY

Musée du Terroir. Local tools, costumes and furniture. Next door is the **Poultry Museum** which shows the the development of Bresse chickens, breeding methods and marketing techniques of modern and early times. Free entry. Open: every afternoon July and August, otherwise by appointment. Tel: 85.40.30.90 (town hall).

SAGY

A **department** of the **Ecomusée de la Bresse Bourguignonne** based in the village communal house. It offers a tour of seven water mills, plus displays of the technical development of hydraulic mills. Information from: the Château de Pierre, tel: 85.76.27.16.

ST-MARTIN-EN-BRESSE

Branch of the **Ecomusée de la Bresse Bourguignonne**, with exhibitions on the Bresse Forest and woodcrafts. Also details of forest paths. Open: Sunday afternoons May–September. Information: tel: 85.76.27.16 (Château de Pierre).

SOLUTRE

Musée de la Préhistoire. Dug into the base of a rock, this recently-built museum displays exhibits from the excavations of the prehistoric site of Solutré. Closed: Tuesdays. Tel: 85.35.85.24.

TOURNUS

Musée Bourguignonne de Perrin de Puycousin. Reconstructed interiors and scenes from traditional Burgundian life; plus Napoleonic souvenirs of the Tournus soldier, Jean-Marie Putigny. Open: daily, except Tuesdays, April–November.
Musée Greuze. Paintings and drawings by Greuze, plus regional archaeology and sculpture. Open: Monday–Saturday, April–October.

VERDUN-SUR-LE-DOUBS

Musée du Blé et du Pain. A branch of the Ecomusée de la Bresse Bourguignonne, depicting the story of wheat and bread through the ages. Also examines the problems of world hunger. Open: daily mid-May–September, other times by appointment Tel: 85.76.27.15 (Château de Pierre).

AIN

BOURG-EN-BRESSE

Musée de Brou, 63 Boulevard de Brou, installed in a former monastery dating from the 16th century, and unique in France for its three cloisters. Good collection of fine arts: Dutch, Flemish, French and Italian paintings from the 16th–20th century, plus sculpture, pottery and old furniture. Tel: 74.22.22.31.

CHATILLON-SUR-CHALARONNE

Apothicairerie de l'Ancien Hospice, Place St-Vincent-de-Paul, former pharmacy, established in 1731 with a remarkable collection of 120 pots made from local faience, and other objects. Open: every afternoon. Closed: Sundays, except June–mid September. Tel: 74.55.02.27.

MONTREVEL-EN-BRESSE

Musée Océanien et de St-Pierre Chanel, Cuet, new museum, opened in the spring of 1991, local art and life story of St Pierre Chanel. Tel: 74.25.40.33.

PONT-DE-VAUX

Musée Chintreuil, Hôtel de Ville, local paintings, and natural history, plus collections of weapons and coins and memorial to Général Joubert. Closed: Sunday. Tel: 85.30.31.01.

RHONE

AMPLEPUIS

Musée Barthélémy-Thimonier, unusual museum displaying the complete history of the sewing-machine, with some unique examples. Open: after-noons: Wednesday and Friday–Sunday. Tel: 74.89.08.90.

LIVE ARTS

Son-et-lumière displays are now a popular way of presenting historical events; in Autun, for example, an historical Gallo-Roman show at the ancient Roman theatre, the largest of its kind in the world. Performances normally start at 10pm and there are several shows in July and August. For information and reservation contact: the Office de Tourisme, 3 Avenue Charles de Gaulle, 71400 Autun. Tel: 85.86.30.00.

Another impressive setting for a sound and light show is the Hôtel-Dieu in Beaune which tells the story of the creation of the famous Hospices. Performances in English and French, from Easter until October. Information and booking: Office de Tourisme, Rue de l'Hôtel-Dieu, 21200 Beaune. Tel: 80.22.24.51.

The **historical pageant** at the **Château of St-Fargeau** uses 600 local "actors" and 50 horses and it has an audience capacity of 6,000. Tickets also include entry to the château's farm, reconstructed in local style. Information and booking: Château de St-Fargeau, 89170 St-Fargeau. Tel: 86.74.05.67.

La Clayette (Saône-et-Loire) is the setting for the Chantemerle Theatre Company's *son-et-lumière* pres-entations in July and August. For reservations and information, tel: 85.88.16.35

The Eglise de Brou, **Bourg-en-Bresse**, presents *son-et-lumière* on Fridays during July and August; enquire at the tourist office, Centre Culturel Albert Camus, 6 Avenue Alsace-Lorraine, 01005 Bourg-en-Bresse. Tel: 74.22.49.40.

The Cultural Affairs department of Dijon Town Hall publishes a monthly programme of events, the main venues being the Grand Théâtre (for plays, opera and musical programmes), the Atheneum (mostly music and dance), the Centre Arts et Loisirs Fontaine-d'Ouche and the Salle des Jacobins which both put on a variety of performances. Dijon has a full cultural programme all year round; summer visitors can enjoy outdoor events during the Estivade. Beaune too presents outdoor performances at the Hospices during its summer music festival.

Listed here are brief details of events throughout the region. For more specific information, contact the local tourist offices.

JANUARY

Festivals of St Vincent, patron saint of wine growers, take place in Puligny-Montrachet (Côte d'Or) and Fontenay (Yonne) towards the end of the month.

FEBRUARY

Chablis: Yonne, St Vincent Tournante festival (*as above*).

MARCH

Chalon-sur-Saône: Saône-et-Loire, Carnival, with the "Goniots" people in fancy dress (sometimes held in February).
Nevers: Nièvre, Foire de Nevers – annual fair.
Nuits-St-Georges: Côte d'Or, Wine Sale of the Hospices (sometimes held in April).

APRIL

Châtillon-sur-Seine: Côte d'Or, Spring Fair.
Cluny: Saône-et-Loire, Chamber Music Festival.

MAY

Nevers: Nièvre, Spring Fair.
Mâcon: Saône-et-Loire, Foire des Vins de France – wine fair.
Rouvray: Côte d'Or, Wine Fair.
Saulieu: Côte d'Or, Journées gourmandes du Grand Morvan – local produce fair.
St-en-Puisaye: Yonne, Fête de Saint-Prix.

JUNE

Auxerre: Yonne, Festival de Jazz.
Beaune: Côte d'Or, Music Festival (continues into July).
Cublize: Rhône, Display of model boats at the Lac des Sapins.
Dijon: Côte d'Or, Été Musicale – music festival.
Donzy: Nièvre, Festival de Musique.
Esolives Ste-Camille: Yonne, Foire aux Cerises – cherry fair.
St-Jean-de-Losne: Côte d'Or, Grand Pardon des Mariniers – boatmen's annual festival.
Villefranche-sur-Saône: Rhône, Festival du Beaujolais, from mid-June to mid-July.

JULY

Anzy-le-Duc: Saône-et-Loire, Été Musical – summer music festival.
Autun: Saône-et-Loire, Musique en Morvan.
Chalon-sur-Saône: Saône-et-Loire, Festival National des artistes des rues – street performers everywhere in the town.
Dijon: Côte d'Or, L'Estivade – all kinds of arts and music events throughout the summer, some out of doors.
Flagy: Saône-et-Loire, Flagy-Mâcon Festival – what started as the "smallest theatre festival in the world" has now gained considerable prestige and national support.
Meursault: Côte d'Or, Festival des Grands Crus – music festival.
Vézelay: Yonne, Pélerinage de la Madeleine – religious pilgrimage and music concert.

AUGUST

Bouhans: Saône-et-Loire, Fête de la Balme – centuries old fair, created in 1645, originally just a sale of horses, now also a cattle market, plus lively entertainment.
Clamecy: Nièvre, Fête des Vaux d'Yonne.
Cluny: Saône-et-Loire, Festival des Grands Crus – "Les Grandes Heures" – five classical music concerts under the vaults of the abbey cloister.
Étigny: Yonne, Fête des Moissons – harvest festival.
Glux-en-Glenne: Nièvre, Fête de la Myrtille – bilberry fair.
Montbard: Côte d'Or, Regional Fair.
Pouilly-sur-Loire: Nièvre, Foire aux Vins – wine fair.
Rogny-les-Sept-Ecluses: Yonne, Fête du Canal du Nivernais – events along the canal and fireworks at Rogny.
St-Honoré-les-Bains: Nièvre, Fête des Fleurs – flower festival.
Saulieu: Côte d'Or, Fête du Charolais – festival of Charolais cattle.
Tournus: Saône-et-Loire, Festival des Églises Romanes – celebration of Romanesque churches.

SEPTEMBER

Alise-Ste-Reine: Côte d'Or, Martyr de Ste-Reine – religious festival.
Amplepuis: Rhône, old car rally.
Beaune: Côte d'Or, wine rally.
Cosne-sur-Loire: Nièvre, Foire de la Saint Michel.
Dijon: Côte-d'Or, Folkloriades Internationales et Fêtes de la Vigne – international folk and wine festival (some events in Beaune). Also in Dijon the start of the winter music concert season.
Gevrey-Chambertin: Côte d'Or, Festival des Grands Crus "Musique au Chambertin"; Fête du Roi Chambertin – wine prize-giving.
Joigny: Yonne, Foire aux melons et oignons – produce fair.

Sully: Saône-et-Loire, Fête de la Chasse et de la Nature – festival of hunting and nature at Château de Sully.

OCTOBER

Auxerre: Yonne, Montgolfiades – hot-air ballooning festival.
Chalon-sur-Saône: Saône-et-Loire, Festival de l'Image de Film – pays homage to the technicians who shoot films.
Châtillon-sur-Seine: Côte d'Or, Autumn Fair.
Dijon: Côte d'Or, Foire Internationale et Gastronomique – starts at the end of October and continues well into November.
Nevers: Nièvre, Salon des Fleurs et des Animaux – flower and animal show.
St-Léger-sous-Beuvray: Saône-et-Loire, Foire aux Marrons – chestnut fair.

NOVEMBER

The most important event in November is "Les Trois Glorieuses" – three days dedicated to wine, the third weekend in November:
Clos de Vougeot: Côte d'Or, the Chapter meeting;
Beaune: Côte d'Or, Vente des Vins – the famous auction at the Hospices de Beaune;
Meursault: Côte d'Or, Paulée – wine festival.

Other wine festivals around the region are the Fête de Vin Bourru in Nuits-St-Georges: Côte d'Or; the Fête du Vin in Chablis: Yonne and the Fête du vine de l'Auxerrois in St-Bris-le-Vineux: Yonne.

Louhans: Saône-et-Loire, Fernand Point Gastronomic Exhibition – competition for trainee cooks and raffle of exhibited dishes.
Mâcon: Saône-et-Loire, Festival Européen.
Nevers: Nièvre, Concours agricole – agricultural show.

DECEMBER

Dijon: Côte d'Or, Salon de l'artisanat d'art et du cadeau – art and crafts fair.
Marcigny: Saône-et-Loire – Foire aux dindes et aux oies – poultry fair (turkeys and geese).

ARCHAEOLOGY & ARCHITECTURE

Burgundy has some of the finest Gallo-Roman sites in France; a whole holiday could be devoted just to exploring them. But those who prefer a range of cultural treats will not be disappointed. There are superb examples of religious building, a wealth of Romanesque churches, as well as the famous abbeys such as Fontenay and Paray-le-Monial.

Then there are the Dutch and Flemish influences to be observed, mostly in southern Burgundy. Some of the finest Burgundian buildings with their famous tiled roofs owe much to the artists brought to the region from Flanders, by Philip the Bold in the late 14th century.

Some of the best examples of all types of architecture, religious and secular, are listed here, as well as the most important archaeological sites, which often include museums. The listing also includes mention of particularly beautiful towns or villages, with no specific notable buildings.

Opening times are similar to those in museums (*see above*). All the monuments listed below are open daily, unless otherwise mentioned.

YONNE

ANCY-LE-FRANC

Renaissance château whose austere facade belies its elegant inner courtyard and sumptuously decorated apartments (the work of the School of Fontainebleau). Automobile and carriage museum in the grounds. Open: April–November.

ARCY-SUR-CURE

Château de Chastenay, near the famous caves (*see Things to Do*), this Renaissance château was rebuilt in 1549, and is still inhabited. Notable alchemical symbolic decoration. Open: daily July and August (except Sunday morning); weekends only at Easter, May and September. Tel: M de la Varende 86.81.93.41.

AUXERRE

Beautifully preserved medieval town, in particular the pedestrianised quarter at the heart of the town with its timbered houses and 14th-century clock tower. Two notable religious buildings: **Cathédrale St-Étienne**, the present Gothic building replaced the Romanesque church destroyed in the 13th century; **Abbaye St-Germain**, built around the tomb of St-Germain who was born in Auxerre – of particular interest are the carolingian frescoes in the crypt.

AVALLON

An attractive old fortified town whose ramparts, planted with lime trees, provide fine views over the Morvan hills. The Romanesque **Church of St-Lazare** (built 11th century and enlarged in the 12th century by monks from Cluny) boasts some fine sculpures on its main doorways.

DRUYES-LES-BELLES-FONTAINES

Château des Comtes d'Auxerre et de Nevers, imposing ruins of a fortified castle, dating back to the 12th century. Open: Saturday and Sunday afternoons, July to mid-September. In the village below the castle visit the Romanesque church.

ESCOLIVES-ST-CAMILLE

Important archaeological site, on the Roman road where evidence of man's presence can be traced back, without a break, to Neolithic times. Among the excavations are 3rd-century baths, covering an area of 10,765 sq. ft (1,000 sq. metres). Open: June–September, Wednesday–Sunday (daily in August). Tel: 86.53.39.09.

JOIGNY

Delightful medieval town on the River Yonne, overlooked by a ruined **Renaissance château**. **St-Thibault church** is built in flamboyant Gothic style, whilst **St-Jean church** boasts a remarkable vault which took 40 years to complete and was built to house the tomb of Countess Aléis. Note too the rare wooden house, **Maison du Bailli** which escaped the 1530 fire which destroyed much of the town.

NOYERS-SUR-SEREIN

Extremely well preserved little medieval town with fine half-timbered houses and fortifications. In summer there are processions through the town with local people in medieval dress.

PONTIGNY

Potigny abbey, built in 1114, is one of the finest remaining examples of Cistercian architecture in France. Closed to the public during services.

ST-FARGEAU

The château dates back to the 10th century, but has been rebuilt, extended and decorated by many owners since that time. It is now a huge pentagon of rose-coloured brick with six towers. Its impressive inner court was built by Le Vau, architect of Versailles. *Son-et-lumière* presentations in summer (*see Live Arts*). Open: April to mid-November. Tel: 86.74.05.67.

ST-PERE-SOUS-VEZELAY

Fontaines Salées, archaeological site and museum. Natural mineral springs, rich in salt, were used as an early cult site, and many devotional relics have been found. Discovered in 1934, it is one of the largest and richest archaeological sites in the region. Open: March–November. Closed: Wednesday. Tel: 86.33.23.14.

SENS

Gateway to Burgundy, Sens enjoys an impressive history: first as the capital of a powerful Gallic tribe, then of a Gallo-Roman province, and more recently as the seat of an archbishopric (the former archbish-op's palace now houses the museum – *see Museum listing*). St-Étienne was the first of France's grand Gothic cathedrals, and boasts beautiful stained glass and ironwork.

TANLAY

The **Renaissance château** is one of the finest residences in Burgundy. It is surrounded by a moat and a beautiful park. Of particular note are its richly decorated apartments and frescoes. Regular exhibitions of contemporary art are held in the summer in a building in the château grounds. Open: April to mid-November. Closed: Tuesday. Tel: 86.75.70.61.

TONNERRE

An old town, built-up around the site of the Fosse Dionne, an ancient water source. The old hospital has been well preserved and is open to the public; it has a vast ward (300 ft/91 metres long), dominated by a superb sculpture, the Entombment. Open: April–October. Closed: Tuesday. Tel: 86.55.14.48 (tourist office).

TOUCY

The **birthplace of Pierre Larousse**, editor of France's most well-known dictionary, boasts an unusual fortified church.

TREIGNY-RATILLY

Château de Ratilly, fortified medieval castle which has a permanent exhibition of Puisaye pottery, ranging from the 16th century to contemporary pieces; also stages concerts and modern art exhibitions in summer. Open: every afternoon, also mornings in July–September. Closed: Sundays November–March. Tel: 86.74.79.54.

VEZELAY

Ancient place of pilgrimage, recognised by UNESCO as a sanctuary. Its abbey, the **Basilique Ste-Madeleine** is a superb example of Romanesque art; early pilgrims used to come here before setting off on the road to Compostela, or the crusades. The former monks' dormitory now houses a **lapidary museum**.

NIEVRE

ANTHIEN

Château de Villemolin, fairytale château, set in parkland with its own chapel. Open to the public by appointment only April–November. Tel: 86.22.01.09.

BREVES

Site of a Merovingian necropolis where more than 200 tombs have recently been discovered; exhibition of burial objects. Open: in summer only.

CHAMPALLEMENT

In the Compierre wood on the road to St-Révérien stand the remains of a large Gallo-Roman village, showing shops, workshops and a theatre.

CHASSY

Ensemble of 18th-century castle and outbuildings where regular exhibitions are held. Open: every afternoon July–August. Tel: 86.84.72.87.

CHATEAU-CHINON

Near the town on Mount Beuvray is the former *oppidum* which served as a stronghold for the Gallic troops before the Battle of Alésia in 52 BC. The site is to become a leading archaeological base in Europe. Excavations continue. Information from: Base Archéologique du Mont-Beuvray, 58370 Glux-en-Glenne. Tel: 86.78.61.55.

ENTRAINES-SUR-NOHANS

Entrains was a prosperous Gallo-Roman town, and many of the objects found during excavations are on view during the summer, although the digs themselves are no longer open to the public.

NEVERS

The old town, still much enclosed by its defensive ramparts, leads down to the river Loire. The **Church of St-Étienne** (11th-century) is particularly noted for its purity of design and unity of style; by contrast the huge **St-Cyr Cathedral** incorporates every ecclesiastical style from the 10th–16th centuries. See too the **Ducal Palace**, a fine example of Renaissance architecture, now housing part of the law courts.

COTE D'OR

ALISE-STE-REINE

Site of Alésia, excavations of a substantial Gallo-Roman city with theatre, forum, commercial and craftwork districts clearly marked on a map to be found near the statue of Vercingétorix. Also a museum, and viewpoint over the battleground of Alésia (52 BC). Open: Spring–November.

AUXONNE

An old fortified town where Napoleon Bonaparte served in the army; the castle now houses a museum

dedicated to him. See too the Church of Notre Dame with its wealth of statuary and numerous gargoyles.

BAUBIGNY

Dracty is an archaeological site of a medieval vineyard village which disappeared in the early 15th century. Excavations allow visitors to have a vision of the everyday life of a rural community in the Middle Ages. Access is by a path to the cliffs from the wash-house in Baubigny.

BEAUNE

The city boasts some of the finest examples of Gothic/Flemish art in the region, of which the most famous is undoubtedly the Hôtel-Dieu, often mistakenly referred to as the Hospices de Beaune (the building actually belongs to the Hospices de Beaune Foundation). It was built as an hospital for the poor by Nicolas Rolin, Chancellor to Duke Phillippe-le-Bon in 1443, and many of its original fittings remain intact, including the pharmacy and the wards. See too the altarpiece of the Last Judgement by van der Weyden.

Other notable buildings include the **Church of Notre Dame**, a fine example of Cluniac architecture, with some good tapestries; the **Church of St-Nicolas**, built during the transition from the Romanesque to Gothic periods; and the **Demeure St-Martin**, 4 Avenue Foch, an 18th-century residence open to the public, with wine-tastings possible.

Archéodrome, just south of Beaune (at the A6 Beaune-Tailly motorway services or via the D18 to Tailly, then D23 to Merceuil). Outdoor exhibition with life-sized reconstructions of Burgundy's early history: neolithic huts, fortification works of the battle at Alésia, Gallo-Roman temple and villa and even a necropolis. Also a museum. Tel: 80.21.48.25.

BUSSY-RABUTIN

Château du Comte de Bussy, a 13th-century fortress, much altered over the centuries. Closed: Tuesday and Wednesday October–April. Tel: 80.96.00.03.

CHATEAUNEUF-EN-AUXOIS

The castle is a well-preserved example of 15th-century military architecture. Closed: Tuesday and Wednesday October–April. Tel: 80.49.21.89.

CITEAUX

Cîteaux Abbey, birthplace of the Cistercian order of monks; remains of 15th-century buildings; the 19th-century church is all that is open to the public. Slide show (in English) about the life of the monks. Closed: Sunday mornings. Tel: 80.61.11.53.

COLLONGES-LES-BEVY

Seventeenth and 18th-century castle with fine interior décor and mementoes of General Gassendi, of Monge and the Empire. Open: weekends and public holidays July–September. Tel: 80.61.40.05.

COMMARIN

Castle dating back to the 15th century with later additions. Note the heraldic tapestries; the furniture, decorations and arrangements are unchanged since the 18th century. Open: April–October. Closed: Tuesday. Tel: 80.49.23.67.

CORGOLOIN

Château de Cussigny, L-shaped castle, rebuilt around 1743 and later modified. Fine 18th-century gardens with bowers and arbours. Open: mid-July to September. Tel: 80.62.98.28.

DIJON

Dijon boasts many notable buildings. **Rue des Forges**, which was once the city's main street, has a row of medieval and Renaissance facades, while the **Rue Verrerie** boasts many half-timbered houses and decorative sculptures. Others include the **Hôtel Chambellan**, which now houses the tourist office, the **Maison des Cariatides** in Rue Chaudronnerie and **Maison Millière**, decorated with animals on the roof. The **St-Bénigne Cathedral** boasts an 11th-century crypt; see too the Romanesque **St-Philibert Church**.

EGUILLY

Twelveth-century castle, rebuilt in the 18th century, now housing a permanent exhibition of paintings, sculptures and lithographs. Closed: Tuesday except May–October. Tel: 80.90.72.90.

EPOISSES

A former royal residence, this moated medieval fortress (11th-century) was designed to house the local population in times of danger, so there is a church and various other buildings within its walls. Much modified in later years; half its buildings were lost during the Revolution. Closed: Tuesday. Tel: 80.96.40.56.

ESSAROIS

Abbaye de Val des Choux, set right at the heart of the Châtillon forest, the abbey was the head of an order run by a mixture of Benedictine, Cistercian and Carthusian rules. Some old buildings remain and the walled gardens and orchards. Tel: 80.81.01.09.

FROLOIS

The old fortified castle built on a rocky spur in a particularly picturesque spot. Little remains of the original 14th-century building, but it was rebuilt in the 18th century with painted beamed ceilings and Venetian painted tapestries. Open: July–August. Tel: 80.96.22.92.

GEVREY-CHAMBERTIN

The ancient fortress (10th-century) which originally belonged to Cluny abbey was rebuilt by the abbot Yves de Chasan in 1280 to protect the famous local wine. Remarkable interior. Tel: 80.34.36.13.

LANTILLY

Known as the **"castle of 100 windows"**, the château has scarcely been altered since it was built in the early 18th century. Note the dining room, decorated with Corinthian pilasters. Open: Easter holidays, then July–September. Closed: Tuesday. Tel: 80.97.11.57.

NUITS-ST-GEORGES

The ruins of the large Gallo-Roman town of Bolards have been partly excavated: in particular the Temple of Apollo and the sanctuary of Mithra. Also a museum (open during summer).

MARMAGNE

Abbaye de Fontenay, designated as a World Heritage site, this 12th-century abbey is the best known and best preserved of all the Cistercian abbeys. Founded by St Bernard, it is a perfect example of Romanesque art. Tel: 80.92.15.00.

MOLESMES

Molesmes Abbey, dates back to the 13th century and is notable for its different styles of vault. Visit the prior's apartments, store-room, cellars and refectory. The cloister terraces and gardens are also open to the public. Open: April–October. Closed: Monday. Tel: 80.81.44.47.

SEMUR-EN-AUXOIS

A medieval city with its towers and ramparts still in evidence, the **Tour de l'Orle d'Or** being the most imposing of the four corner towers of the keep. The **municipal museum** is housed in a former Dominican convent; while the **Church of Notre Dame** is fine example of Burgundian Gothic architecture.

TALANT

An historic site – a 13th-century listed village, with notable church and Confrairie Tower.

VOUGEOT

hâteau du Clos de Vougeot, dating back to the 12th century, the castle is the headquarters of the Confrérie des Chevaliers du Tastevin. It has four fine original store rooms and a collection of antique wine-tasting cups. Tel: 80.62.86.09.

SAONE-ET-LOIRE

ANZY-LE-DUC

With its three-tiered octagonal tower dominating the Brionnais countryside, this is one of the most beautiful Romanesque churches to be found in southern Burgundy.

AUTUN

Founded by Emperor Augustus and named Augustodonum in his honour, almost 2,000 years ago, Autun was an important Roman city although not many of its buildings have survived: the theatre was the largest in Roman Gaul, has been well preserved and is still in use today; parts of its ramparts and gateways are also visible. See too the **Temple of Janus**, built in Celtic style nearby.

The town also boasts one of the finest Cluniac churches, the **Cathedral of St-Lazare**. Although it now sports a 15th-century stone tower, the original church was almost entirely built in 10 years in the early 12th century. Note the "Last Judgement" triptych over the central doorway, and its sculpted capitals.

BERZE-LA-VILLE

Chapelle priorale du Château des Moines, a small chapel of the residence of the Cluny abbots, it has remarkable Romanesque paintings and superb Cluniac murals, discovered in 1887. Open: mid-March to mid-November.

BRANCION

Medieval village with the remains of a vast castle dating back to the 10th century, once the most important fortress in southern Burgundy. There is also an excellent Romanesque church nearby. Château open: daily March–November, Sundays only the rest of the year.

CHALON-SUR-SAONE

A charming old town, full of flowers, with picturesque streets and paved quarters. **Cathedral of St-Vincent** – not much remains of the original 12th-century structure; it has been rebuilt many times.

CLUNY

Ancienne Abbaye St-Pierre et St-Paul, remains of the abbey founded in 910 which extended an amazing influence over Europe, with 1,500 religious establishments and 10,000 monks under its control. Only the south transept is still standing, but there is much fragmentary evidence and some fine sculptured capitals remain. Guided tours. Tel: 85.59.12.79.

CORMATIN

The château was the former home of one of Louis XIII's noblemen. Well-preserved apartments with original decoration; in the grounds there are a moat, ponds and recreated gardens including the largest maze in France (planted just recently). Open: daily during Easter holidays and mid-June to end-October; May to mid-June open weekends and public holidays. Tel: 85.50.16.55.

COUCHES

Château de Marguerite de Bourgogne, fortified castle with high defensive walls; note the glazed tiles and Gothic chapel. Open: July–September. Tel: 85.49.68.02. At the crossroads of the D225 and CV4 is the **Megaliths of Époigny**, six menhirs of which the largest, at 24 ft, is the highest in eastern France.

CURTIL-SOUS-BURNAND

Munot is the site of a **Merovingian cemetery** where over 400 tombs (6th and 7th-century) were discovered. Some remain on view here, others are exhibited at the Denon Museum in Chalon-sur-Saône.

MACON

The old town can be best seen by walking the pedestrianised area parallel to Quai Lamartine. Of particular note is the **Maison de Bois** which has carved heads with gruesome expressions.

MELLECEY

Château de Germolles, 13th-century fortified manor which became the favourite residence of Marguerite of Flanders and Philip the Bold. Fine murals (being restored) and decorated floor tiles. Open: July–September. Closed: Tuesday. Tel: 85.45.10.55.

PARAY-LE-MONIAL

Famous as a place of pilgrimage to the great **Basilica of the Sacré Coeur**, built in imitation of the abbey church of Cluny. A park behind the basilica leads down to the recently restored old quarter whose town hall is a fine Renaissance mansion. Note the former belltower, **Tour St-Nicolas**, all that remains of the old parish church.

PERRECLOS

Château de Pierreclos, associated with the poet Lamartine; the 12th-century castle is surrounded by terraced gardens and offers splendid views over the Petite Grosne valley. Medieval kitchens, and a bakehouse (now a museum – *see listing*). Tastings and sale of wine made on the property. Tel: 85.35.73.73.

ST-AUBIN-SUR-LE-LOIRE

A remarkable site: monumental buildings pierced by a barrel-vaulted passageway lead up to an 18th-century castle of immaculate proportions. Balustraded terraces slope down from the castle to the River Loire. Open: July–September.

ST-PIERRE-DE-VARENNES

Château de Brandon, a former stronghold of the dukes of Burgundy, perched on a hilltop. A well-restored example of defensive architecture. Visits by appointment only. Tel: 85.55.45.16.

ST-POINT

Original 12th-century castle with neo-Gothic additions, ordered by Lamartine, the poet who lived there. His study is as he left it. His grave can also be visited. Open: March to mid-November. Closed: Wednesday and Sunday morning.

SEMUR-EN-BRIONNAIS

Heralded as **one of the most beautiful villages in France**, its church is a late, very fine example of Cluniac architecture. The ruined castle was the **birthplace of St-Hugh**, Abbot of Cluny; the jailer's house displays a collection of Revolutionary posters. Open: April–November.

SOLUTRE

A remarkable archaeological site at the foot of the famous **Rock of Solutré**, where local tribes set up their hunting camps to track horses. This practice went on for 20,000 years (from 30,000–10,000 BC) and there is a great accumulation of remains. Also a museum (*see Museum listing*).

SULLY

Château de Sully, moated 16th-century mansion, called by the famous 17th-century diarist Mme de Sévigné, the "Fontainebleau of Burgundy". With additions over the years, it now displays a colourful mixture of periods and styles. Open: Easter–October. Tel: 85.82.01.08.

AIN

BOURG-EN-BRESSE

The old quarter is in the centre of the town and well worth a visit; in particular the nearby **Église de Brou** built in flamboyant Gothic style with fine stained glass and its neighbouring **museum** should not be missed.

CHATILLON-SUR-CHALARONNE

Well-preserved medieval town, and one of the most flower-filled in France. It boasts **17th-century market halls** (market Saturday morning), timbered houses and a cultural centre housed in the former hospital.

PONT-D'AIN

Old town set on the River Ain at the junction of the Bresse, Dombes and Bugey regions. Note the 15th-century houses and the former château of the dukes of Savoy.

ST-TRIVIER-DE-COURTES

A very picturesque Bresse village which has been well restored and is now a protected site. Many old houses and remains of the fortifications. Visit the **Ferme de la Forêt** at nearby Courtes – a completely restored 17th-century farm which is now open as a museum. Open: daily mid-June to mid-September, also Sundays from Easter–October. Tel: 74.30.71.89.

TREVOUX

Former capital of the old principality of the Dombes region, with many reminders of its earlier importance: the remains of the château, the **Hôtel du Gouverneur** and, of particular note, the former seat of the parliament – **l'Ancien Parlement de la Dombes**, 1 Rue du Palais. This has a painted ceiling and murals created by Pierre-Paul Sevin in the 12th century. Open: Monday–Friday. Free entry. Tel: 74.00.06.49.

GLOSSARY OF ARCHITECTURAL TERMS

chancel	altar, sanctuary and choir
narthex	porch
nave	central space of church, often flanked by aisles
transept	wings of the cruciform at right-angles to the nave
apse	half-domed or vaulted semi-circular recess at east end
apsidal chapels	chapels radiating from the apse
chevet	semi-circular east end often with attached apses

ambulatory	aisle running round east end behind the sanctuary
tympanum	recessed space above a doorway, triangular or semi-circular and ornamented
lintel	horizontal beam over door or window
pilaster	rectangular column attached to the face of a wall
capitals	top of a column, often elaborately carved
clerestory	row of windows above the aisle roof lighting the nave
triforium	arcade of windows above the arches of the nave
retable	ornamental screen behind the altar
corbel	supporting bracket

NIGHTLIFE

For most evening entertainment you need to be in the major towns, such as Dijon or Beaune; although in summer there are plenty of concerts, *son-et-lumière* displays, etc. around the region (*see Live Arts*). If you intend to take young children to such displays, note that they often start quite late, around 10pm.

Santenay (Côte d'Or) at the heart of the region, 12 miles (20 km) south of Beaune, boasts a **Casino** which is open every evening except Monday. It also has a **restaurant** and **discothèque**. Tel: 80.20.61.00.

For something more out of the ordinary, and absolutely typical of the region, it is possible to attend initiation ceremonies at some of the wine-drinking brotherhoods. Of particular interest is the **Confrérie des Chevaliers du Tastevin** which holds its initiation ceremonies at the beautiful Clos de Vouget Château, midway between Beaune and Dijon. Small groups of visitors are admitted on prior request; information from the Côte d'Or departmental tourist office (*see Useful Addresses*).

In the main, though, nightlife in rural Burgundy, as in country areas everywhere, is limited to a local level – small bars, cafés and restaurants, village hops, harvest festivals and other gatherings. Do not expect bars to be open very late in the country.

Everybody celebrates on the **14th of July**, of course – even the smallest villages often have their own **fireworks** displays, and nearly all towns and villages in France have a **summer fête** of some kind. If you are staying in a *gîte* or in other family accommodation you are likely to be warmly encouraged to join in the festivities.

Information about nightclubs, cinemas and other entertainment is available from the tourist offices, or at your hotel.

SHOPPING

Over the past couple of decades most major towns in France have made the sensible decision to keep the town centre for small boutiques and individual shops. Many of these areas, such as in Beaune and Dijon, are pedestrianised and attractive (although beware – some cars ignore the *voie piétonnée* signs). The large supermarkets, hypermarkets, furniture stores and do-it-yourself outlets are grouped on the outskirts of the town, mostly designated as a *Centre Commercial*.

These centres, although aesthetically quite unappealing, are fine for bulk shopping for self-catering or for finding a selection of wine to take home at reasonable prices. The biggest selection of such stores in Burgundy is on the southern outskirts of Dijon. But for gifts and general window-shopping the town centres are far more interesting. It is here that you will find the individual souvenirs that give a taste of the region, alongside the beautifully dressed windows of delicatessens and *pâtisseries*.

China-lovers can have a field day in Nevers, which is full of shops selling faïence. Only three small factories remain, Du Bout du Monde (10 Rue de la Porte du Croux); Georges (20 Rue Bovet); and Bernard (1 Rue Sabatier).

The heart of every French town is its market; they mostly start early in the morning and close at midday. The French themselves usually visit early to get the best of the produce. In a region which prides itself on the quality of its food production, it is hardly surprising that even local markets are seen as very serious events. There is a whole series of special fairs and auctions for instance in Charolles (Saône-et-Loire), mostly devoted to the sale of their famous Charolais cattle. Similarly, the Bresse region, whose chickens carry their own *appellation contrôlée*, has regular poultry markets. The lovely old town of Louhans, for example, has a market every Monday where the poultry has pride of place amongst the 200 stalls which offer all kinds of wares.

Other particularly interesting markets include the following:

Autun (Saône-et-Loire); Wednesdays and Saturdays

in the Champ de Mars.

Auxerre (Yonne); Tuesday.

Avallon (Yonne); Wednesday and Friday.

Bourg-en-Bresse (Ain); Wednesdays, plus livestock market on Tuesday afternoons.

Beaune (Côte d'Or); Saturday.

Chagny (Saône-et-Loire); Sunday market with bric-à-brac and local produce.

Chalon-sur-Saône (Saône-et-Loire); by the cathedral on Fridays and Sundays, fruit, vegetables and bric-à-brac.

Dijon (Côte d'Or); Friday and Sunday best days, also open Tuesday and Saturday.

Donzy (Nièvre); Saturday is best, also Thursday.

Joigny (Yonne); Saturday.

Mâcon (Saône-et-Loire); extensive Saturday market on Lamartine promenade and the quayside.

Marcigny (Saône-et-Loire); the Monday market was instituted by a charter of 1266; noted for its poultry.

St-Christophe-en-Brionnais (Saône-et-Loire) dates back to the 16th century; in the autumn up to 4,000 heads of cattle are sold each week.

St-Honoré-les Bains (Nièvre); Thursday is best; also open and Saturday.

Sens (Yonne); Monday.

Villefranche-sur-Saône (Rhône) the town's covered market in its famous old halls is held on Friday, Sunday and Monday.

Villeneuve-sur-Yonne (Yonne); Friday.

There are also antique and craft fairs and *marchés exceptionnels*, held at various times throughout the year, such as harvest times. Some of the most important, such as wine sales, are listed in the *Diary of Events* section (*see Culture Plus*), for others check with the local tourist office for details.

BUYING DIRECT

You may be tempted by all the signs you see along the road for *dégustations* (tastings). Many wine producers and farmers will invite you to try their wines and other produce with an eye to selling you a case, or, for instance, a few jars of pâté. This is a good way to try before you buy and can sometimes include a visit to a wine cellar. Sometimes farm produce is more expensive to buy this way than in the supermarkets – do not forget that it is home-produced and not factory-processed. For a selection of wine cellars open to the public, *see Wines*.

PRACTICAL INFORMATION

Food shops, especially bakers, tend to open early; boutiques and department stores open from 9am, but sometimes not until 10am. In town centres, just about everything closes from noon until 2.30 or 3pm apart from the department stores which usually stay open. Most shops close in the evening at 7pm. Out of town, the hypermarkets are usually open all day until 8 or even 9pm. Most shops are closed Monday mornings and large stores generally all day. If you want to buy a picnic lunch, remember to buy everything you need before midday. Good delicatessens (*charcuteries*) have a selection of delicious ready-prepared dishes, which make picnicking a delight.

On most purchases, the price includes TVA (VAT or purchase tax). The base rate is currently 18.6 percent, but can be as high as 33 percent on luxury items. Foreign visitors can claim back TVA; worth doing if you spend more than FF2,400 (FF1,200 for non-EC residents) in one place. Some large stores and hypermarkets have information bureaux where you can obtain a refund form. This must be completed to show (with the goods purchased) to customs officers on leaving the country (pack the items separately for ease of access). Then mail the form back to the retailer who will refund the TVA in a month or two. Certain items purchased (e.g., antiques) may need special customs clearance.

If you have a complaint about any purchase, return it in the first place to the shop as soon as possible. In the case of any serious dispute, contact the Direction Départementale de la Concurrence et de la Consommation et de la Répression des Fraudes (see telephone directory for number).

CLOTHING

Most shops are happy to let you try clothes on (*essayer*) before buying. Children's clothes sizes, in particular, tend to be small compared with British and US age ranges.

SPORTS

You are likely to find opportunities for most sports within the region. Most medium-sized towns have swimming-pools and even small villages often have a tennis court, but you may have to become a temporary member to use it – enquire at the local tourist office or *mairie* (town hall) which will also provide details of all other local sporting activities.

It seems to be a quirk of the French tourist industry that they do not always take full advantage of their facilities. Even though there may be good weather in early summer and autumn, open-air swimming-pools and other venues often limit their seasons to the period of the school holidays.

Although land-locked, the region offers some opportunities for water sports, on man-made or natural lakes (particularly in the Morvan Regional Park), or sometimes on safe stretches of a river. Often called a *Base de Loisirs*, these centres offer all kinds of leisure activities – not just water sports. They usually have a café or bar, maybe even a restaurant, as well as picnic areas.

Many offer tuition in the various sports available – canoeing, wind-surfing etc; fees are usually charged at an hourly or half hourly rate. Where boating and windsurfing is permitted, equipment is often available for hire, or you may take your own.

Listed below are the main *Bases de Loisirs* in the region, with details of their facilities/activities (*see also Things to Do for Leisure Parks*).

NIEVRE

Châtillon-en-Bazois: Base Nautique de l'Étang de Baye. Sailing, windsurfing, canoeing and fishing; as well as mountain bikes, volleyball and horse-riding. Accommodation and restaurant available on the site. Open: April–September. Tel: 86.84.51.98.
Decize: At the end of the Nivernais canal, the stade nautique offers good facilities for water sports, also for bathing. Tel: 86.25.00.99.
Lormes: Base Nautique de Chaumeçon. A beautiful lake in the west of the Morvan Park, which connects by means of the River Cure to the Lac du Crescent to the north. Sailing and canoeing, campsite and other accommodation. Open: April–October. Tel: 86.84.51.98.
Étang du Goulot, sailing and windsurfing. Tel: 86.22.85.47.
Montsauche-les-Settons: Base Nautique des Settons. Leisure centre on the Settons Lake, at the heart of the Morvan Park. Swimming, sailing, windsurfing, water-skiing and canoeing, plus riding, tennis and mini-golf. Campsite and other accommodation available. Open: April–October. Tel: 86.84.51.98.
Pannecière: Centre Nautique de Pannecière, in the Morvan Regional Park, sailing and windsurfing. Open: weekends only from 1st June, daily in July and August. Tel: 86.78.20.11 (tourist office); 86.78.22.64 (out of season).

COTE D'OR

Auxonne: Water sports on a stretch of the River Saône; also bathing.
Dijon: Base Nautique du Lac Kir, 21370 Plombières-les-Dijon. Canoeing and other amenities, including a restaurant on the Chanoine Kir reservoir.
Nuits-St-Georges: Plans d'eau de Saule-Guillaume. Windsurfing and other water sports.
Pontailler-sur-Saône: Leisure centre and campsite on a stretch of the River Saône; various water sports and bathing; also good for fishing.

Saulieu: Lac de Chamboux, in the Morvan Regional Park, is the HQ of the Club Nautique de Saulieu – sailing possible.
Semur-en-Auxois: Lac du Pont, man-made reservoir, 3 km (2 miles) south of town. Various water sports and good bathing.

SAONE-ET-LOIRE

Autun: Centre de Loisirs du Moulin du Vallon, a large man-made lake located on the outskirts of town with safe bathing, fishing, sailing and windsurfing; also facilities for horse-riding, golf and mini-golf, tennis and climbing.
Chalon-sur-Saône:
Pleasure boating and other water sports on a stretch of the River Saône.
Gigny-sur-Saône: Lac de Laives leisure centre. Sailing and other water sports, not far from Châlon-sur-Saône.
Mâcon: Excellent boating facilities on a stretch of the River Saône.

AIN

Montrevel-en-Bresse: Montrevel-Malafretaz leisure centre, all kinds of sporting activities as well as water sports at this large site. Camping possible. For information: tel: 74.25.48.74 (tourist office).
Thoissey: All kinds of water sports and bathing on a stretch of the River Saône; campsite. For information tel: 74.04.04.25 (tourist office).

RHONE

Cublize: Lac des Sapins, large man-made lake between Amplepuis and Thizy. Water sports include canoeing, sailing, pedalos and bathing; also horse-riding, mountain bikes and mini-golf. Snack bars, restaurants, camping and wooden chalets also on the site. Tel: 74.89.54.05.
Villefranche-sur-Saône:
A large lake, right next to the municipal campsite on the Route de Riottier, offers supervised bathing, angling and other sporting activities. For information: tel: 74.68.05.18 (tourist office).

Both the Côte d'Or and the Nièvre Loisirs Accueil services (*see Useful Addresses*) offer courses and all-in holidays in canoeing and other water sports. In the latter case, these are mostly on the River Loire where there is an annual canoe rally.

For more details of canoeing, contact the Ligue Régionale de Canoë-Kayak, Rue St-Pellerin, 89000 Auxerre, tel: 86.51.52.61; the national associations are the Canoë-Kayak Club de France, 47 Quai Ferber, 94360 Bry-sur-Marne, tel: 48.81.54.26; and the Fédération Française de Canoë-Kayak, 17 Route de Vienne, 69007 Lyon, tel: 78.61.32.74.

A good source of information for all leisure activities on the rivers and lakes of Burgundy is

Navigation et Technique, Port du Canal, 21370 Plombières-les-Dijon. Tel: 80.45.44.60. Also for the waterways of the Morvan park, contact the Maison du Parc (*see Useful Addresses*).

ANGLING

With its wealth of waterways and lakes, fishing is a popular activity in the region. Again, the Morvan Regional Park is a very popular venue, and it is possible to book fishing holidays (a weekend or longer) with accommodation in the park. Contact the following organisations for information and booking:

JPR Tourisme, 21430 Brazey-en-Morvan. Tel: 80.84.03.65.

Autun Morvan Voyages, 13 Rue de l'Arbalète, 71400 Autun. Tel: 85.86.14.41.

Domaine du Manoir de Tarperon, Tarperon, 21510 Aigny-le-Duc. Tel: 80.93.83.74.

Les 4 Chemins, 25 Rue aux Rax, 71400 Autun. Tel: 85.54.47.19.

CYCLING

To take your own *vélo* to France is easy – they are carried free on most ferries and trains – or you can rent cycles for a reasonable cost; main railway stations usually have them for hire and you can often arrange to pick up at one station and leave the bike at a distant one. Alternatively try bicycle retailers/ repairers or ask at the local tourist office.

Some youth hostels rent cycles and also arrange tours with accommodation in hostels or under canvas. For more information, contact the YHA (*see Where to Stay*). French Routes, 1 Mill Green Cottages, Newbridge, Yarmouth, Isle of Wight, PO41 0TZ, tel: 0983-78392, offers a route planning service for individual tourists and will also arrange bicycle hire and accommodation.

"Packaged" cycling holidays are offered by various organisations; with campsite or hotel accommodation with the advantage that your luggage is normally transported for you to your next destination. The Nièvre Loisirs Accueil service (*see Useful Addresses*) offers a six-night tour of the upper Loire Valley. Other options are given below.

Susi Madron's Cycling for Softies, Lloyds House, 22 Lloyd Street, Manchester M2 5WA. Tel: 061 834 6800. A choice of tours in the Beaujolais area, with hotel accommodation and fine food.

Bourgogne Tour Incoming, 14 Rue du Chapeau Rouge, 21000 Dijon. Tel: 80.30.49.49; fax: 80.30.69.87. Various tours around Dijon/Beaune, also a one-day tour of the vineyards.

Les 4 Chemins, 25 Rue au Raz, 71400 Autun. Tel: 85.52.07.91. Tours in the Morvan Regional Park.

La Peurtentaine, École du Bourg, 71550 Anost. Tel: 85.82.77.74. Also based in the Morvan.

Horizon Aventure, 5 Place Jacques Prévert, 21000 Dijon. Tel: 80.30.38.64.

It is advisable to take out insurance before you go. Obviously the normal rules of the road apply to cyclists (*see Getting Around*). Advice and information can be obtained from The Touring Department, Cyclists Touring Club, Cotterell House, 69 Meadrow, Godalming, Surrey GU7 3HS, tel: 0483-417217. Their service to members includes competitive cycle and travel insurance, free detailed touring itineraries and general information sheets about France whilst their tours brochure often lists trips to the region, organised by members. The club's French counterpart, Fédération Française de Cyclotourisme, offers a similar service, including holidays. Contact them at: 8 Rue Jean-Marie-Jego, 75013 Paris, tel: 1-45.80.30.21. Rob Hunter's book *Cycle Touring in France* is also useful as a handbook.

Such is the French passion for cycling that local clubs organise many trips lasting a day or more and visitors are often more than welcome to join in. Weekend or longer tours are organised by the national Bicyclub, 8 Place Porte de Champerret, 75017 Paris, tel: 1-42.27.28.82. Lists of clubs and events are also available from the Ligue Régionale de Bourgogne de Cyclotourisme, 2 Rue des Corroyeurs, 21000 Dijon, tel: 80.45.04.87. This organisation also produces leaflets giving suggested cycle tours for independent travellers, ranging from easy terrain, to very hard-going for the more experienced cyclist, with details of accommodation en route, cycle repairers and other facilities.

MOUNTAIN BIKING

This sport has really taken off in recent years, particularly among the French, many of whom are already dedicated cyclists. Once again, the Morvan attracts many devotees of the sport, its hilly landscapes providing ideal routes. The organisations listed under Cycling above (Nièvre Loisirs Accueil service, Les 4 Chemins and La Puertentaine) all offer mountain bike holidays.

Mountain bikes (known in French as VTT – *Vélo Tout Terrain*) and protective gear can be hired locally, try the local tourist office, or cycle shops/ repairers.

HORSE-RIDING

All riding holidays in France come under the umbrella of the National Association of Equestrian Tourism and Leisure Riding (ARTE) based at 14 Rue de Bruxelles, 75009 Paris, tel: 1-42.81.82. For local information contact the regional branch: M Ramillon, Château de Lantilly, 58800 Corbigny, tel: 86.20.18.85. There are two other regional associations with similar interests: the Association Régionale de Tourisme Équestre de Bourgogne, La Croix-Maillot, 58140 Lormes, tel: 86.22.85.26; and the Association Bourguignonne d'Equitation de Loisirs, Corlay-Nanton, 71240 Sennecey-le-Grand, tel: 85.92.22.94. These organisations can also provide information about marked bridleways, maps, riding centres and insurance.

Treks lasting a day or more and also longer holidays on horseback can be organised locally. Information can be obtained from the organisations mentioned above, from tourist offices and from the Loisirs Accueil services of the individual *départements* (*see Useful Addresses*). Holidays in the Morvan park are organised by Les 4 Chemins (*see Cycling*).

Local tourist offices will provide details of stables (of which there are plenty in the region) if you simply wish to hire a horse by the hour or day. Expect to pay around FF75 per hour/FF350 per day.

FROM BIBRACTE TO ALESIA

An annual event is held each year in the region, which is quite particular to Burgundy. This is a five-day trek following the footsteps of the Gauls, in their march against Caesar. It takes you through some of the most delightful Morvan scenery and is open to participants on foot, horseback, cycle or mountain bike. Luggage is transported and accommodation is provided in hostels. More information and booking from Nièvre Loisirs Accueil (*see Useful Addresses*) or from Les 4 Chemins (*see Cycling*).

GOLF

In recent years, golf has caught on in a big way in France and the Regional Tourist Boards have joined forces with the French Golf Federation in an effort to promote it better and set standards. General information can be obtained from the Comité Régional au Tourisme (*see Useful Addresses*). For the serious golfer, who can expect to pay around FF165 for green fees (this is for the whole day), the following courses (18-hole unless otherwise indicated) are open to the public and all offer good facilities:

YONNE

Golf du Roncemay, Aillant-sur-Tholon, 89110 Chassy. Tel: 86.73.69.87. New course with 9 additional holes opening in 1992.
Golf de Tanlay, Château de Tanlay, 89430 Tanlay. Tel: 86.75.72.92.

NIEVRE

Golf de Nevers, 58470 Magny-Cours. Tel: 86.58.18.30.
Golf du Château d'Azy, Parc du Château, 58270 Saint-Benin d'Azy. Tel: 86.58.50.00. 9 holes.

COTE D'OR

Golf de Beaune Levernois, 21200 Beaune. Tel: 80.24.10.29.
Golf Club du Château de Chailly, Château de

Chailly sur Armancon, 21320 Pouilly-en-Auxois. Tel: 80.90.30.40.
Golf du Cap Vert, Parc Urbain d'Activities et de Loisirs, 21800 Quétigny. Tel: 80.46.69.00. New 9-hole course in Quétigny Leisure Park near Dijon (*see Things to Do*).

SAONE-ET-LOIRE

Golf d'Autun, Plan d'Eau du Vallon, 71400 Autun. Tel: 85.52.09.28. 9 holes.
Golf Club de la Frédière, Céron, 71110 Marcigny. Tel: 85.25.27.40.
Golf de la Salle Mâcon, 71260 Lugny. Tel: 85.36.09.71.
Chalon-sur-Saône Golf Course, Zone de Loisirs de St-Nicolas, Chatenoy-en-Bresse, 71380 St-Marcel. Tel: 85.48.61.64.

AIN

Golf de la Bresse, Domaine de Mary, Condessiat, 01400 Châtillon-sur-Chalaronne. Tel: 74.51.42.09.

HANG-GLIDING

Hang-gliders (ULM) are quite popular in the region. For safety, always use an authorised or listed site. For information contact the nearest tourist office or contact Club-ULM-Bourgogne, tel: 85.26.84.02, who will give advice and may be able to hire equipment. For hang-gliding in the Morvan, contact: Jean-Michel Dizier, tel: 86.84.54.55.

SPECTATOR SPORTS

The Dijon-Prenois motor racing circuit stages many important events throughout the year, including the **Formula 3 French Championship**, the **Grand Prix Historique**, and the **European Lorry Grand Prix**. A full calendar is available from Circuit Dijon-Prenois, BP 8 21380 Messigny-et-Vantoux, tel: 80.35.32.22; fax: 80.35.33.22.

In Nièvre, the **Grand Prix Formula 1 race** takes place in July at the Magny-Cours racing circuit, which in October stages the **World Superbike Championship**. For more details of these and other events at the track, tel: 86.21.20.74.

Another bike race is held in the Morvan Regional Park in September – the **Morvan Rallye** VTT (mountain bike rally). For details: tel: 86.36.02.44. Also in the Morvan in August is the **Grand Prix Cycliste International**, held during the Fête du Morvan (tel: 86.85.06.58 for details).

Semur-en-Auxois stages some prestigious horse races; in particular the **Course des Chausses et des Damoiselles**, and the oldest horse race of them all (since 1639), the **Fête de la Bague**, both in May. More information from the Maison du Tourisme, Place Gustave Gaveau, 21140 Semur-en-Auxois, tel:

80.97.05.96; or from the town hall, tel: 80.97.01.11. Other races (with official betting) takes place in mid-July and mid-August at Vitteaux, near Dijon.

In Nièvre a **horse show** combines with a **water sports festival** in Decize in July (tel: 86.25.03.23), while in the same month, a **canoe rally** takes place on the Loire, from St-Hilaire to Cosne; for information: tel: 86.36.39.80.

More unusual water sports – water jousting – are on display in Clamecy (Nièvre) in July, tel: 86.27.02.51; and at Coulanges-sur-Yonne in August, tel: 86.81.70.32.

Details of these and other local sporting events can be obtained from the nearest tourist office.

Special Information

DOING BUSINESS

Business travel is now such an important part of the tourist economy that the French Government Tourist Office in London and Chicago (*see Useful Addresses*) has a department set up just to deal with business enquiries. They will help organise hotels, conference centres and incentive deals for any group, large or small.

For general information about business travel and facilities contact the regional tourist offices (*see Useful Addresses*). Another good source of business information and local assistance, are the Chambres de Commerce et d'Industrie in the individual *départements*. Here you can obtain details about local companies, assistance with the technicalities of export and import, interpretation/translation agencies and conference centres – indeed, most chambers of commerce have conference facilities of some kind themselves. The main Chambres de Commerce et d'Industrie are located at the following addresses:
Chambre Régionale de Commerce et d'Industrie, 68 Rue Chevreul, 21000 Dijon. Tel: 80.63.52.52.

Ain: 3 Place Pierre Goujon, 01000 Ain. Tel: 74.21.35.11; fax: 74.21.42.63.
Côte d'Or: 1 Place du Théâtre, 21000 Dijon. Tel: 80.65.91.00.
Nièvre: Place Carnot, 58000 Nevers. Tel: 86.57.22.14.
Rhône: 317 Boulevard Gambetta, 69400 Villefranche-sur-Saône. Tel: 74.65.10.11.
Saône-et-Loire: Place Gérard Genevès, 71000 Mâcon. Tel: 85.38.93.33.

Yonne: 26 Rue Étienne-Dolet, 89000 Auxerre. Tel: 86.46.46.14.

There is also a French Chamber of Commerce in London (tel: 071 225 5250) which exists to promote business between the two countries, and at the same address is French Trade Exhibitions: 2nd floor, Knightsbridge House, 197 Knightsbridge, London SW7 1RB. Tel: 071-225 5566.

CONFERENCE HALLS

There are plenty of conference halls available in the region. Some very modern, while others are in the prestigious surroundings of châteaux or old wine cellars. A selection of the most interesting is given below:

YONNE

Auxerre: Caves de l'Hôtel de Ville. Ancient cellars under the town hall, accommodating 170 people. Information from M and Mme Morot, 50 Rue du Pont, 89000. Tel: 86.52.92.11.
Sens: Caves du Marché Couvert. Cellar beneath the old covered market, 150-seat capacity. Tel: 86.95.67.00 (Town Hall).
La Poterne. An ancient room with fine décor, seating 150. Information from M Serrurier, 21 Boulevard du 14 juillet. Tel: 86.65.11.38.

COTE-D'OR

Beaune: La Maison des Confréries. Cellar seating 300 for banqueting (catering service available) in the House of Brotherhoods, plus a modern lecture hall. Information: 20–24 Rue du Faubourg Madeleine, 21200. Tel: 80.24.05.05.
Dijon: Espace Grévin. Arched cellar beneath the new waxworks museum, catering service for banqueting, plus 100-seat capacity for seminars. Information from Espace Grévin, 13b Avenue Albert 1er, BP 148, 21004 Dijon Cedex. Tel: 80.42.03.03; fax: 80.41.76.37.
Vougeot: Château du Clos de Vougeot. Rooms catering for 100–700 people, in a splendid setting near Beaune. Information from Château du Clos Vougeot, 21640. Tel: 80.62.35.81; fax: 80.62.82.75.

SAONE-ET-LOIRE

Le Creusot: Château de la Verrerie. Prestigious banqueting rooms. Information from the Town Hall. Tel: 85.55.17.63.

Important trade fairs are held in Nevers (Nièvre) in March and May/June, in Mâcon (Saône-et-Loire) in May, Chalon-sur-Saône (Saône-et-Loire) in June and in Dijon (Côte d'Or) in November.

In France generally, children are treated as people, not just nuisances. It is pleasant to be able to take them to restaurants (even in the evening) without heads being turned in horror at the invasion. It has to be said, however, that French children, being accustomed to eating out from an early age, are on the whole well-behaved in restaurants so it helps if one's own offspring are able to understand that they can't run wild. Many **restaurants** offer a children's menu; if not they will often split a *prix-fixe* menu between two children. If travelling with very young children, you may find it practical to order nothing specific at all for them but just to request an extra plate and give them tasty morsels to try from your own dish. It is a good introduction to foreign food for them, without too much waste. French meals are generally generous enough (*nouvelle cuisine* excepted) to allow you to do this without going hungry yourself, and you are unlikely to encounter any hostility from *le patron* (or *la patronne*). Another option is to order a single simple, inexpensive dish from the à la carte menu, such as an omelette, which most childen will happily eat.

Most **hotels** have family rooms so children do not have to be separated from parents and a cot (*lit bébé*) can often be provided for a small supplement, although it is a good idea to check availability if booking in advance.

Family **leisure activities** in the region are somewhat limited; but there are some parks which offer a variety of amusements, particularly La Toison d'Or in Dijon, the water park at Quétigny, also in Côte d'Or, and Touro-Parc leisure park at Romanèche-Thorins (Saône-et-Loire). The best area for family holidays is the Morvan which offers plenty of outdoor pursuits. For more details of other places to take children, *see Things to Do*.

The tourist offices in each *département* also organise events for **unaccompanied children**, including stays in *gîtes d'enfants* or on farms. Naturally, children would be happy to be left only if they have a reasonable command of French, but it is quite common in France, as in the US, for children to spend at least part of their summer vacation at a holiday centre. For more information, contact the tourist office or the Loisirs Accueil service in individual *départements* (*see Useful Addresses*).

Gay organisations and social centres are not widely advertised in the region, but general information is available from the national *Gai Pied Guide* (published in French, sold in the UK). If you need urgent help or information, try the Paris-based gay switchboard (SOS Homosexualité, tel: 16.1-46.27.49.36) where there are English-speakers; please note this service is only active Wednesday and Fridays from 6pm to midnight.

Most disabled travellers will be keen to book accommodation in the region rather than arriving "on spec". The region's official list of hotels (available from the FGTO or the regional tourist office – *see Useful Addresses*) includes a symbol to show if rooms are easily accessible to the disabled, but it is always adivisable to check directly with the chosen hotel as to exactly what facilities are available. Balladins is a chain of newly-built, budget-priced hotels throughout France which all have at least one room designed for disabled guests and restaurants and all other public areas are accessible. They have hotels in Beaune, Dijon, Mâcon, Villefranche-sur-Saône and Auxerre. For a complete list contact Hotels Balladins, 20 Rue du Pont des Halles, 94656 Rungis Cedex. Tel: 49.78.24.00; fax: 46.86.41.44.

There is a guide, *Où Ferons Nous Étape?* (published 1990 in French only), which lists accommodation, throughout France, suitable for the disabled, including wheelchair users, but again if you have specific needs you would need to double-check when booking. It is available (for FF40 by post) from the Association des Paralysés de France, Service Information, 17 Boulevard August Blanqui, 75013 Paris. Tel: 1-45.80.82.40. This organisation may also be able to deal direct with specific enquiries and can provide addresses of their branches throughout France.

The Michelin red guide *France*, for hotels, and their *Camping-Caravanning – France* both include symbols for disabled welcome.

The **Royal Association for Disability and Rehabilitation** (RADAR), 25 Mortimer Street, London WIN 8AB, tel: 071-637 5400, has some useful information for tourists, including a guidebook, *Holidays and Travel Abroad* (£3 including postage). This is a general country by country guide and provides information about France as a whole, including hotel chains offering suitable accommodation, and tour operators offering specialist holidays. In particular, try Village Vacances Famille, Tour Maine Montparnasse, 33 Avenue du Maine, 75755 Paris Cedex 15, tel: 45.38.28.28, who run holiday villages especially adapted for disabled people in Semur-en-Auxois.

France's sister organisation to RADAR, the **Comité National Français de Liaison pour la Réadaption des Handicapés** (CNFLRH), is based at 38 Boulevard Raspail, 75007 Paris, tel: 1-45.48.90.13. They offer a good information service for disabled visitors to France and publish a useful free guide in French/English entitled *Touristes Quand Même* which gives information about access at airports, stations, tourist sites, restaurants, etc., as well as where to hire wheelchairs and other aids.

Specifically for young people, the **Centre d'Information et de Documentation Jeunesse**, 101 Quai Branly, 75740 Paris Cedex 15 provides information on services for young disabled. It publishes *Vacances pour Personnes Handicapées* and annual leaflets on acitivity and sports holidays for young disabled people. The Youth Hostel at Vézelay (Yonne) has some suitable accommodation for the disabled.

The **Comité de Liaison pour le transport des personnes handicapées**, Conseil National des Transports, 34 Avenue Marceau, 75009 Paris publishes a booklet called *Guide des Transport à l'usage des Personnes à Mobilité Réduite*. This gives brief information on the accessibility and arrangements for disabled passengers on all forms of public transport and contacts for special transport schemes throughout France.

Brittany Ferries offers free passage for cars of registered disabled travellers on all their routes (except Plymouth–Santander). More information about air and sea travel is also available in a guide entitled *Door-to-Door*. For a free copy write to Department of Transport, Door-to-Door Guide, Freepost, Victoria Road, South Ruislip, Middlesex HA4 0NZ who can also provide copies on cassette for the vision-impaired.

In the US, the following organisations offer services to disabled travellers:
Travel Information Service, Moss Rehabilitation Hospital, 1200 West Tabor Rd., Philadelphia, PA 19141-3099. Tel: 215-329 5715; ext: 2233. General information for would-be travellers.
Society for the Advancement of Travel for the Handicapped (SATH). 26 Court Street, Brooklyn, New York 11242. Tel: 718-858 5483. Offers advice and assistance in travel matters.
Evergreen Travel Service, 19505 44th Avenue West, Lynnwood, WA 98036. Tel: 206-776 1184. A private company with over 30 years' experience of organising holidays for the disabled.
Accessible Journeys, 412 South 45th Street, Philadelphia, PA 19104. Tel: 215-747 0171. Offers tours using wheelchair-accessible transport in Europe.
Flying Wheels Travel Inc., PO Box 383, 143 West Bridge Street, Owatonna MN 55060. Tel: 507-451 5005. Has been organising worldwide travel for over 20 years.
In Canada:
Canadian Rehabilitation Council for the Disabled, 45 Sheppard Avenue E, Toronto, Ontario, M2N 5W9. Tel: 416-250 7490. A national organisation producing some material relating to travel.
Association for Specialised Services Involving Special Travellers, c/o ACTA, Suite 1106, 75 Albert Street, Ottawa, Ontario K1P 5E7. Tel: 613-238 1361.

STUDENTS & YOUNG PEOPLE

Students and young people under the age of 26 can benefit from cut-price travel to France and rail cards for getting around the region – for details *see Getting There*.

If you wish to have a prolonged stay in the region, it may be worth finding out about an exchange visit or study holiday. Several organisations exist to provide information or arrange such visits. In the UK, the Central Bureau for Educational Visits and Exchanges, Seymour Mews House, Seymour Mews, London WlH 9PE, tel: 071-486 5101, produces three books: *Working Holidays* (opportunities in the region are limited; the grape harvest is still a big draw for young people and employment opportunities are listed here); *Home from Home* (a wealth of useful information about staying with a French family) and *Study Holidays* (details of language courses).

Volunteers are welcome at the workcamps organised on several on the archaeological and cultural sites in Burgundy (mainly during the summer). For information contact: the Direction Régionale des Affaires Culturelles, 39 Rue Vannerie, 21000 Dijon. Tel: 80.67.22.23. Although unpaid, this is a good way of meeting other young people of all nationalities and an opportunity to learn the language.

Organisations in the US include the Council on International Educational Exchange (CIEE), 205 E. 42nd Street, New York, NY 10017, tel: 212 661 1414 – a wide range of services, including travel; American Council for International Studies Inc., l9 Bay State Road, Boston, Mass. 02215, tel: 617 236 2051; and Youth for Understanding International Exchange, 3501 Newark Street, NW, Washington DC 20016, tel: 202 966 6800.

There are also several French tour operators which organise study tours in the region, and language courses:
Centre Internationale d'Études Françaises, 36 Rue Chabot-Charny, 21000 Dijon. Tel: 80.30.50.20. All-year language courses and summer courses for all levels.
Accueil France International, 3 Rue Philbert Delorme, 75017 Paris. Tel: 1-46.22.02.97. Arranges stays with French families for individuals or groups and optional language courses.
Accueil des Jeunes en France, 12 Rue des Barres, 75004 Paris. Tel: 1-42.72.72.09. Offers French study programmes, inexpensive accommodation (or with a family), and tours for individuals or groups.
Centre des Échanges Internationaux, 104 Rue de Vaugirard, 75006 Paris. Tel: 1-45.49.26.25. Sporting and cultural holidays and educational tours for 15–30 year olds. Non-profit making organisation.

A complete list of private language schools is obtainable from the regional tourist office (*see Useful Addresses*).

Once in France, students will find a valid student identity card is useful in obtaining discounts on all sorts of activities, including admission to museums and galleries, cinema, theatre, etc. If you do not happen to have your ID card with you reductions may sometimes be allowed by proving your status with a passport.

The Centre d'Information et Documentation de Jeunesse (CIDJ), based at 101 Quai Branly, 75740 Paris, tel: 1-45.67.35.85, is a national organisation which disseminates information pertaining to youth and student activities.

For individual holidays, the cheapest way to stay is generally under canvas, or in a hostel (expect to pay around FF55 per night without meals).

FURTHER READING

Ardagh, John. *France Today*. London: Secker and Warburg. Up-to-date, hefty tome on modern France.

Cole, Robert. *A Traveller's History of France*. London: The Windrush Press. Slim volume for background reading.

Hamilton, Ronald. *A Holiday History of France*. London: The Hogarth Press. Illustrated guide to history and architecture.

Braudel, Fernand. *The Identity of France*. London: Fontana Press.

Wells, Patricia. *The Food Lover's Guide to France*. London: Methuen. The best restaurants, food shops and markets in France, plus regional recipes.

Busselle, Michael. *Burgundy – Wine Lover's Regional Guide*. London: Pavilion. Photographer's guide to the vineyards and countryside of Burgundy.

Sutcliffe, Serena. *The Wines of Burgundy*. London: Mitchell Beazley. Pocket guide to the appellations and châteaux of Burgundy.

Pomerol, Charles (ed). *The Wines and Winelands of France*. London: Robertson McCarta. Guide to the wine regions of France, paying particular attention to the geology and science of the subject, plus itineraries and history.

Johnson, Hugh and Duijker, Hubrecht. *Wine Atlas of France*. London: Mitchell Beazley. Well-illustrated atlas, concentrating on wine and vineyards, but also supplementary information on history, architecture and culture.

Parker, Robert. *Burgundy*. London: Dorling Kindersley.

Dunlop, Ian. *Burgundy*. London: Hamish Hamilton. Traces the architectural development of the region from 1000–1789.

Bourgogne Romane. Zodiaque Press. Romanesque architecture.

USEFUL ADDRESSES

IN FRANCE

Air France, 119 Champs Elysées, 75384 Paris Cedex 08. Tel: 1-43.23.81.81; central reservation, tel: 1-45.35.61.61.

Maison de la France, 8 Avenue de l'Opéra, 75001 Paris. Tel: 1-42. 96.10.23.

Comité Régional de Tourisme de Bourgogne, Conseil Régional, BP 1602, 21035 Dijon Cedex. Tel: 80.50.10.20; fax: 80.30.48.74.

DEPARTEMENTAL TOURIST OFFICES

Ain: 34 Rue Général Delestraint, BP 78, 01002 Bourg-en-Bresse Cedex. Tel: 74.21.95.00; fax: 74.21.45.69.

Côte d'Or: Hôtel du Département, BP 1601, 21035 Dijon Cedex. Tel: 80.63.66.00; fax: 80.30.48.74.

Nièvre: 3 Rue du Sort, 58000 Nevers. Tel: 86.36.39.80; fax: 86.36.36.63.

Rhône: Office de Tourisme, Place Bellecour, BP 2254, 69214 Lyon Cedex 02. Tel: 78.42.25.75; fax; 78.37.02.06.

Saône-et-Loire: 389 Avenue de Lattre de Tassigny, 71000 Mâcon. Tel: 85.39.47.47.

Yonne: Maison du Tourisme, 1–2 Quai de la République, 89000 Auxerre. Tel: 86.52.26.27; fax: 86.51.68.47.

SERVICES RESERVATION LOISIRS ACCUEIL

Nièvre: Service de Réservation Loisirs Accueil du Nivernais-Morvan, 3 Rue du Sort, 58000 Nevers. Tel: 86.59.14.22; fax: 86.36.36.63.

Yonne: 1–2 Quai de la République, 89000 Auxerre Tel: 86.51.12.05.

Maison du Parc Natural Régional du Morvan, 58230 Saint-Brisson. Tel: 86.78.70.16.

Ligue Française pour la Protection des Oiseaux (LPO), La Corderie Royale, BP 263, 17305 Rochefort.

IN THE UK & EIRE

Air France, 158 New Bond Street, London W1Y 0AY. Tel: 071-499 9511 (reservations 071-750 4308); 29–30 Dawson Street, Dublin 2. Tel: 77-8272 (reservations: 77-8899).

Consulat Général de France, College House, 29/31 Wrights Lane, London W8 5SH. Tel: 01-937 1202. **Maison de la France/French Government Tourist Office**, 178 Piccadilly, London W1V 9DB. Tel: 071-491 7622; fax: 071-493 6594.

IN THE US & CANADA

Air France, 666, Fifth Avenue, New York NY 10019. Tel: 212-315 1122 (toll-free reservations: 800 237 2747); 850l Wilshire Boulevard, Beverly Hills, Los Angeles, Ca. Tel: 213-274 8364; 979 Ouest Boulevard de Maisonneuve, Montreal, Quebec. Tel: 514-284 2825; 151 Bloor Street West, Suite 600, Toronto, Ontario. Tel: 922-3344.
Maison de la France/French Government Tourist Office, 610 Fifth Avenue, Suite 222, New York, NY 10020-2452. Tel: 212-757 1125; fax: 212-247 6468; 9454 Wilshire Boulevard, Beverley Hills, Los Angeles Ca. 90212-2967. Tel: 213-272 2661. 645 North Michigan Avenue, Suite 630, Chicago, Illinois 60611-2836. Tel: 337 6301 (Business Travel Division 751 7804). Cedar Maple Plaza, 2305 Cedar Springs Road, Suite 205, Dallas, Texas 75201. Tel: 214-720 4010; fax: 214-702 0250.
Maison de la France/French Government Tourist Office, 1981 McGill College, Tour Esso, Suite 490, Montreal H3A 2W9, Quebec. Tel: 514-288 4264; fax: 514-845 4868; Suite 2405, 1 Dundas Street West, Toronto M5G 1Z3 Ontario. Tel: 416-593 4723.

EMBASSIES & CONSULATES

In most cases, the nearest consular services are in Paris.
American Embassy: 2 Avenue Gabriel, 75382 Paris Cedex 08. Tel: 16-1.42.96.12.02.
Australian Embassy: 4 Rue Jean Rey, 75015 Paris. Tel: 16-1. 45.75.62.00.
British Consulate: 16 Rue d'Anjou, 75008 Paris: Tel: 1-42.66.91.42 **British Embassy**: 35 Rue du Faubourg St-Honoré, 75008 Paris. Tel: 16-1.42.66.91.42.
Canadian Embassy: 35 Avenue Montaigne, 75008 Paris. Tel: 16-1.47.23.01.
Irish Embassy: 12 Avenue Foch, 75116 Paris. Tel: 16-1.00.20.87.

ART/PHOTO CREDITS

Photography by **LYLE LAWSON**
except for:

INDEX

INSIGHT *Pocket* GUIDES

United States: **Houghton Mifflin Company, Boston MA 02108**
Tel: (800) 2253362 Fax: (800) 4589501

Canada: **Thomas Allen & Son, 390 Steelcase Road East**
Markham, Ontario L3R 1G2
Tel: (416) 4759126 Fax: (416) 4756747

Great Britain: **GeoCenter UK, Hampshire RG22 4BJ**
Tel: (256) 817987 Fax: (256) 817988

Worldwide: **Höfer Communications Singapore 2262**
Tel: (65) 8612755 Fax: (65) 8616438

"I was first drawn to the Insight Guides by the excellent "Nepal" volume. I can think of no book which so effectively captures the essence of a country. Out of these pages leaped the Nepal I know – the captivating charm of a people and their culture. I've since discovered and enjoyed the entire Insight Guide Series. Each volume deals with a country or city in the same sensitive depth, which is nowhere more evident than in the superb photography.**"**

Sir Edmund Hillary